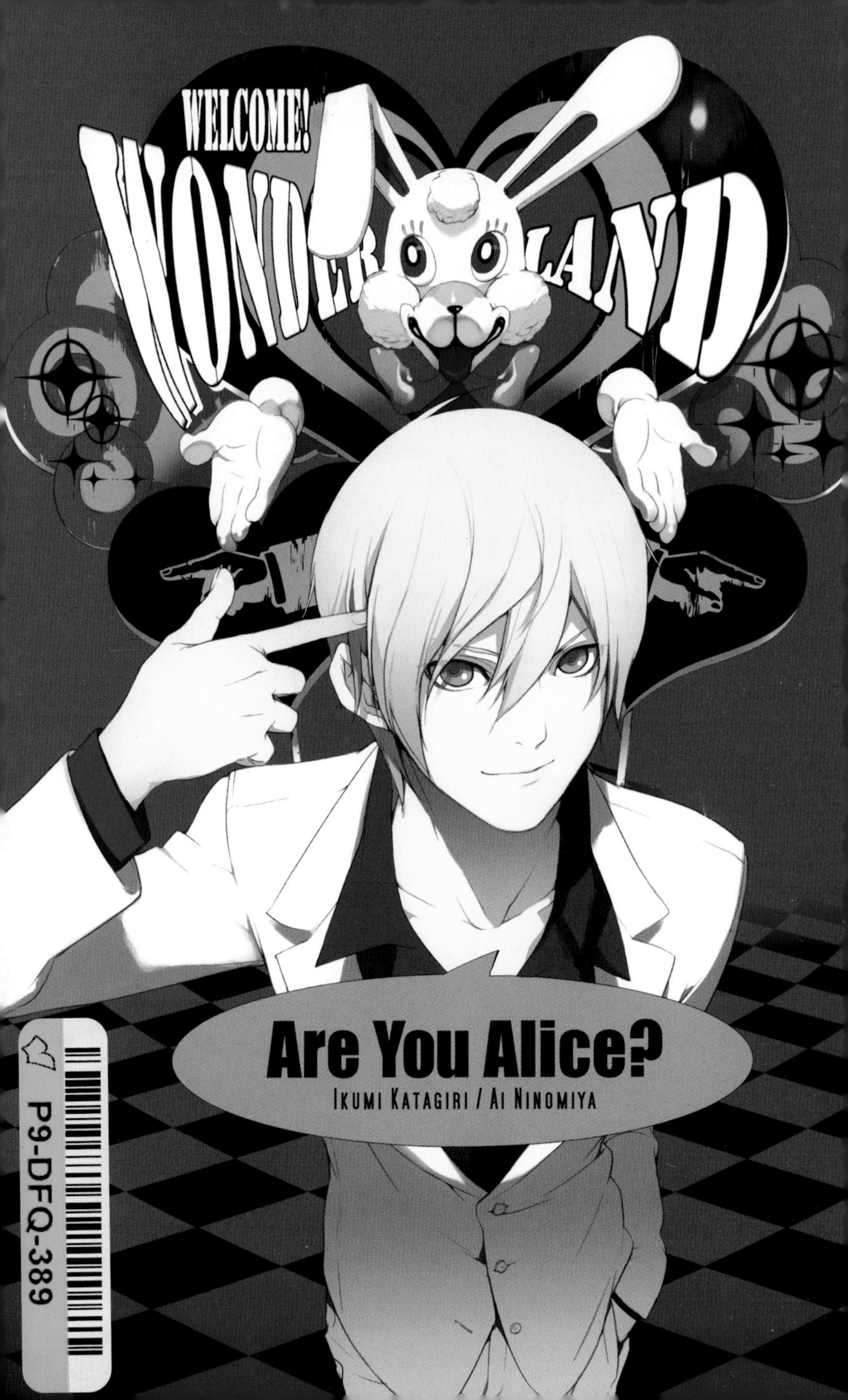
WELCOME!
WONDERLAND
Are You Alice?
IKUMI KATAGIRI / AI NINOMIYA

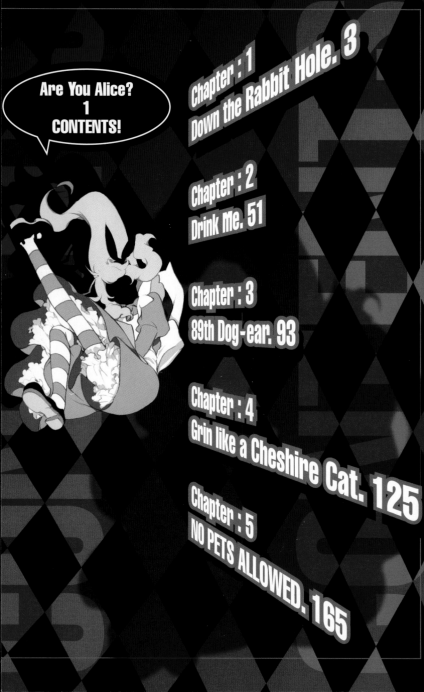

Are You Alice?
1
CONTENTS!

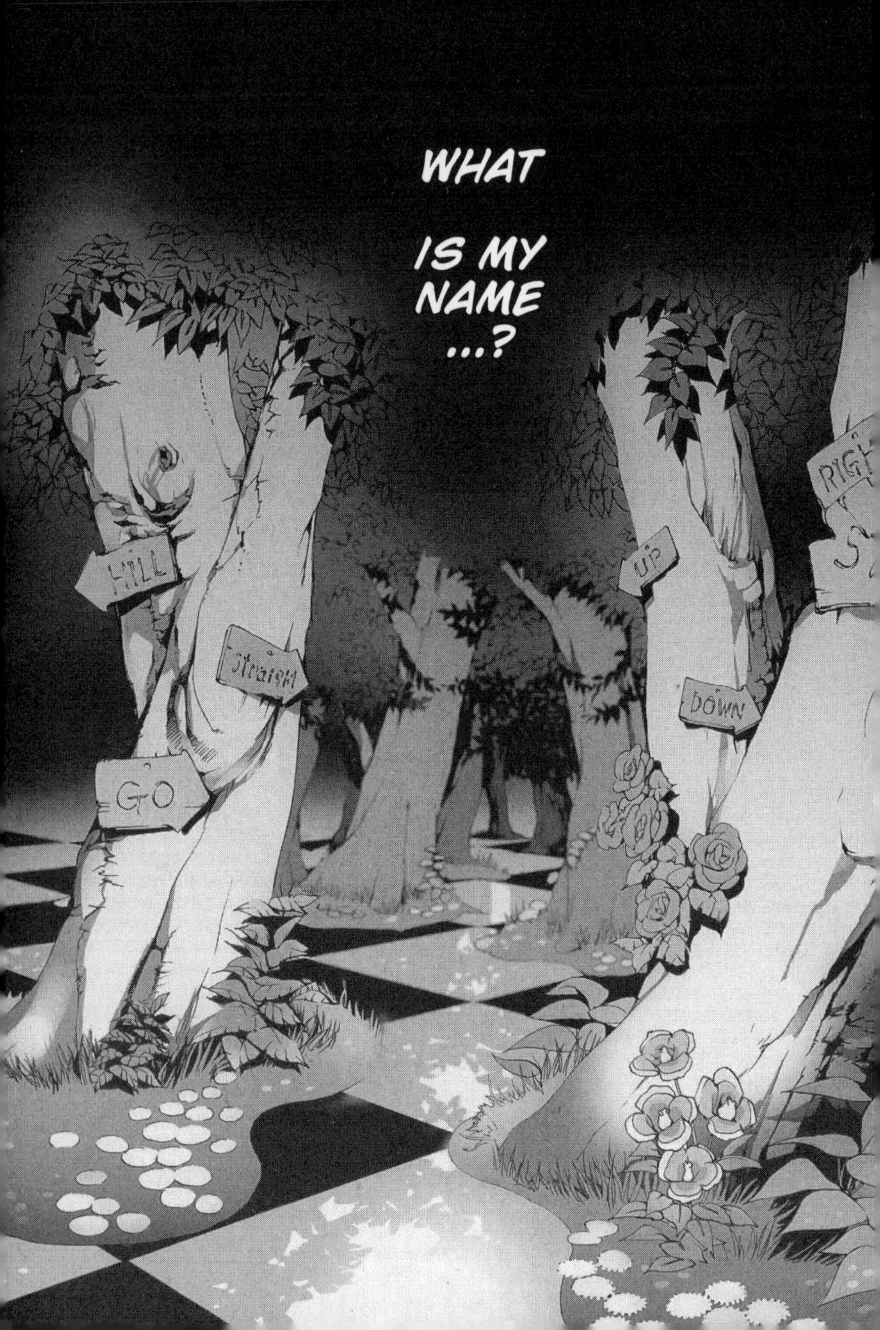
WHAT
IS MY NAME ...?
straight
GO
UP
DOWN

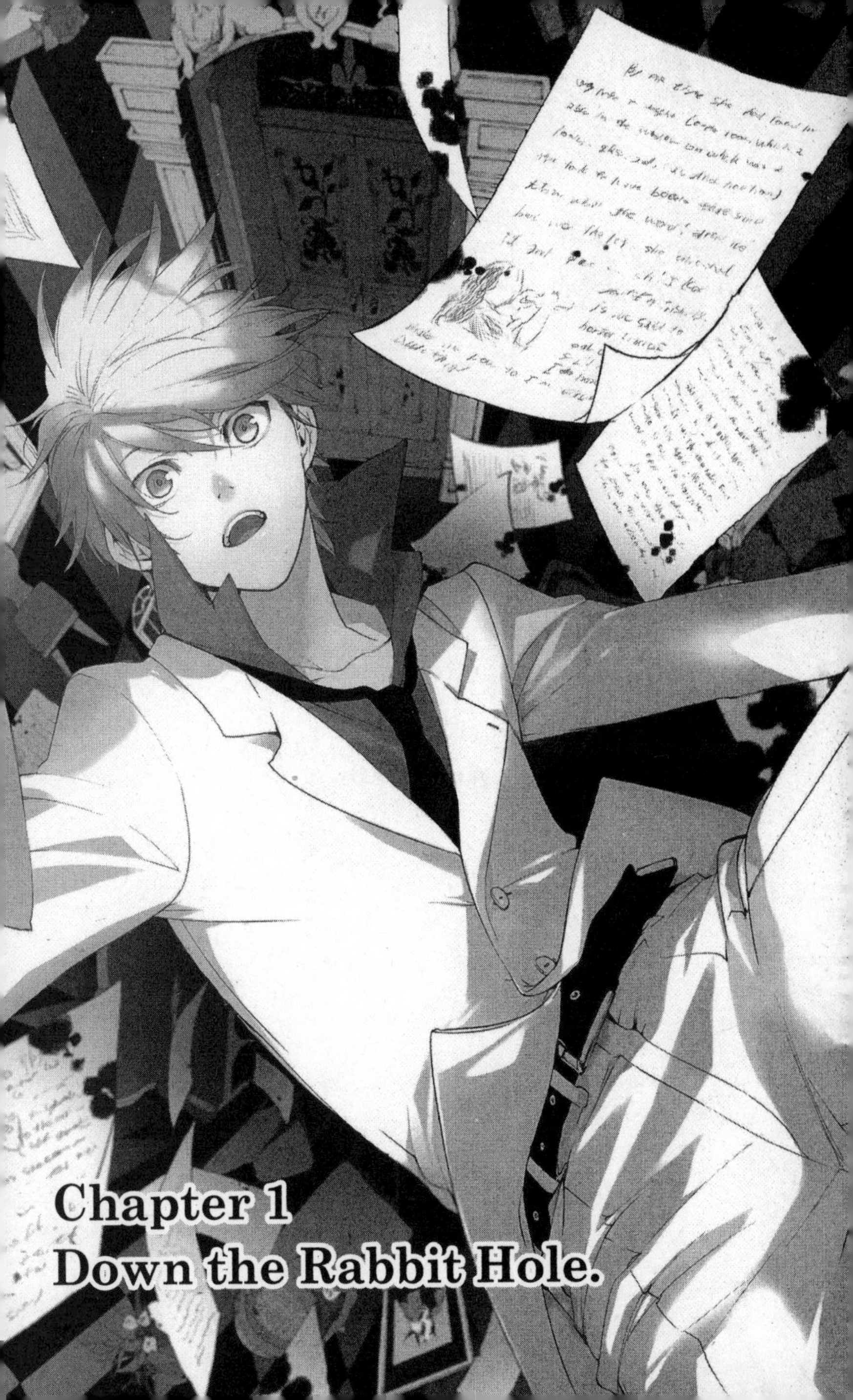
Chapter 1
Down the Rabbit Hole.

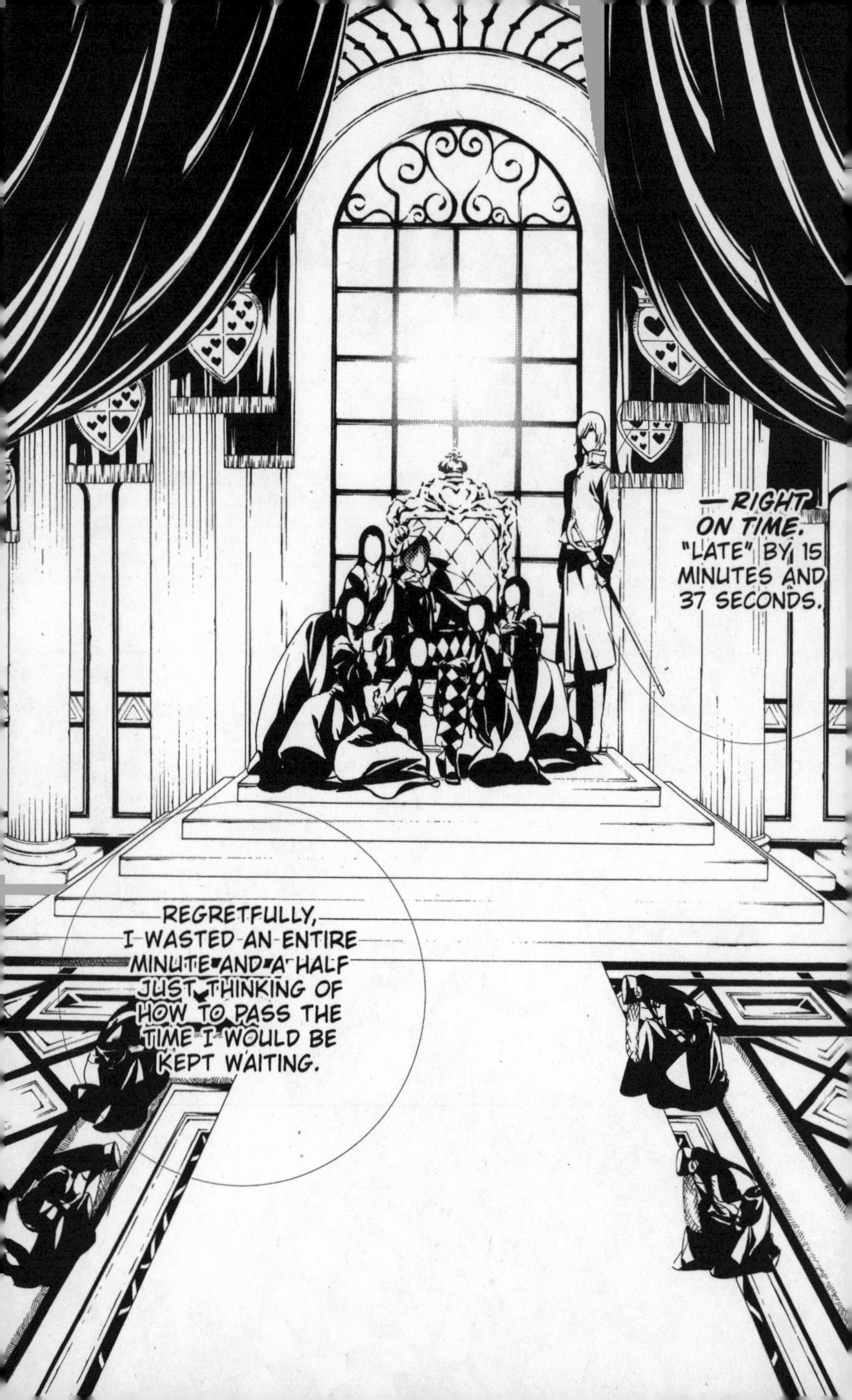
—RIGHT ON TIME. "LATE" BY 15 MINUTES AND 37 SECONDS.
REGRETFULLY, I WASTED AN ENTIRE MINUTE AND A HALF JUST THINKING OF HOW TO PASS THE TIME I WOULD BE KEPT WAITING.

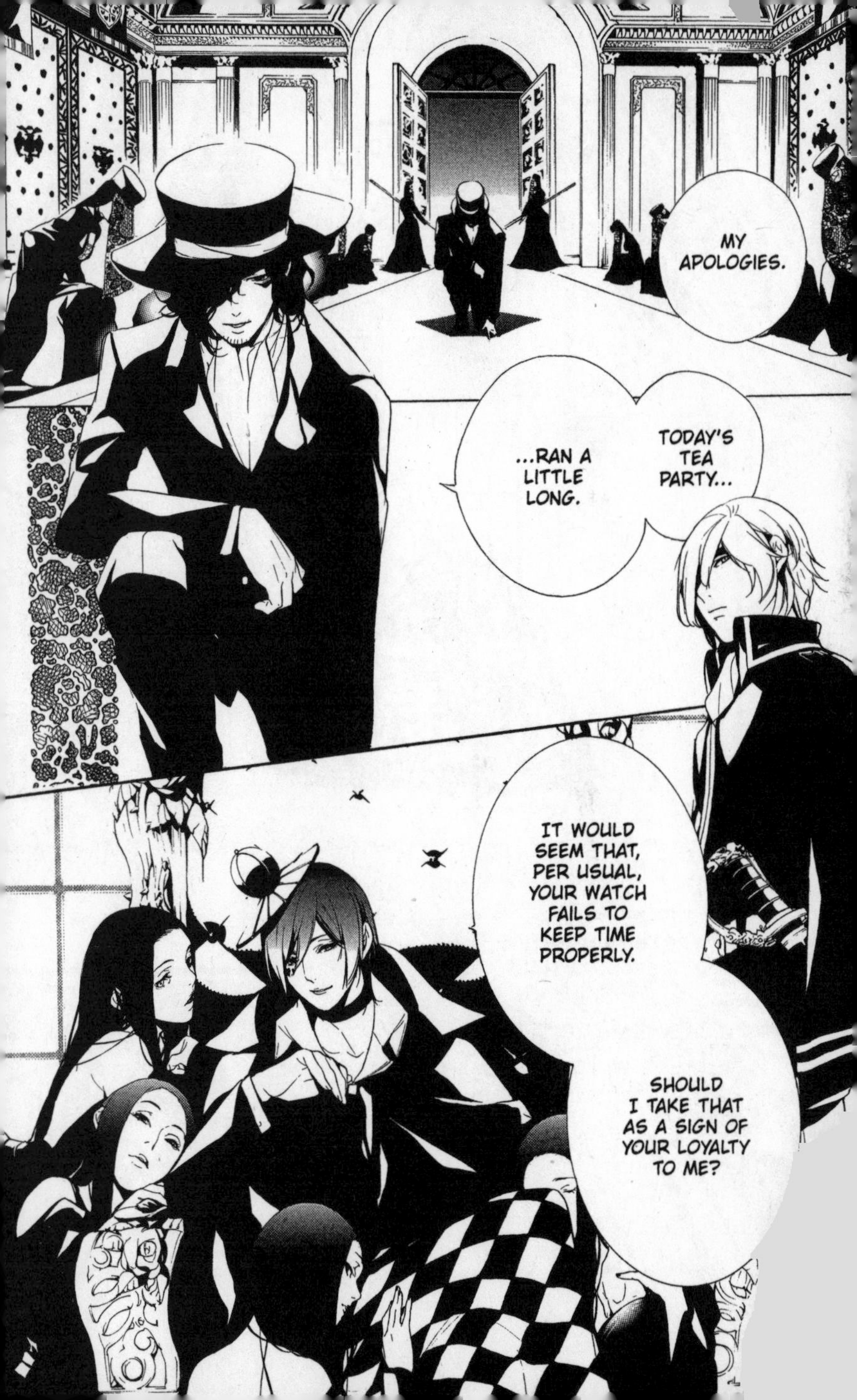
MY APOLOGIES.
TODAY'S TEA PARTY...
...RAN A LITTLE LONG.
IT WOULD SEEM THAT, PER USUAL, YOUR WATCH FAILS TO KEEP TIME PROPERLY.
SHOULD I TAKE THAT AS A SIGN OF YOUR LOYALTY TO ME?

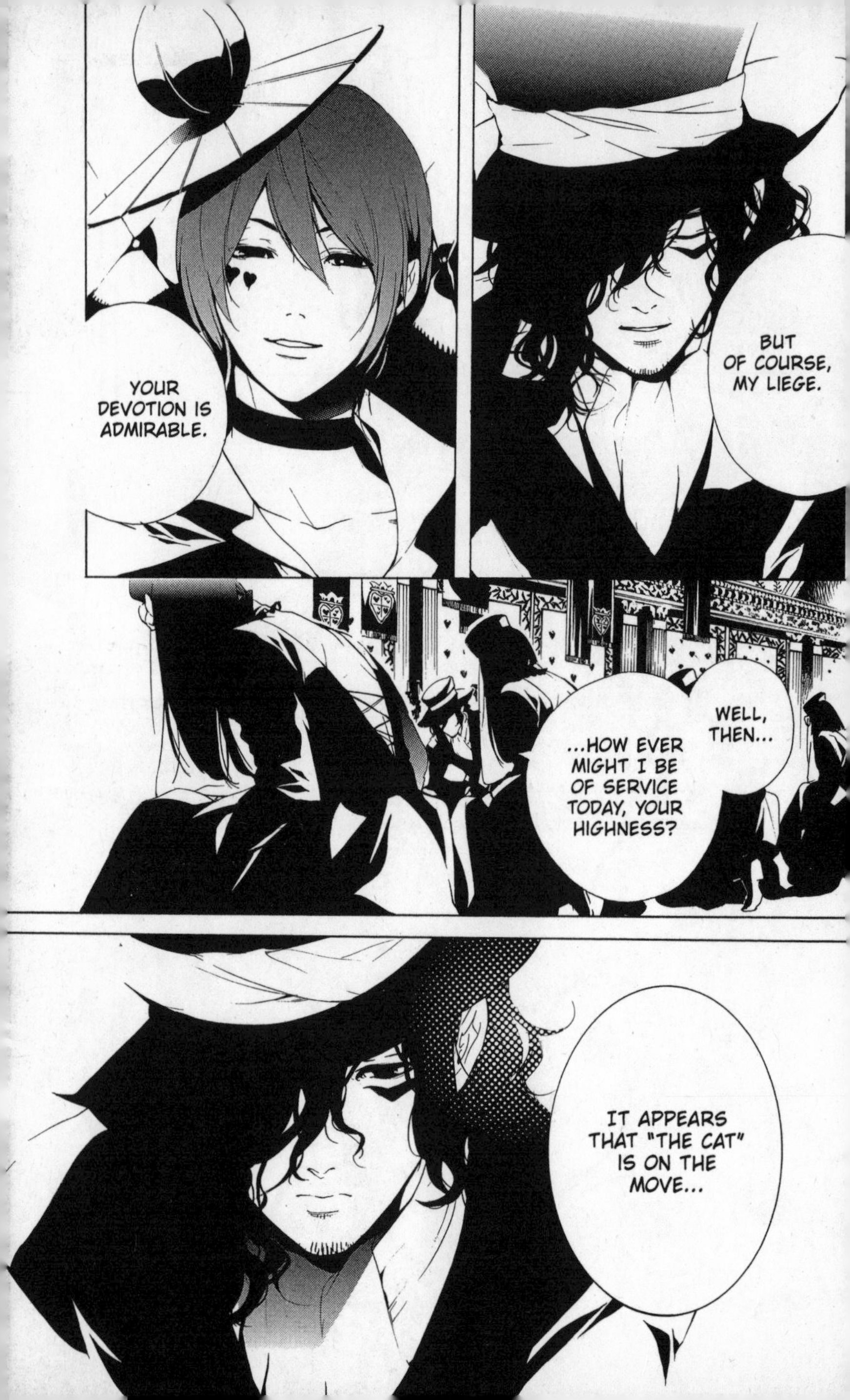
BUT OF COURSE, MY LIEGE.
YOUR DEVOTION IS ADMIRABLE.
WELL, THEN...
...HOW EVER MIGHT I BE OF SERVICE TODAY, YOUR HIGHNESS?
IT APPEARS THAT "THE CAT" IS ON THE MOVE...

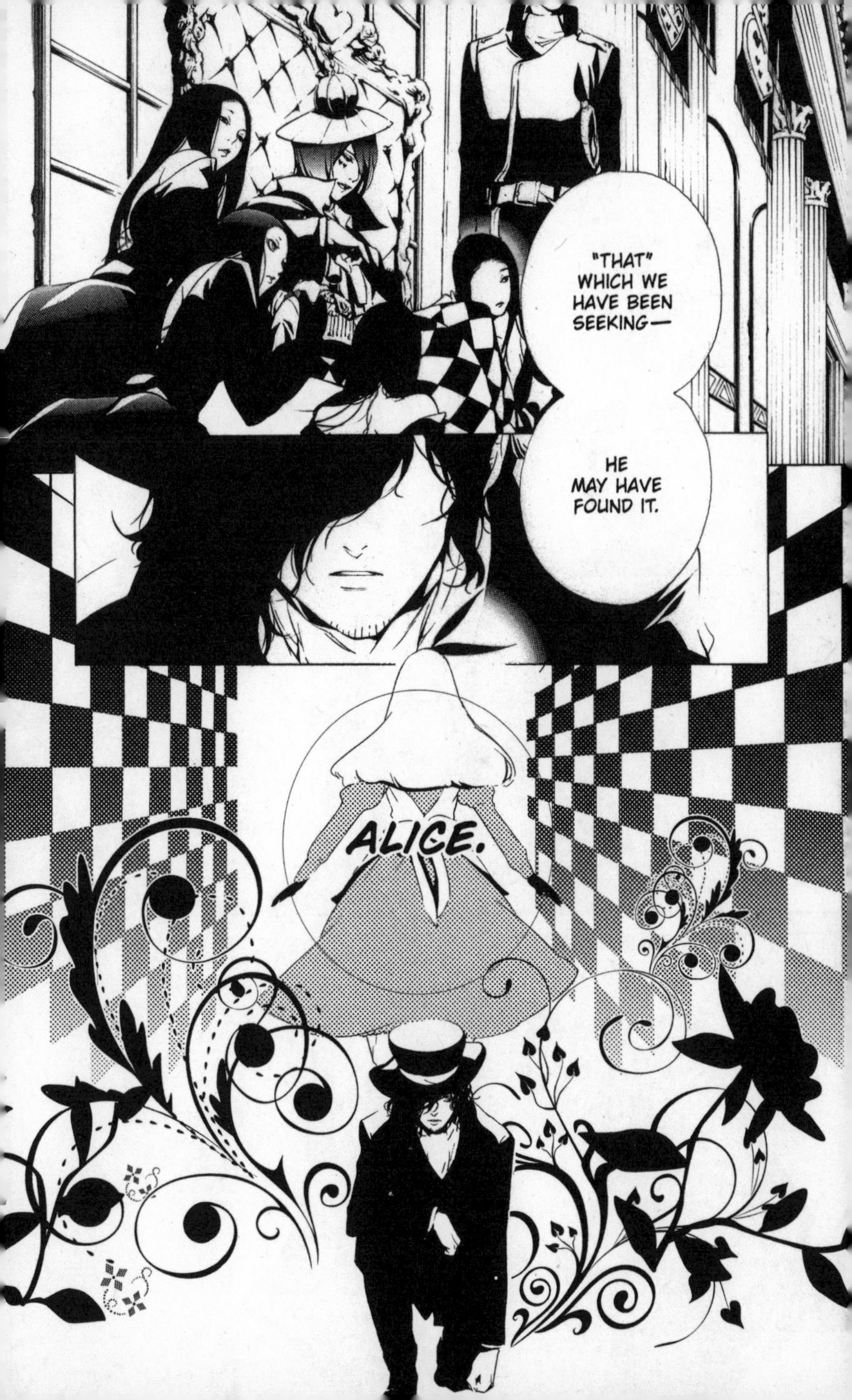
"THAT" WHICH WE HAVE BEEN SEEKING—
HE MAY HAVE FOUND IT.
ALICE.

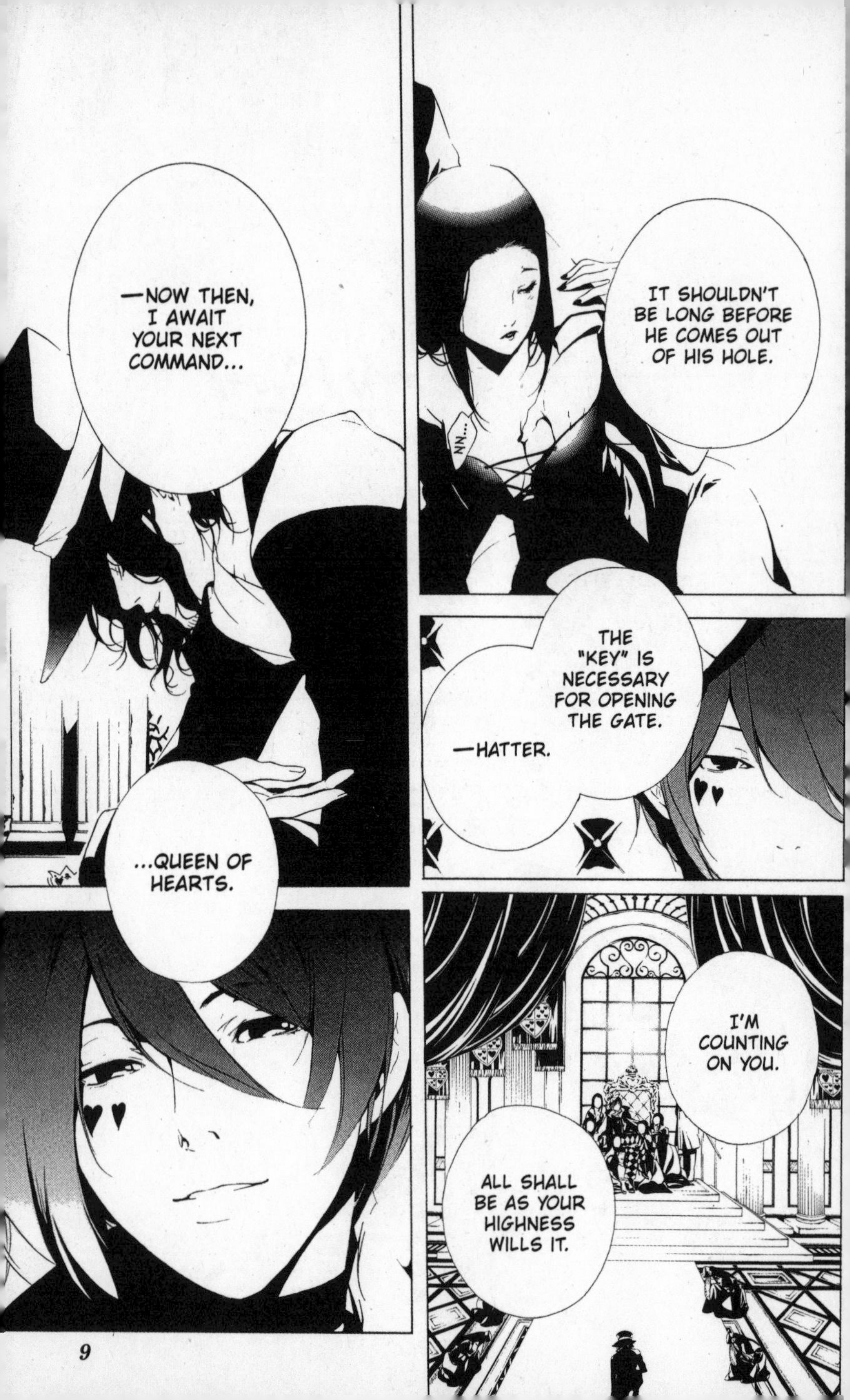
IT SHOULDN'T BE LONG BEFORE HE COMES OUT OF HIS HOLE.
NN...
THE "KEY" IS NECESSARY FOR OPENING THE GATE.
—HATTER.
—NOW THEN, I AWAIT YOUR NEXT COMMAND...
...QUEEN OF HEARTS.
I'M COUNTING ON YOU.
ALL SHALL BE AS YOUR HIGHNESS WILLS IT.

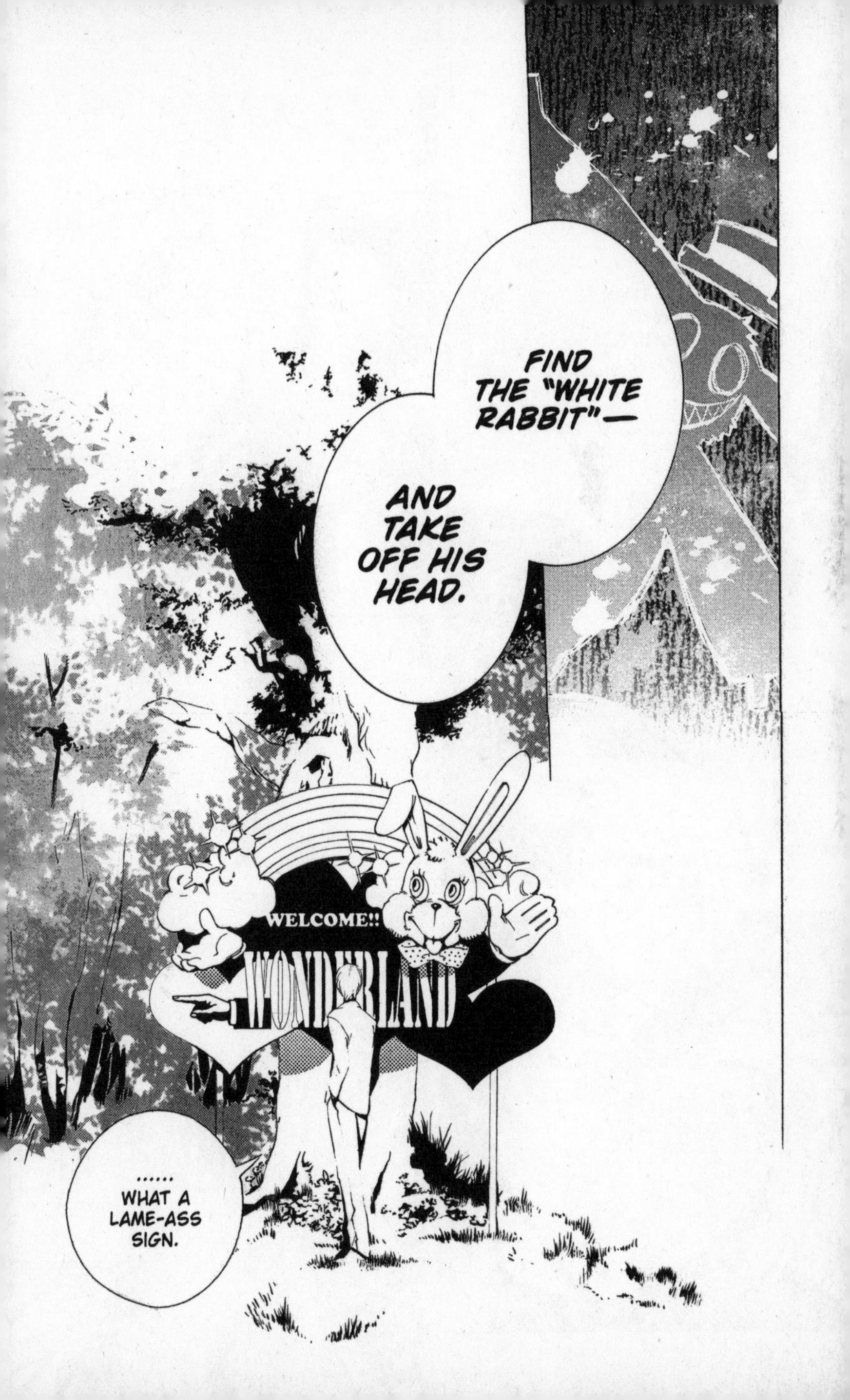
FIND THE "WHITE RABBIT"—
AND TAKE OFF HIS HEAD.
WELCOME!!
WONDERLAND
...... WHAT A LAME-ASS SIGN.

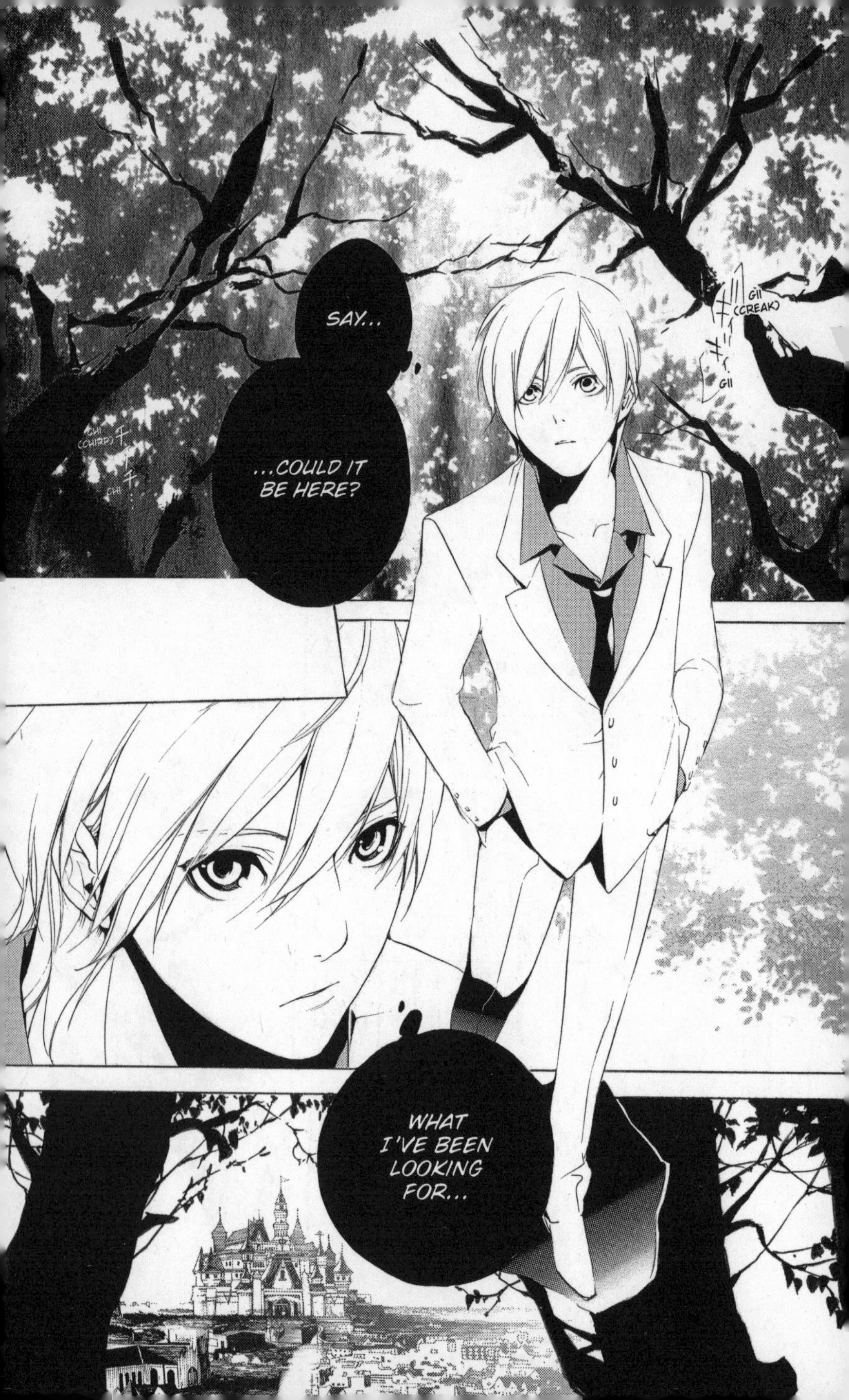
GII (CREAK)
GII
SAY...
...COULD IT BE HERE?
CHI (CHIRP)
CHI
WHAT I'VE BEEN LOOKING FOR...

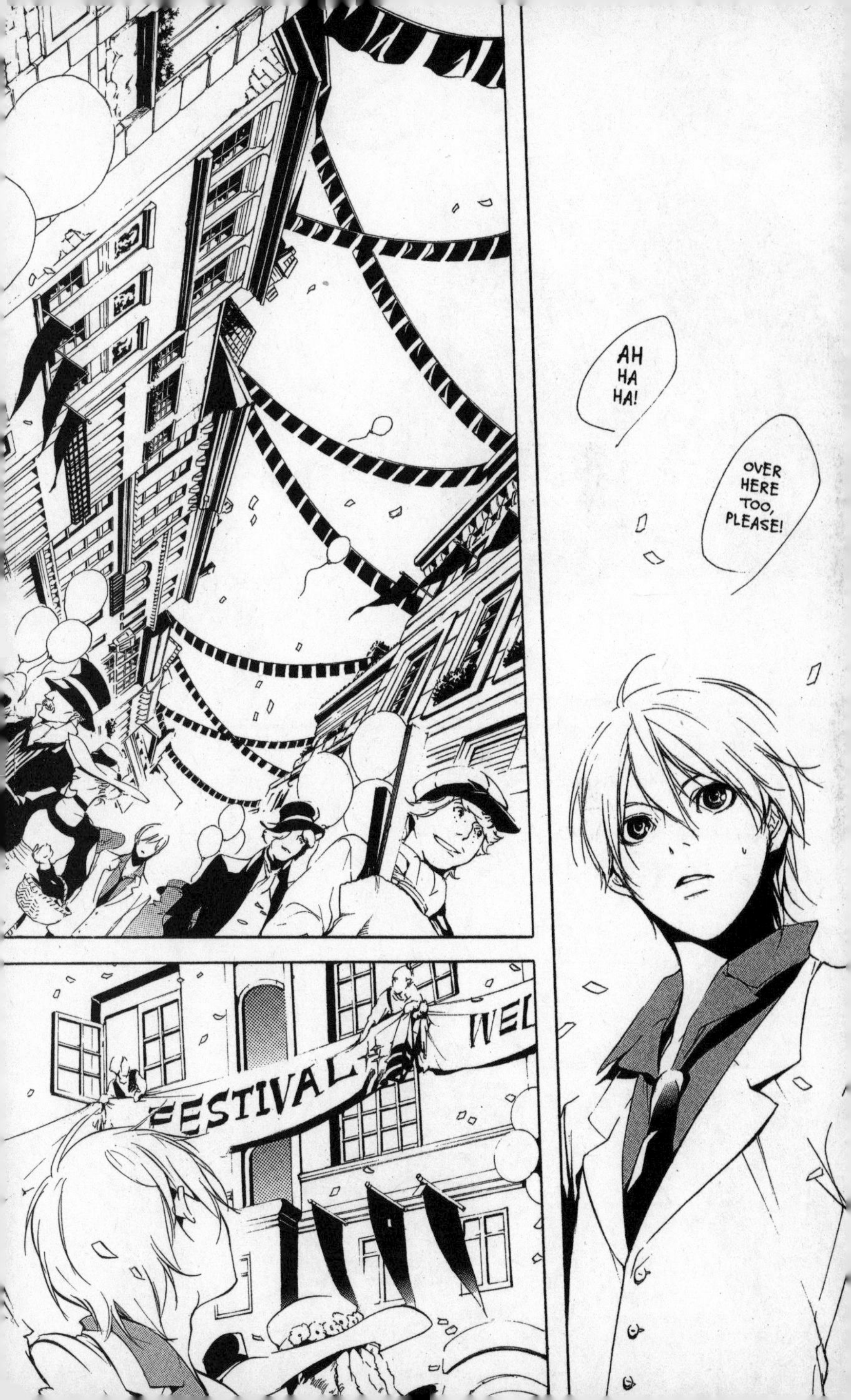
AH HA HA!
OVER HERE TOO, PLEASE!
WEL
FESTIVAL

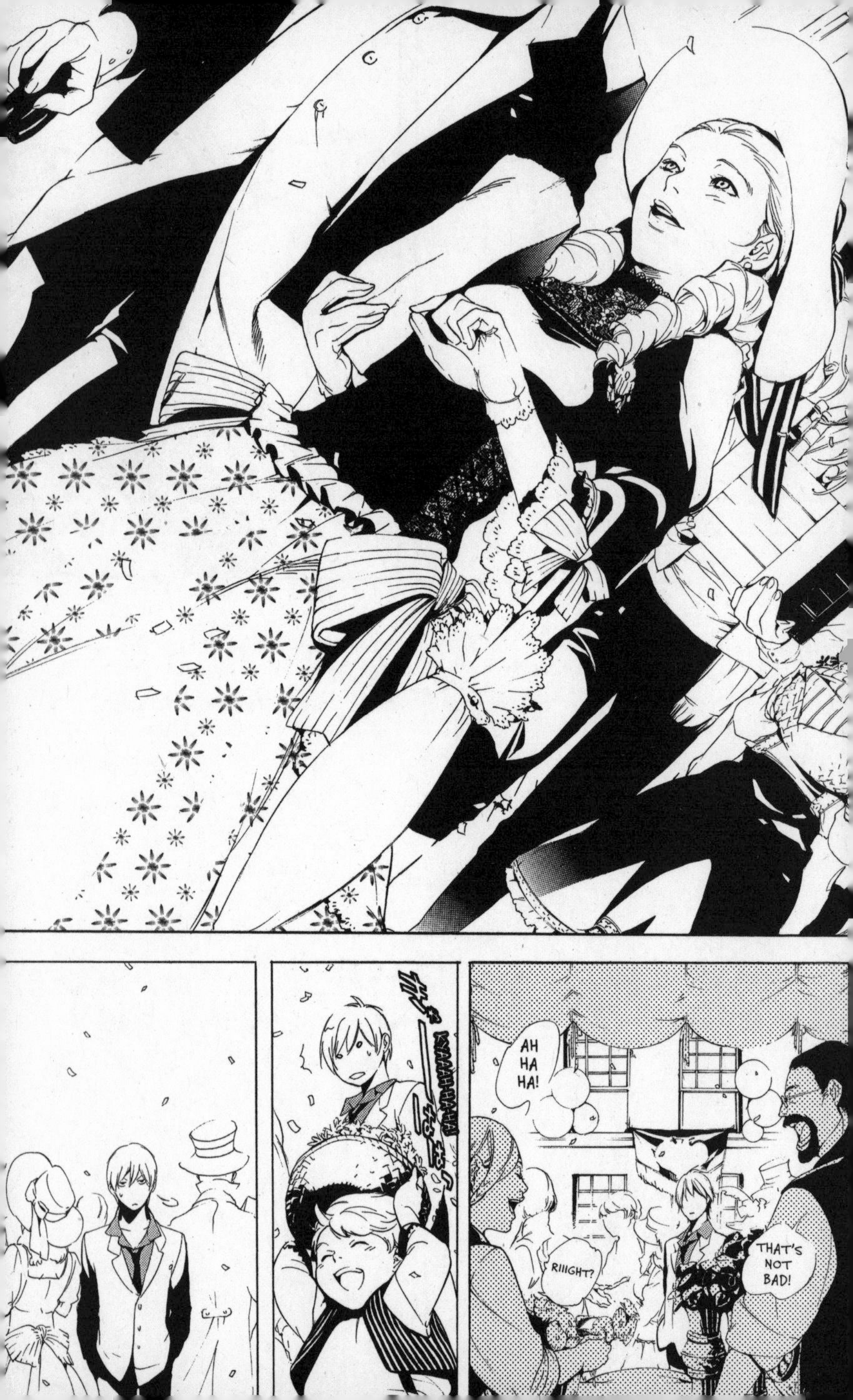
AH HA HA!
THAT'S NOT BAD!
RIIIGHT?
KYAAAH-HA-HA-HA!

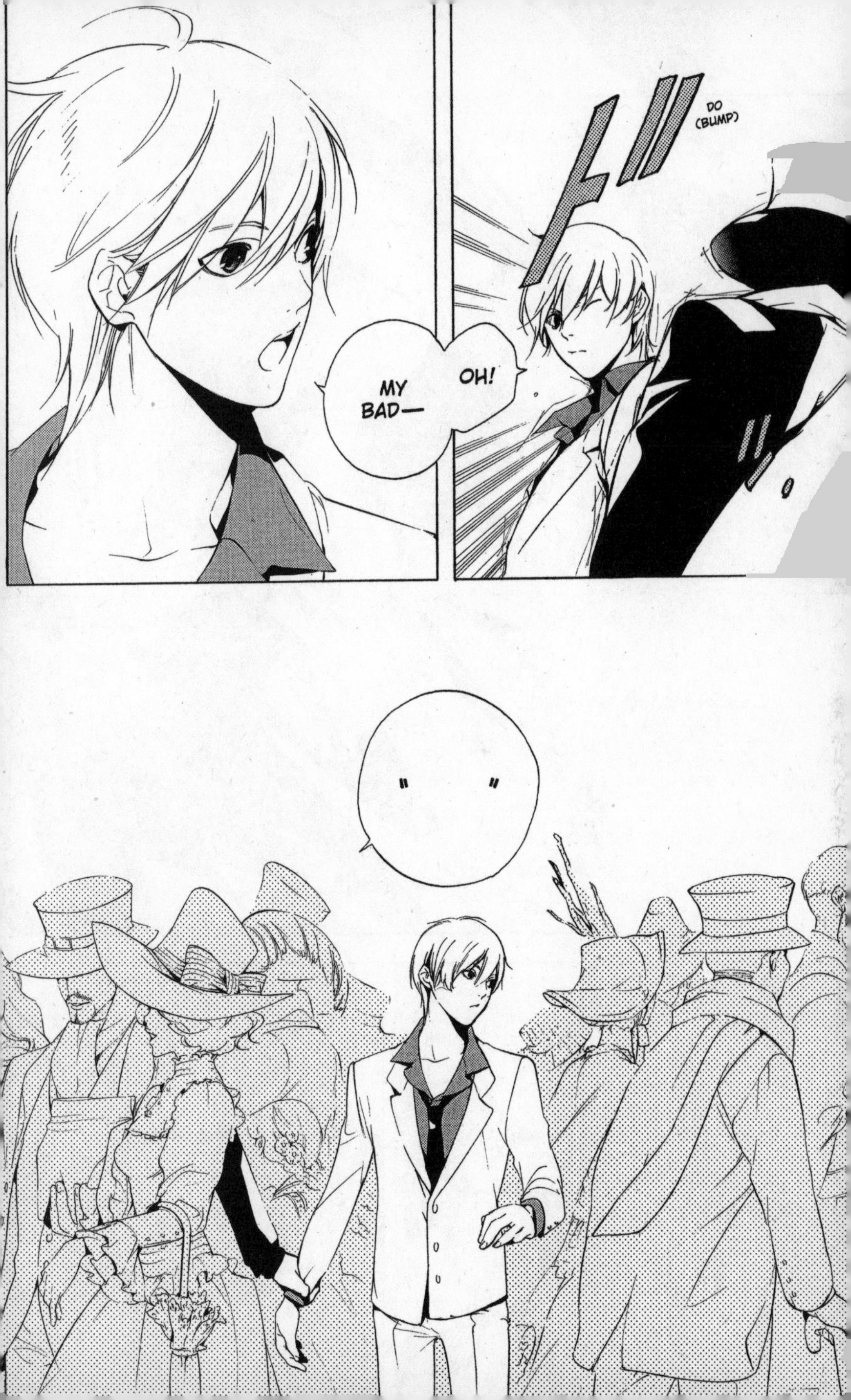
DO
(BUMP)
OH!
MY BAD—

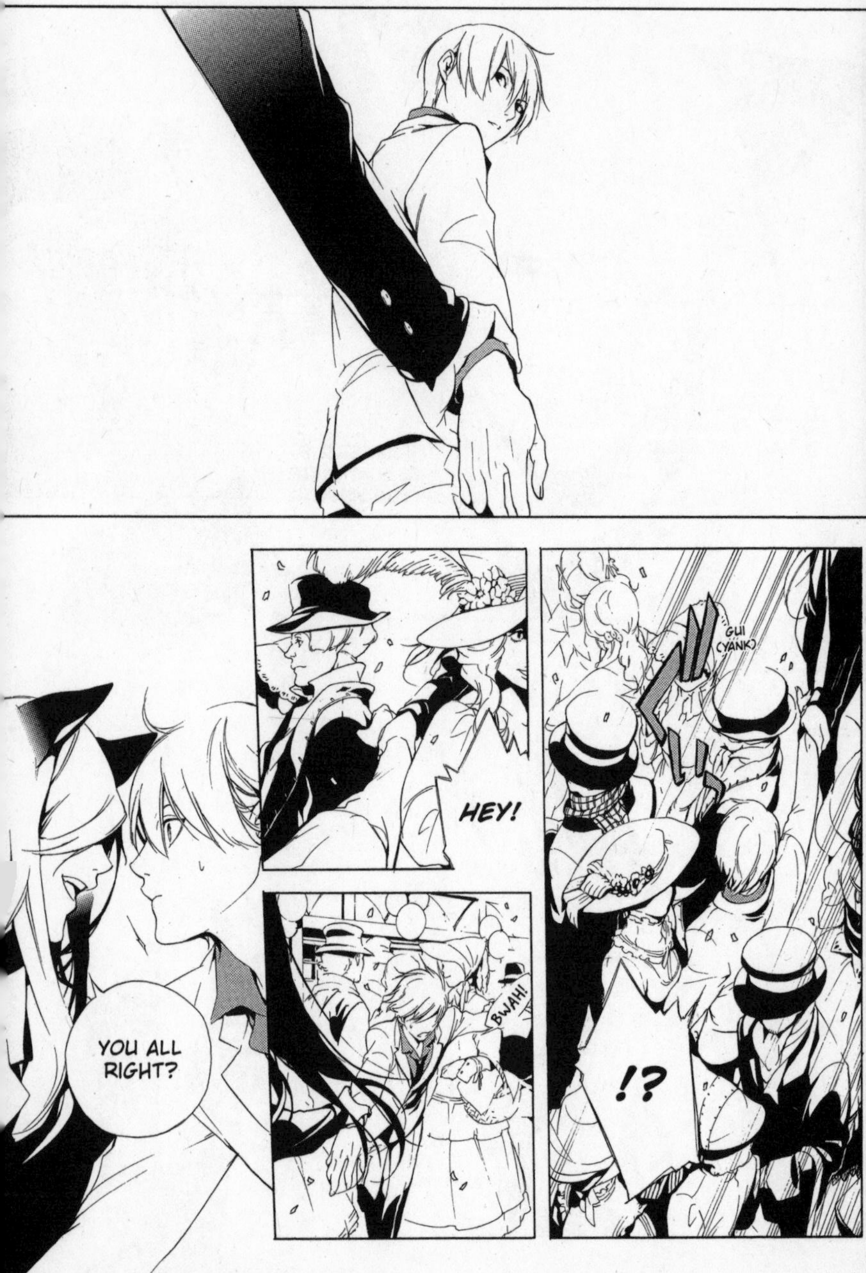
GUI (YANK)
!?
HEY!
BWAH!
YOU ALL RIGHT?

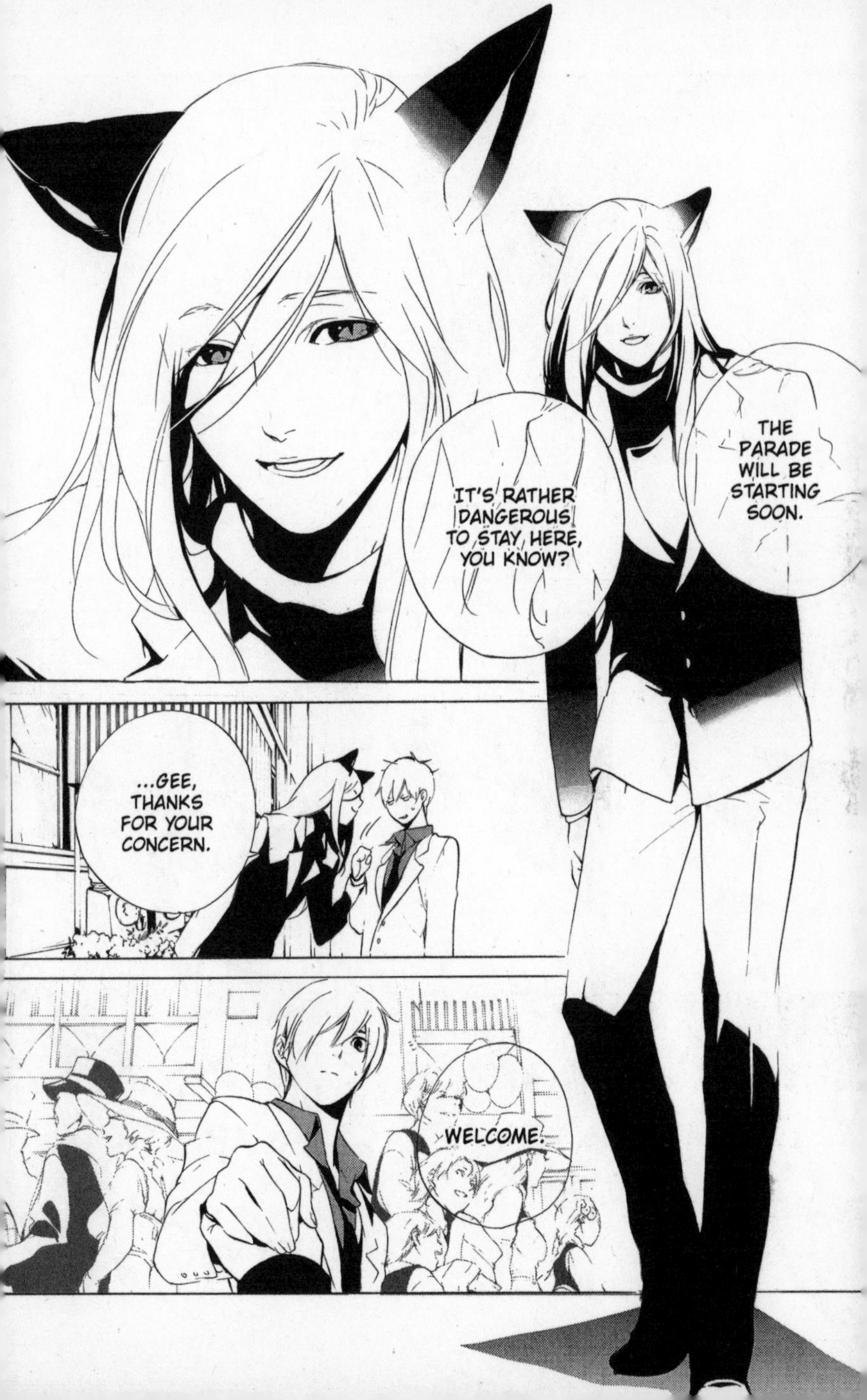
THE PARADE WILL BE STARTING SOON.
IT'S RATHER DANGEROUS TO STAY HERE, YOU KNOW?
...GEE, THANKS FOR YOUR CONCERN.
WELCOME.

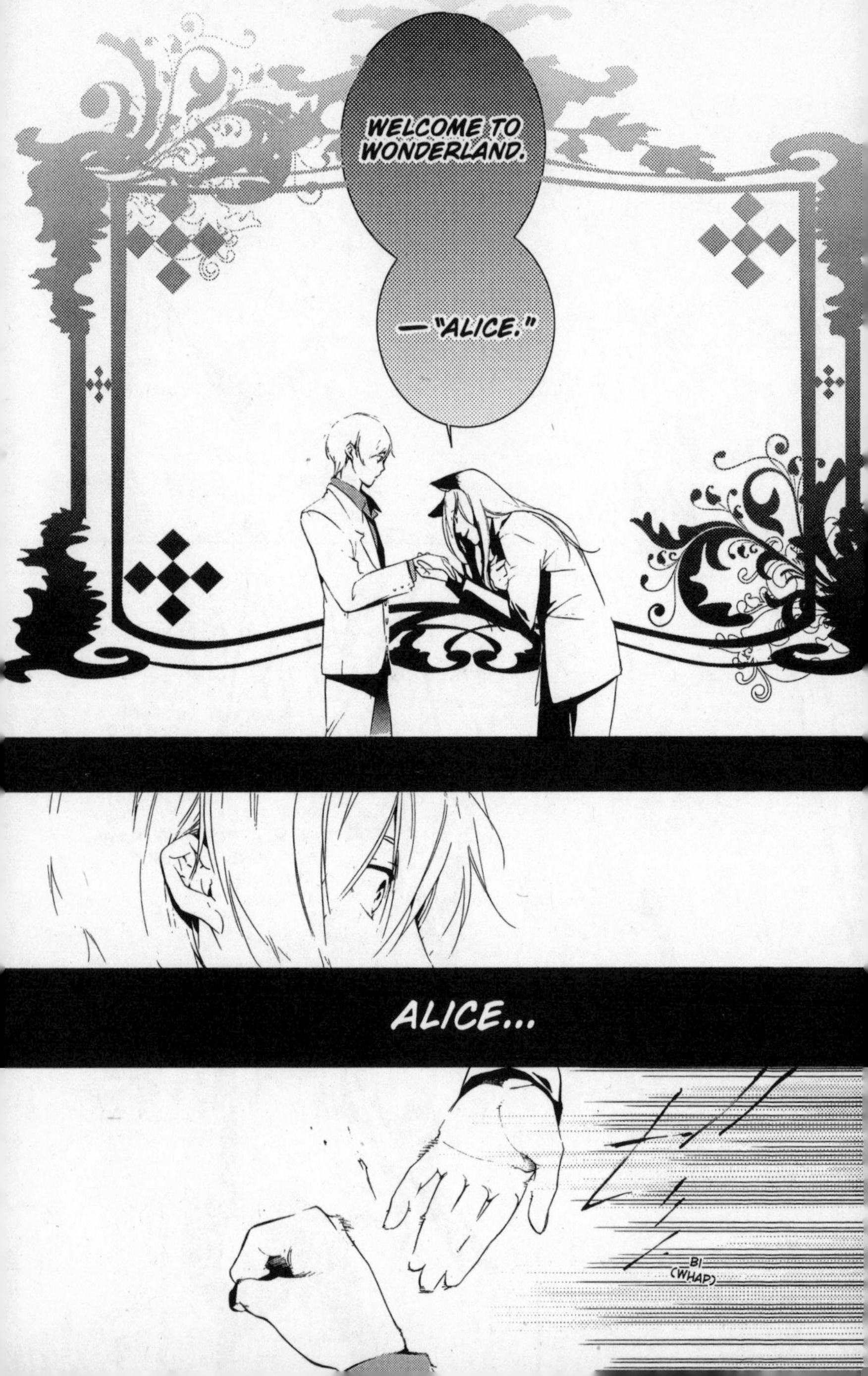
WELCOME TO WONDERLAND.
—"ALICE."
ALICE...
BI (WHAP)

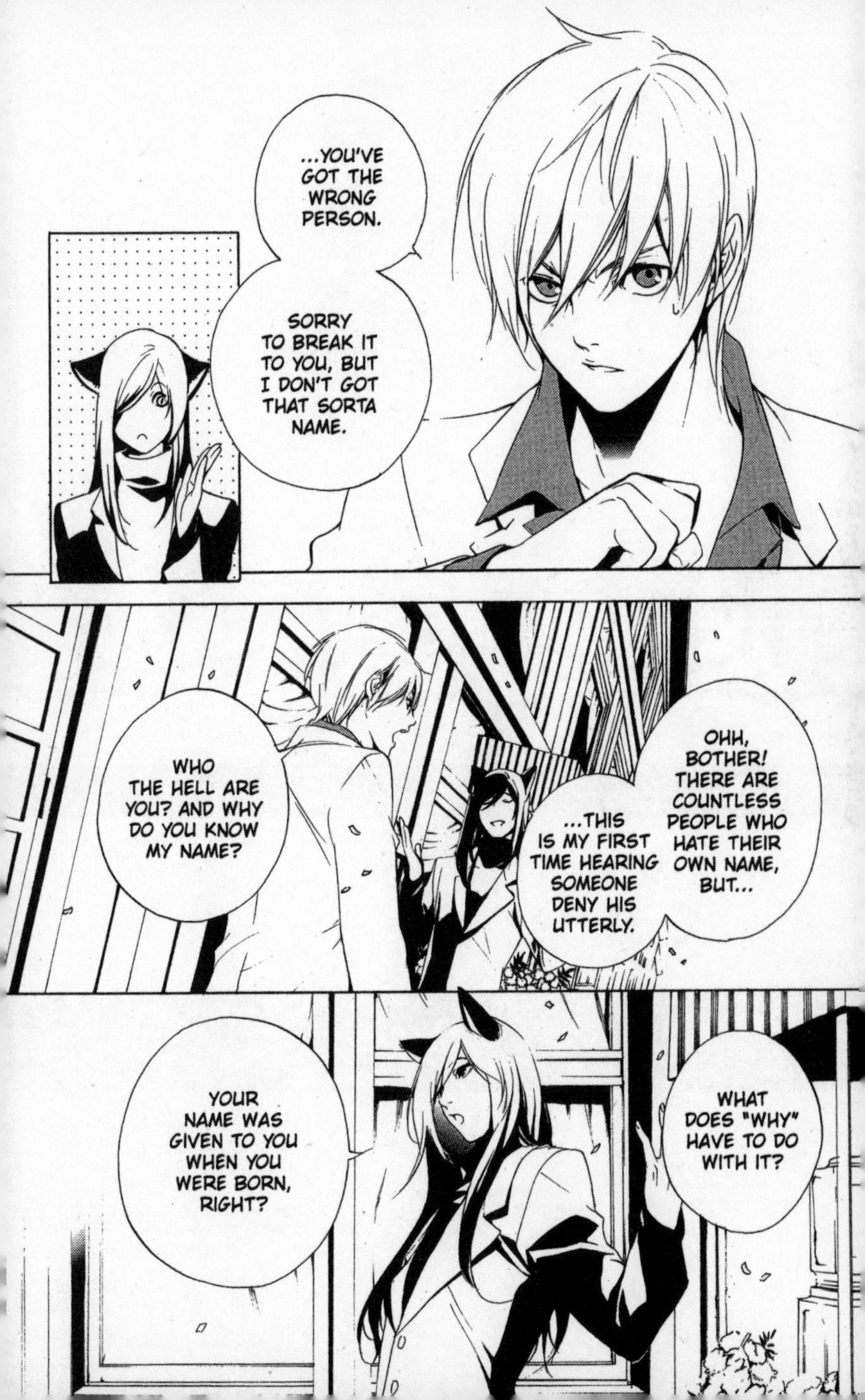
...YOU'VE GOT THE WRONG PERSON.
SORRY TO BREAK IT TO YOU, BUT I DON'T GOT THAT SORTA NAME.
OHH, BOTHER! THERE ARE COUNTLESS PEOPLE WHO HATE THEIR OWN NAME, BUT...
...THIS IS MY FIRST TIME HEARING SOMEONE DENY HIS UTTERLY.
WHO THE HELL ARE YOU? AND WHY DO YOU KNOW MY NAME?
WHAT DOES "WHY" HAVE TO DO WITH IT?
YOUR NAME WAS GIVEN TO YOU WHEN YOU WERE BORN, RIGHT?

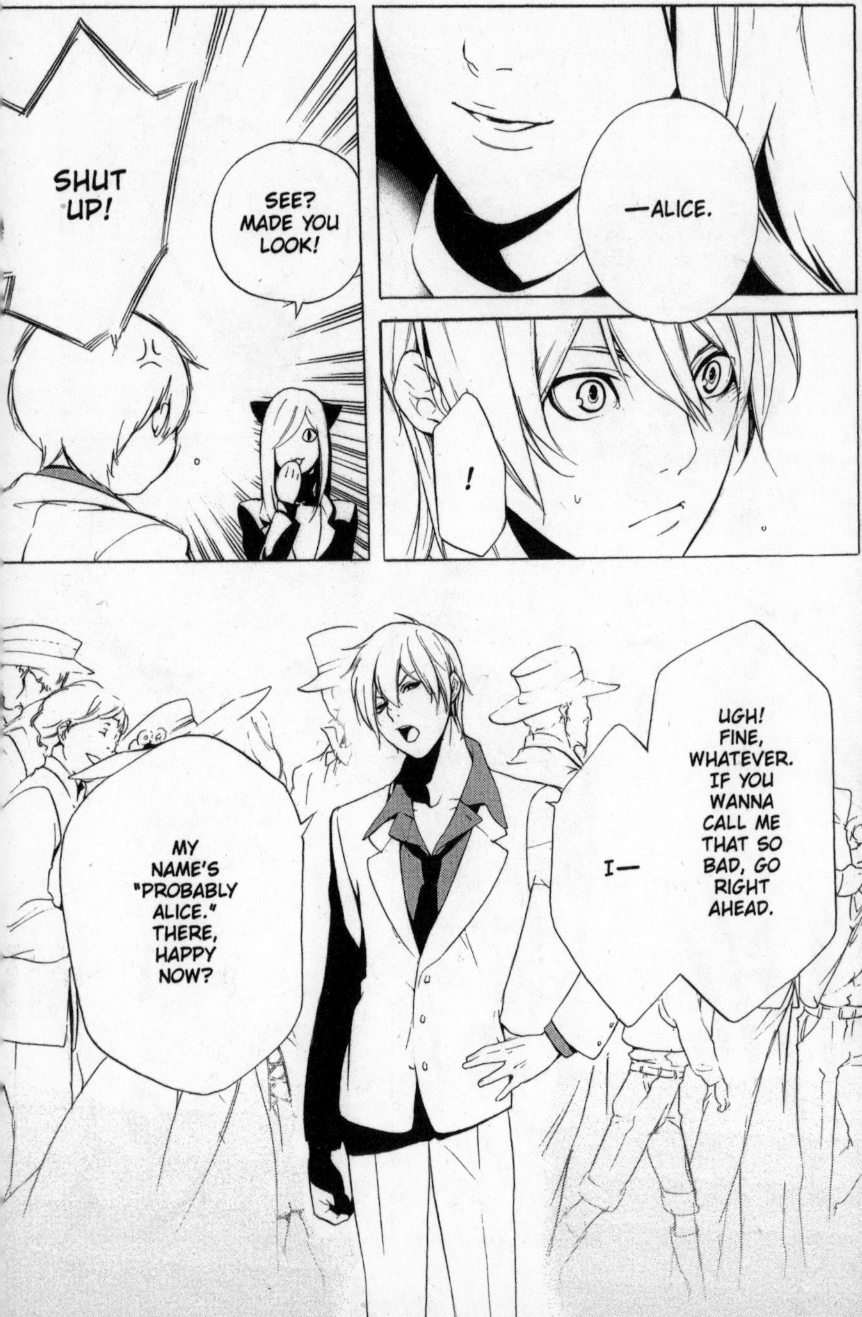
—ALICE.
!
SEE? MADE YOU LOOK!
SHUT UP!
UGH! FINE, WHATEVER. IF YOU WANNA CALL ME THAT SO BAD, GO RIGHT AHEAD.
I—
MY NAME'S "PROBABLY ALICE." THERE, HAPPY NOW?

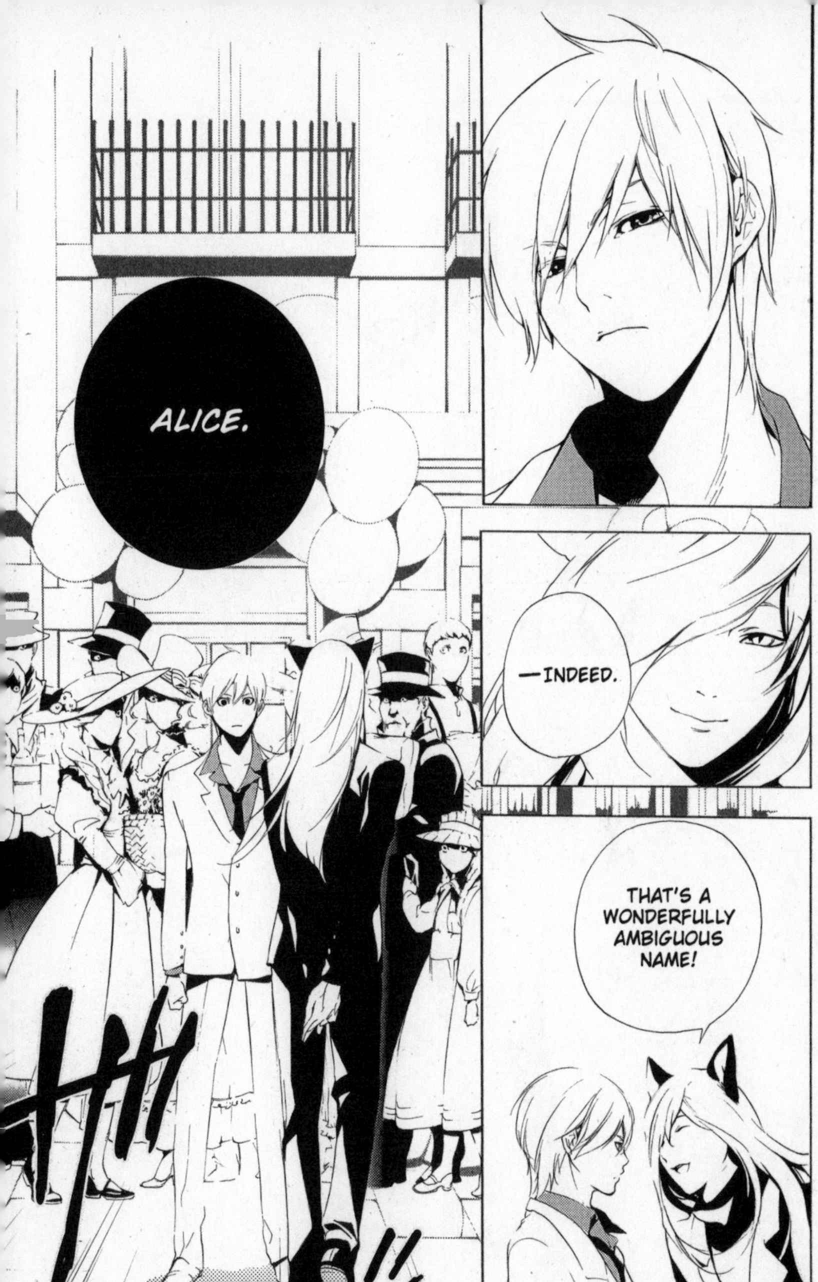
—INDEED.
THAT'S A WONDERFULLY AMBIGUOUS NAME!
ALICE.
ZA (FWOOSH)

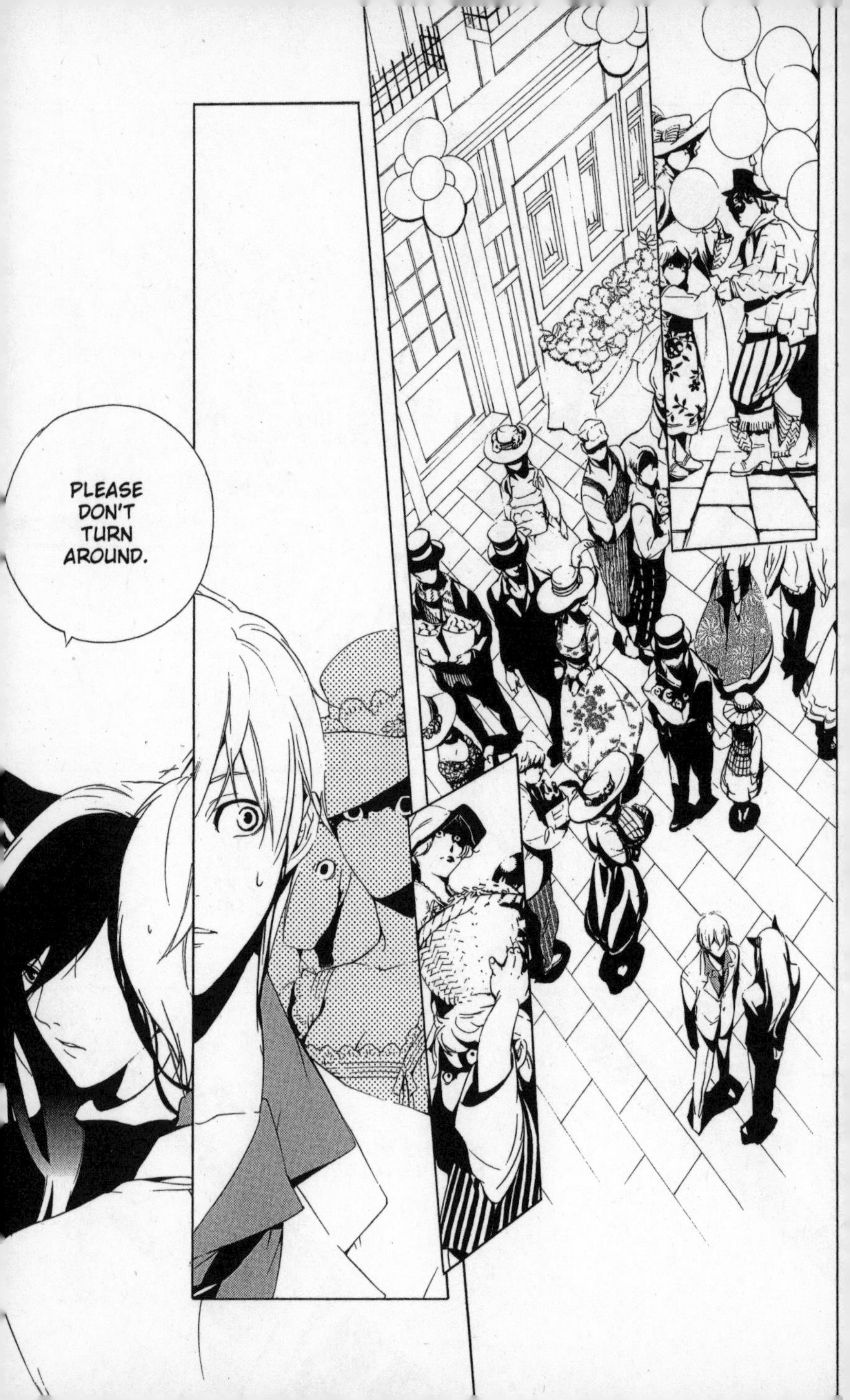
PLEASE DON'T TURN AROUND.

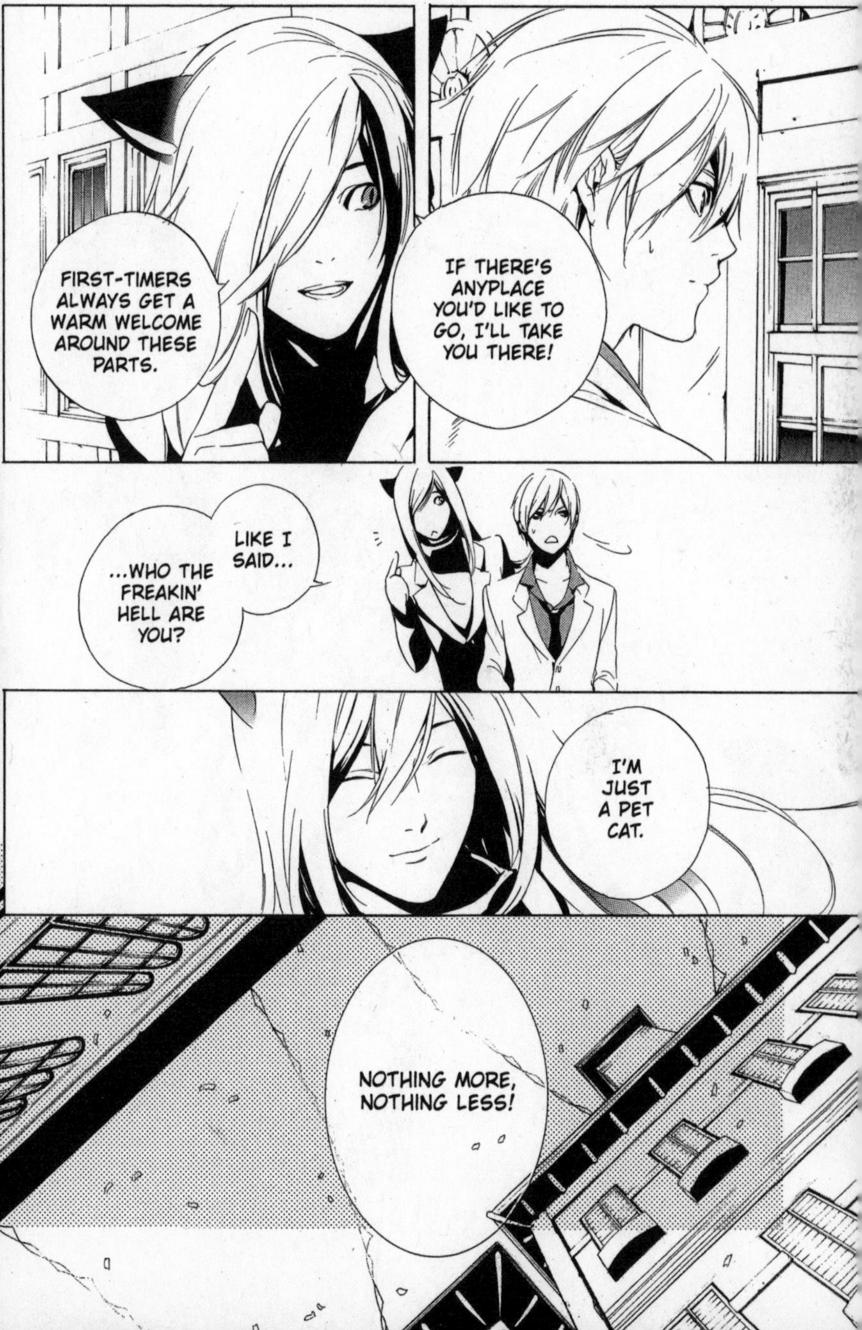
IF THERE'S ANYPLACE YOU'D LIKE TO GO, I'LL TAKE YOU THERE!
FIRST-TIMERS ALWAYS GET A WARM WELCOME AROUND THESE PARTS.
LIKE I SAID...
...WHO THE FREAKIN' HELL ARE YOU?
I'M JUST A PET CAT.
NOTHING MORE, NOTHING LESS!

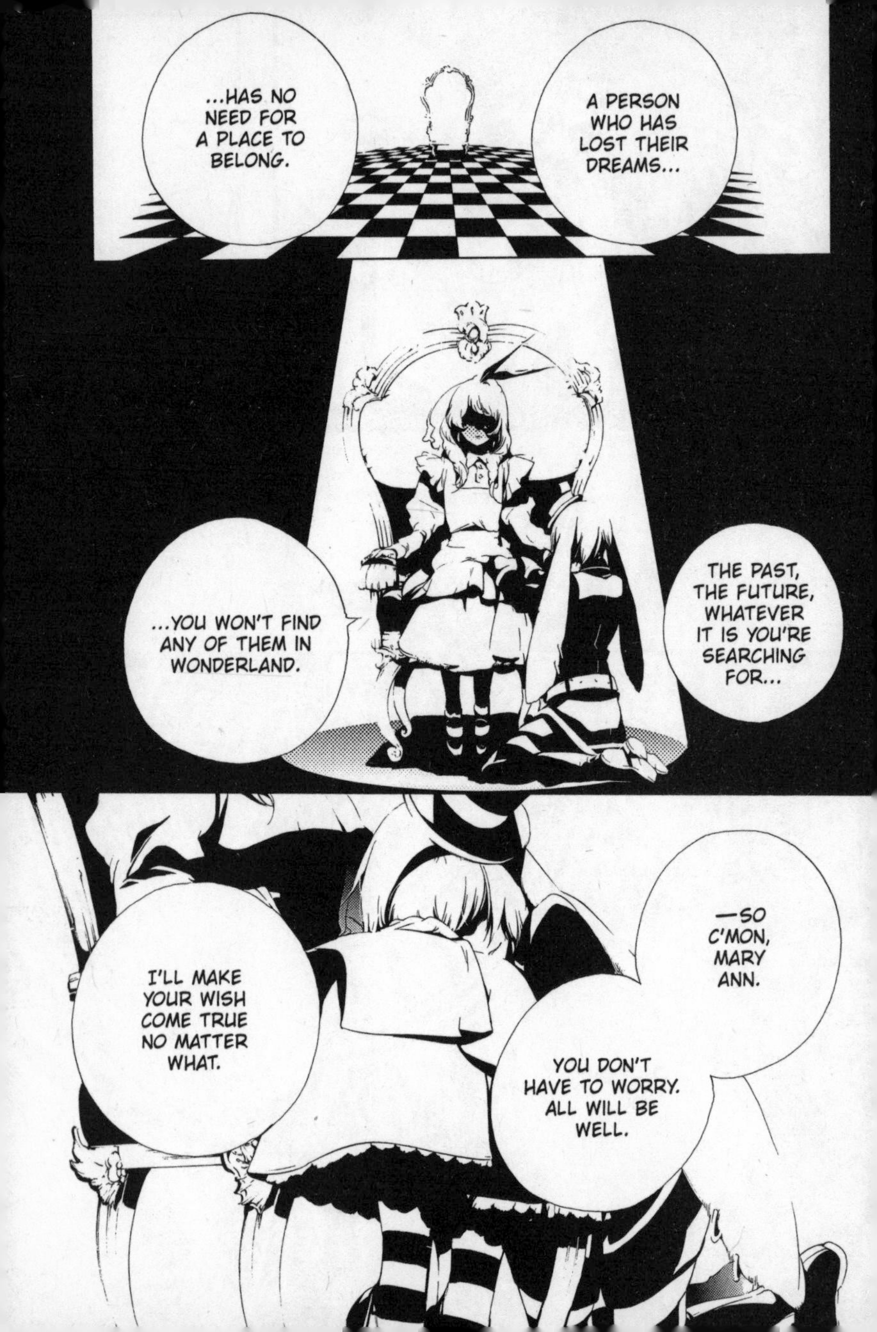
A PERSON WHO HAS LOST THEIR DREAMS...
...HAS NO NEED FOR A PLACE TO BELONG.
THE PAST, THE FUTURE, WHATEVER IT IS YOU'RE SEARCHING FOR...
...YOU WON'T FIND ANY OF THEM IN WONDERLAND.
—SO C'MON, MARY ANN.
YOU DON'T HAVE TO WORRY. ALL WILL BE WELL.
I'LL MAKE YOUR WISH COME TRUE NO MATTER WHAT.

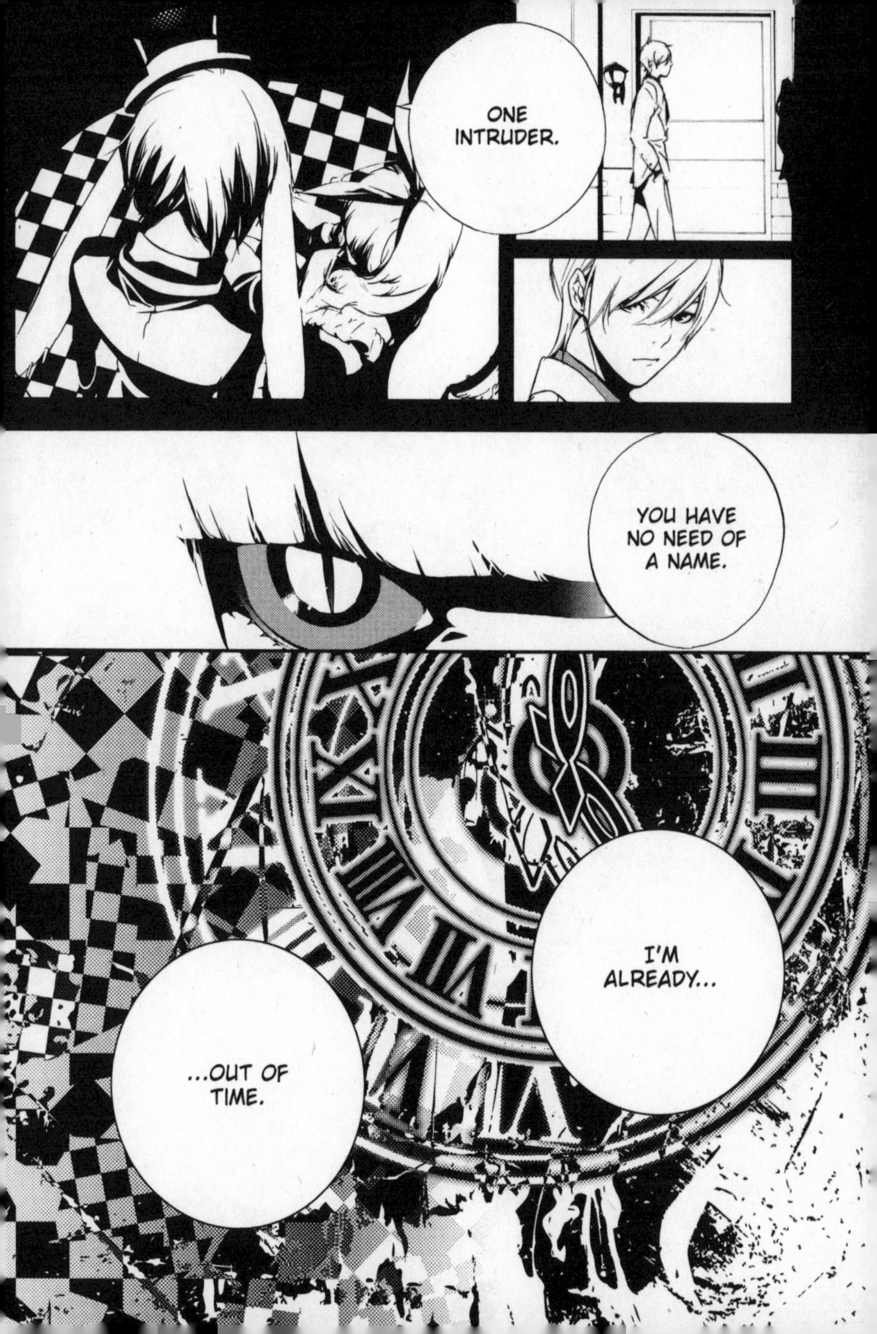
ONE INTRUDER.
YOU HAVE NO NEED OF A NAME.
I'M ALREADY...
...OUT OF TIME.

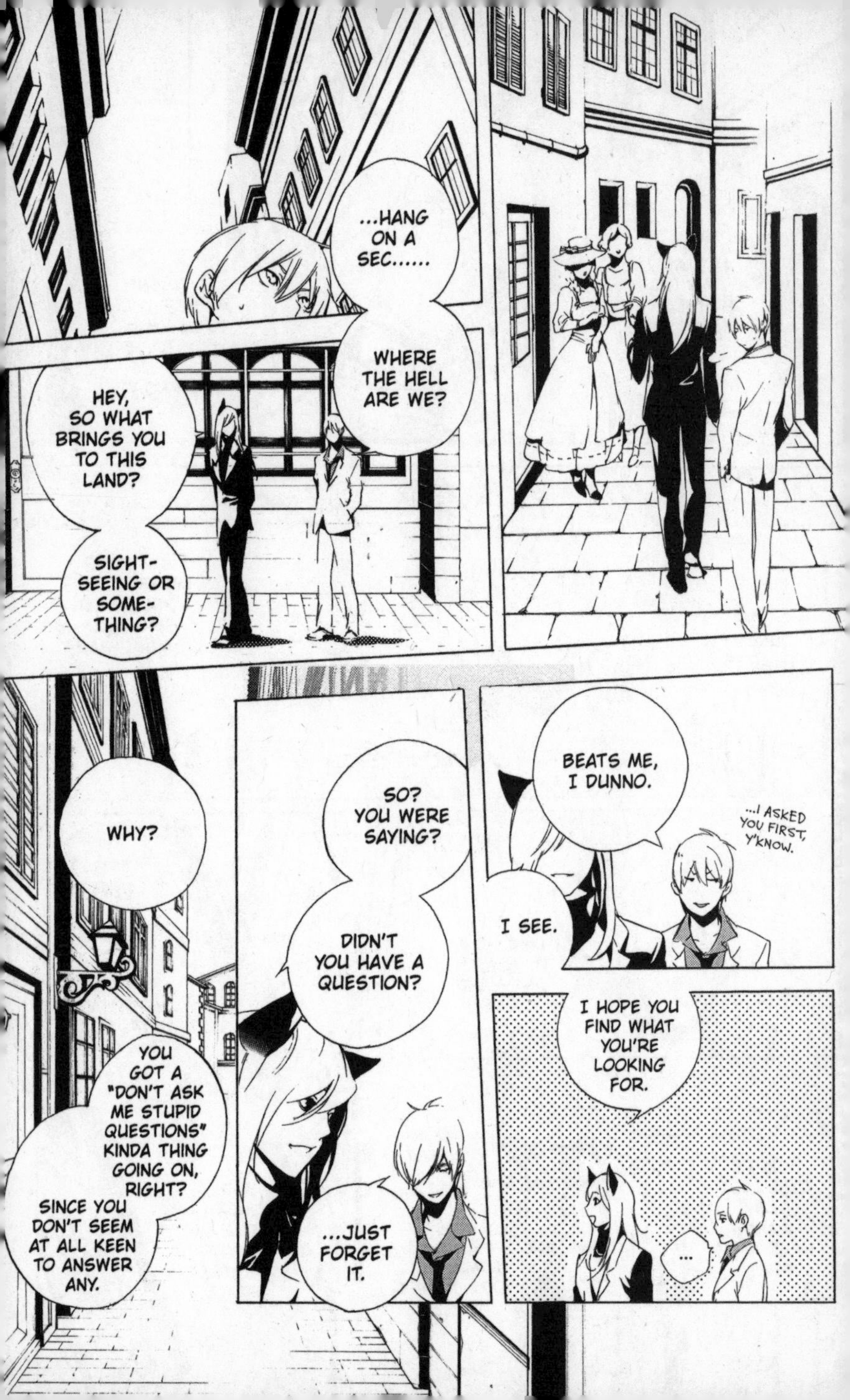
...HANG ON A SEC......
WHERE THE HELL ARE WE?
HEY, SO WHAT BRINGS YOU TO THIS LAND?
SIGHT-SEEING OR SOME-THING?
BEATS ME, I DUNNO.
...I ASKED YOU FIRST, Y'KNOW.
I SEE.
I HOPE YOU FIND WHAT YOU'RE LOOKING FOR.
...
SO? YOU WERE SAYING?
DIDN'T YOU HAVE A QUESTION?
...JUST FORGET IT.
WHY?
YOU GOT A "DON'T ASK ME STUPID QUESTIONS" KINDA THING GOING ON, RIGHT?
SINCE YOU DON'T SEEM AT ALL KEEN TO ANSWER ANY.

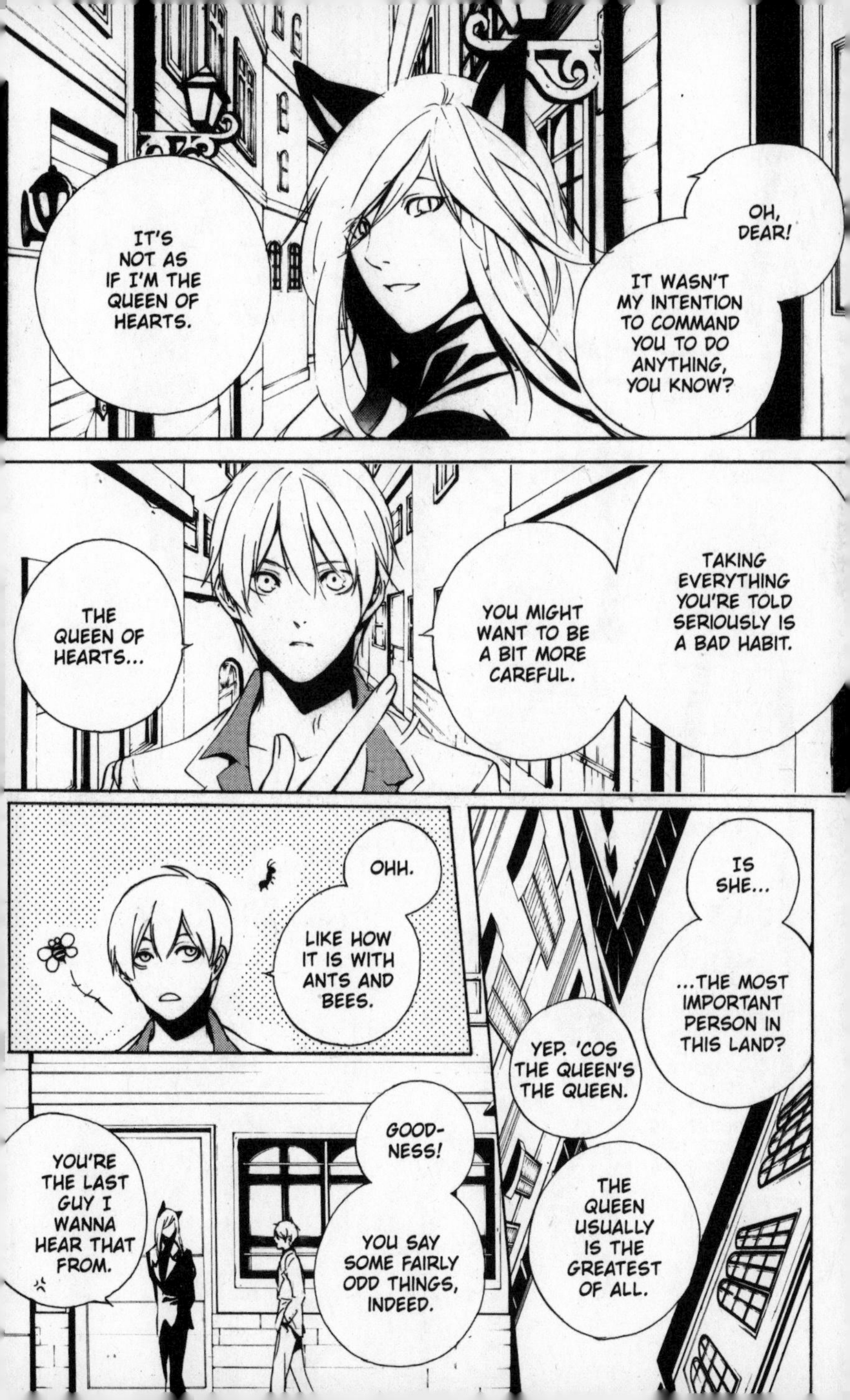
OH, DEAR!
IT WASN'T MY INTENTION TO COMMAND YOU TO DO ANYTHING, YOU KNOW?
IT'S NOT AS IF I'M THE QUEEN OF HEARTS.
TAKING EVERYTHING YOU'RE TOLD SERIOUSLY IS A BAD HABIT.
YOU MIGHT WANT TO BE A BIT MORE CAREFUL.
THE QUEEN OF HEARTS...
IS SHE...
...THE MOST IMPORTANT PERSON IN THIS LAND?
YEP. 'COS THE QUEEN'S THE QUEEN.
THE QUEEN USUALLY IS THE GREATEST OF ALL.
OHH.
LIKE HOW IT IS WITH ANTS AND BEES.
GOOD-NESS!
YOU SAY SOME FAIRLY ODD THINGS, INDEED.
YOU'RE THE LAST GUY I WANNA HEAR THAT FROM.

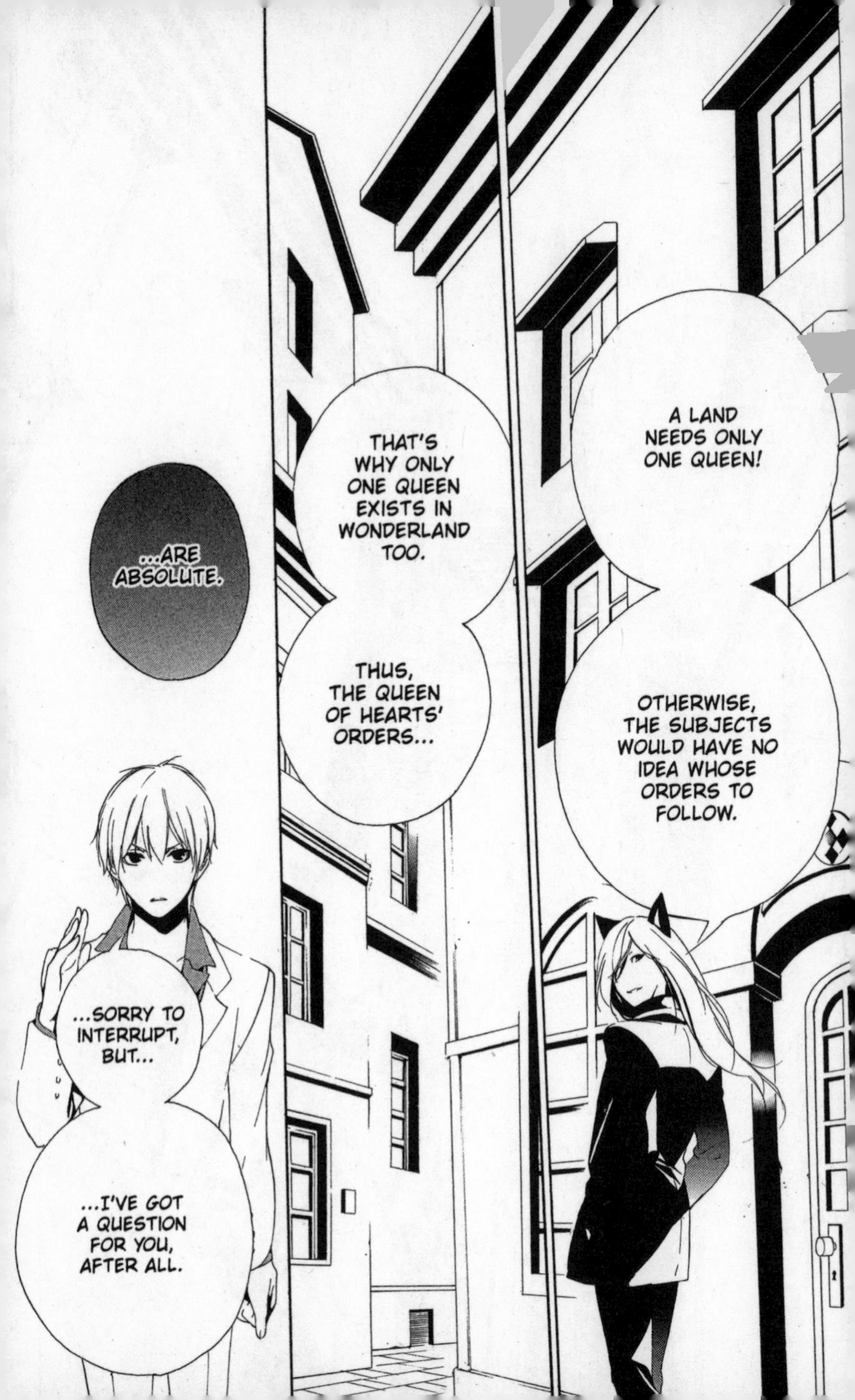
A LAND NEEDS ONLY ONE QUEEN!
OTHERWISE, THE SUBJECTS WOULD HAVE NO IDEA WHOSE ORDERS TO FOLLOW.
THAT'S WHY ONLY ONE QUEEN EXISTS IN WONDERLAND TOO.
THUS, THE QUEEN OF HEARTS' ORDERS...
...ARE ABSOLUTE.
...SORRY TO INTERRUPT, BUT...
...I'VE GOT A QUESTION FOR YOU, AFTER ALL.

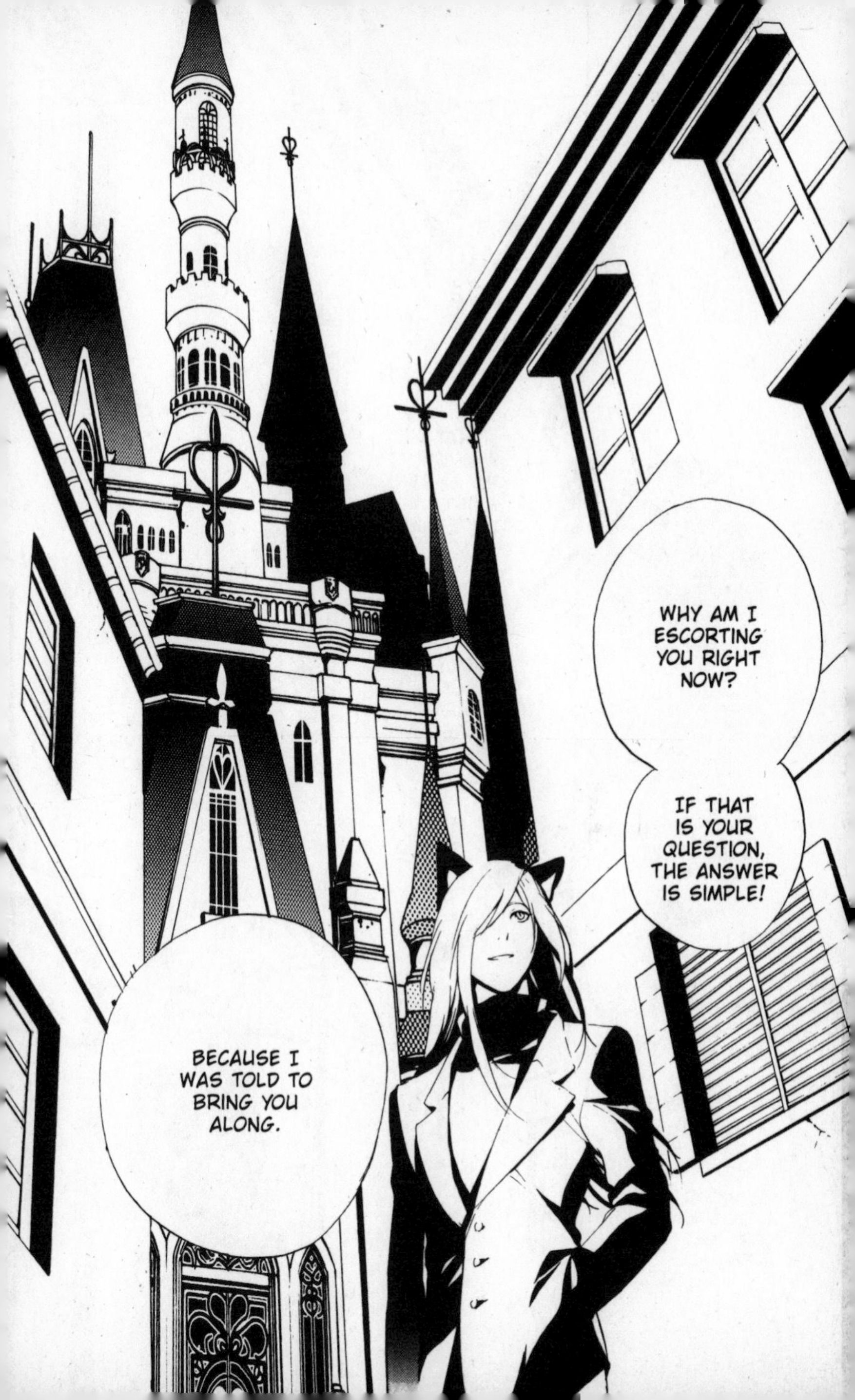
WHY AM I ESCORTING YOU RIGHT NOW?
IF THAT IS YOUR QUESTION, THE ANSWER IS SIMPLE!
BECAUSE I WAS TOLD TO BRING YOU ALONG.

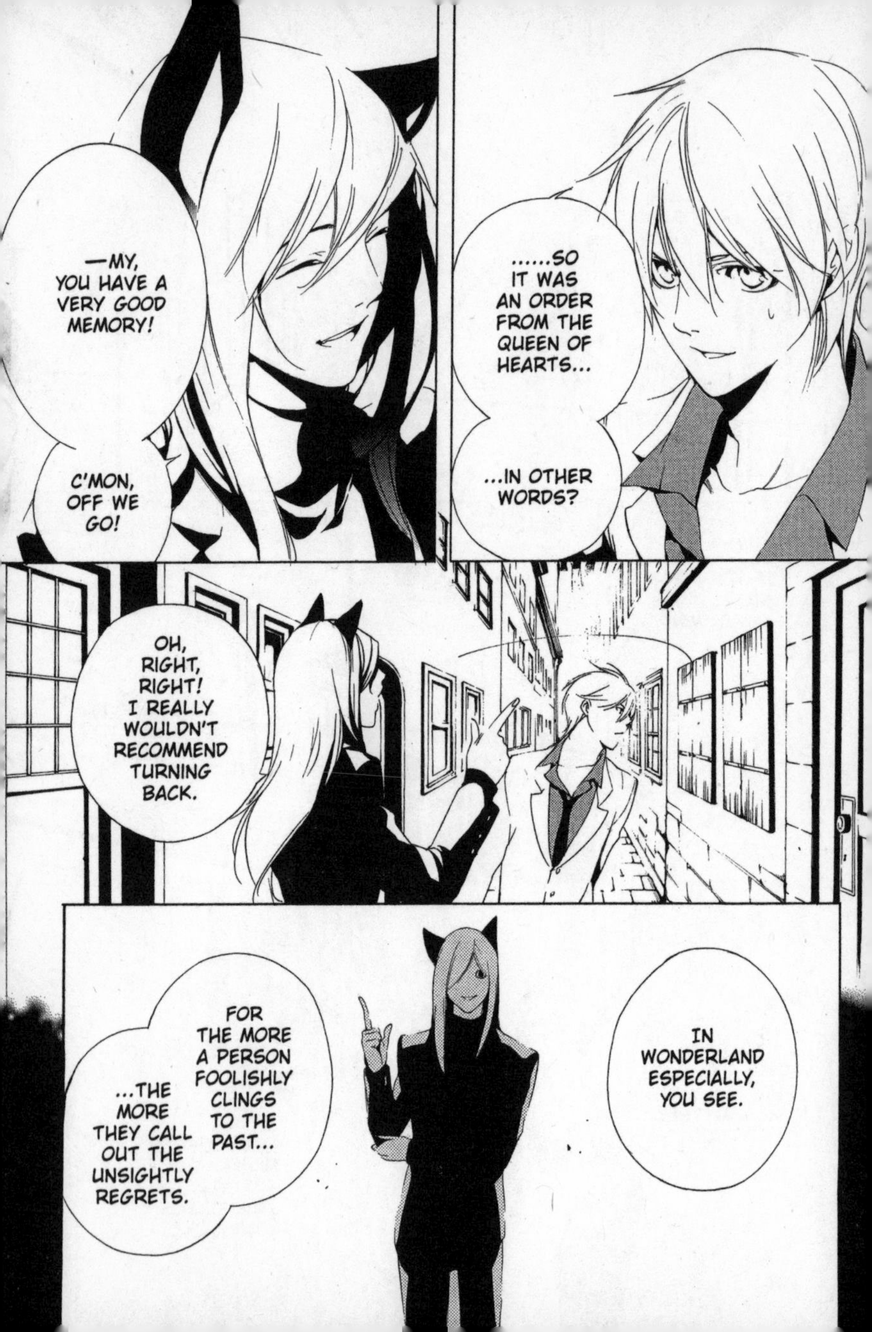
......SO IT WAS AN ORDER FROM THE QUEEN OF HEARTS...
...IN OTHER WORDS?
—MY, YOU HAVE A VERY GOOD MEMORY!
C'MON, OFF WE GO!
OH, RIGHT, RIGHT! I REALLY WOULDN'T RECOMMEND TURNING BACK.
IN WONDERLAND ESPECIALLY, YOU SEE.
FOR THE MORE A PERSON FOOLISHLY CLINGS TO THE PAST...
...THE MORE THEY CALL OUT THE UNSIGHTLY REGRETS.

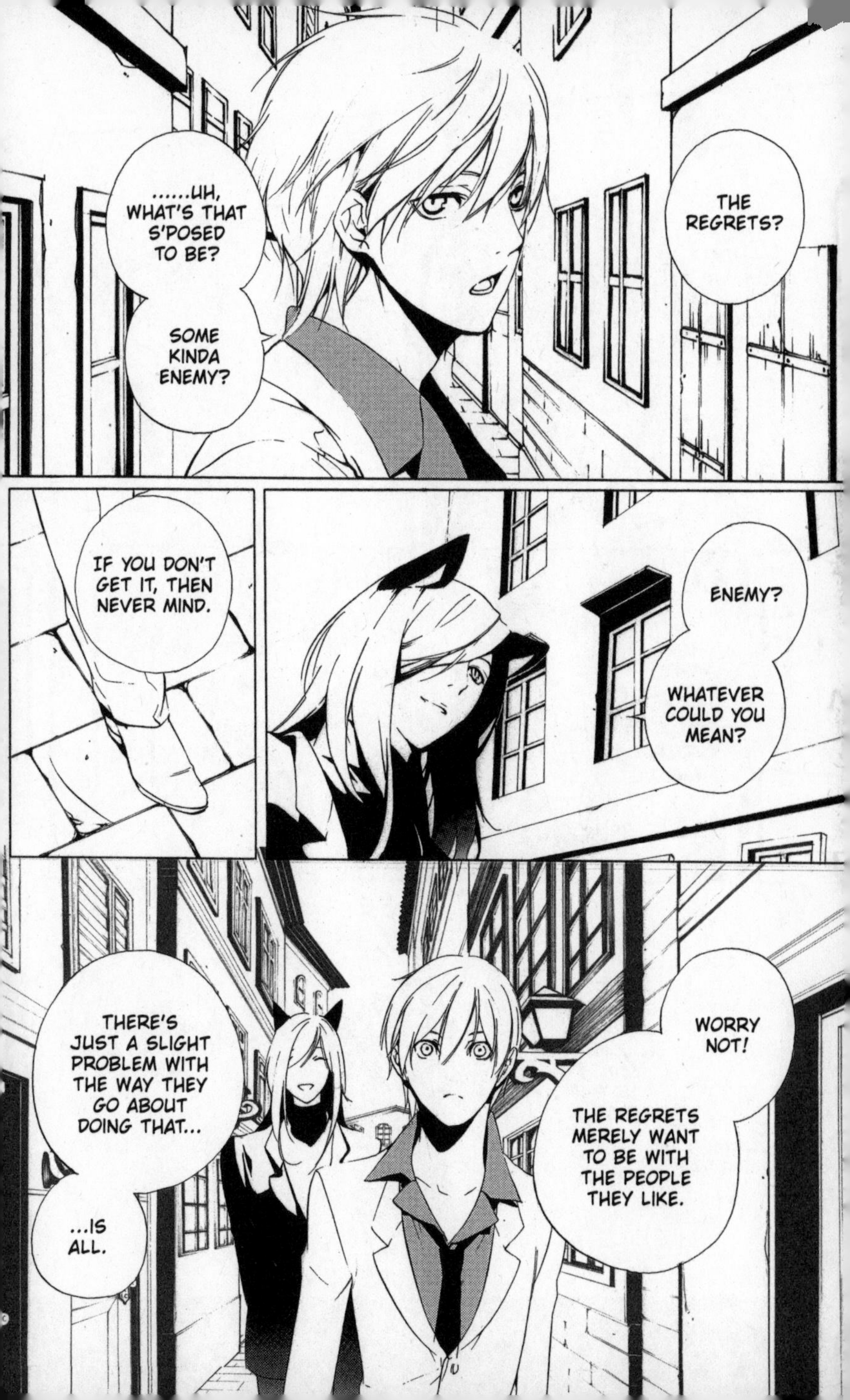
THE REGRETS?
......UH, WHAT'S THAT S'POSED TO BE?
SOME KINDA ENEMY?
ENEMY?
WHATEVER COULD YOU MEAN?
IF YOU DON'T GET IT, THEN NEVER MIND.
WORRY NOT!
THE REGRETS MERELY WANT TO BE WITH THE PEOPLE THEY LIKE.
THERE'S JUST A SLIGHT PROBLEM WITH THE WAY THEY GO ABOUT DOING THAT...
...IS ALL.

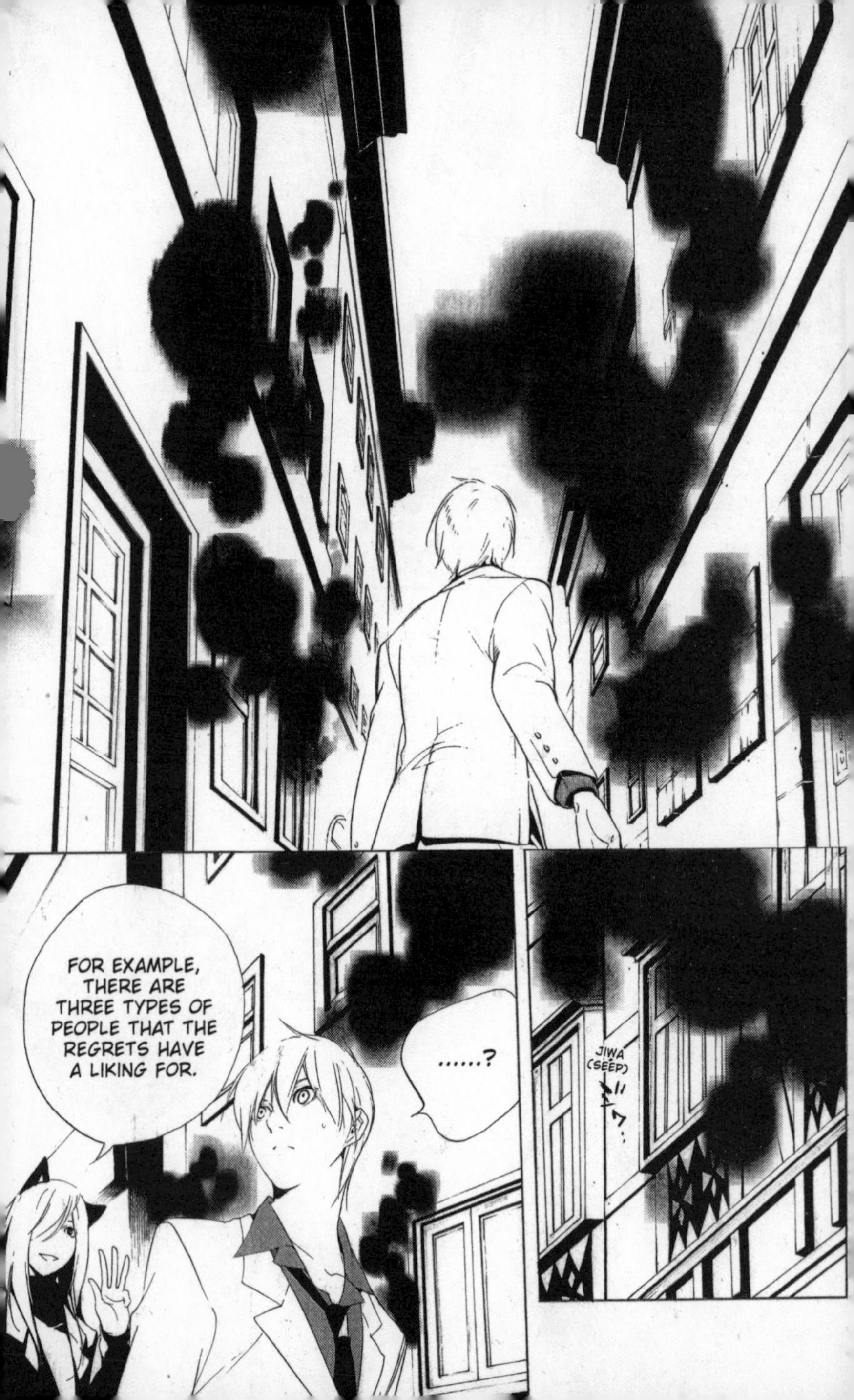
JIWA (SEEP)
FOR EXAMPLE, THERE ARE THREE TYPES OF PEOPLE THAT THE REGRETS HAVE A LIKING FOR.
......?

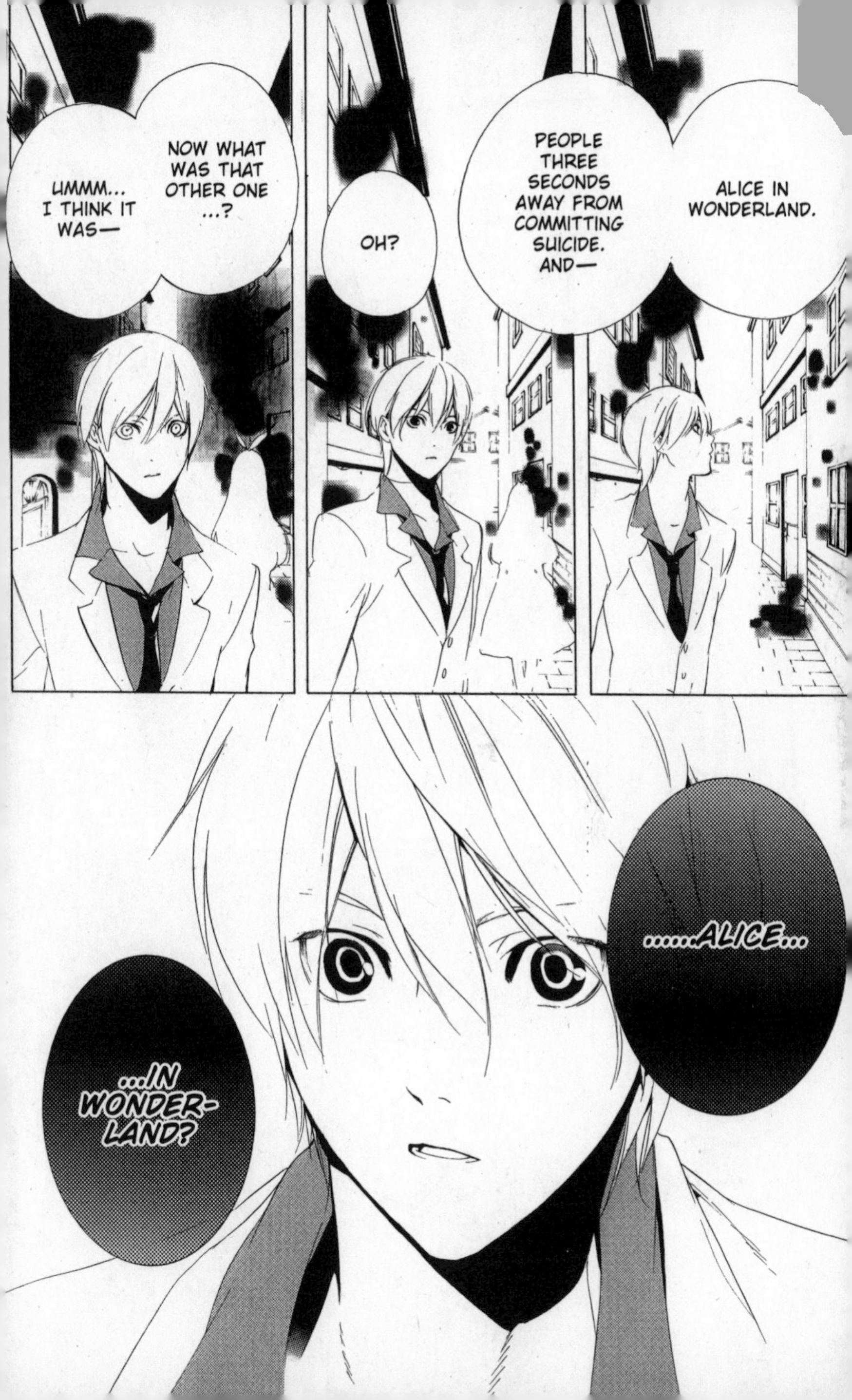
ALICE IN WONDERLAND.
PEOPLE THREE SECONDS AWAY FROM COMMITTING SUICIDE. AND—
OH?
NOW WHAT WAS THAT OTHER ONE ...?
UMMM... I THINK IT WAS—
......ALICE...
...IN WONDERLAND?

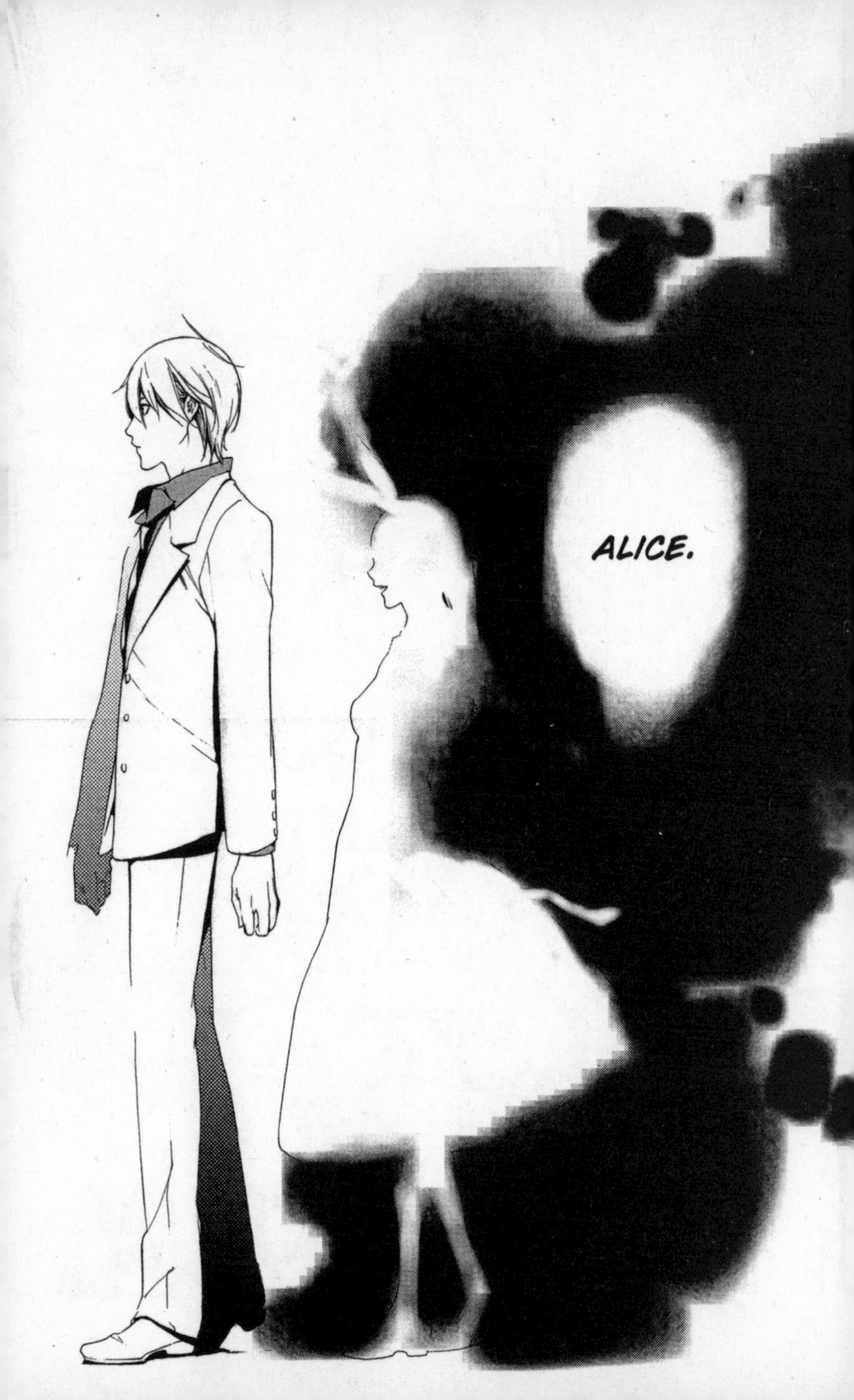
ALICE.

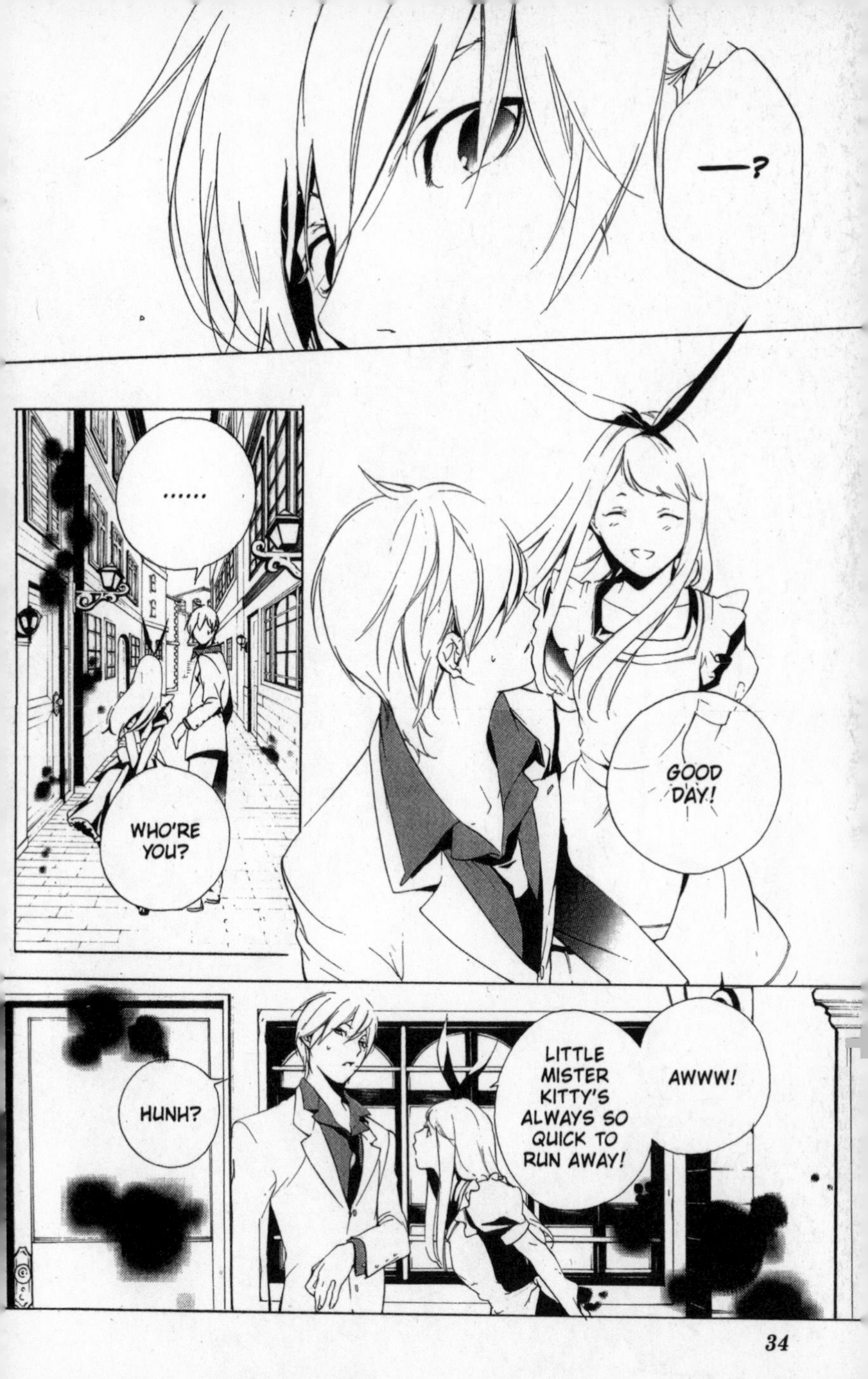
—?
GOOD DAY!
......
WHO'RE YOU?
AWWW!
LITTLE MISTER KITTY'S ALWAYS SO QUICK TO RUN AWAY!
HUNH?

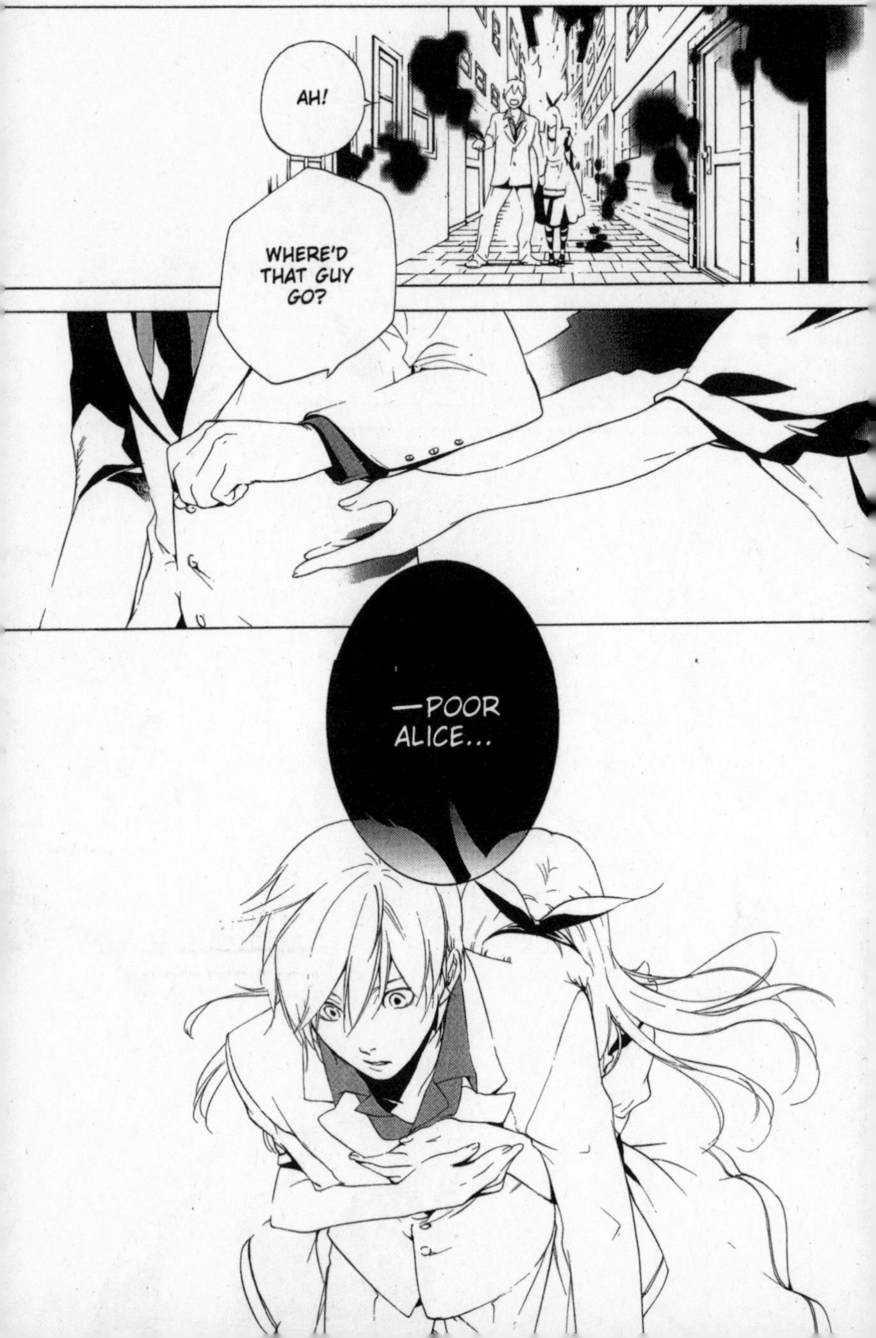
AH!
WHERE'D THAT GUY GO?
—POOR ALICE...

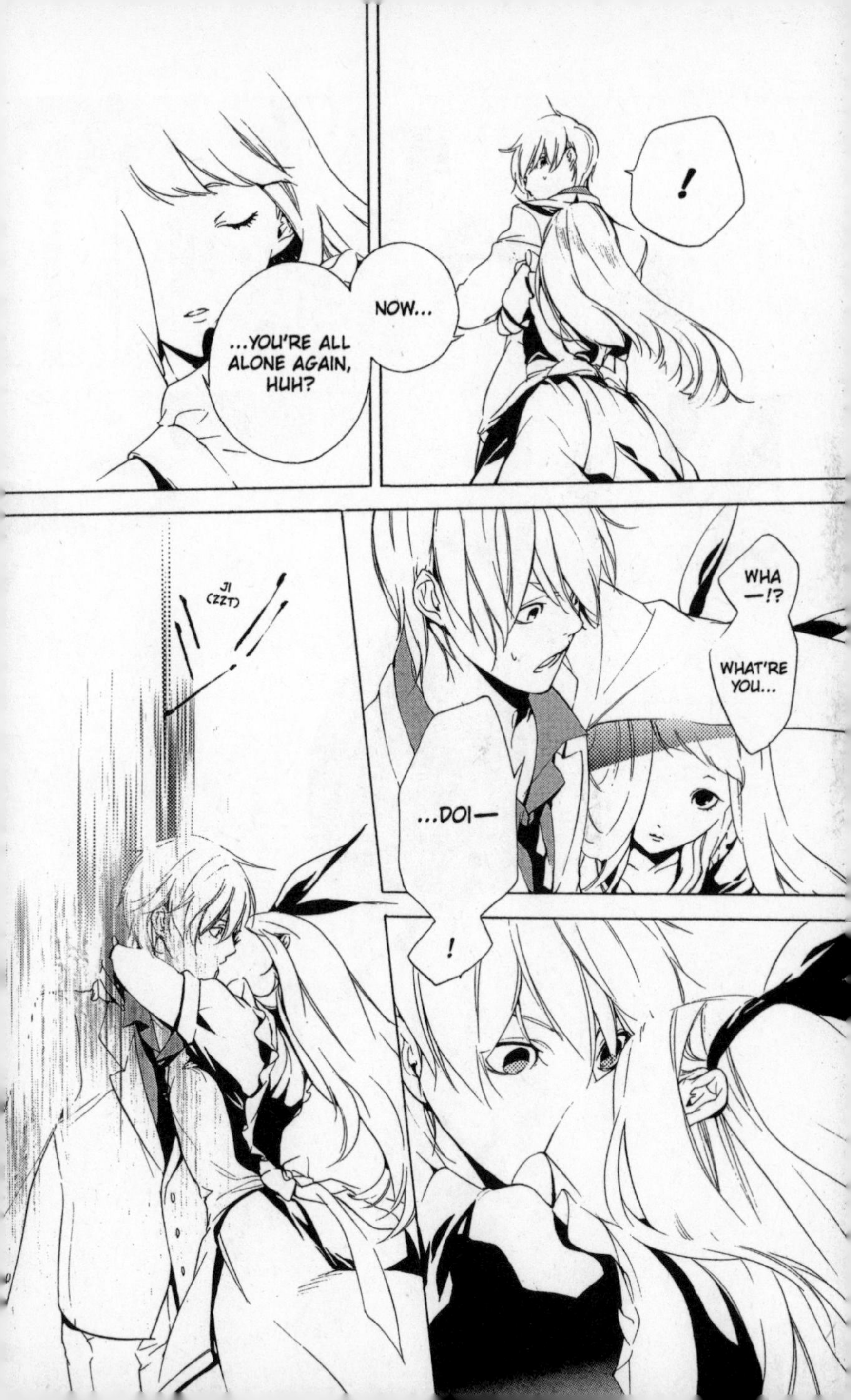
!
NOW...
...YOU'RE ALL ALONE AGAIN, HUH?
WHA—!?
WHAT'RE YOU...
...DOI—
!
JI (ZZT)

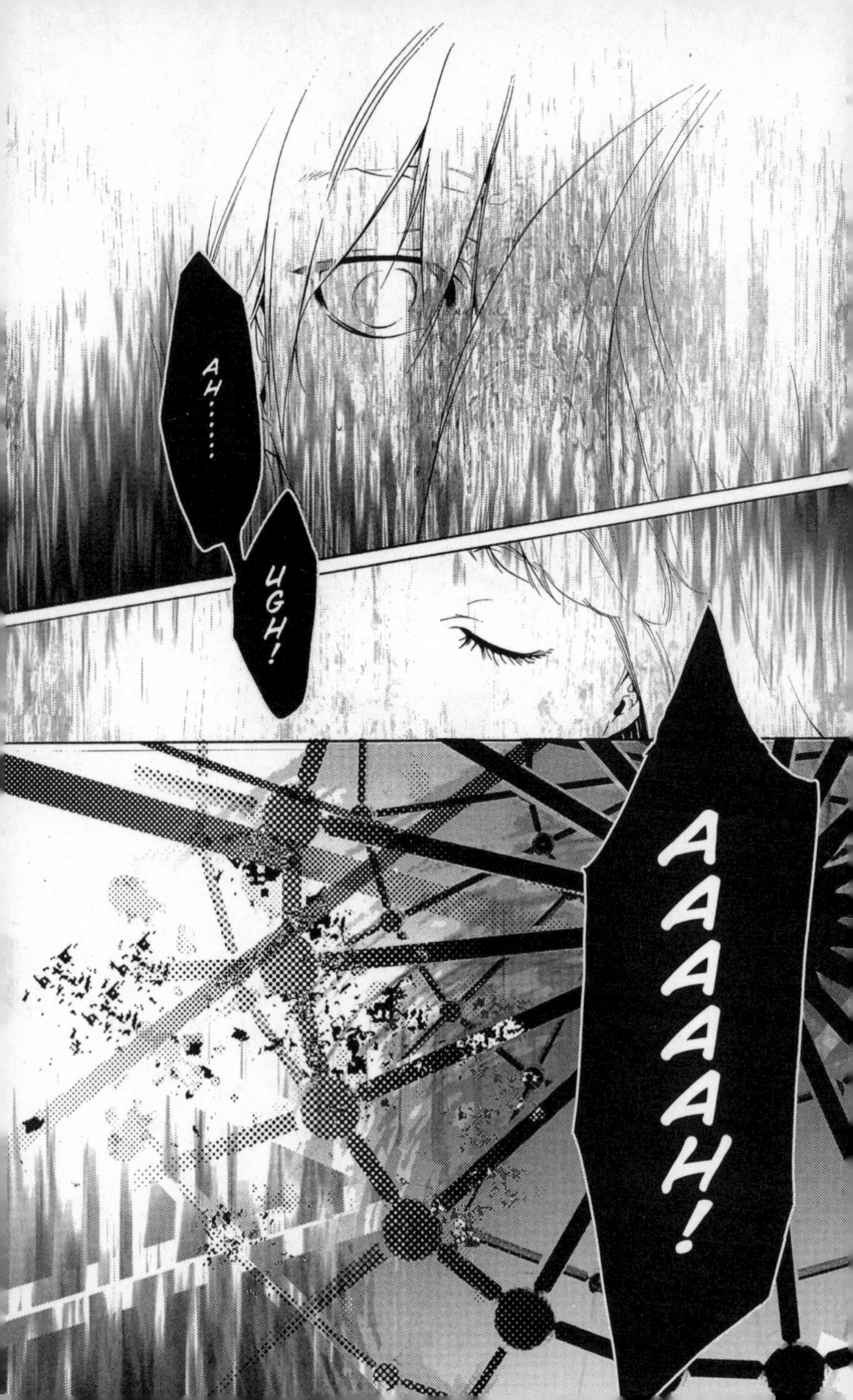
AH......
UGH!
AAAAAH!

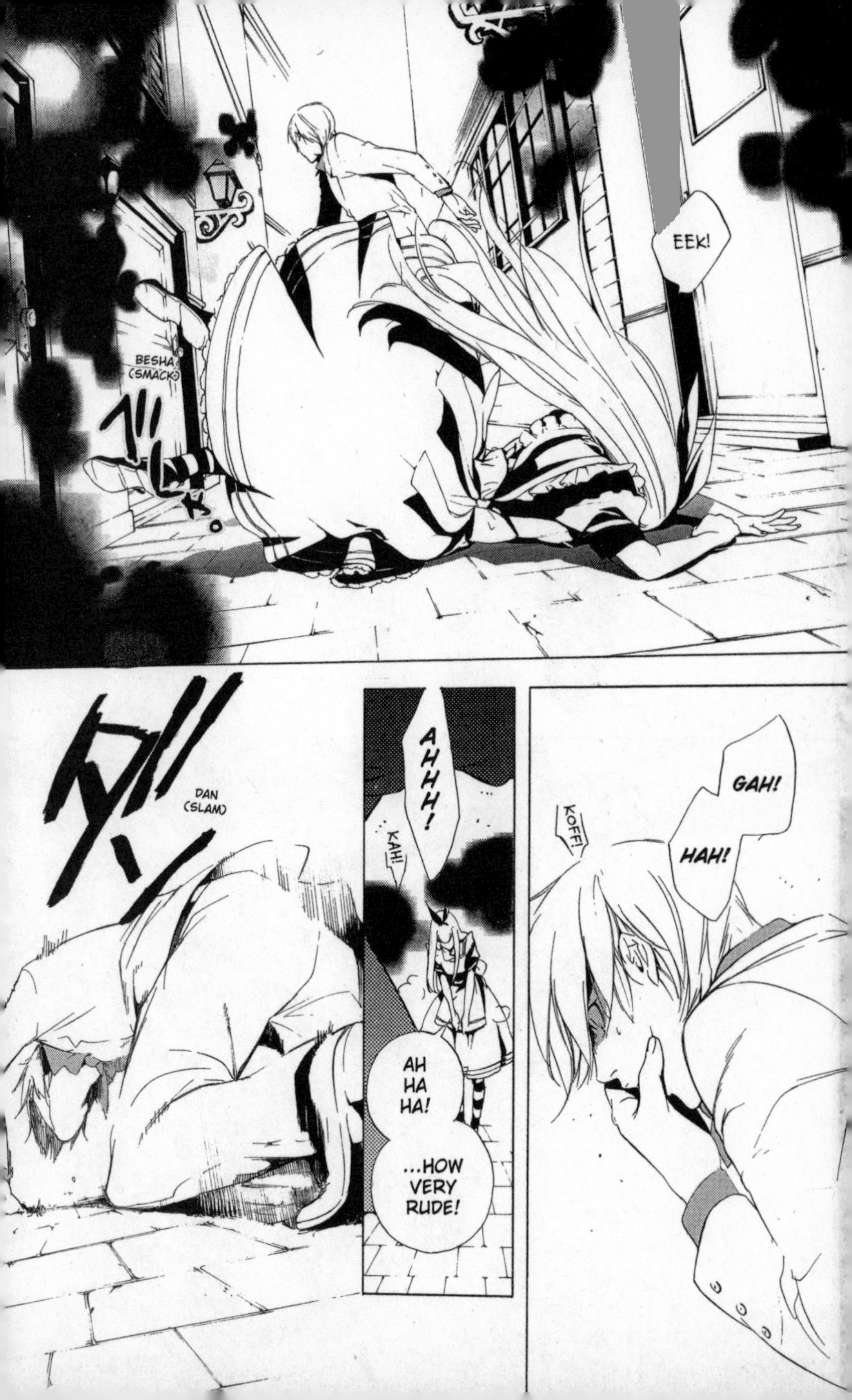
EEK!
BESHA (SMACK)
GAH!
HAH!
KOFF!
AHHHH!
KAH!
AH HA HA!
...HOW VERY RUDE!
DAN (SLAM)

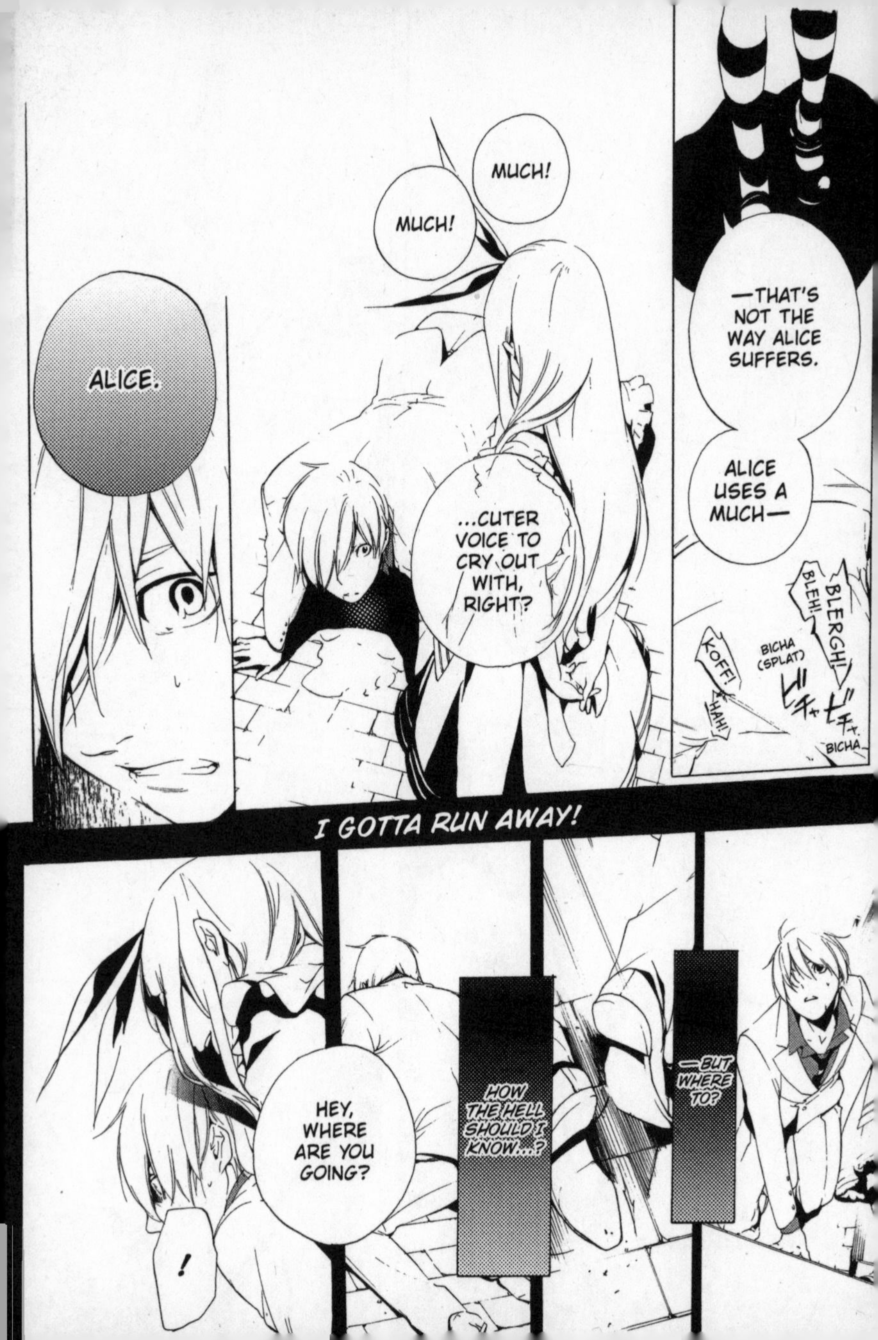
—THAT'S NOT THE WAY ALICE SUFFERS.
ALICE USES A MUCH—
BLERGH!
BLEH!
BICHA (SPLAT)
KOFF!
HAH!
BICHA
MUCH!
MUCH!
...CUTER VOICE TO CRY OUT WITH, RIGHT?
ALICE.
I GOTTA RUN AWAY!
—BUT WHERE TO?
HOW THE HELL SHOULD I KNOW...?
HEY, WHERE ARE YOU GOING?
!

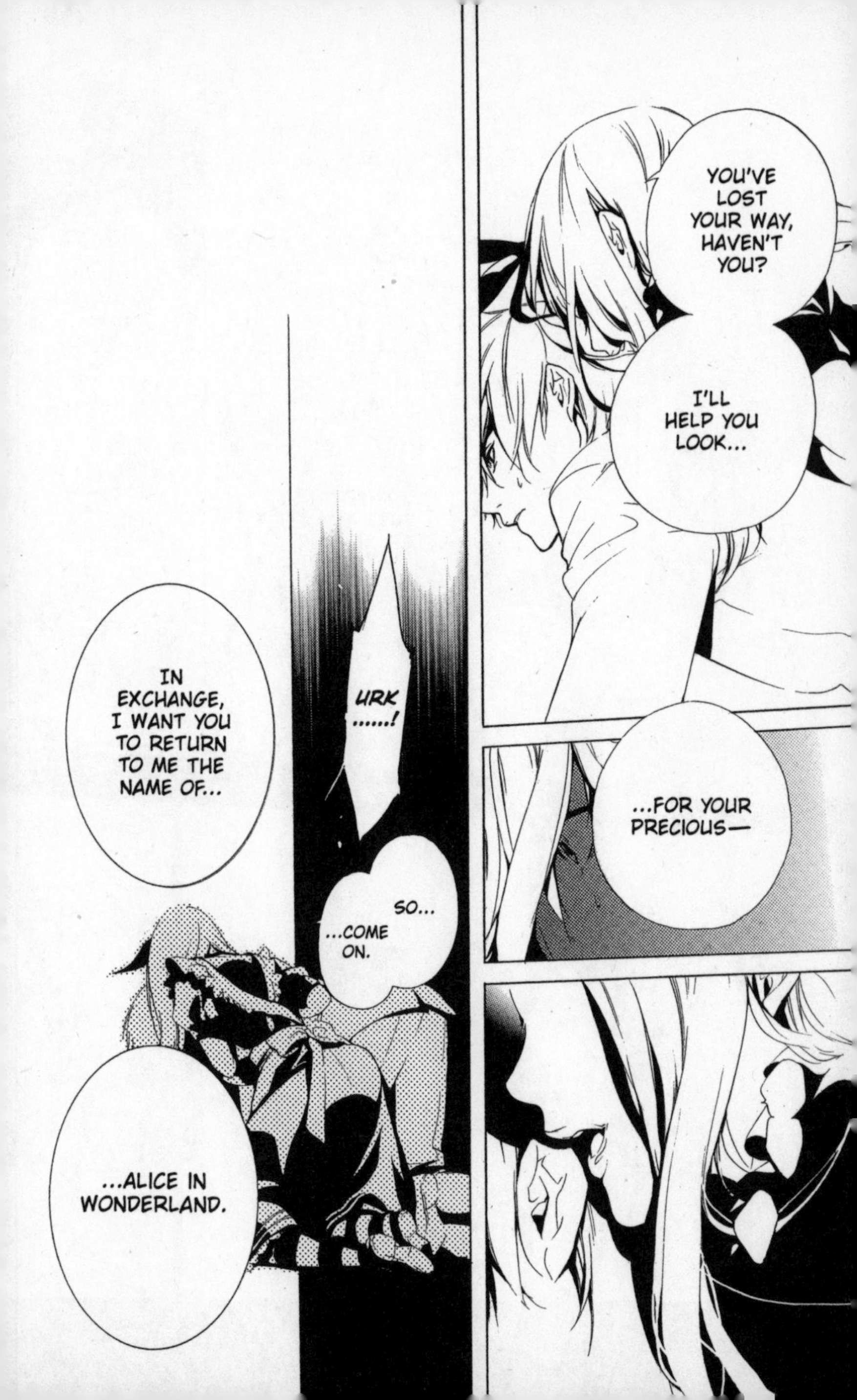
YOU'VE LOST YOUR WAY, HAVEN'T YOU?
I'LL HELP YOU LOOK...
...FOR YOUR PRECIOUS—
URK ......!
IN EXCHANGE, I WANT YOU TO RETURN TO ME THE NAME OF...
SO... ...COME ON.
...ALICE IN WONDERLAND.

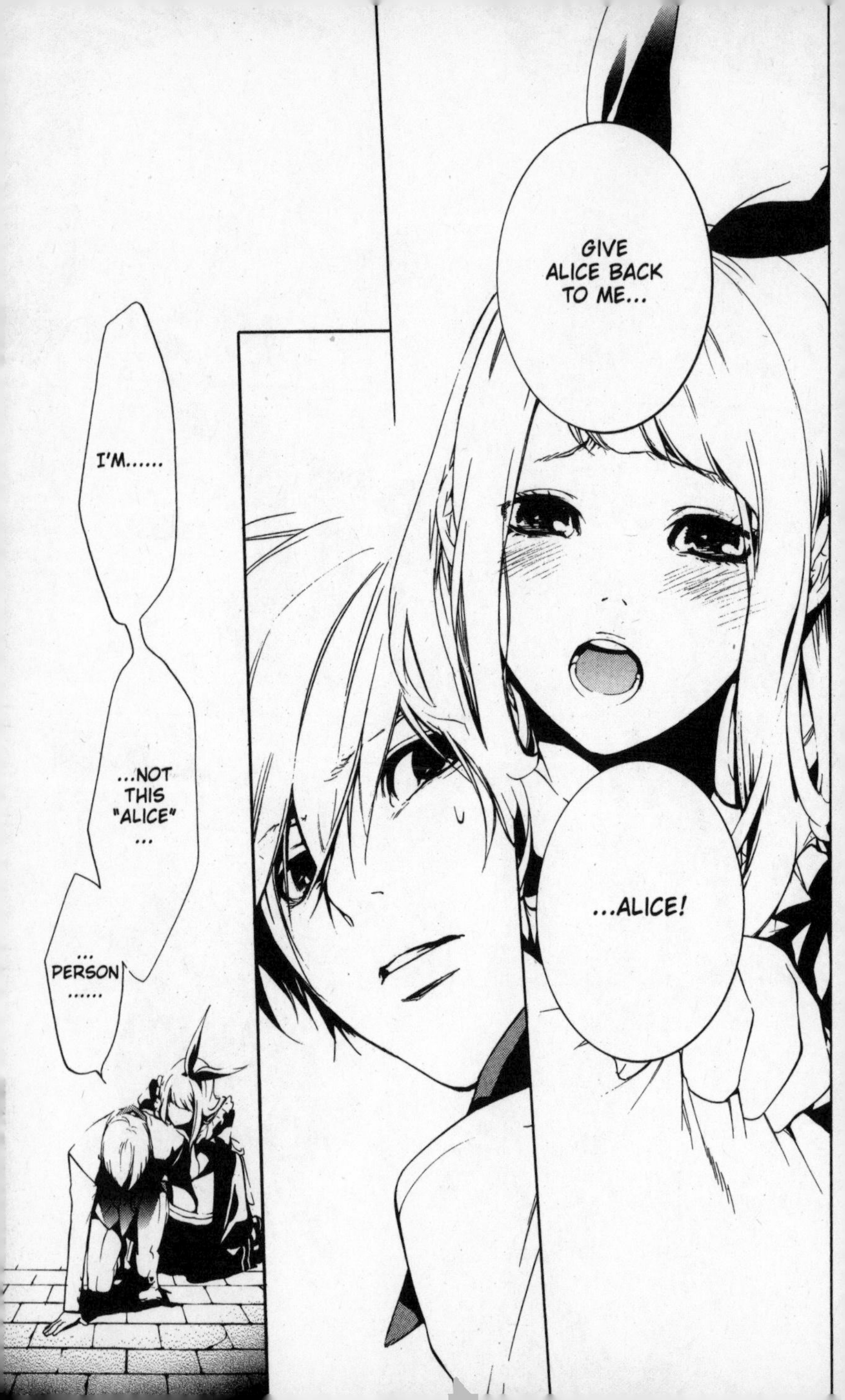
GIVE ALICE BACK TO ME...
...ALICE!
I'M......
...NOT THIS "ALICE" ...
... PERSON ......

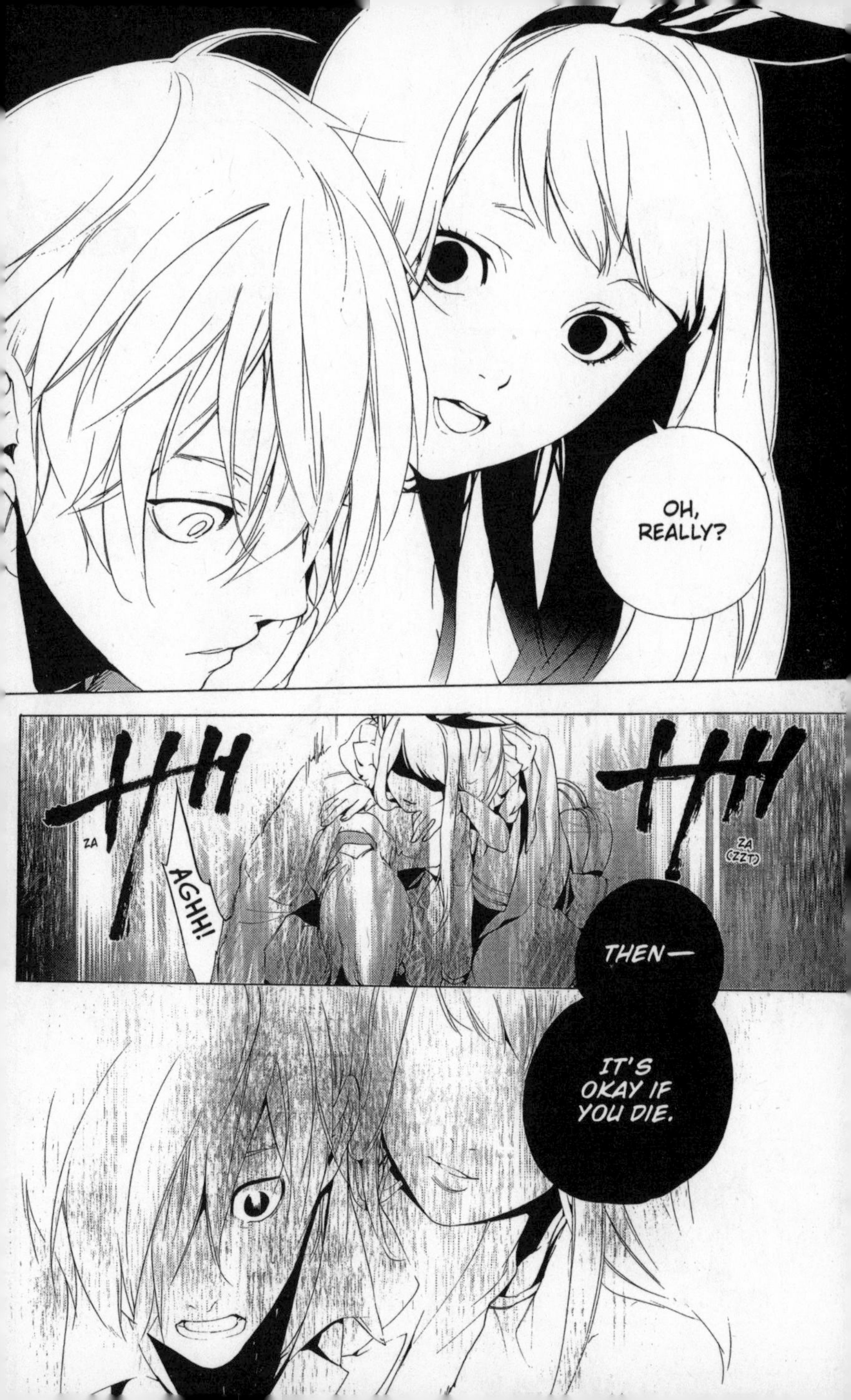
OH, REALLY?
ZA (ZZT)
ZA
AGHH!
THEN—
IT'S OKAY IF YOU DIE.

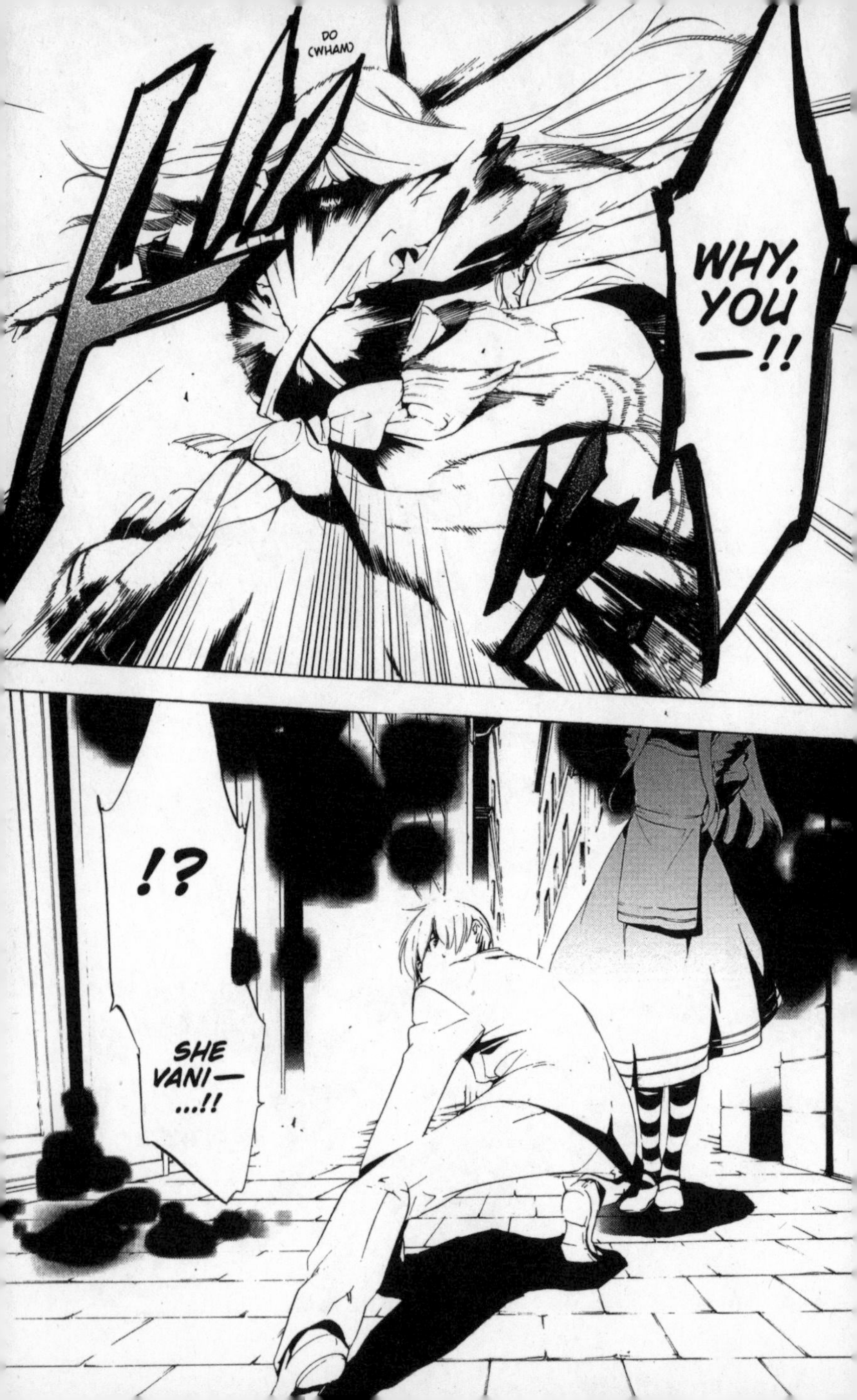
DO (WHAM)
WHY, YOU—!!
!?
SHE VANI—...!!

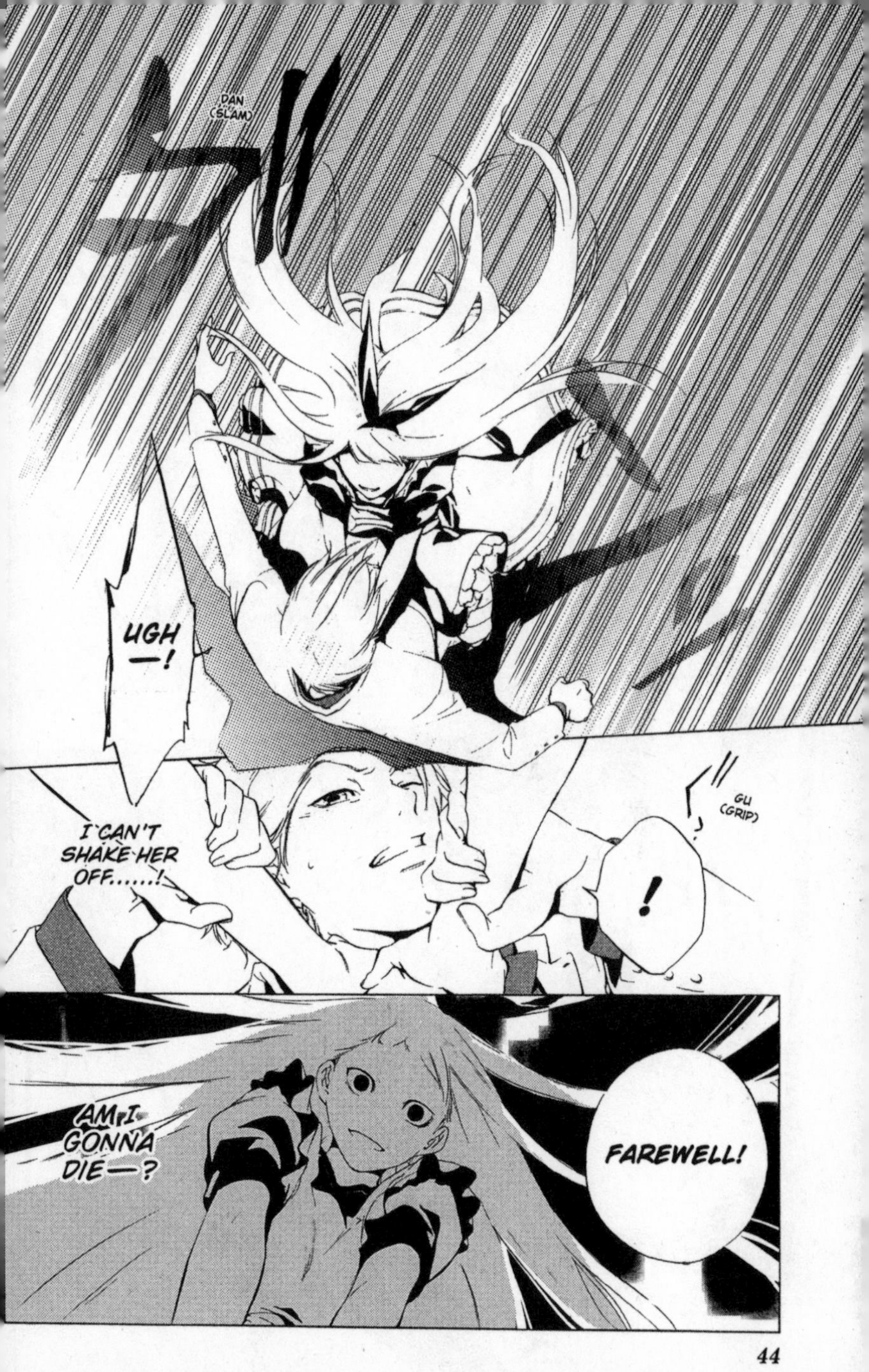
DAN (SLAM)
UGH—!
GU (GRIP)
!
I CAN'T SHAKE HER OFF......!
FAREWELL!
AM I GONNA DIE—?

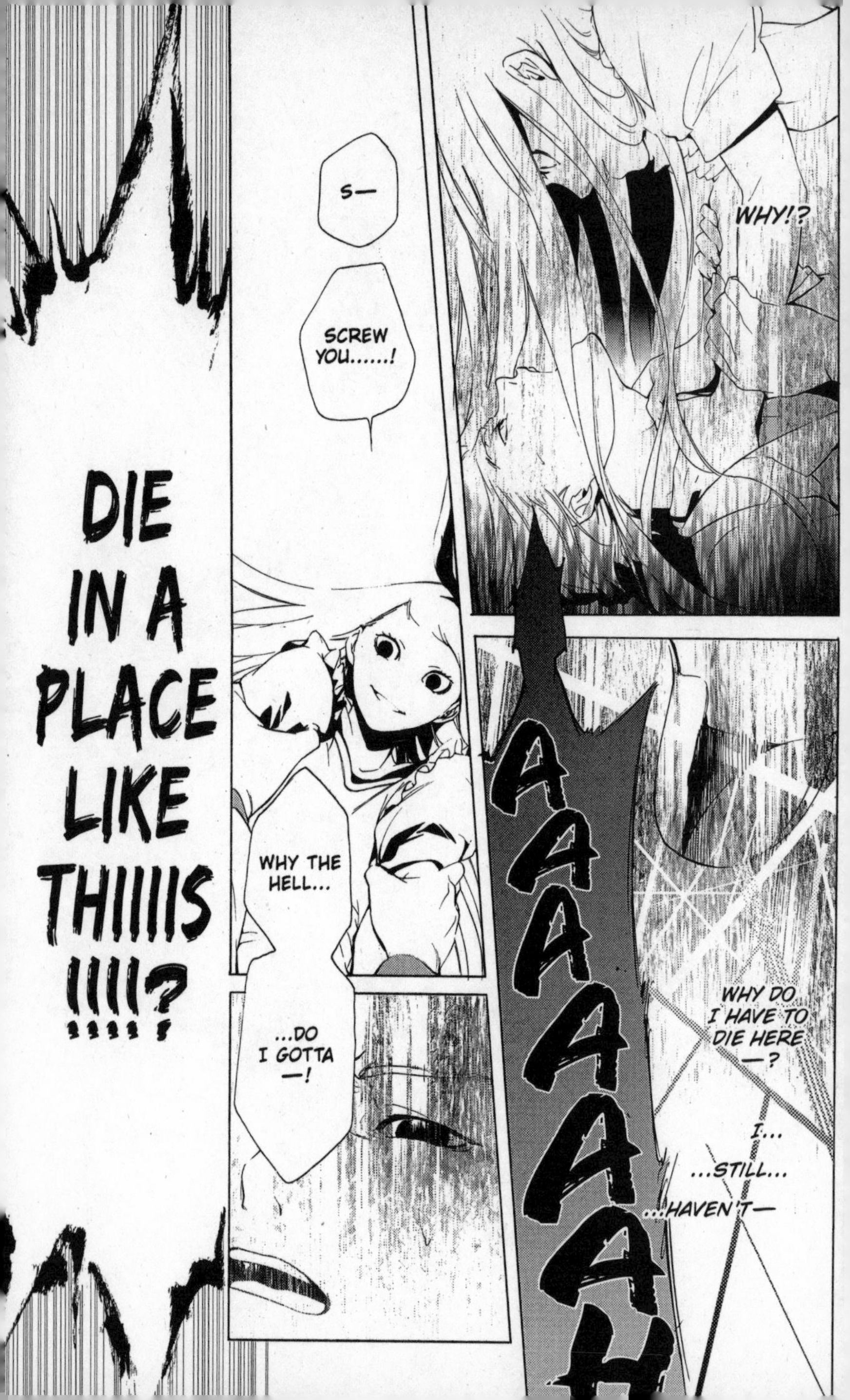
WHY!?
AAAAAAAH
WHY DO I HAVE TO DIE HERE —?
I...
...STILL...
...HAVEN'T—
S—
SCREW YOU.......!
WHY THE HELL...
...DO I GOTTA —!
DIE IN A PLACE LIKE THIIIIS !!!!?

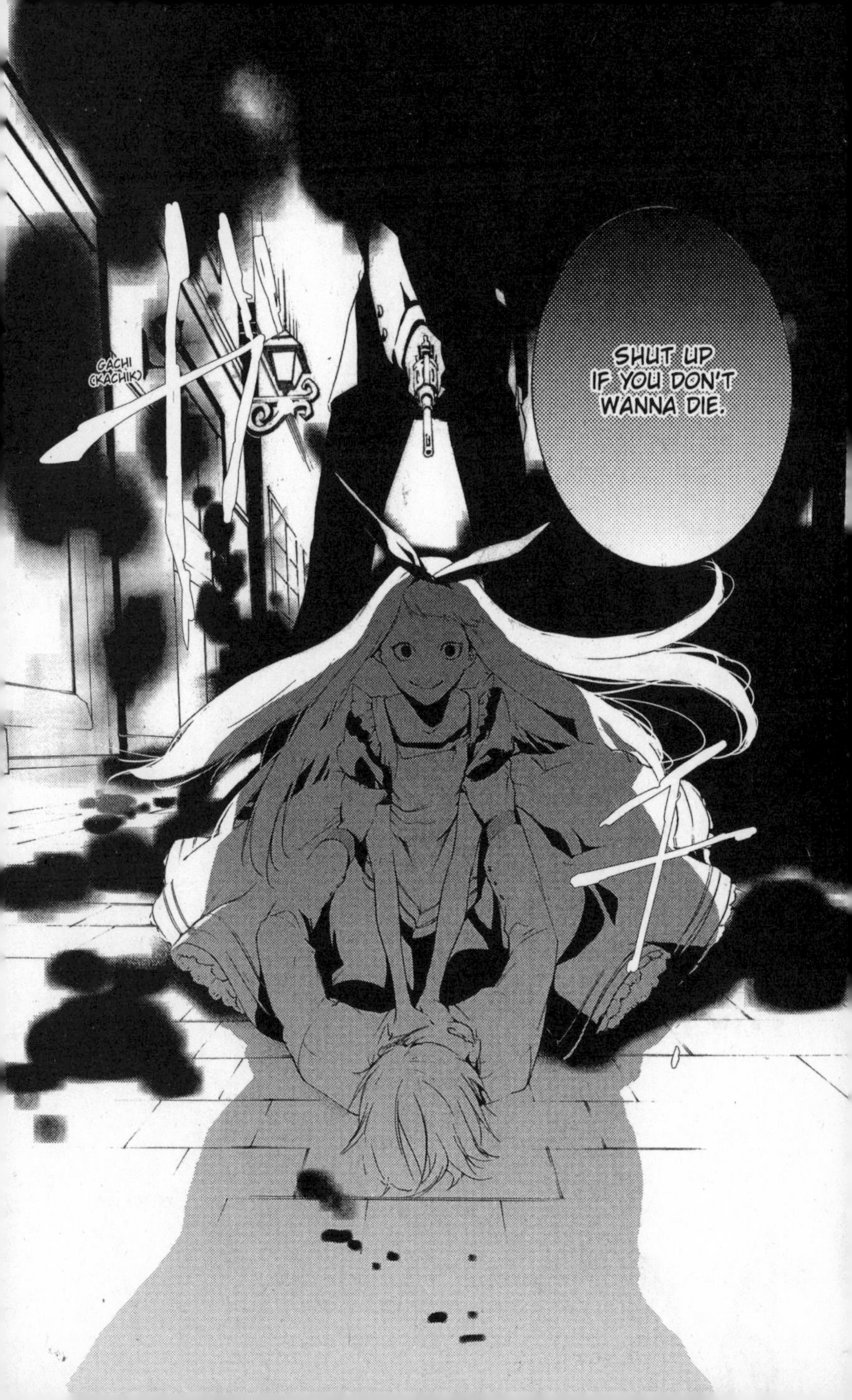
SHUT UP IF YOU DON'T WANNA DIE.
GACHI (KACHIK)

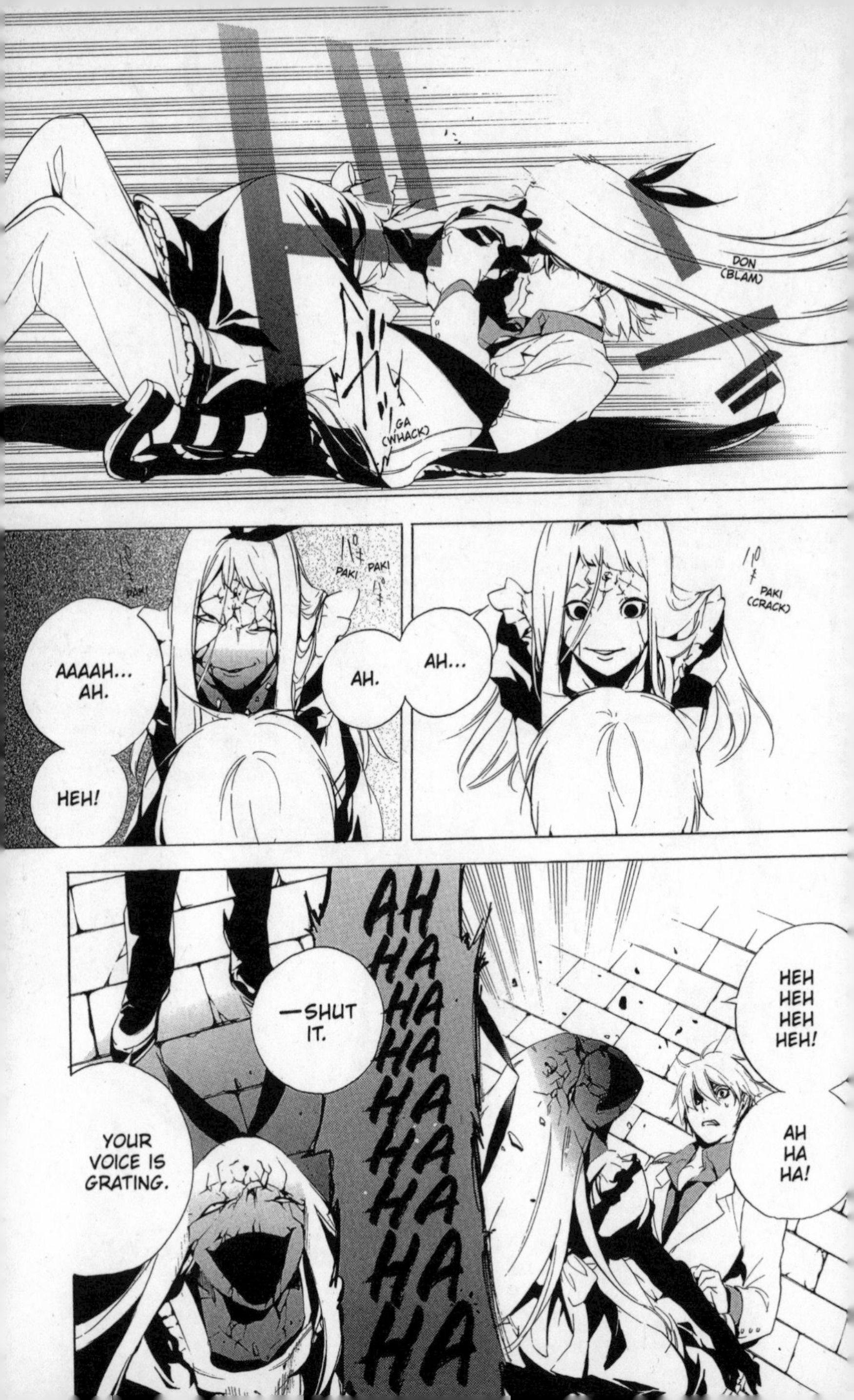
DON (BLAM)
GA (WHACK)
PAKI (CRACK)
AH...
AH.
PAKI PAKI
PAKI
AAAAH... AH.
HEH!
HEH HEH HEH HEH!
AH HA HA!
AH HA HA HA HA HA HA HA HA HA HA HA HA
—SHUT IT.
YOUR VOICE IS GRATING.

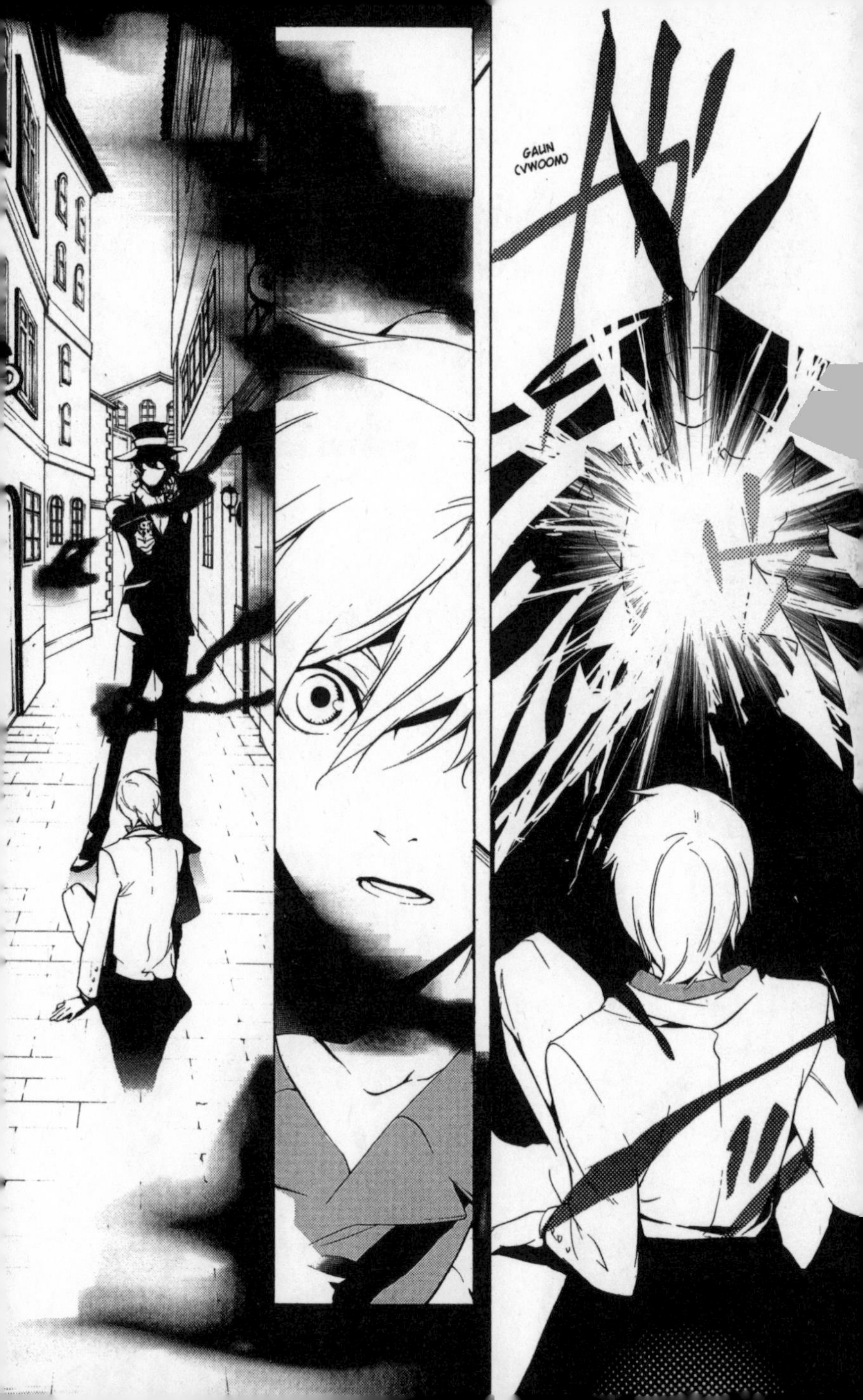
GAUN
(VWOOM)

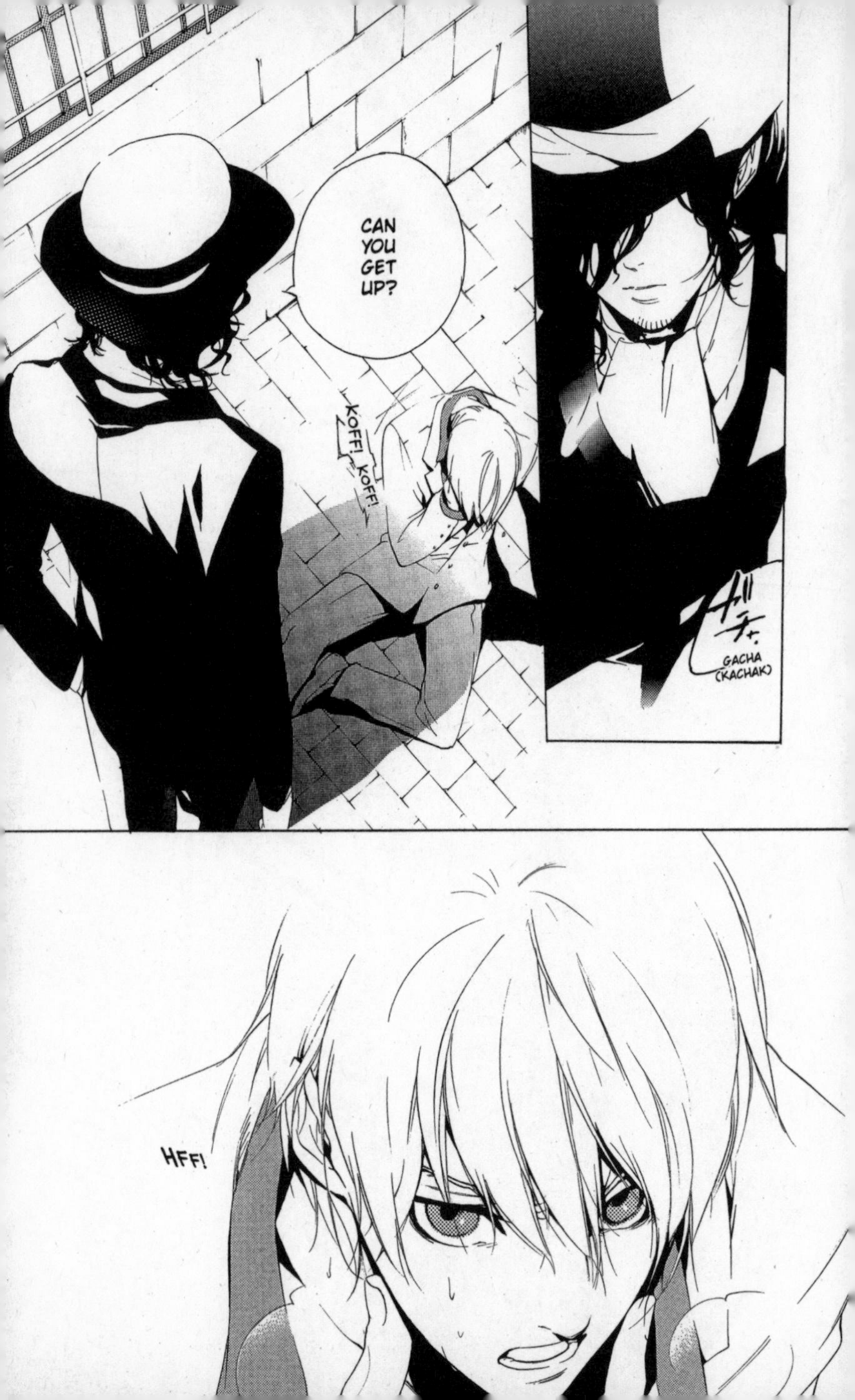

GACHA (KACHAK)
CAN YOU GET UP?
KOFF! KOFF!
HFF!

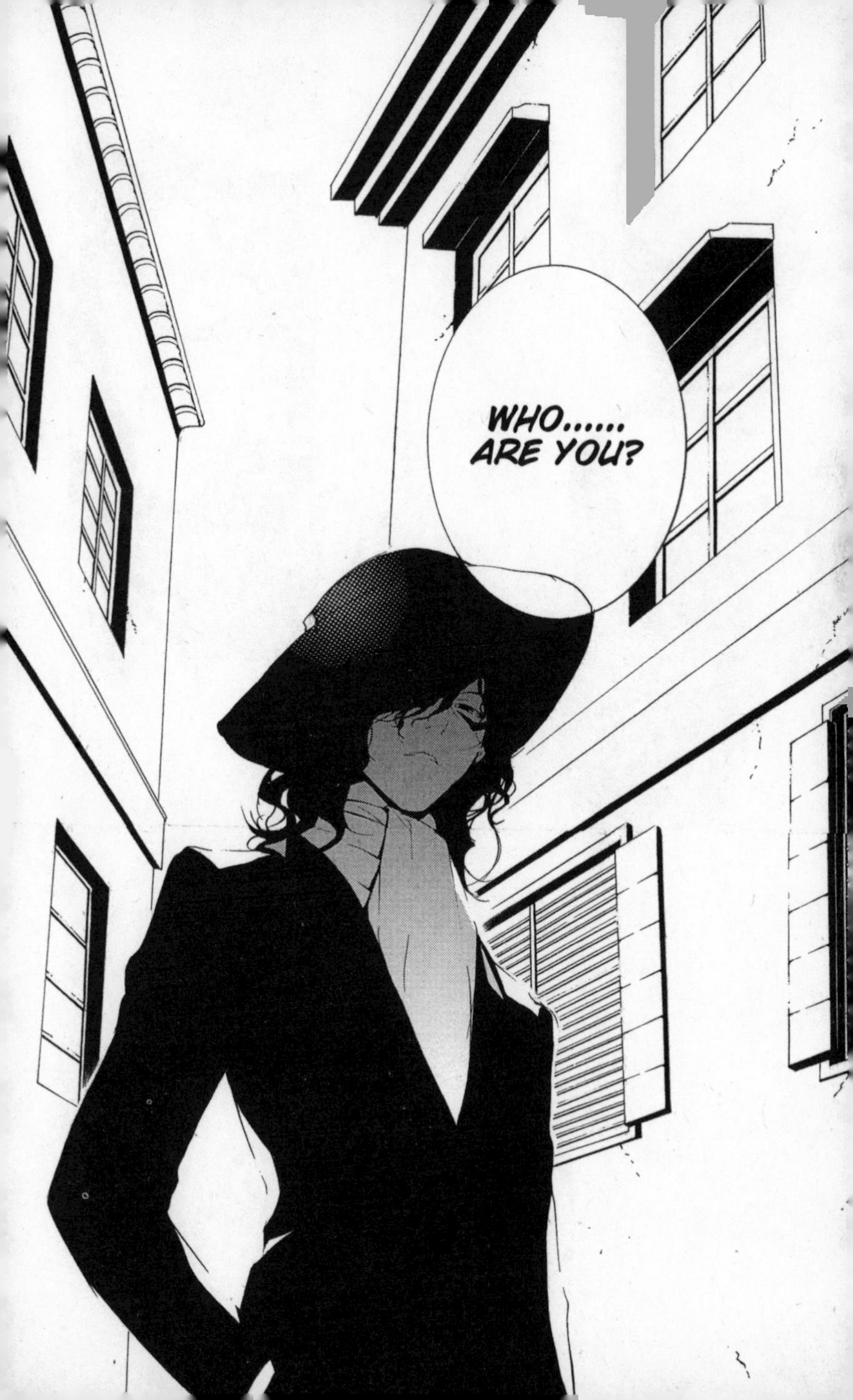
WHO...... ARE YOU?

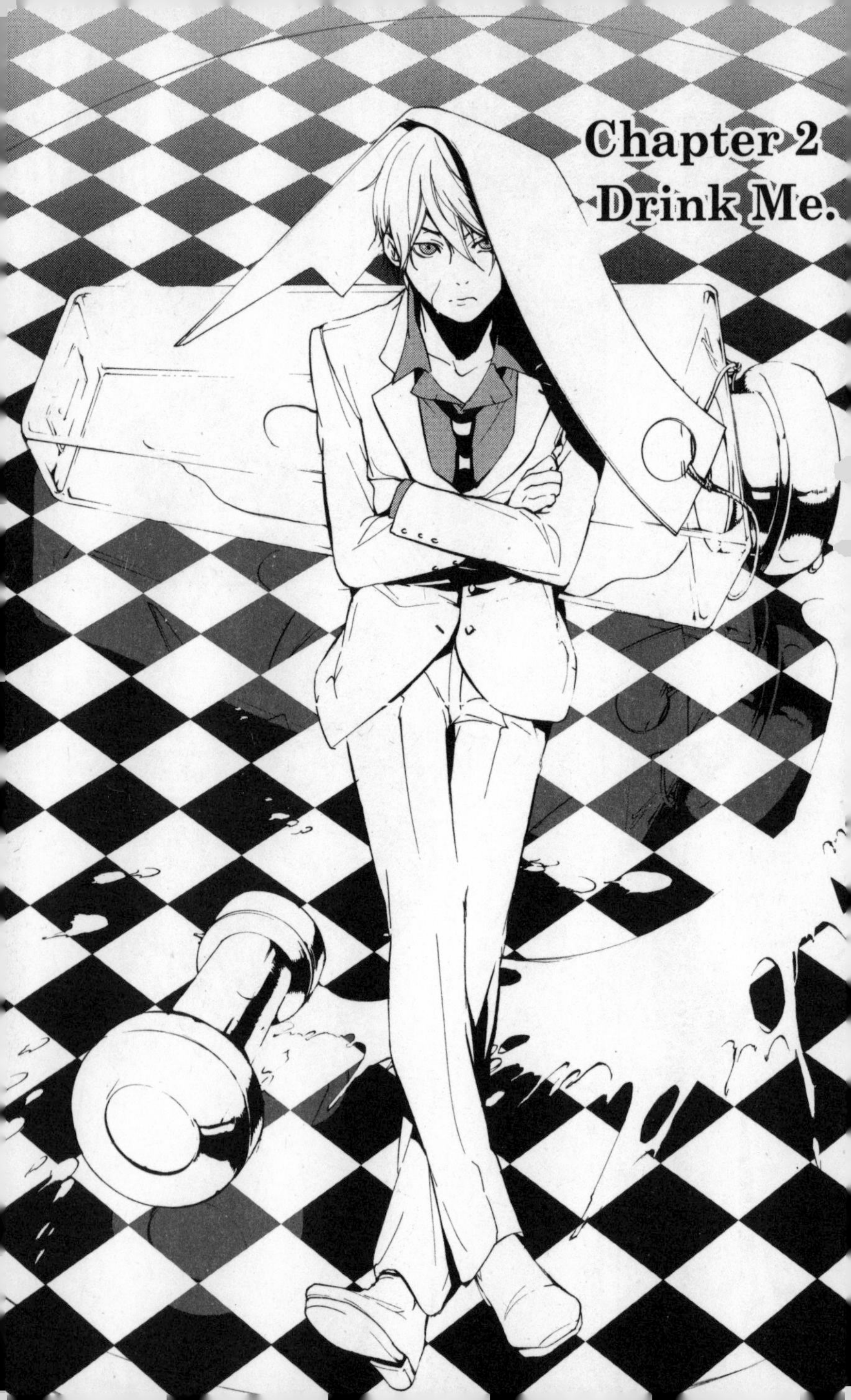
Chapter 2
Drink Me.

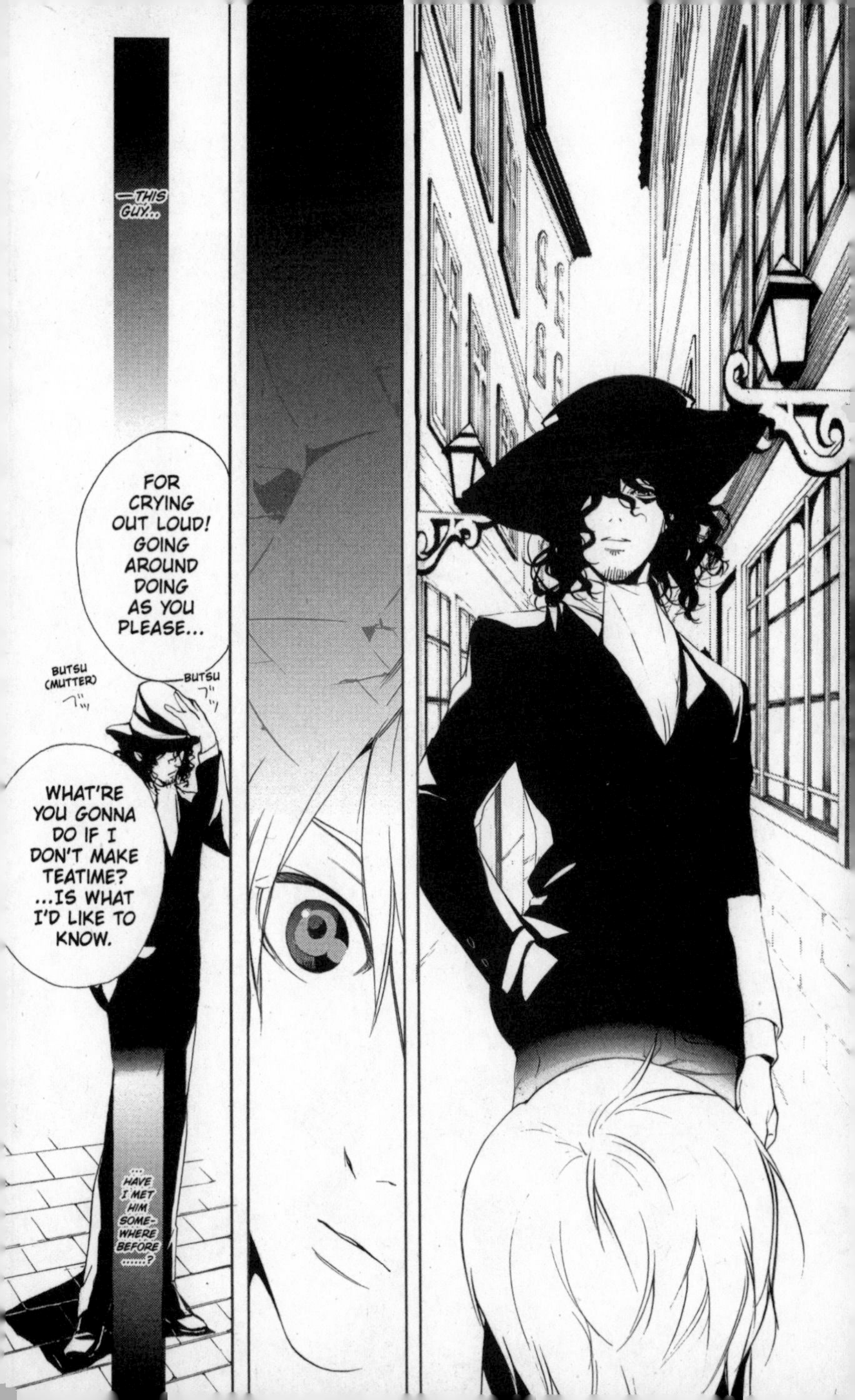
—THIS GUY...
FOR CRYING OUT LOUD! GOING AROUND DOING AS YOU PLEASE...
BUTSU ブツ
BUTSU (MUTTER) ブツ
WHAT'RE YOU GONNA DO IF I DON'T MAKE TEATIME? ...IS WHAT I'D LIKE TO KNOW.
...HAVE I MET HIM SOME-WHERE BEFORE......?

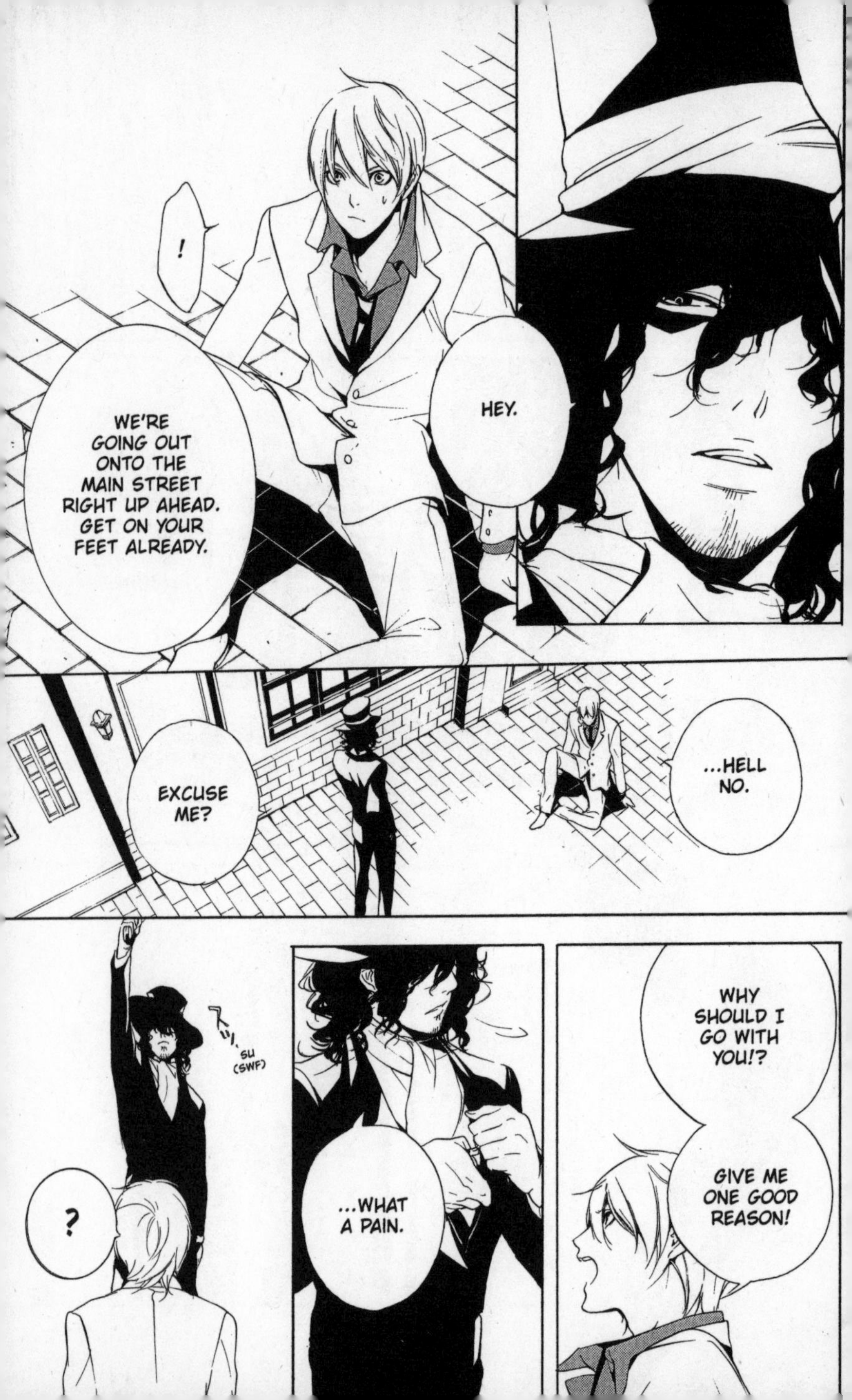
HEY.
!
WE'RE GOING OUT ONTO THE MAIN STREET RIGHT UP AHEAD. GET ON YOUR FEET ALREADY.
...HELL NO.
EXCUSE ME?
WHY SHOULD I GO WITH YOU!?
GIVE ME ONE GOOD REASON!
...WHAT A PAIN.
SU (SWF)
?

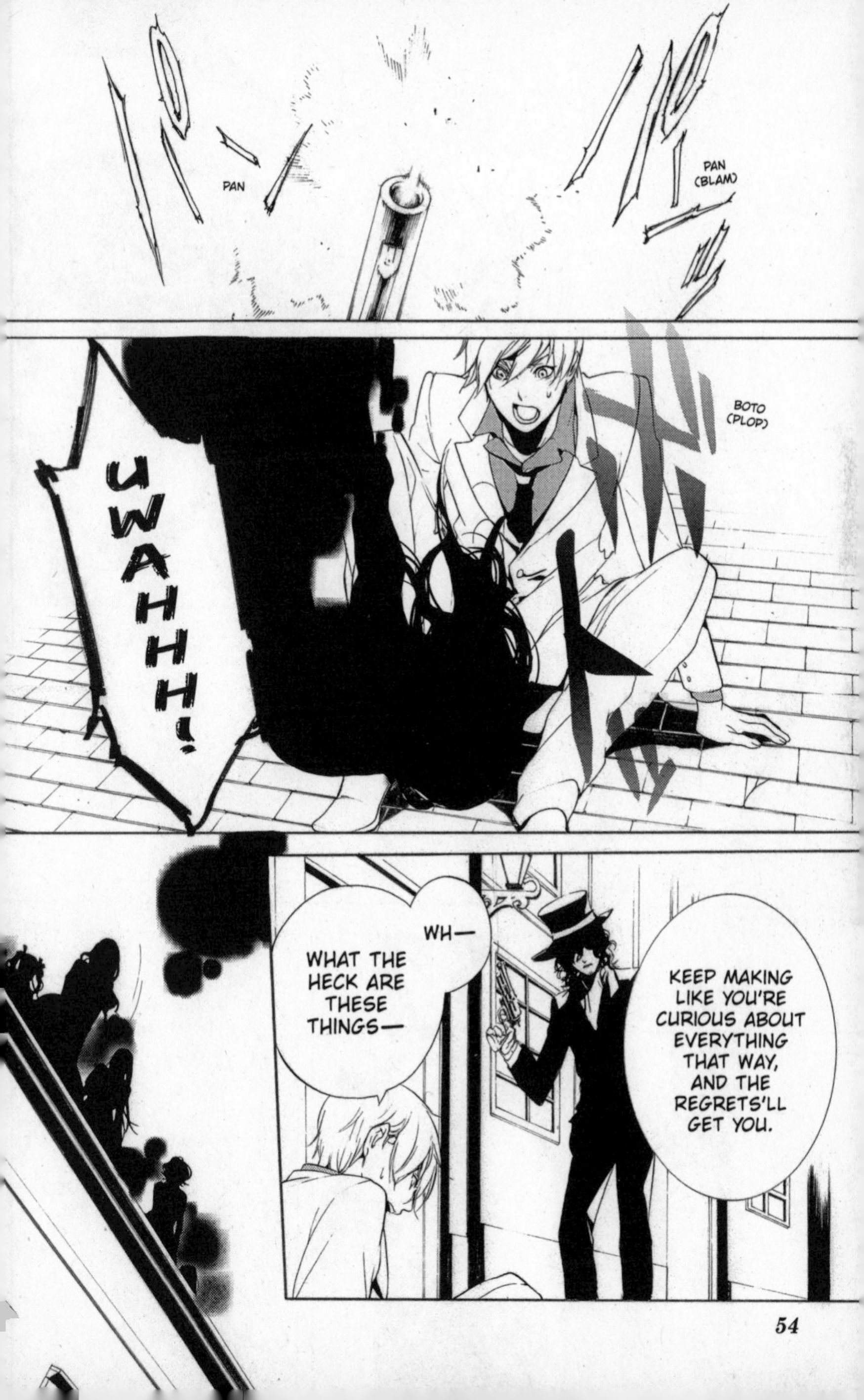
PAN
(BLAM)
PAN
BOTO
(PLOP)
UWAHHH!
KEEP MAKING LIKE YOU'RE CURIOUS ABOUT EVERYTHING THAT WAY, AND THE REGRETS'LL GET YOU.
WH— WHAT THE HECK ARE THESE THINGS—

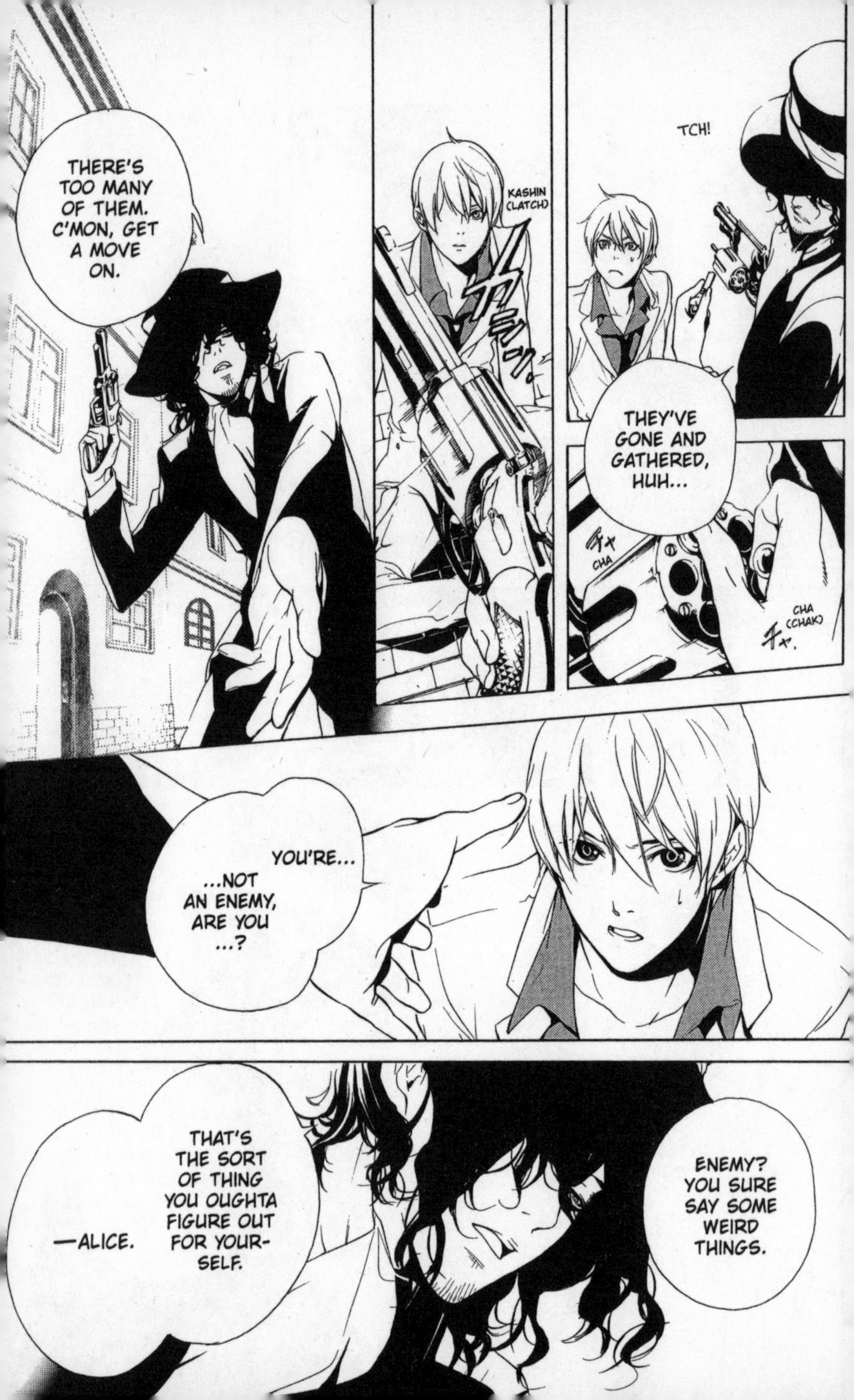
TCH!
THEY'VE GONE AND GATHERED, HUH...
CHA
CHA (CHAK)
KASHIN (LATCH)
THERE'S TOO MANY OF THEM. C'MON, GET A MOVE ON.
YOU'RE...
...NOT AN ENEMY, ARE YOU ...?
ENEMY? YOU SURE SAY SOME WEIRD THINGS.
THAT'S THE SORT OF THING YOU OUGHTA FIGURE OUT FOR YOURSELF.
—ALICE.

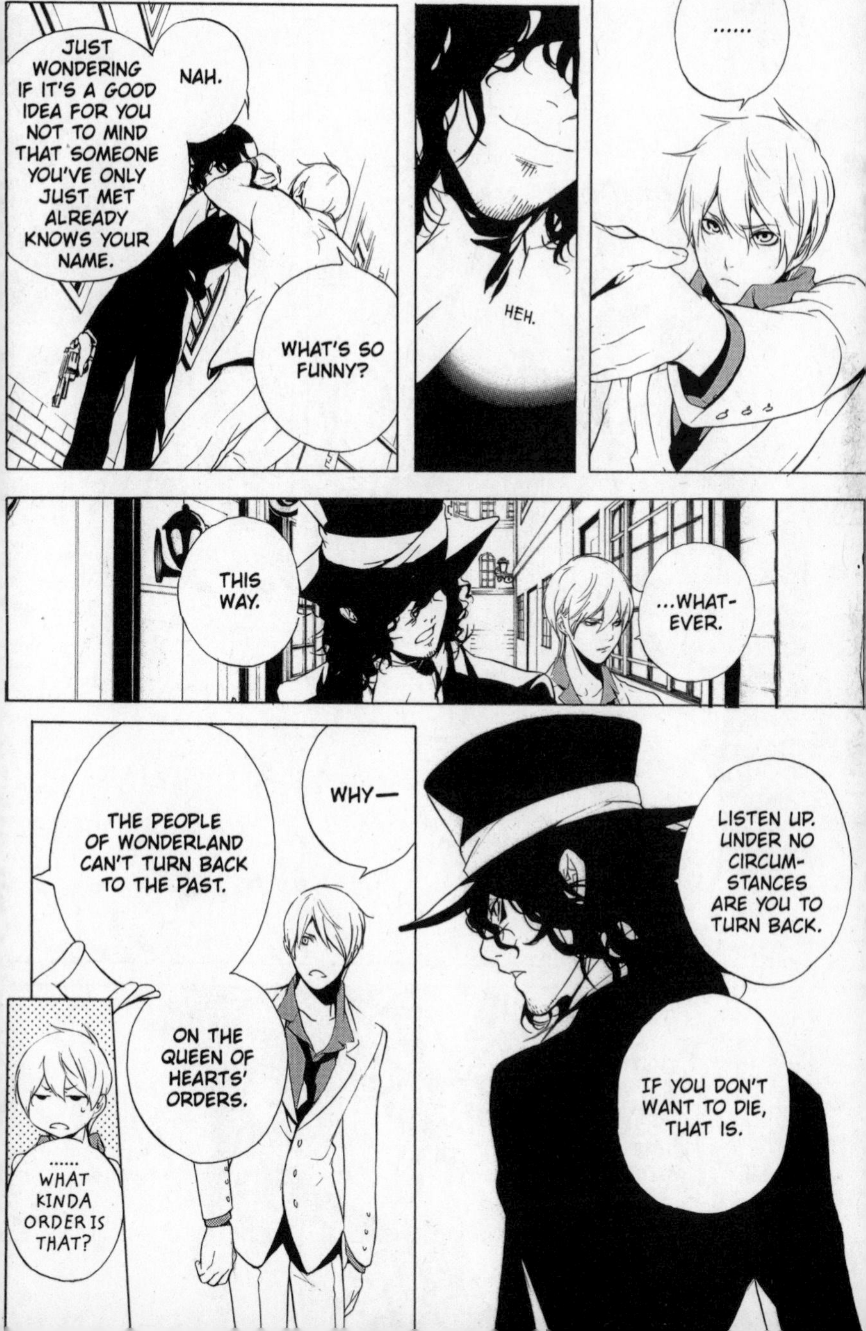
......
HEH.
NAH.
JUST WONDERING IF IT'S A GOOD IDEA FOR YOU NOT TO MIND THAT SOMEONE YOU'VE ONLY JUST MET ALREADY KNOWS YOUR NAME.
WHAT'S SO FUNNY?
...WHAT-EVER.
THIS WAY.
LISTEN UP. UNDER NO CIRCUM-STANCES ARE YOU TO TURN BACK.
IF YOU DON'T WANT TO DIE, THAT IS.
WHY—
THE PEOPLE OF WONDERLAND CAN'T TURN BACK TO THE PAST.
ON THE QUEEN OF HEARTS' ORDERS.
......WHAT KINDA ORDER IS THAT?

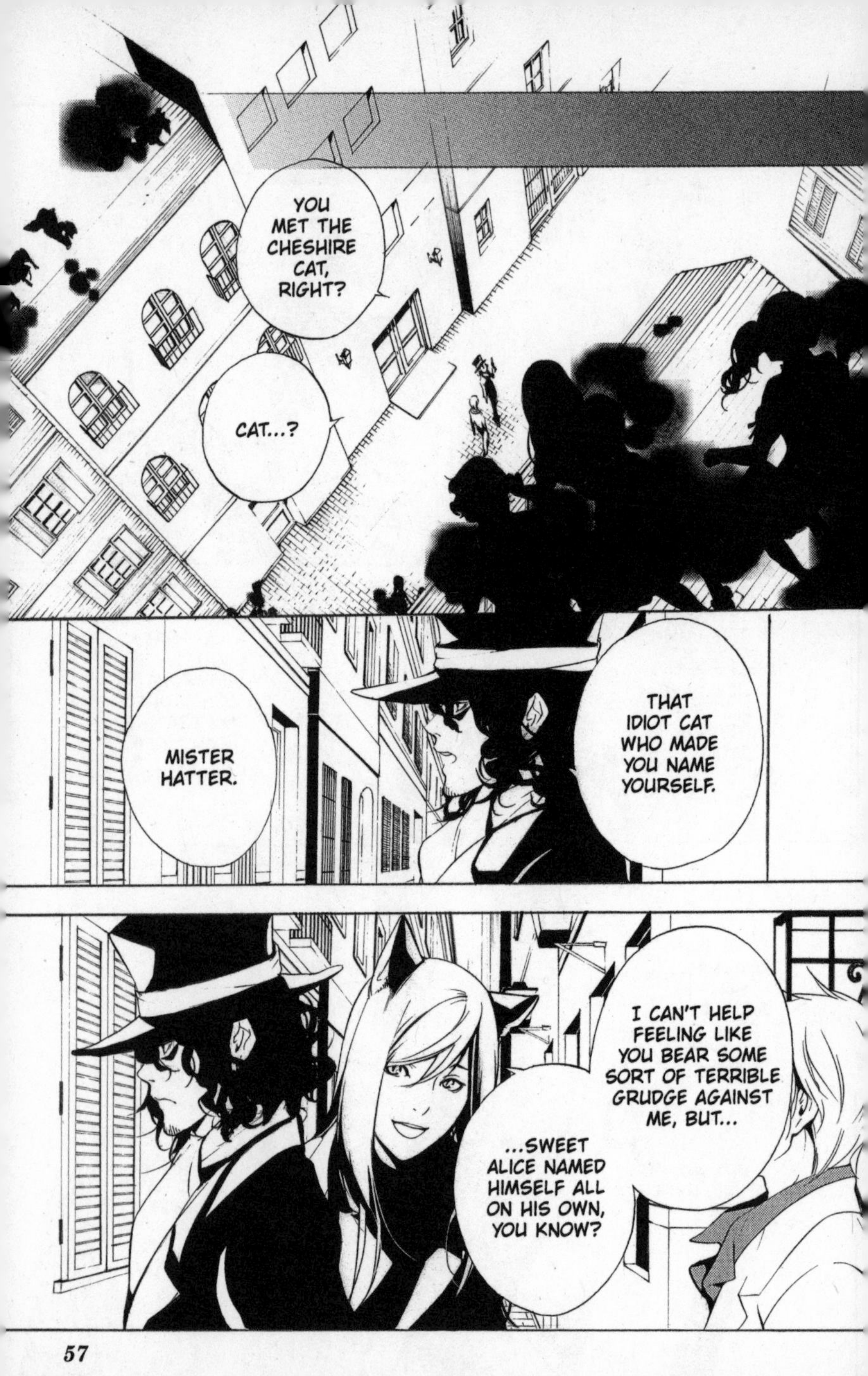
YOU MET THE CHESHIRE CAT, RIGHT?
CAT...?
THAT IDIOT CAT WHO MADE YOU NAME YOURSELF.
MISTER HATTER.
I CAN'T HELP FEELING LIKE YOU BEAR SOME SORT OF TERRIBLE GRUDGE AGAINST ME, BUT...
...SWEET ALICE NAMED HIMSELF ALL ON HIS OWN, YOU KNOW?

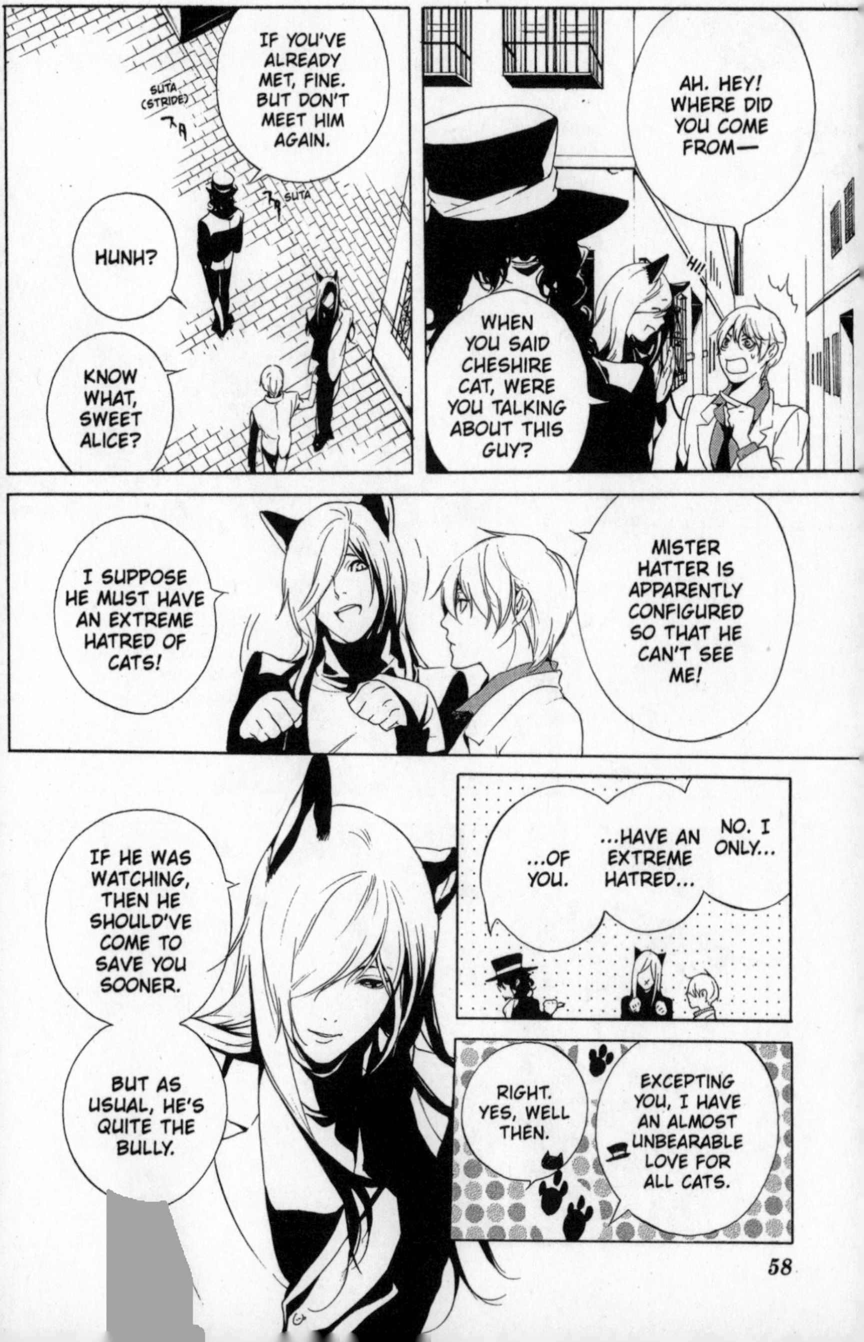
AH. HEY! WHERE DID YOU COME FROM—
H!!
WHEN YOU SAID CHESHIRE CAT, WERE YOU TALKING ABOUT THIS GUY?
IF YOU'VE ALREADY MET, FINE. BUT DON'T MEET HIM AGAIN.
SUTA (STRIDE)
SUTA
HUNH?
KNOW WHAT, SWEET ALICE?
MISTER HATTER IS APPARENTLY CONFIGURED SO THAT HE CAN'T SEE ME!
I SUPPOSE HE MUST HAVE AN EXTREME HATRED OF CATS!
NO. I ONLY...
...HAVE AN EXTREME HATRED...
...OF YOU.
EXCEPTING YOU, I HAVE AN ALMOST UNBEARABLE LOVE FOR ALL CATS.
RIGHT. YES, WELL THEN.
IF HE WAS WATCHING, THEN HE SHOULD'VE COME TO SAVE YOU SOONER.
BUT AS USUAL, HE'S QUITE THE BULLY.

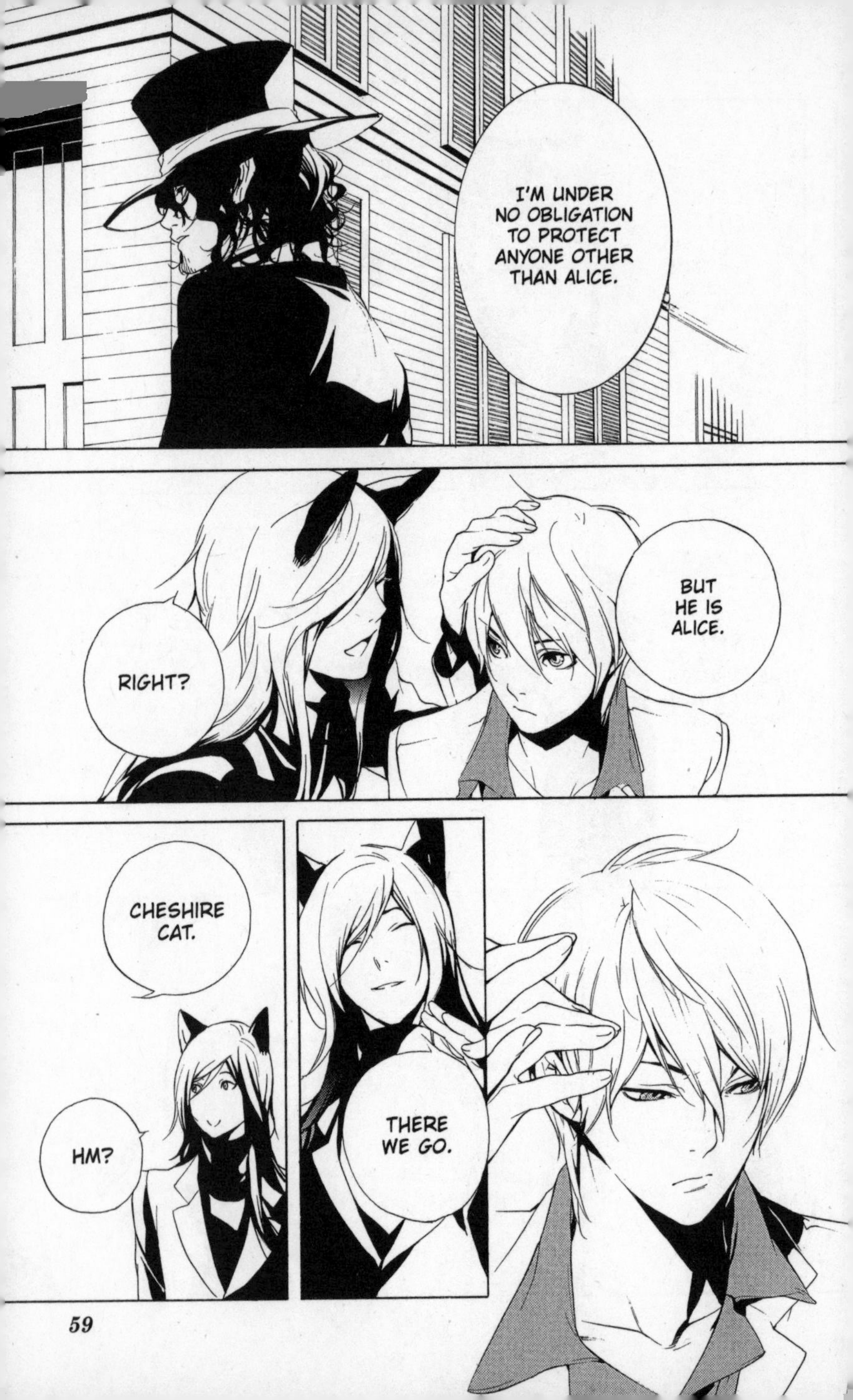
I'M UNDER NO OBLIGATION TO PROTECT ANYONE OTHER THAN ALICE.
BUT HE IS ALICE.
RIGHT?
THERE WE GO.
CHESHIRE CAT.
HM?

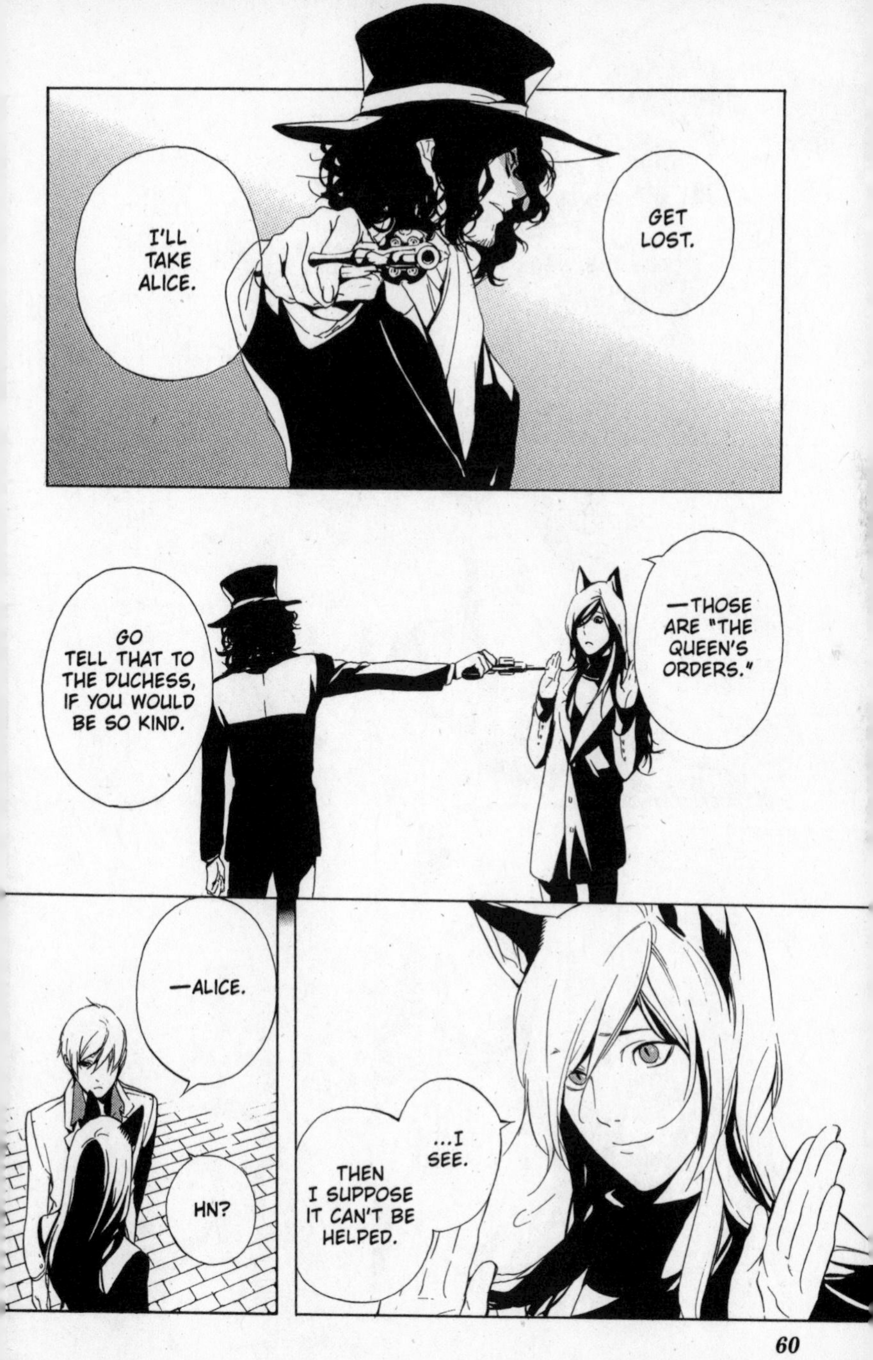
GET LOST.
I'LL TAKE ALICE.
—THOSE ARE "THE QUEEN'S ORDERS."
GO TELL THAT TO THE DUCHESS, IF YOU WOULD BE SO KIND.
...I SEE.
THEN I SUPPOSE IT CAN'T BE HELPED.
—ALICE.
HN?

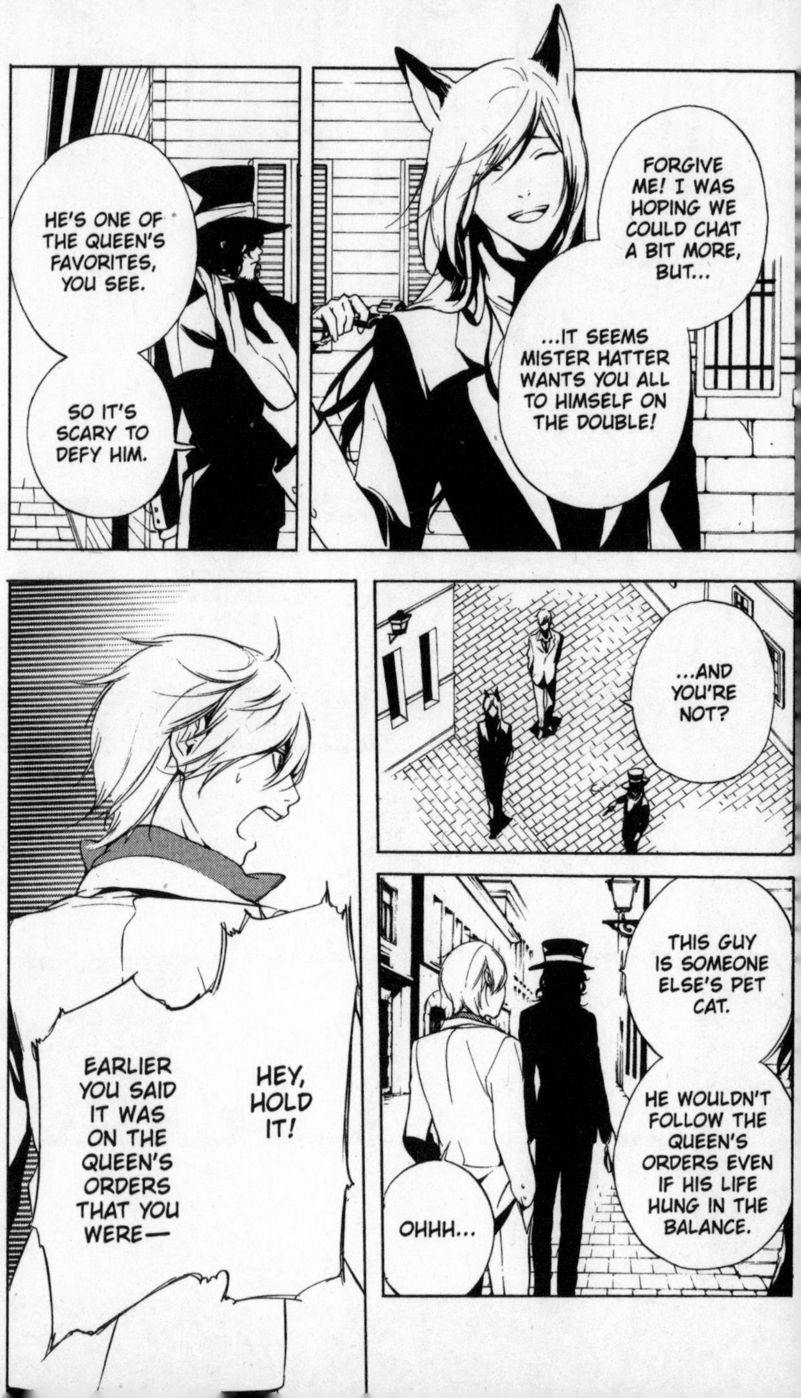
FORGIVE ME! I WAS HOPING WE COULD CHAT A BIT MORE, BUT...
...IT SEEMS MISTER HATTER WANTS YOU ALL TO HIMSELF ON THE DOUBLE!
HE'S ONE OF THE QUEEN'S FAVORITES, YOU SEE.
SO IT'S SCARY TO DEFY HIM.
...AND YOU'RE NOT?
THIS GUY IS SOMEONE ELSE'S PET CAT.
HE WOULDN'T FOLLOW THE QUEEN'S ORDERS EVEN IF HIS LIFE HUNG IN THE BALANCE.
OHHH...
HEY, HOLD IT!
EARLIER YOU SAID IT WAS ON THE QUEEN'S ORDERS THAT YOU WERE—

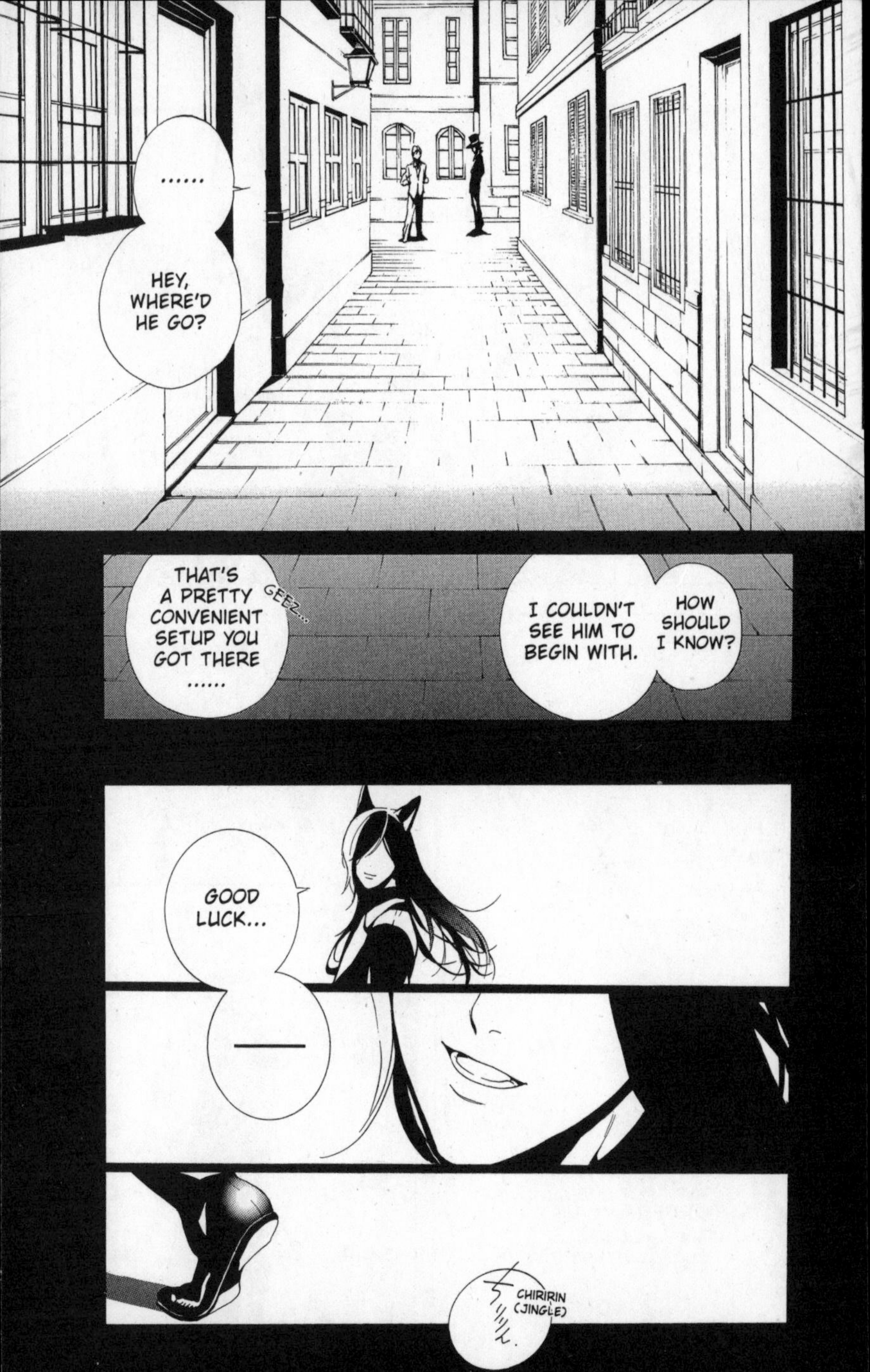
......
HEY, WHERE'D HE GO?
HOW SHOULD I KNOW?
I COULDN'T SEE HIM TO BEGIN WITH.
GEEZ...
THAT'S A PRETTY CONVENIENT SETUP YOU GOT THERE ......
GOOD LUCK...
—
ちりりん
CHIRIRIN (JINGLE)

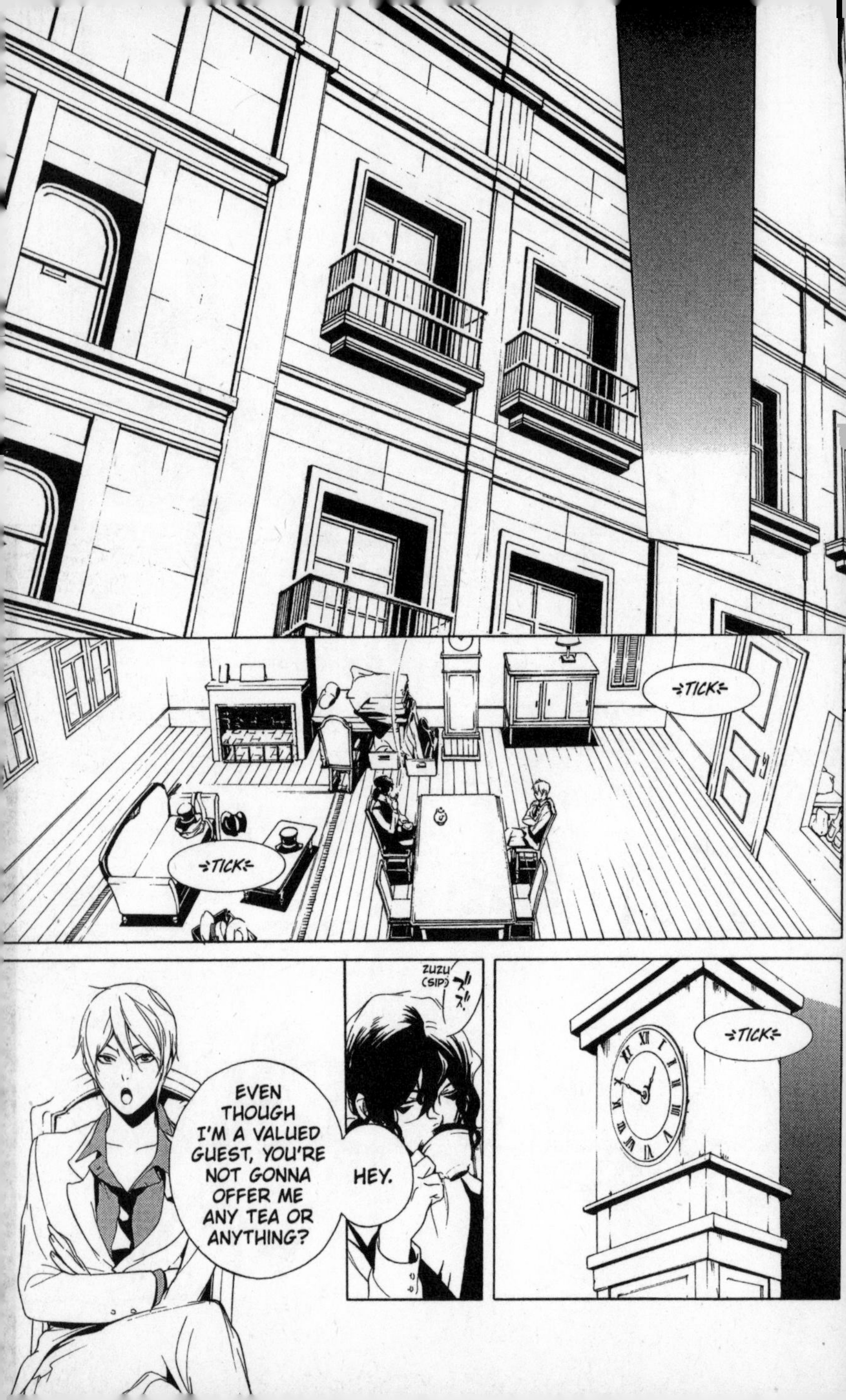
TICK
TICK
TICK
ZUZU (SIP)
HEY.
EVEN THOUGH I'M A VALUED GUEST, YOU'RE NOT GONNA OFFER ME ANY TEA OR ANYTHING?

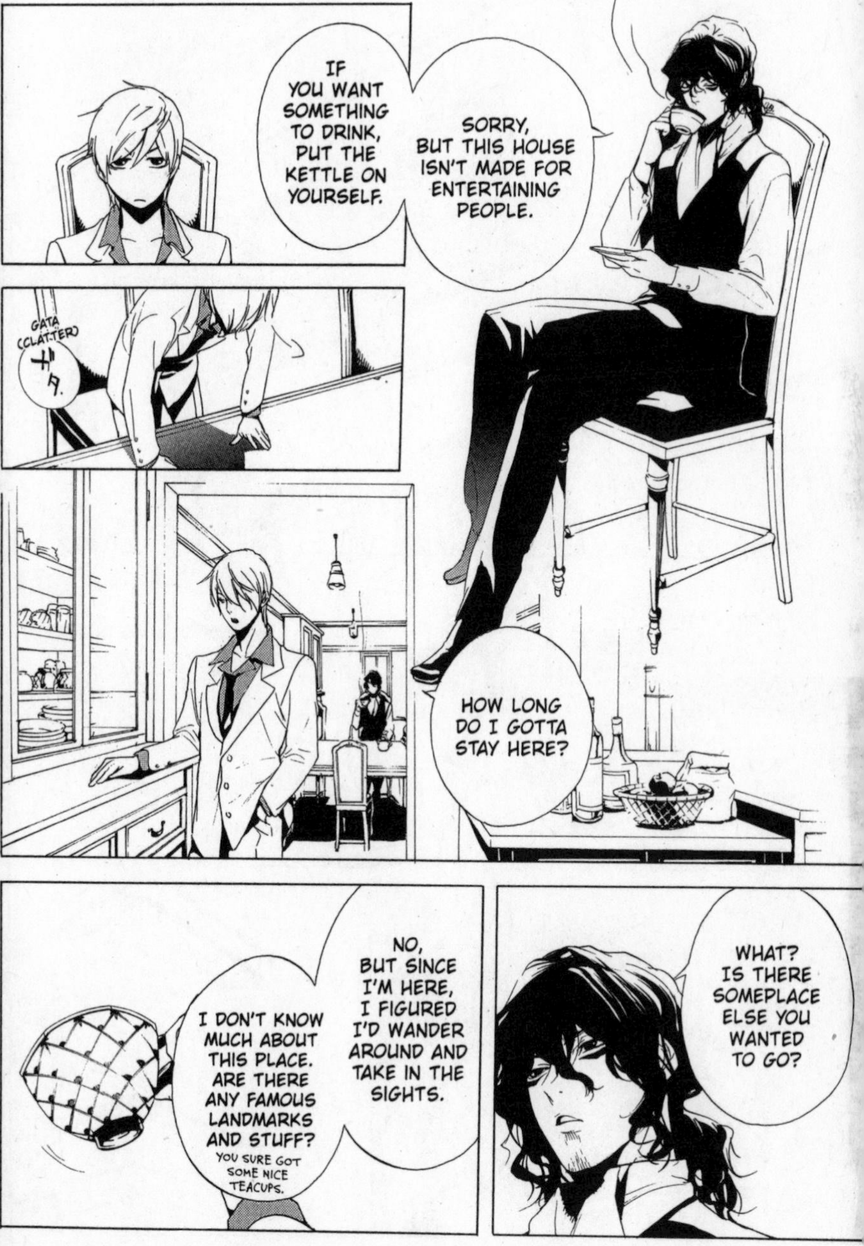
SORRY, BUT THIS HOUSE ISN'T MADE FOR ENTERTAINING PEOPLE.
IF YOU WANT SOMETHING TO DRINK, PUT THE KETTLE ON YOURSELF.
GATA (CLATTER)
ガタ.
HOW LONG DO I GOTTA STAY HERE?
WHAT? IS THERE SOMEPLACE ELSE YOU WANTED TO GO?
NO, BUT SINCE I'M HERE, I FIGURED I'D WANDER AROUND AND TAKE IN THE SIGHTS.
I DON'T KNOW MUCH ABOUT THIS PLACE. ARE THERE ANY FAMOUS LANDMARKS AND STUFF?
YOU SURE GOT SOME NICE TEACUPS.

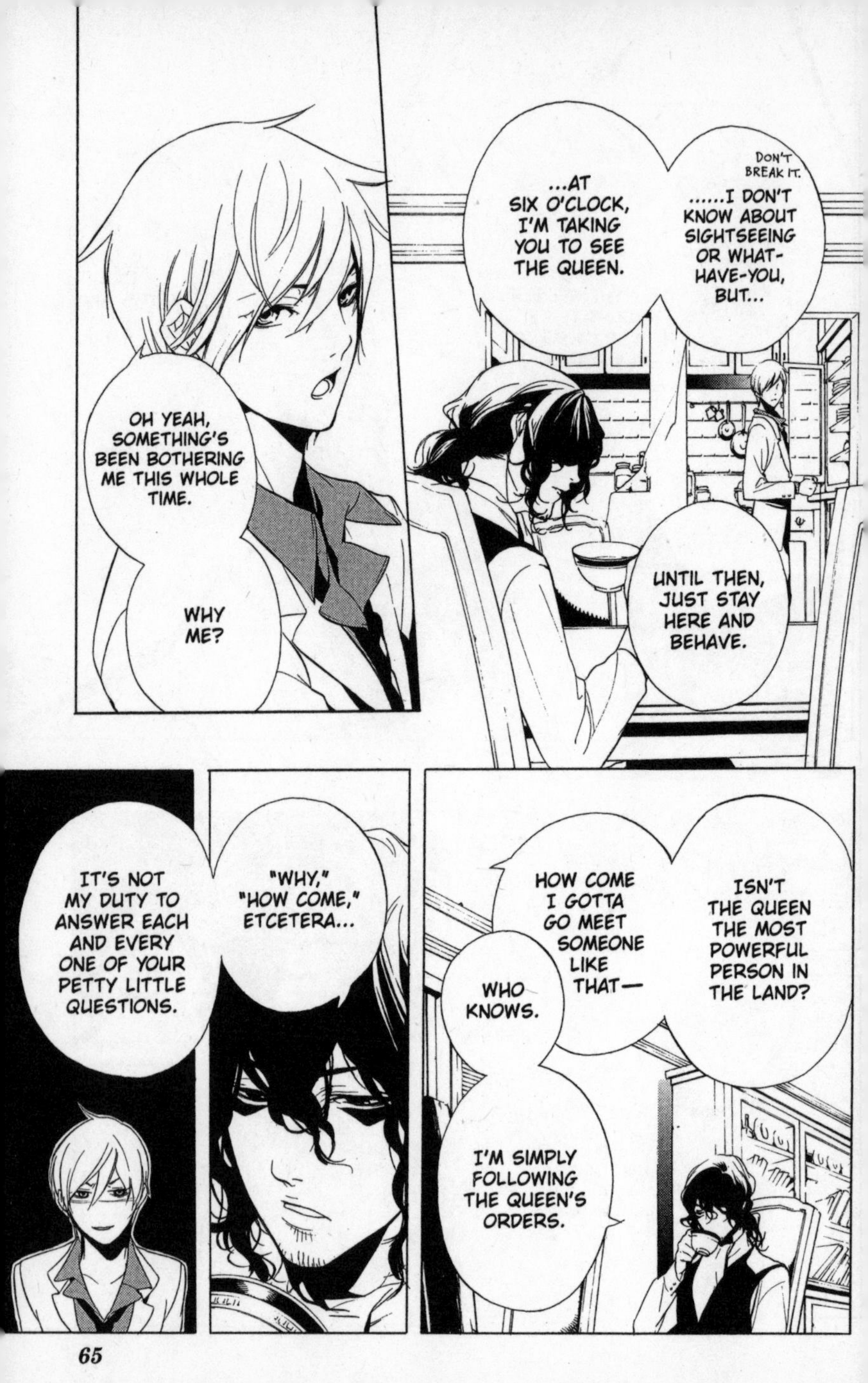
DON'T BREAK IT.
......I DON'T KNOW ABOUT SIGHTSEEING OR WHAT-HAVE-YOU, BUT...
...AT SIX O'CLOCK, I'M TAKING YOU TO SEE THE QUEEN.
UNTIL THEN, JUST STAY HERE AND BEHAVE.
OH YEAH, SOMETHING'S BEEN BOTHERING ME THIS WHOLE TIME.
WHY ME?
ISN'T THE QUEEN THE MOST POWERFUL PERSON IN THE LAND?
HOW COME I GOTTA GO MEET SOMEONE LIKE THAT—
WHO KNOWS.
I'M SIMPLY FOLLOWING THE QUEEN'S ORDERS.
"WHY," "HOW COME," ETCETERA...
IT'S NOT MY DUTY TO ANSWER EACH AND EVERY ONE OF YOUR PETTY LITTLE QUESTIONS.

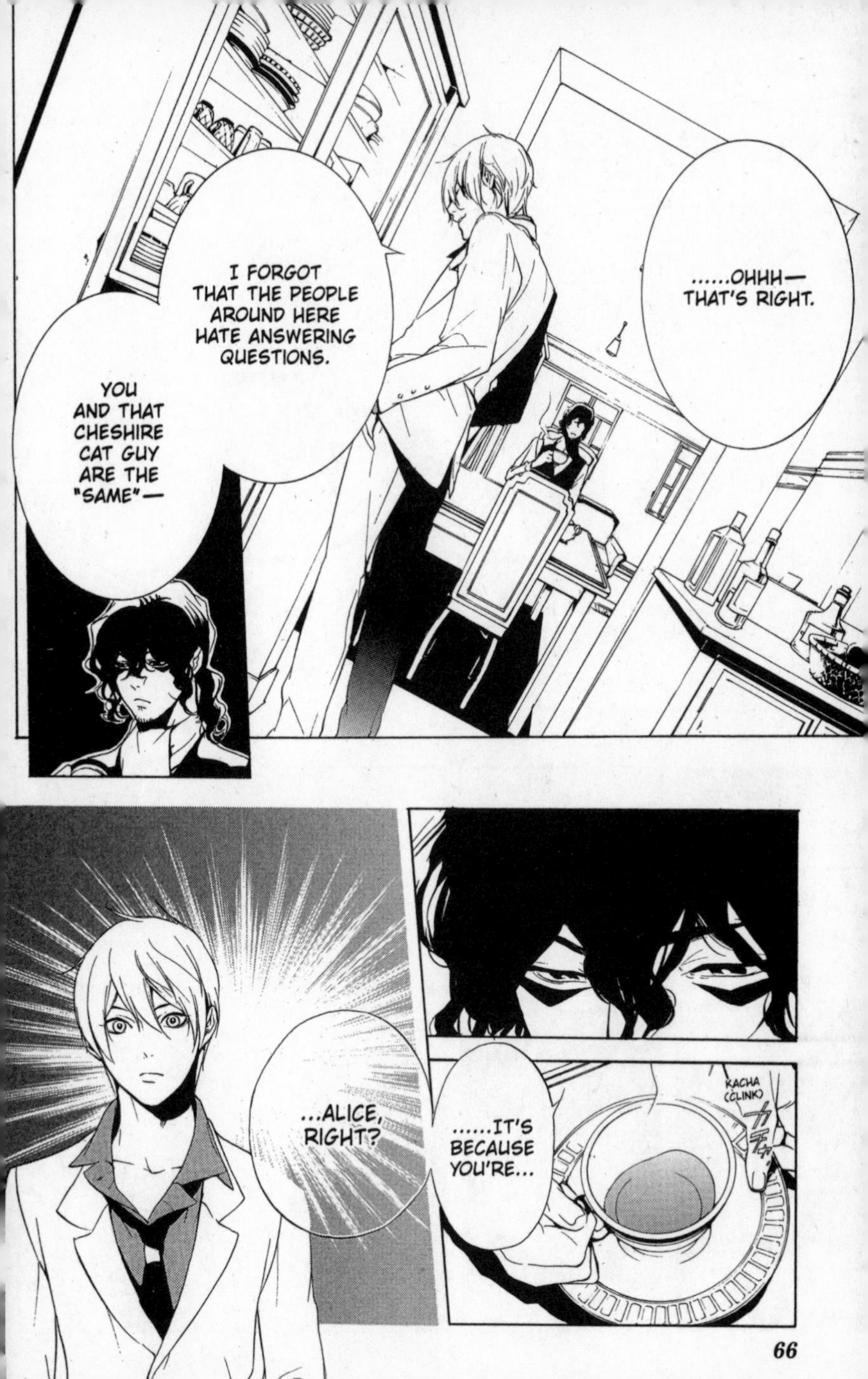
......OHHH— THAT'S RIGHT.
I FORGOT THAT THE PEOPLE AROUND HERE HATE ANSWERING QUESTIONS.
YOU AND THAT CHESHIRE CAT GUY ARE THE "SAME"—
KACHA (CLINK)
......IT'S BECAUSE YOU'RE...
...ALICE, RIGHT?

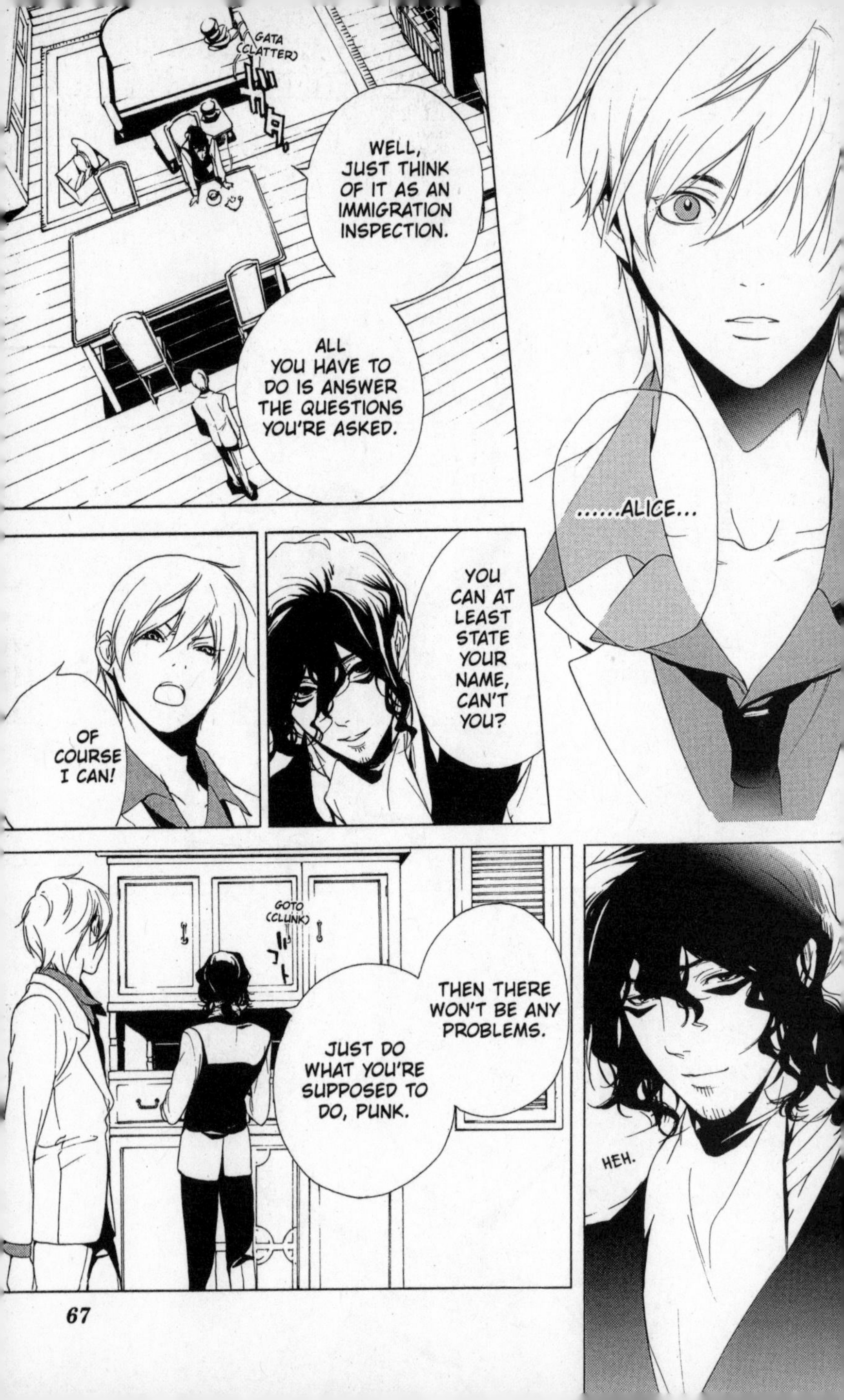
......ALICE...
GATA (CLATTER)
WELL, JUST THINK OF IT AS AN IMMIGRATION INSPECTION.
ALL YOU HAVE TO DO IS ANSWER THE QUESTIONS YOU'RE ASKED.
YOU CAN AT LEAST STATE YOUR NAME, CAN'T YOU?
OF COURSE I CAN!
HEH.
GOTO (CLUNK)
THEN THERE WON'T BE ANY PROBLEMS.
JUST DO WHAT YOU'RE SUPPOSED TO DO, PUNK.

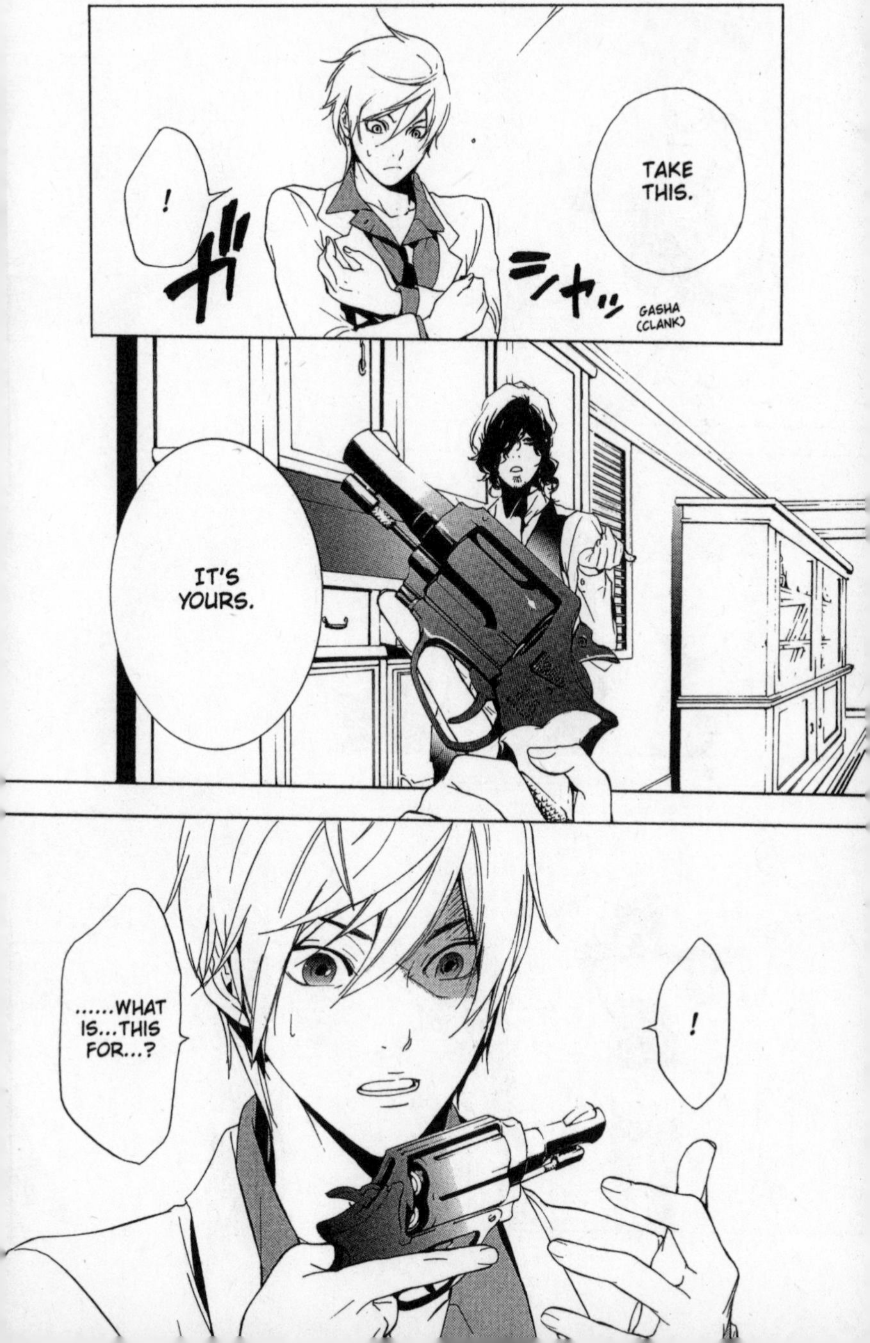
TAKE THIS.
GASHA (CLANK)
!
IT'S YOURS.
!
......WHAT IS...THIS FOR...?

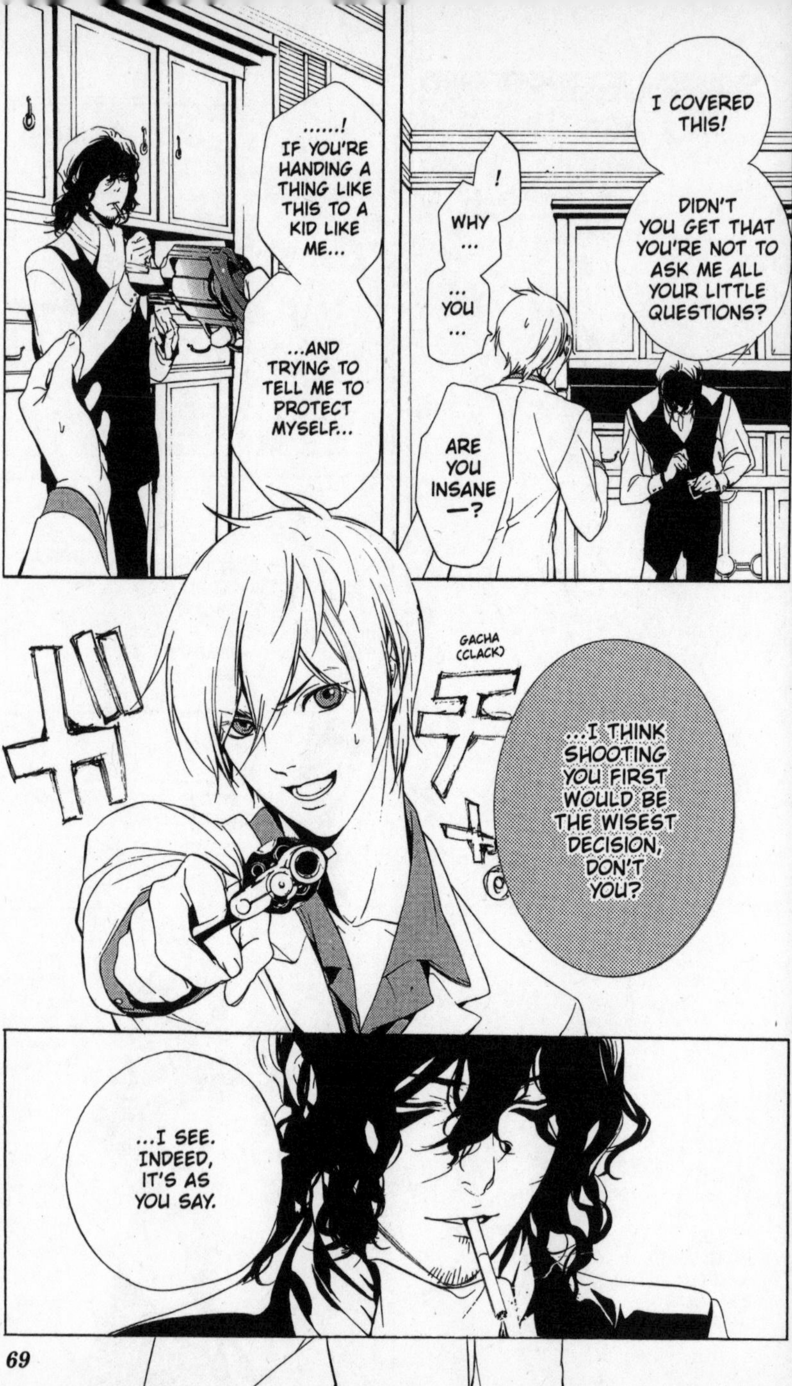
I COVERED THIS!
DIDN'T YOU GET THAT YOU'RE NOT TO ASK ME ALL YOUR LITTLE QUESTIONS?
! WHY ...
... YOU ...
ARE YOU INSANE—?
......! IF YOU'RE HANDING A THING LIKE THIS TO A KID LIKE ME...
...AND TRYING TO TELL ME TO PROTECT MYSELF...
GACHA (CLACK)
...I THINK SHOOTING YOU FIRST WOULD BE THE WISEST DECISION, DON'T YOU?
...I SEE. INDEED, IT'S AS YOU SAY.

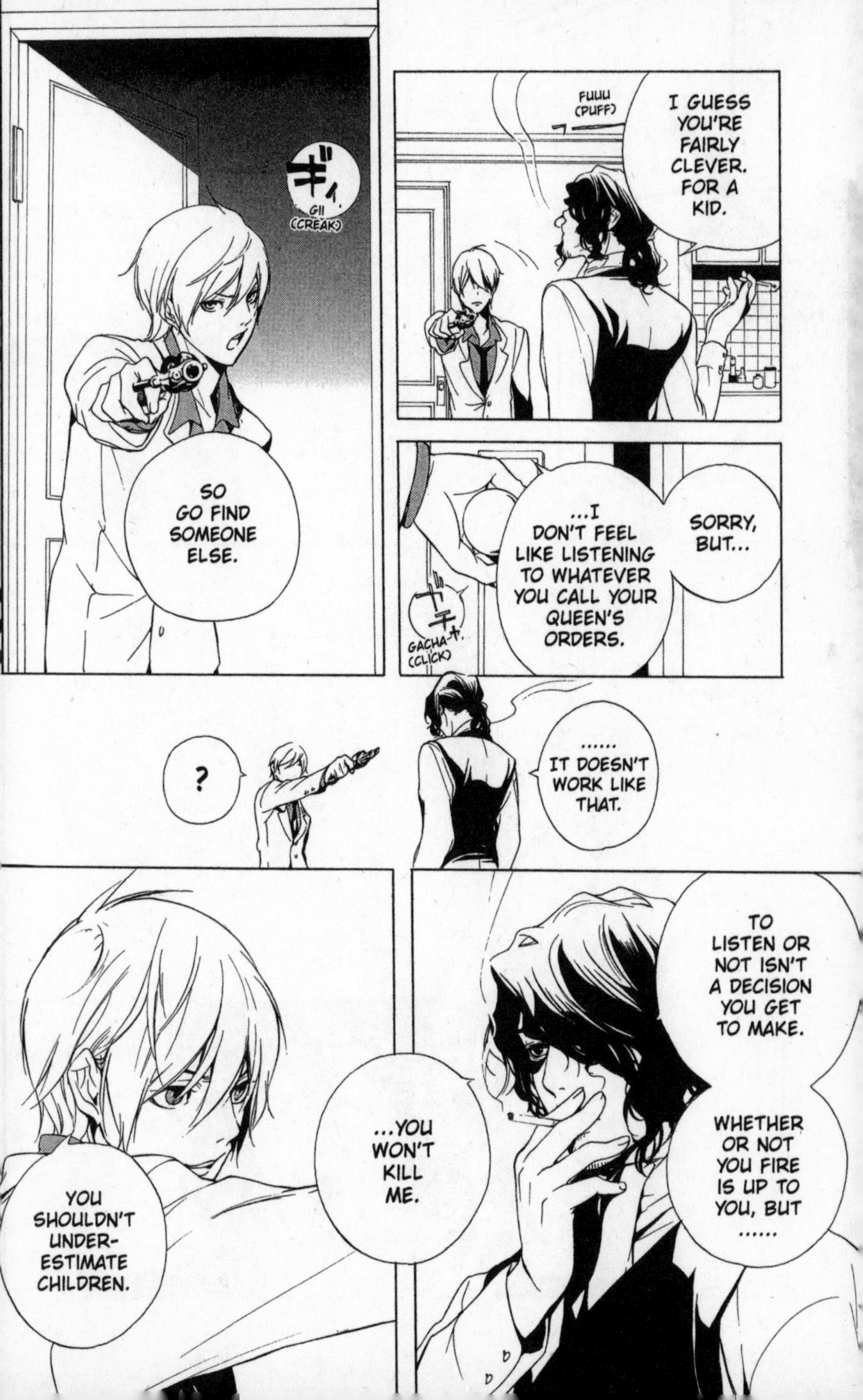
FUUU (PUFF)
I GUESS YOU'RE FAIRLY CLEVER. FOR A KID.
SORRY, BUT...
...I DON'T FEEL LIKE LISTENING TO WHATEVER YOU CALL YOUR QUEEN'S ORDERS.
GACHA (CLICK)
GII (CREAK)
SO GO FIND SOMEONE ELSE.
...... IT DOESN'T WORK LIKE THAT.
?
TO LISTEN OR NOT ISN'T A DECISION YOU GET TO MAKE.
WHETHER OR NOT YOU FIRE IS UP TO YOU, BUT ......
...YOU WON'T KILL ME.
YOU SHOULDN'T UNDER-ESTIMATE CHILDREN.

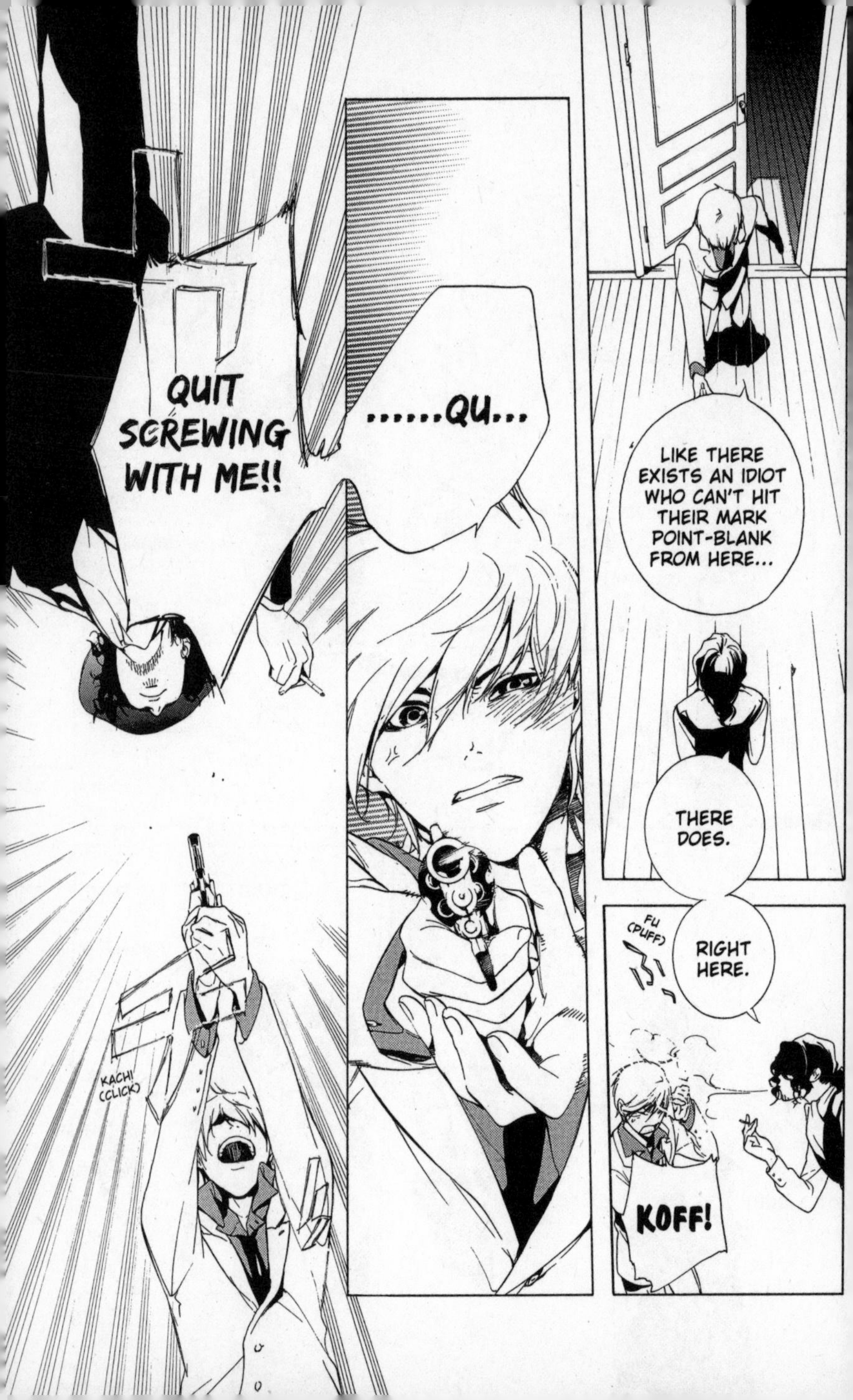
LIKE THERE EXISTS AN IDIOT WHO CAN'T HIT THEIR MARK POINT-BLANK FROM HERE...
THERE DOES.
RIGHT HERE.
FU (PUFF)
KOFF!
......QU...
QUIT SCREWING WITH ME!!
KACHI (CLICK)

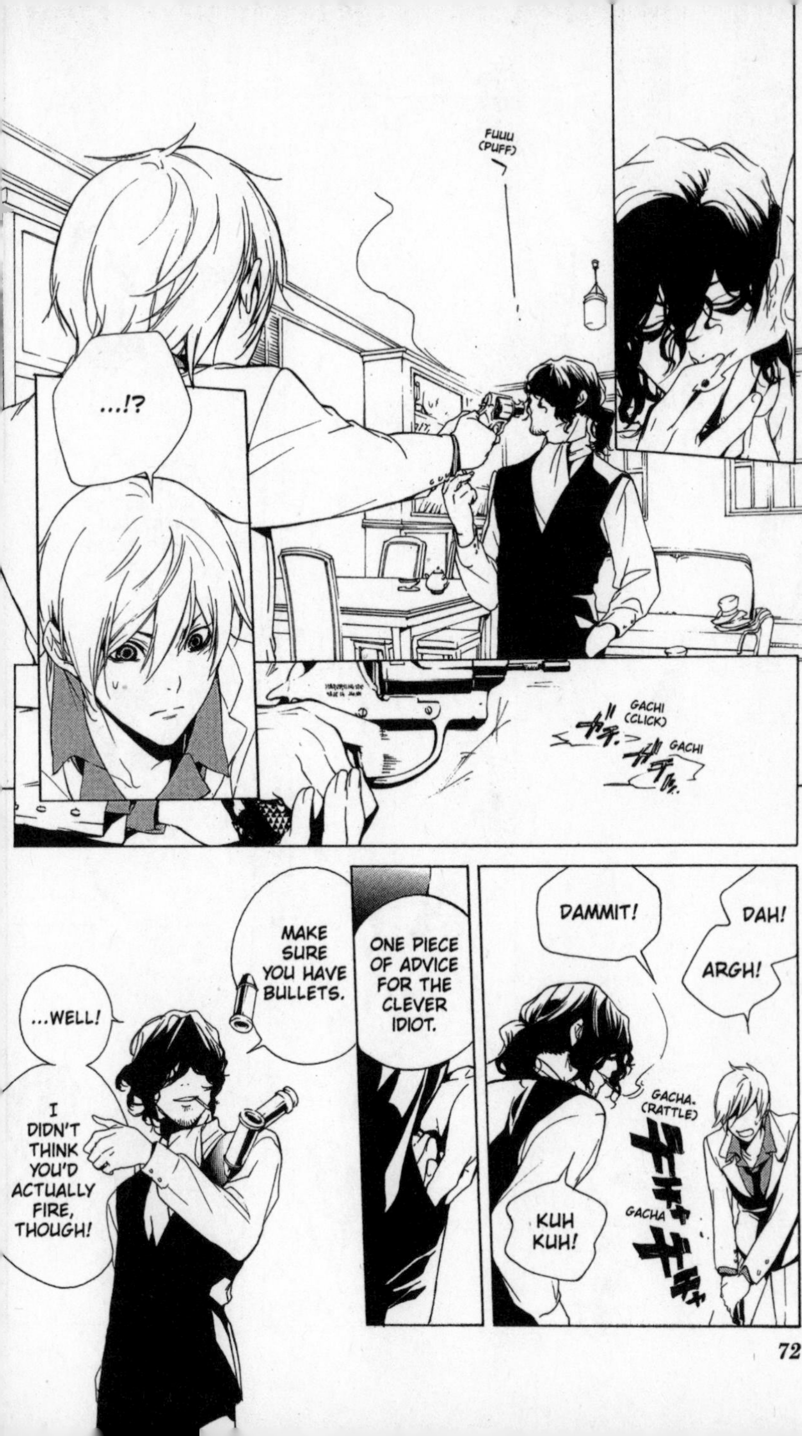
FUUU (PUFF)
...!?
GACHI (CLICK)
GACHI
DAH!
ARGH!
DAMMIT!
GACHA. (RATTLE)
GACHA
KUH KUH!
ONE PIECE OF ADVICE FOR THE CLEVER IDIOT.
MAKE SURE YOU HAVE BULLETS.
...WELL!
I DIDN'T THINK YOU'D ACTUALLY FIRE, THOUGH!

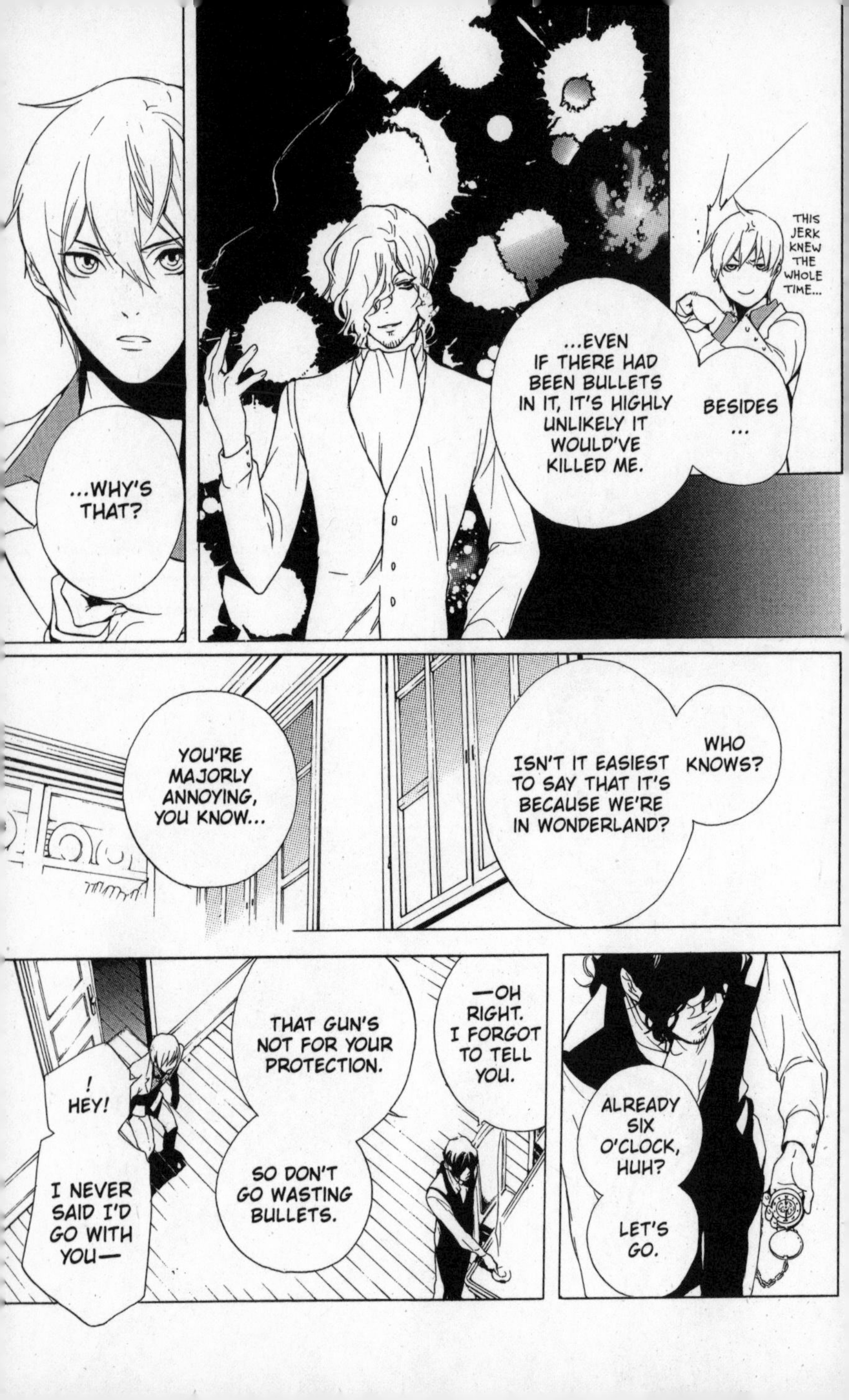
THIS JERK KNEW THE WHOLE TIME...
BESIDES...
...EVEN IF THERE HAD BEEN BULLETS IN IT, IT'S HIGHLY UNLIKELY IT WOULD'VE KILLED ME.
...WHY'S THAT?
WHO KNOWS?
ISN'T IT EASIEST TO SAY THAT IT'S BECAUSE WE'RE IN WONDERLAND?
YOU'RE MAJORLY ANNOYING, YOU KNOW...
ALREADY SIX O'CLOCK, HUH?
LET'S GO.
! HEY!
I NEVER SAID I'D GO WITH YOU—
—OH RIGHT. I FORGOT TO TELL YOU.
THAT GUN'S NOT FOR YOUR PROTECTION.
SO DON'T GO WASTING BULLETS.

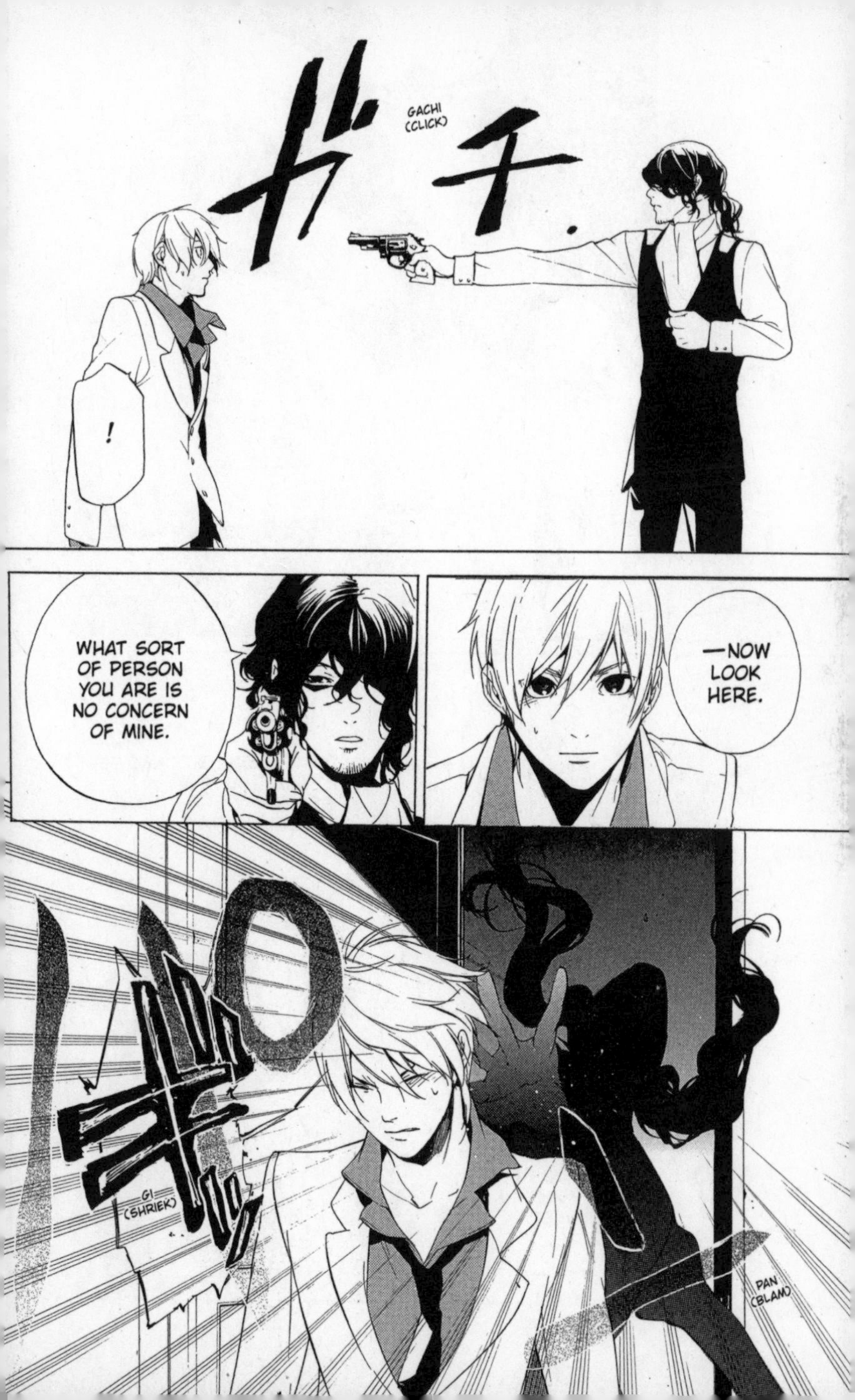
GACHI (CLICK)
!
—NOW LOOK HERE.
WHAT SORT OF PERSON YOU ARE IS NO CONCERN OF MINE.
PAN (BLAM)
GI (SHRIEK)

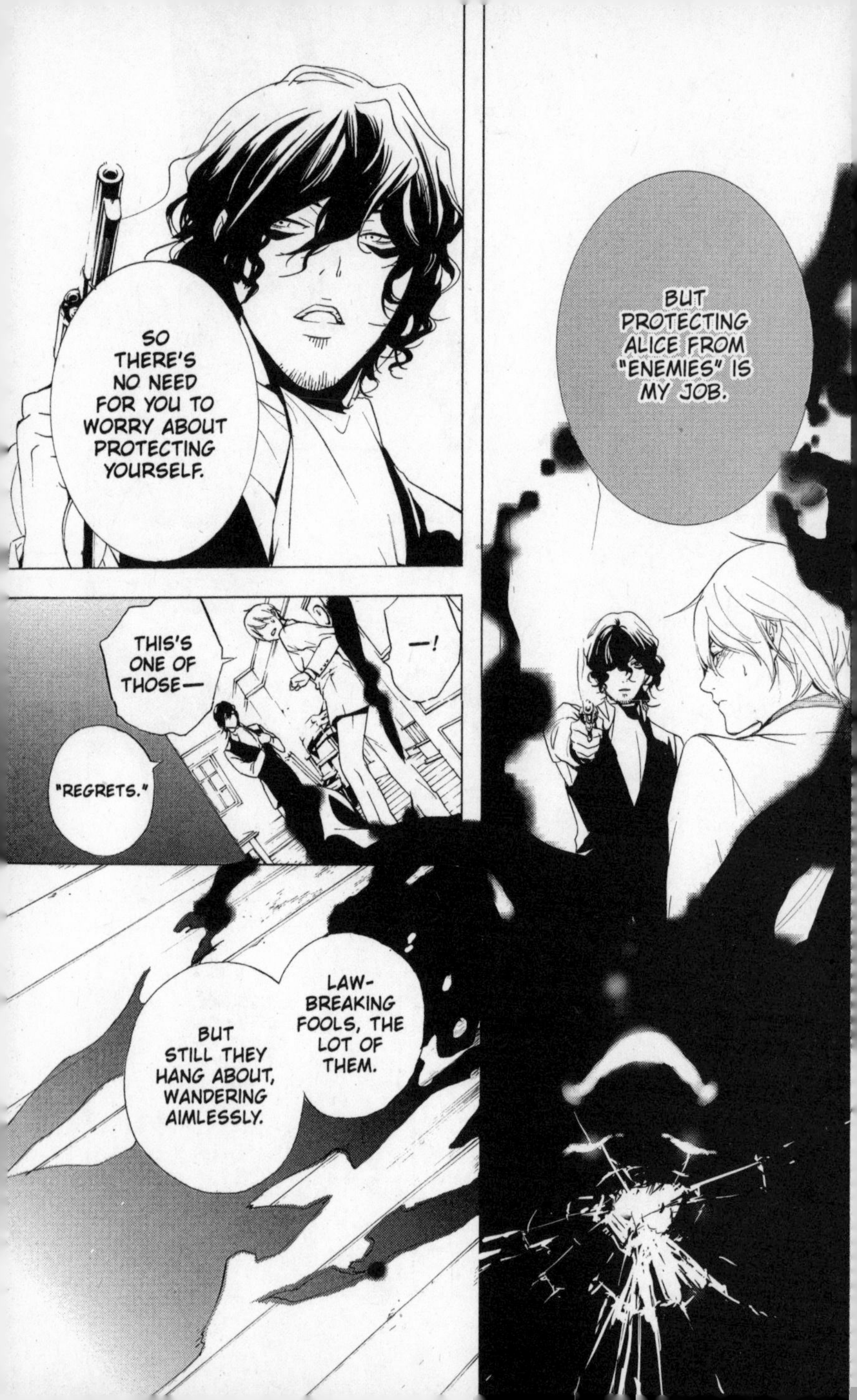
BUT PROTECTING ALICE FROM "ENEMIES" IS MY JOB.
SO THERE'S NO NEED FOR YOU TO WORRY ABOUT PROTECTING YOURSELF.
—!
THIS'S ONE OF THOSE—
"REGRETS."
LAW-BREAKING FOOLS, THE LOT OF THEM.
BUT STILL THEY HANG ABOUT, WANDERING AIMLESSLY.

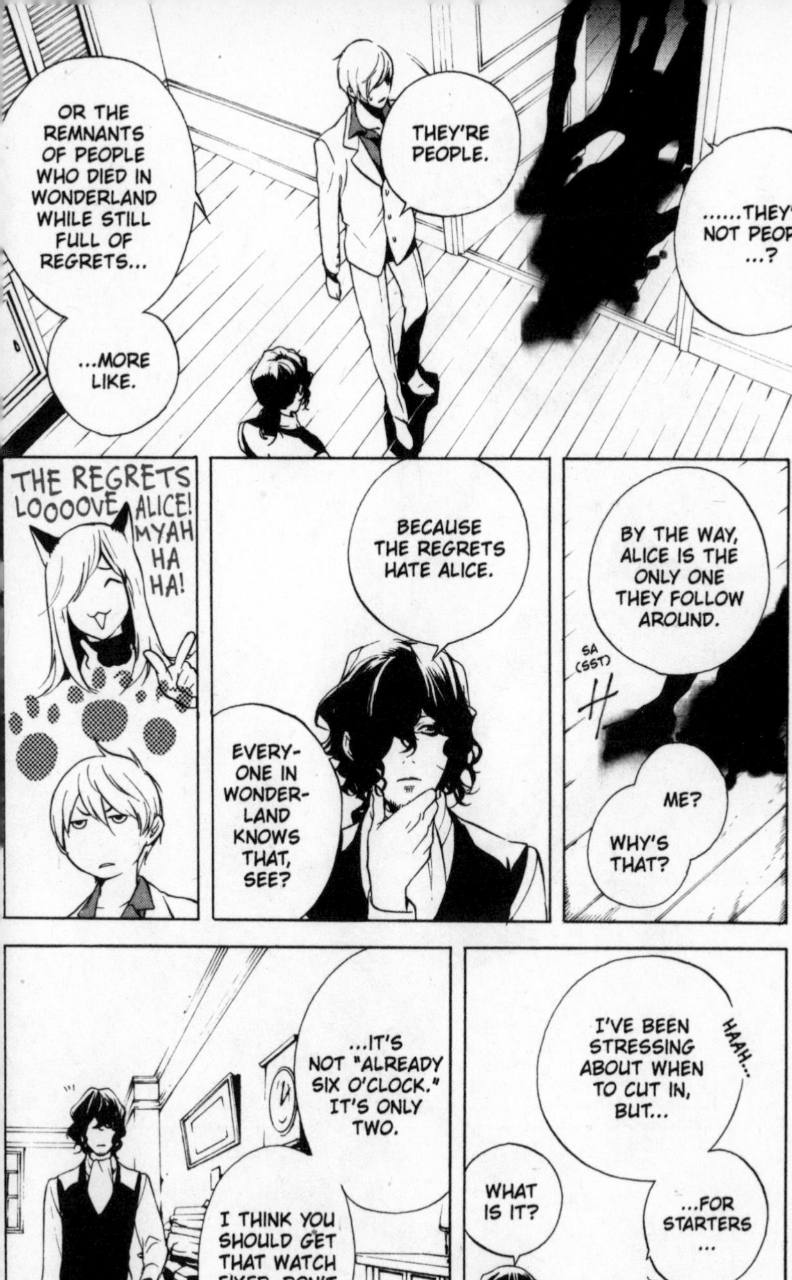
......THEY'RE NOT PEOPLE ...?
THEY'RE PEOPLE.
OR THE REMNANTS OF PEOPLE WHO DIED IN WONDERLAND WHILE STILL FULL OF REGRETS...
...MORE LIKE.
BY THE WAY, ALICE IS THE ONLY ONE THEY FOLLOW AROUND.
SA (SST)
ME?
WHY'S THAT?
BECAUSE THE REGRETS HATE ALICE.
EVERY-ONE IN WONDER-LAND KNOWS THAT, SEE?
THE REGRETS LOOOOVE ALICE! MYAH HA HA!
I'VE BEEN STRESSING ABOUT WHEN TO CUT IN, BUT...
HAAH...
...FOR STARTERS ...
WHAT IS IT?
...IT'S NOT "ALREADY SIX O'CLOCK." IT'S ONLY TWO.
I THINK YOU SHOULD GET THAT WATCH FIXED, DON'T YOU?

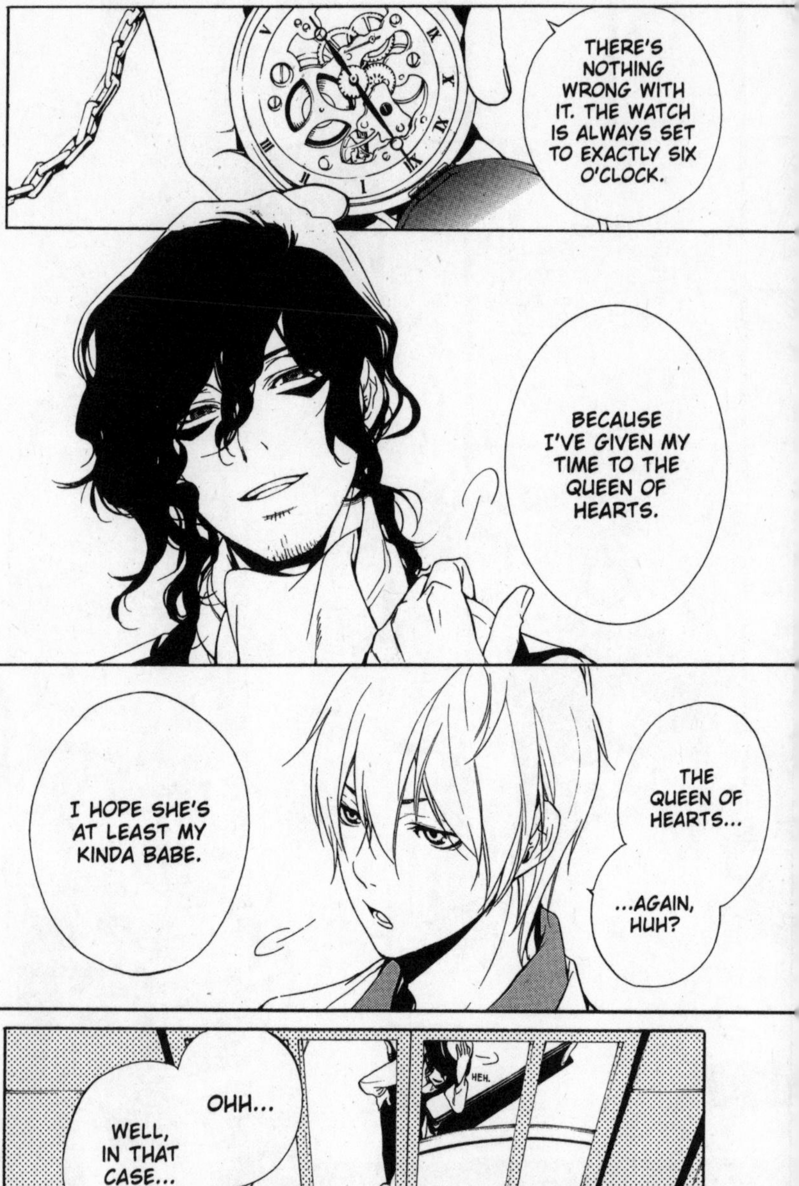
THERE'S NOTHING WRONG WITH IT. THE WATCH IS ALWAYS SET TO EXACTLY SIX O'CLOCK.
BECAUSE I'VE GIVEN MY TIME TO THE QUEEN OF HEARTS.
THE QUEEN OF HEARTS...
...AGAIN, HUH?
I HOPE SHE'S AT LEAST MY KINDA BABE.
HEH.
OHH...
WELL, IN THAT CASE...

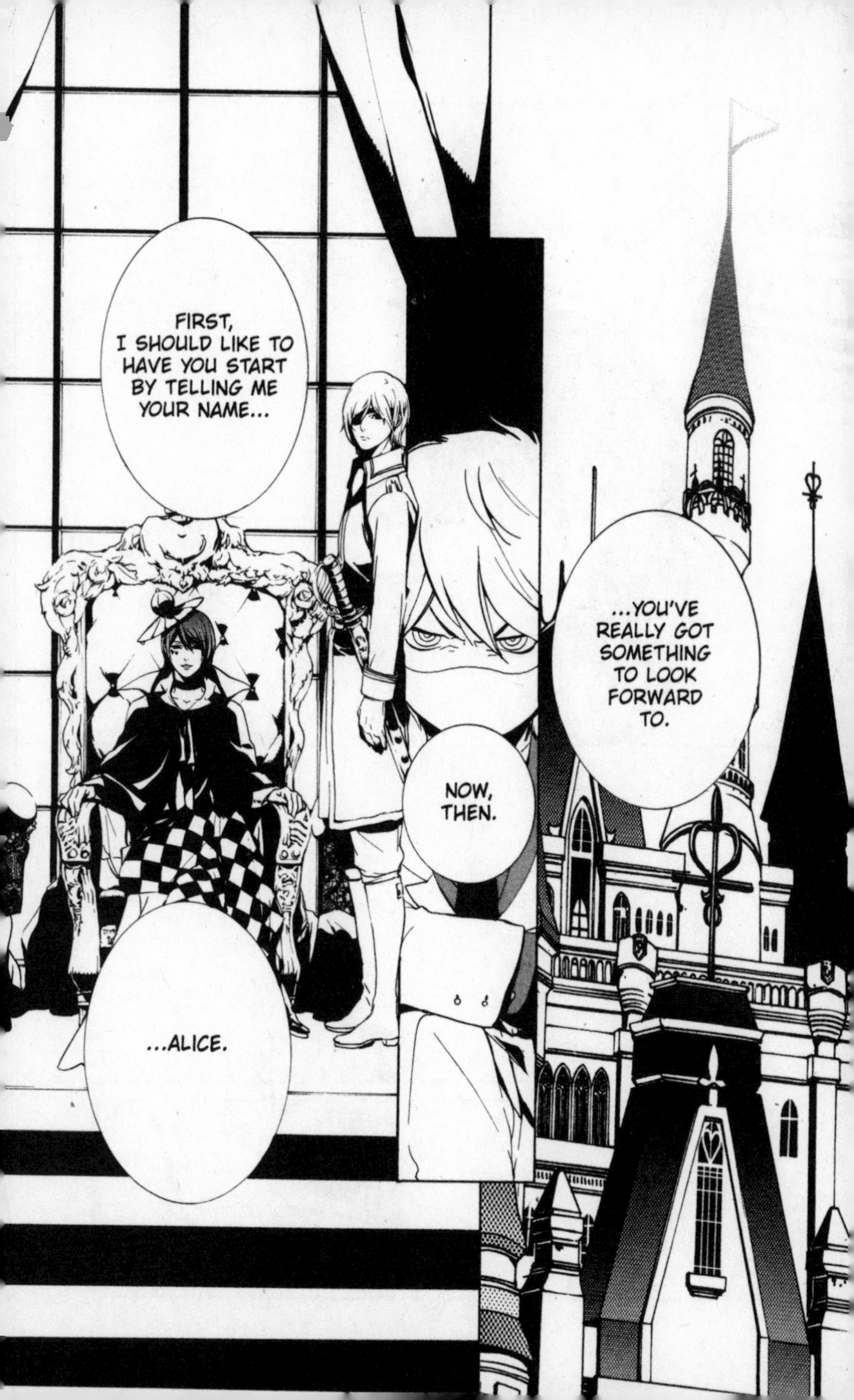
...YOU'VE REALLY GOT SOMETHING TO LOOK FORWARD TO.
NOW, THEN.
FIRST, I SHOULD LIKE TO HAVE YOU START BY TELLING ME YOUR NAME...
...ALICE.

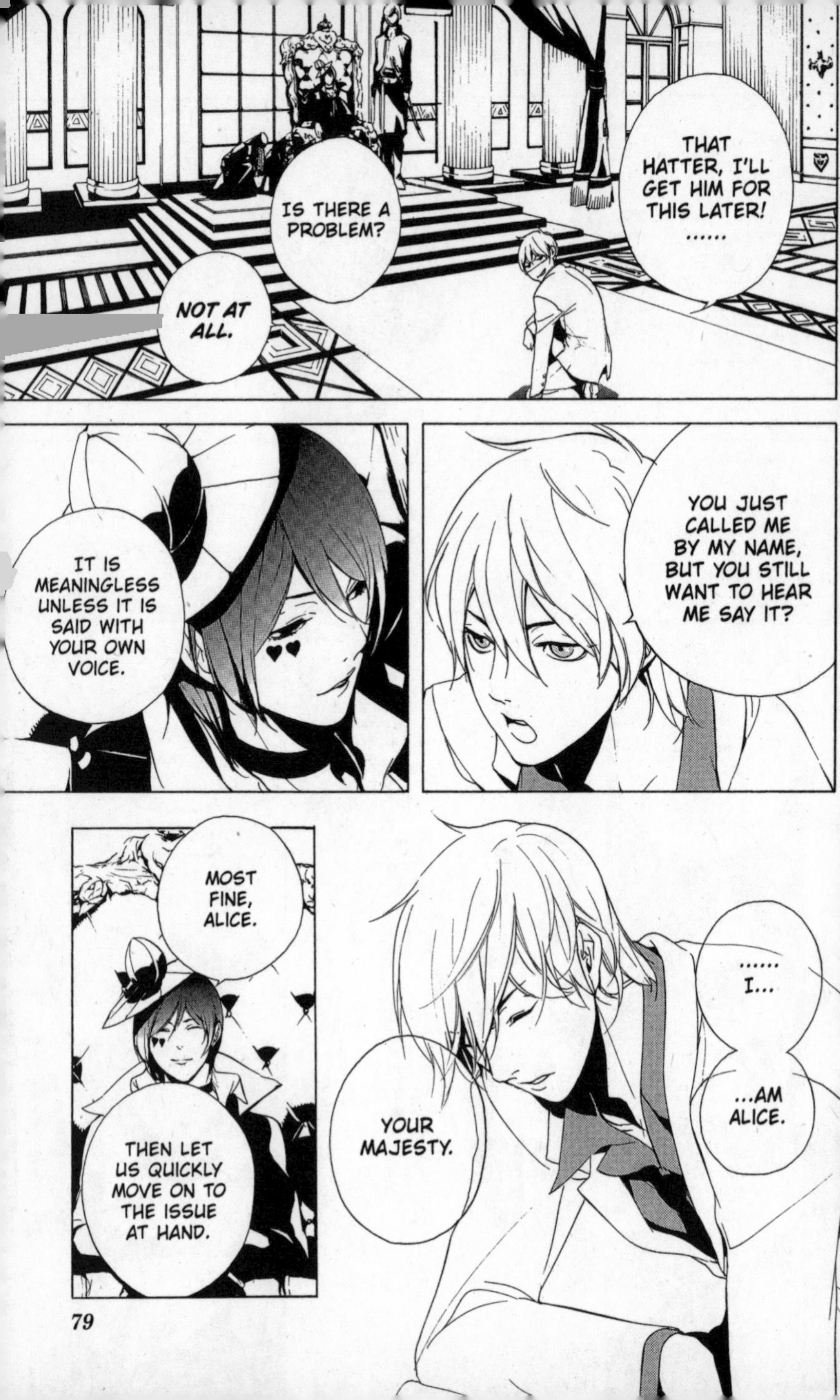
THAT HATTER, I'LL GET HIM FOR THIS LATER! ......
IS THERE A PROBLEM?
NOT AT ALL.
YOU JUST CALLED ME BY MY NAME, BUT YOU STILL WANT TO HEAR ME SAY IT?
IT IS MEANINGLESS UNLESS IT IS SAID WITH YOUR OWN VOICE.
...... I...
...AM ALICE.
YOUR MAJESTY.
MOST FINE, ALICE.
THEN LET US QUICKLY MOVE ON TO THE ISSUE AT HAND.

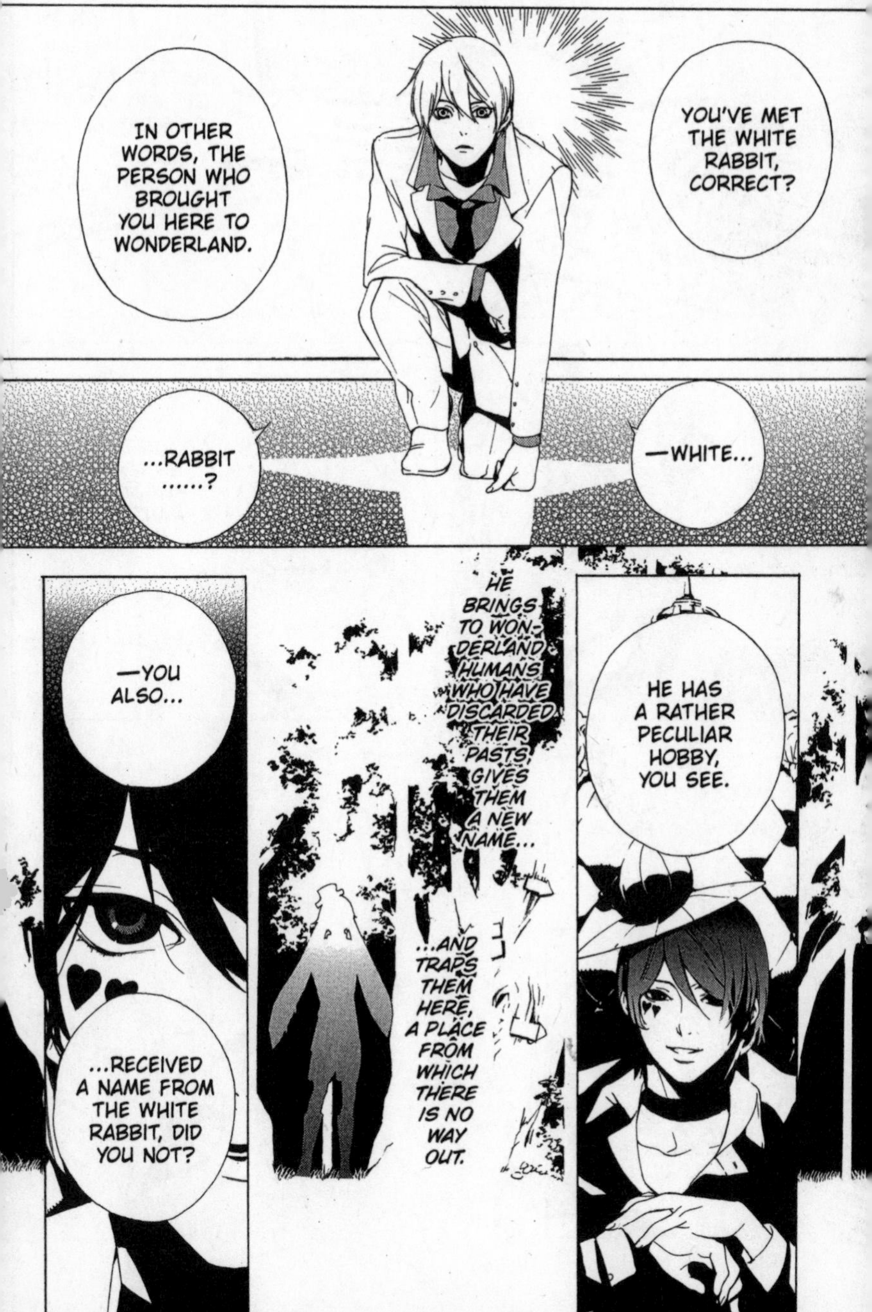
YOU'VE MET THE WHITE RABBIT, CORRECT?
IN OTHER WORDS, THE PERSON WHO BROUGHT YOU HERE TO WONDERLAND.
—WHITE...
...RABBIT ......?
HE HAS A RATHER PECULIAR HOBBY, YOU SEE.
HE BRINGS TO WON-DERLAND HUMANS WHO HAVE DISCARDED THEIR PASTS, GIVES THEM A NEW NAME...
...AND TRAPS THEM HERE, A PLACE FROM WHICH THERE IS NO WAY OUT.
—YOU ALSO...
...RECEIVED A NAME FROM THE WHITE RABBIT, DID YOU NOT?

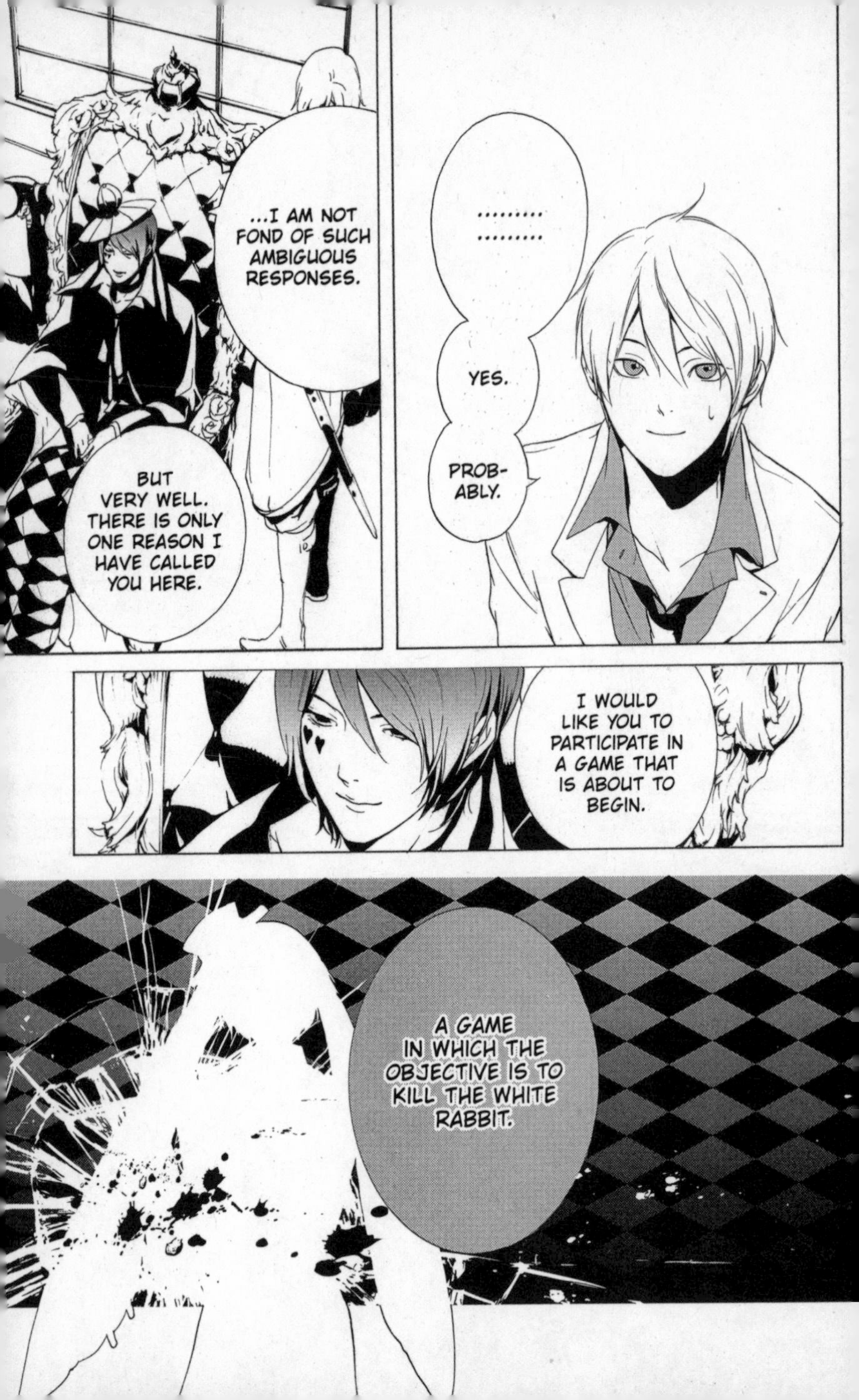
....
....
YES.
PROB-ABLY.
...I AM NOT FOND OF SUCH AMBIGUOUS RESPONSES.
BUT VERY WELL. THERE IS ONLY ONE REASON I HAVE CALLED YOU HERE.
I WOULD LIKE YOU TO PARTICIPATE IN A GAME THAT IS ABOUT TO BEGIN.
A GAME IN WHICH THE OBJECTIVE IS TO KILL THE WHITE RABBIT.

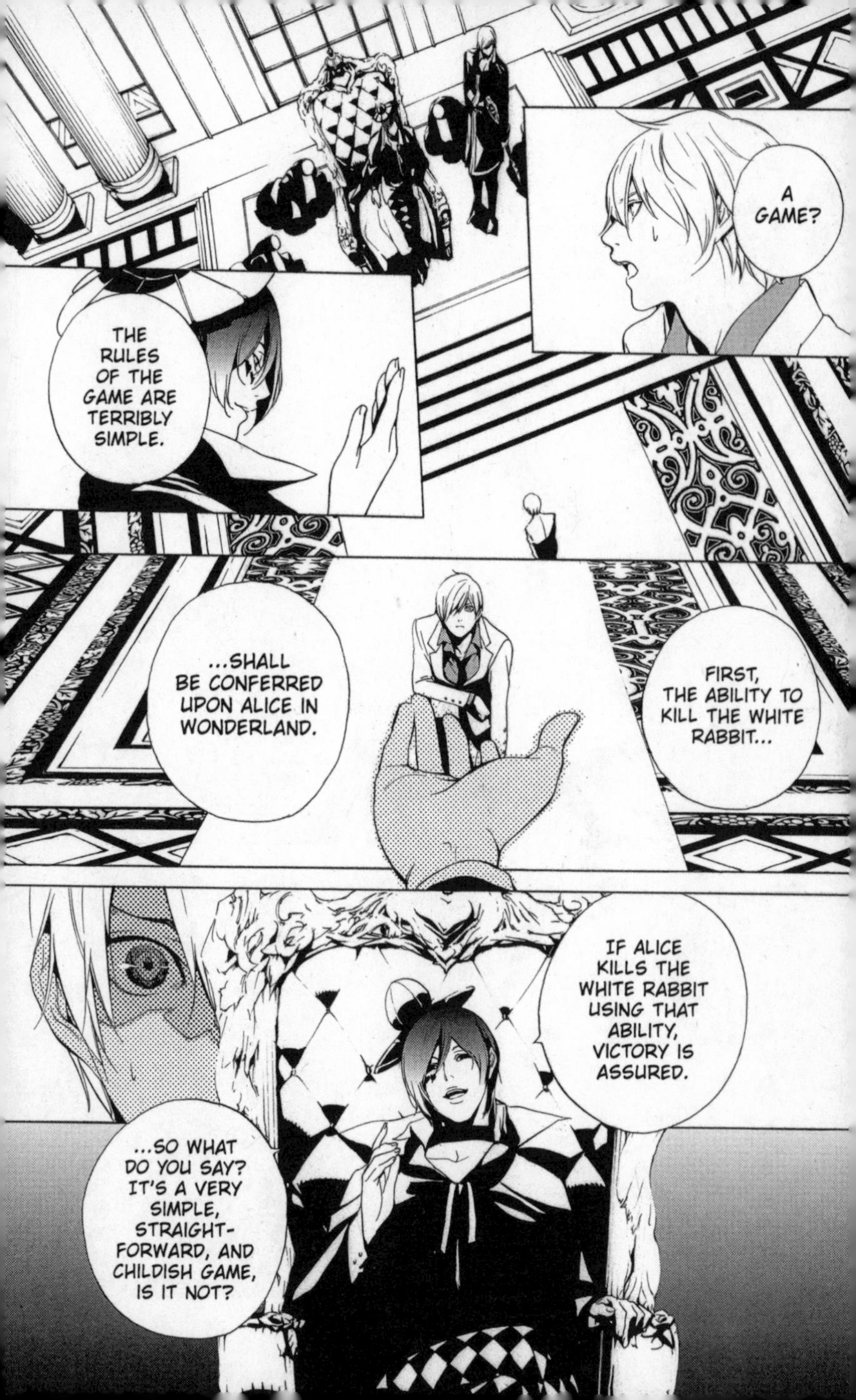
A GAME?
THE RULES OF THE GAME ARE TERRIBLY SIMPLE.
FIRST, THE ABILITY TO KILL THE WHITE RABBIT...
...SHALL BE CONFERRED UPON ALICE IN WONDERLAND.
IF ALICE KILLS THE WHITE RABBIT USING THAT ABILITY, VICTORY IS ASSURED.
...SO WHAT DO YOU SAY? IT'S A VERY SIMPLE, STRAIGHT-FORWARD, AND CHILDISH GAME, IS IT NOT?

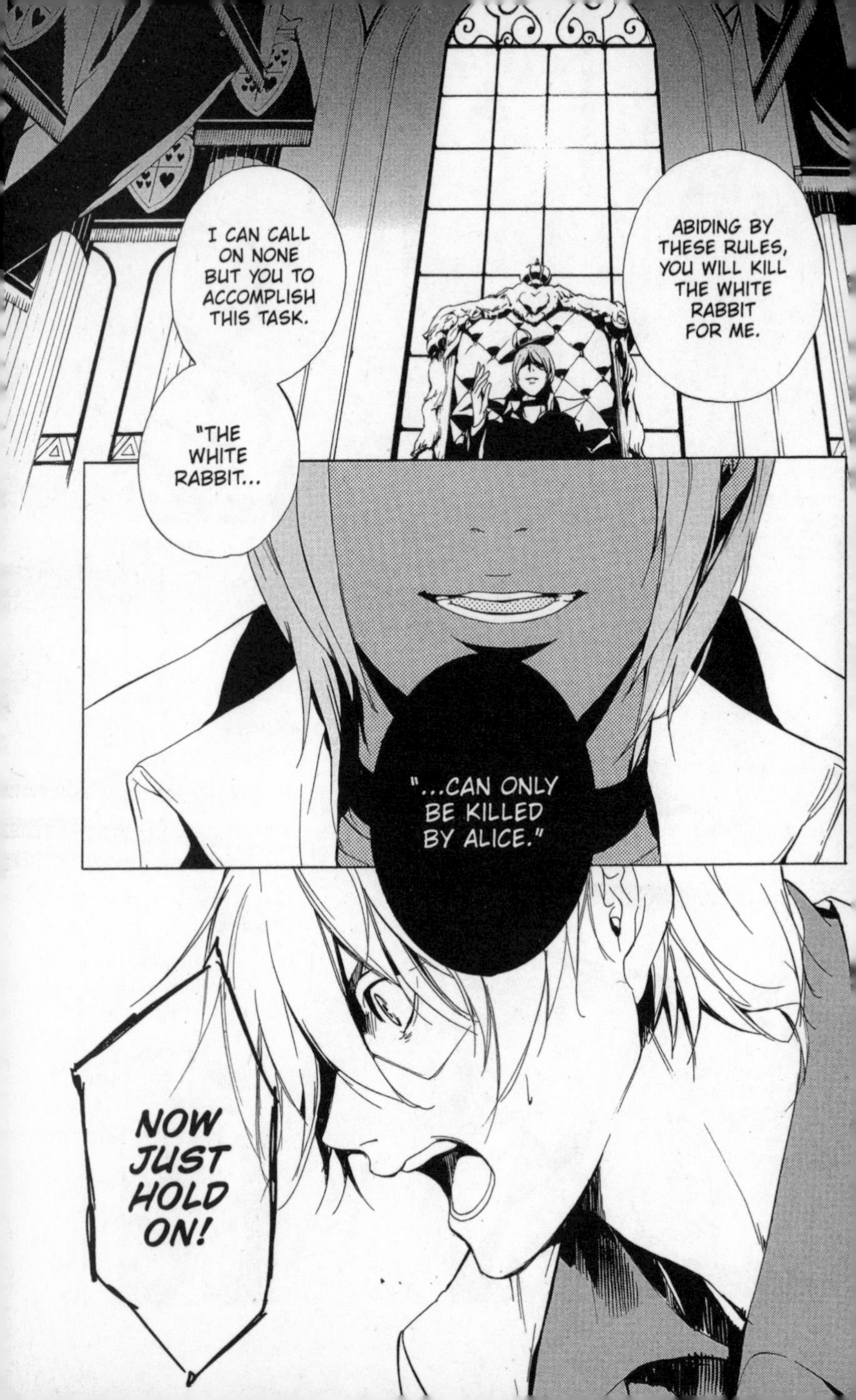
ABIDING BY THESE RULES, YOU WILL KILL THE WHITE RABBIT FOR ME.
I CAN CALL ON NONE BUT YOU TO ACCOMPLISH THIS TASK.
"THE WHITE RABBIT...
"...CAN ONLY BE KILLED BY ALICE."
NOW JUST HOLD ON!

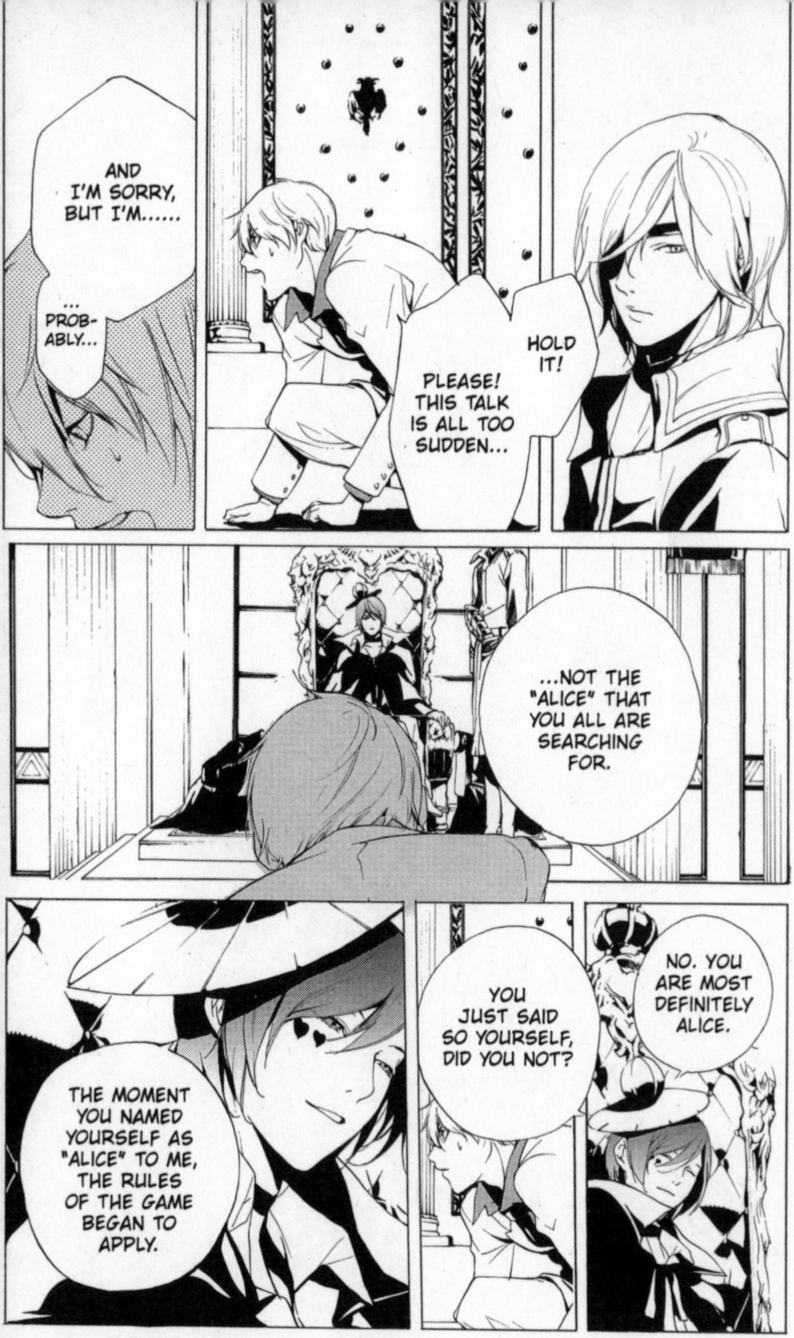
HOLD IT!
PLEASE! THIS TALK IS ALL TOO SUDDEN...
AND I'M SORRY, BUT I'M......
...PROBABLY...
...NOT THE "ALICE" THAT YOU ALL ARE SEARCHING FOR.
NO. YOU ARE MOST DEFINITELY ALICE.
YOU JUST SAID SO YOURSELF, DID YOU NOT?
THE MOMENT YOU NAMED YOURSELF AS "ALICE" TO ME, THE RULES OF THE GAME BEGAN TO APPLY.

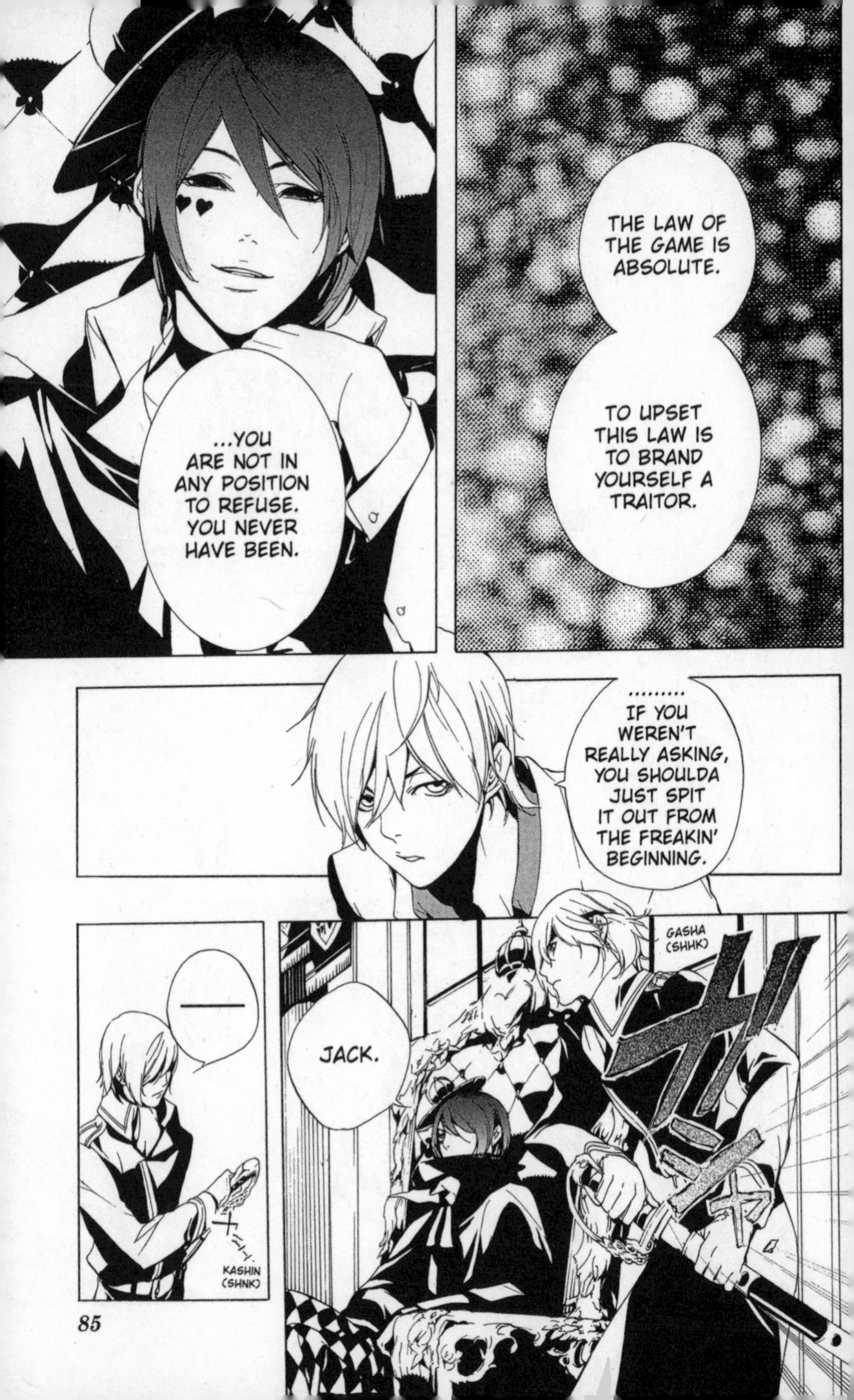
THE LAW OF THE GAME IS ABSOLUTE.
TO UPSET THIS LAW IS TO BRAND YOURSELF A TRAITOR.
...YOU ARE NOT IN ANY POSITION TO REFUSE. YOU NEVER HAVE BEEN.
....
IF YOU WEREN'T REALLY ASKING, YOU SHOULDA JUST SPIT IT OUT FROM THE FREAKIN' BEGINNING.
GASHA (SHHK)
JACK.
———
KASHIN (SHNK)

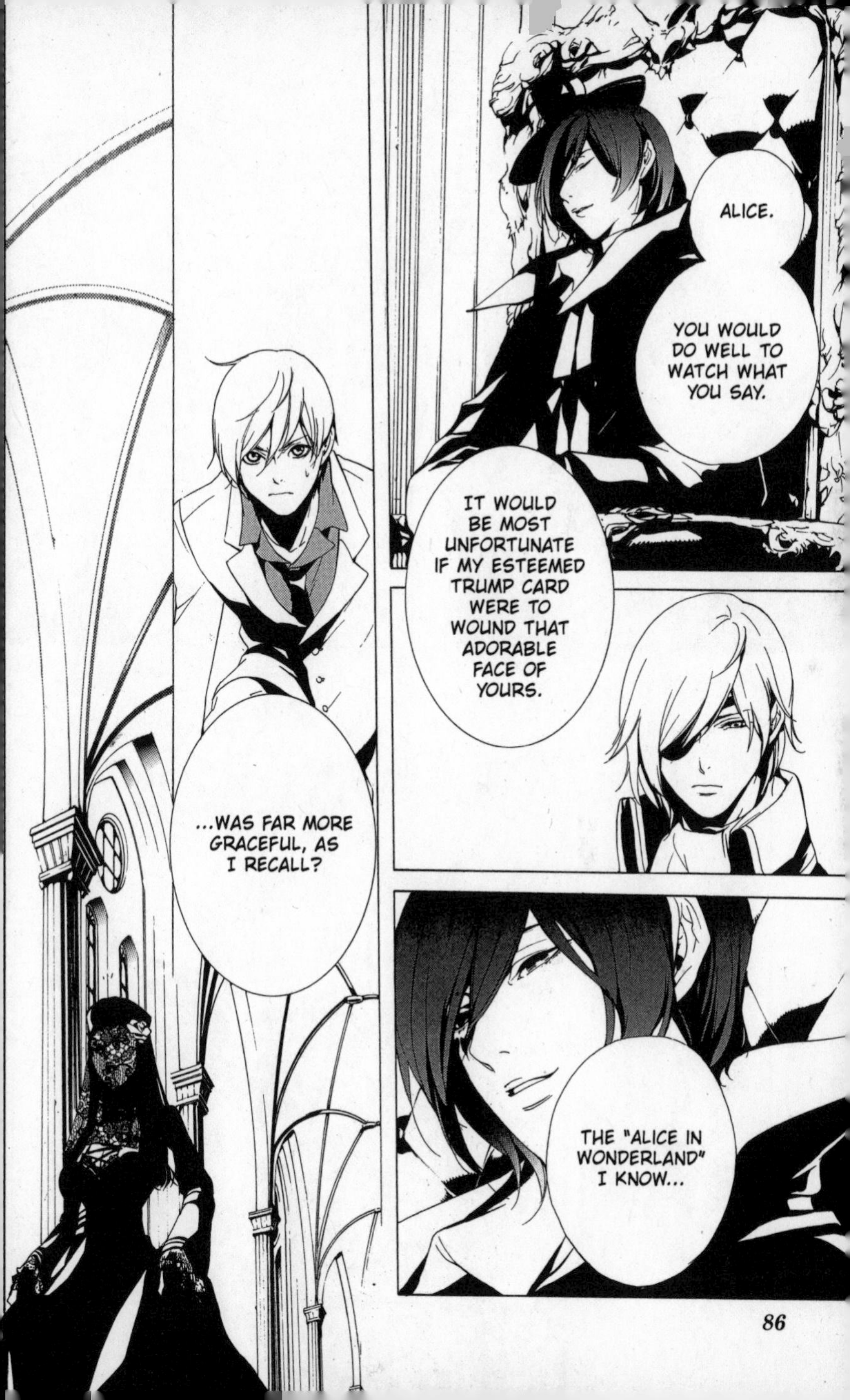
ALICE.
YOU WOULD DO WELL TO WATCH WHAT YOU SAY.
IT WOULD BE MOST UNFORTUNATE IF MY ESTEEMED TRUMP CARD WERE TO WOUND THAT ADORABLE FACE OF YOURS.
THE "ALICE IN WONDERLAND" I KNOW...
...WAS FAR MORE GRACEFUL, AS I RECALL?

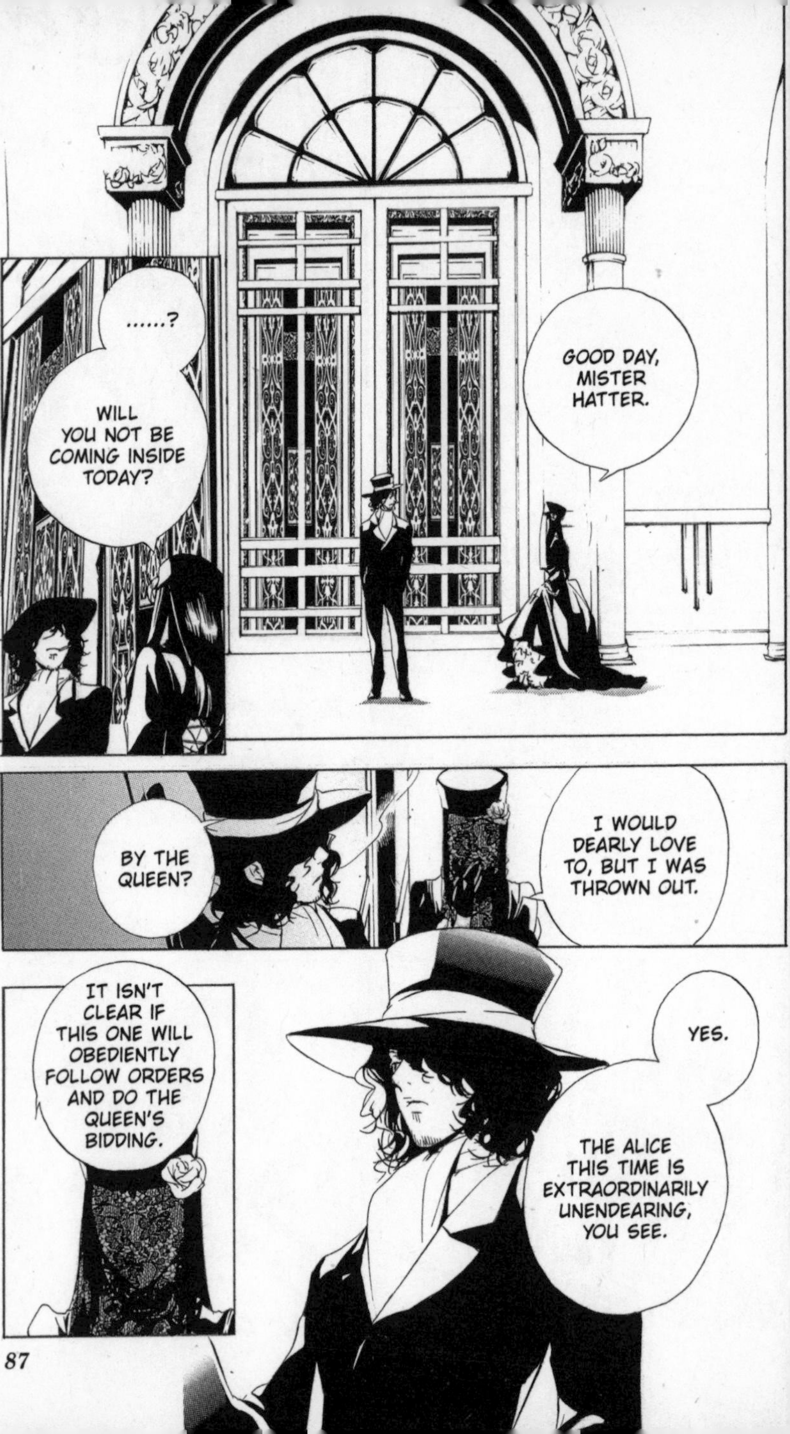
GOOD DAY, MISTER HATTER.
......?
WILL YOU NOT BE COMING INSIDE TODAY?
I WOULD DEARLY LOVE TO, BUT I WAS THROWN OUT.
BY THE QUEEN?
YES.
THE ALICE THIS TIME IS EXTRAORDINARILY UNENDEARING, YOU SEE.
IT ISN'T CLEAR IF THIS ONE WILL OBEDIENTLY FOLLOW ORDERS AND DO THE QUEEN'S BIDDING.

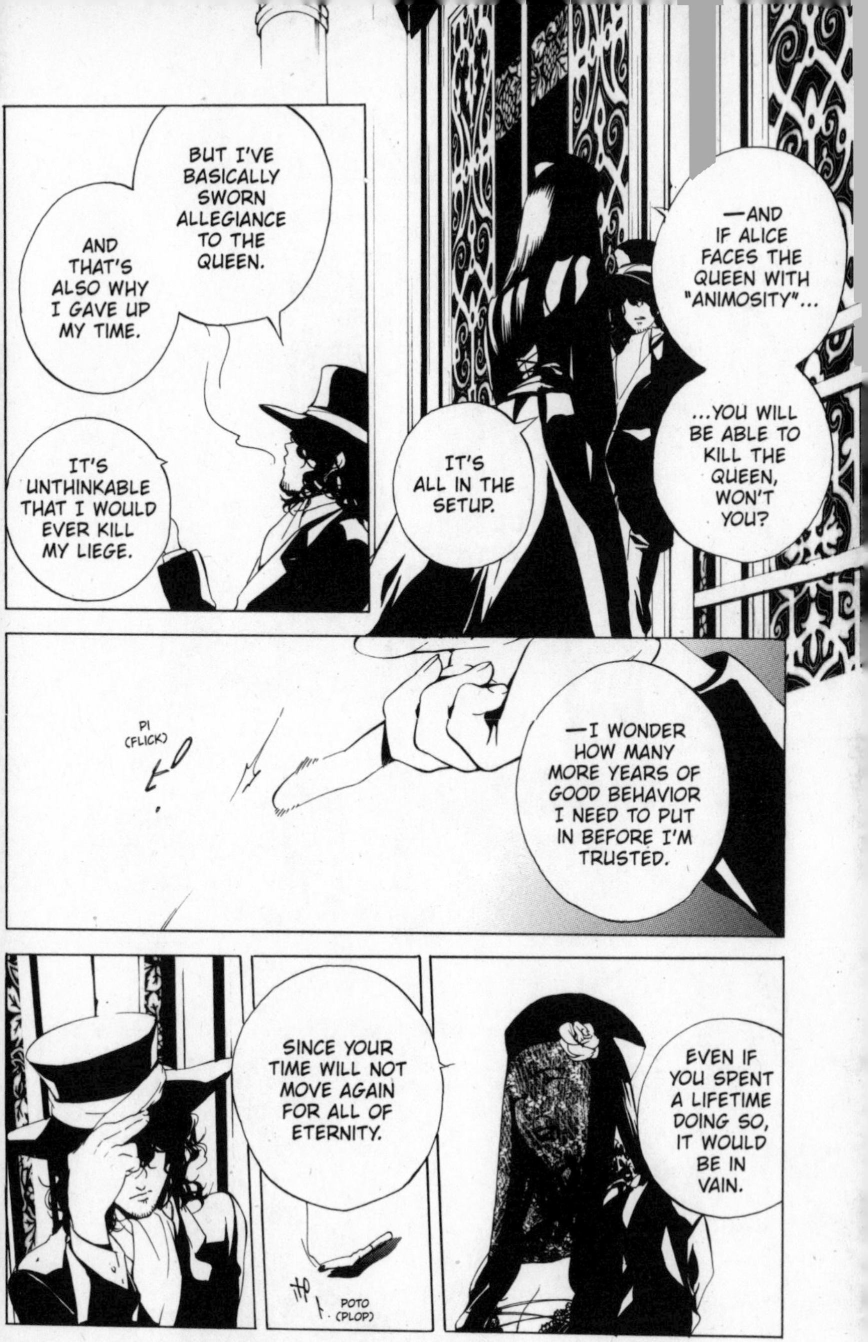
—AND IF ALICE FACES THE QUEEN WITH "ANIMOSITY"...
...YOU WILL BE ABLE TO KILL THE QUEEN, WON'T YOU?
IT'S ALL IN THE SETUP.
BUT I'VE BASICALLY SWORN ALLEGIANCE TO THE QUEEN.
AND THAT'S ALSO WHY I GAVE UP MY TIME.
IT'S UNTHINKABLE THAT I WOULD EVER KILL MY LIEGE.
—I WONDER HOW MANY MORE YEARS OF GOOD BEHAVIOR I NEED TO PUT IN BEFORE I'M TRUSTED.
PI (FLICK)
EVEN IF YOU SPENT A LIFETIME DOING SO, IT WOULD BE IN VAIN.
SINCE YOUR TIME WILL NOT MOVE AGAIN FOR ALL OF ETERNITY.
POTO (PLOP)

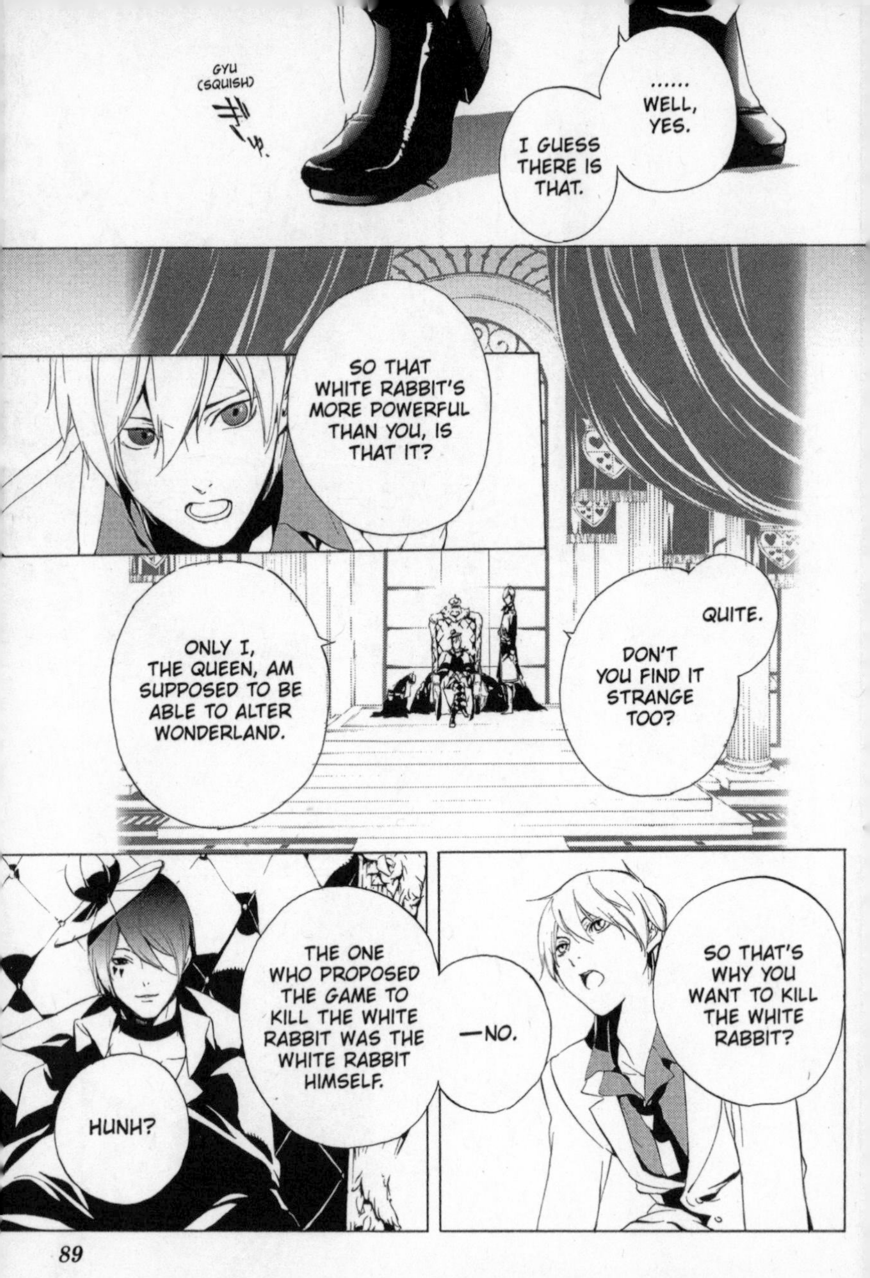
...... WELL, YES.
I GUESS THERE IS THAT.
GYU (SQUISH)
SO THAT WHITE RABBIT'S MORE POWERFUL THAN YOU, IS THAT IT?
QUITE.
DON'T YOU FIND IT STRANGE TOO?
ONLY I, THE QUEEN, AM SUPPOSED TO BE ABLE TO ALTER WONDERLAND.
SO THAT'S WHY YOU WANT TO KILL THE WHITE RABBIT?
—NO.
THE ONE WHO PROPOSED THE GAME TO KILL THE WHITE RABBIT WAS THE WHITE RABBIT HIMSELF.
HUNH?

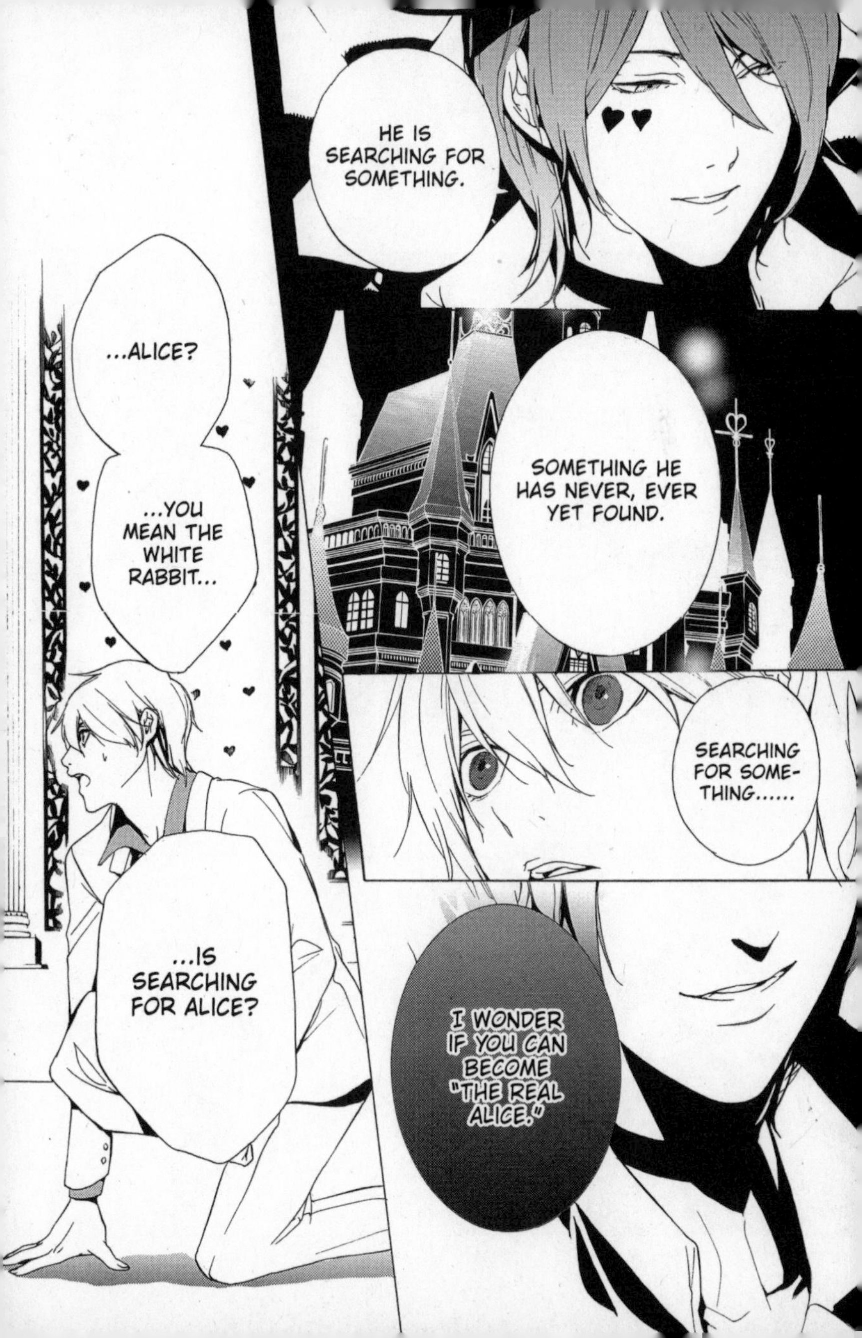
HE IS SEARCHING FOR SOMETHING.
SOMETHING HE HAS NEVER, EVER YET FOUND.
SEARCHING FOR SOME-THING......
I WONDER IF YOU CAN BECOME "THE REAL ALICE."
...ALICE?
...YOU MEAN THE WHITE RABBIT...
...IS SEARCHING FOR ALICE?

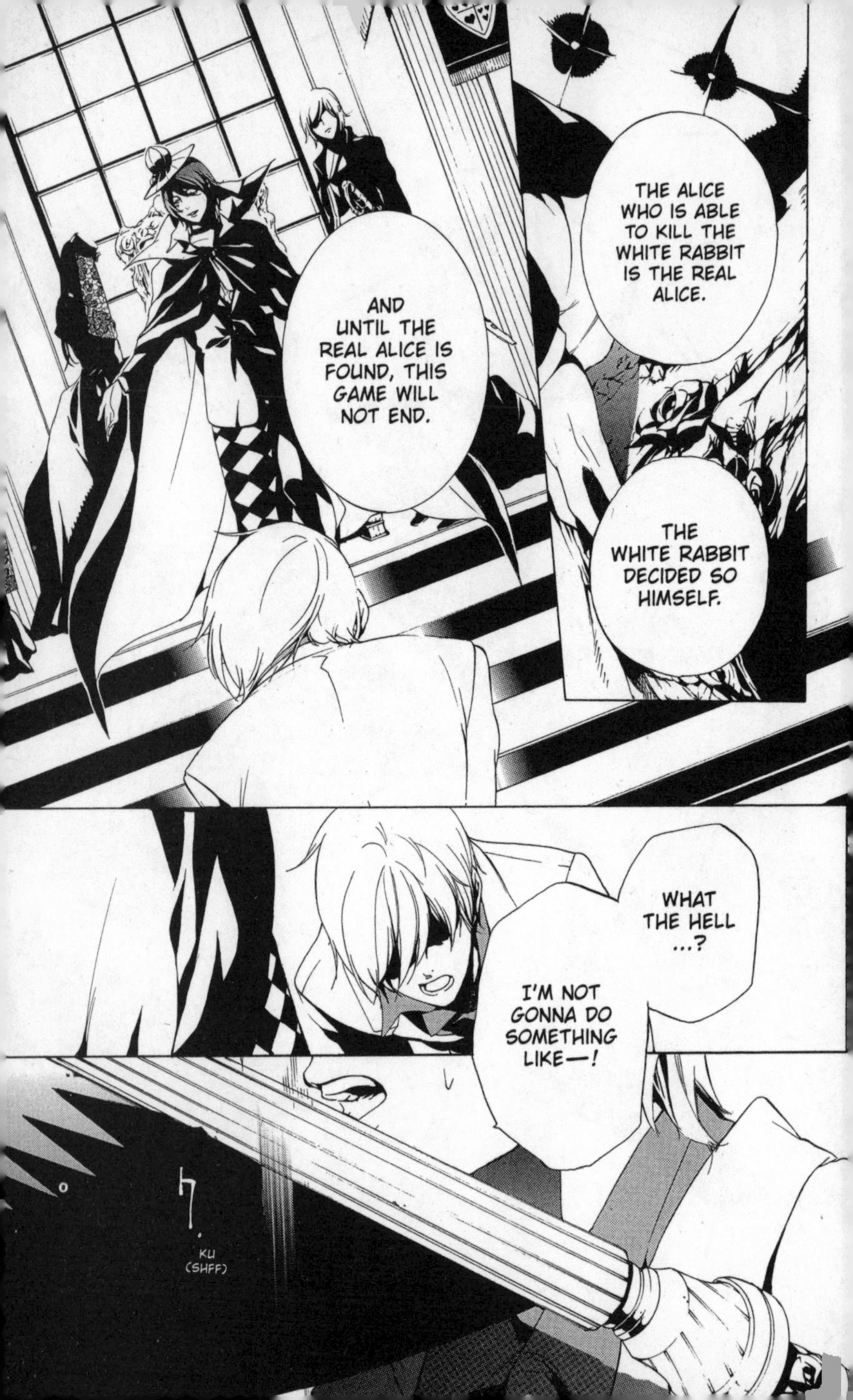
THE ALICE WHO IS ABLE TO KILL THE WHITE RABBIT IS THE REAL ALICE.
THE WHITE RABBIT DECIDED SO HIMSELF.
AND UNTIL THE REAL ALICE IS FOUND, THIS GAME WILL NOT END.
WHAT THE HELL ...?
I'M NOT GONNA DO SOMETHING LIKE—!
ク
KU (SHFF)

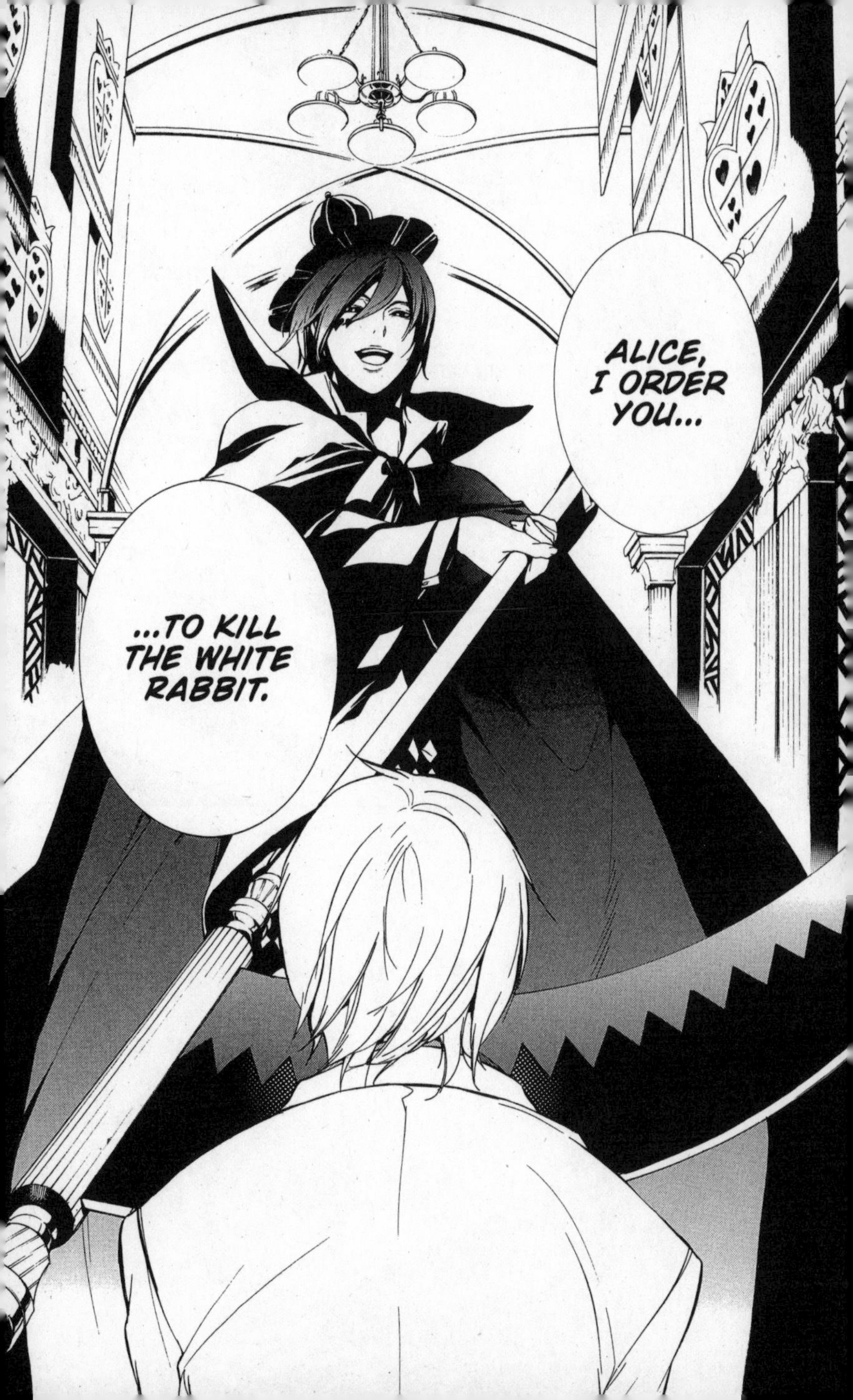
ALICE, I ORDER YOU...
...TO KILL THE WHITE RABBIT.

Chapter 3

Alice was beginning to get very tired of sitting by her sister on the bank, and of having nothing to do, when suddenly a White Rabbit with pink eyes ran close by her. When the Rabbit actually TOOK A WATCH OUT OF ITS WAISTCOAT-POCKET, and looked at it, and then hurried on, Alice started to her feet, for it flashed across her mind that she had never before seen such a curious thing. She ran across the field after it, and fortunately was just in time to see it pop down a large rabbit-hole under the hedge.

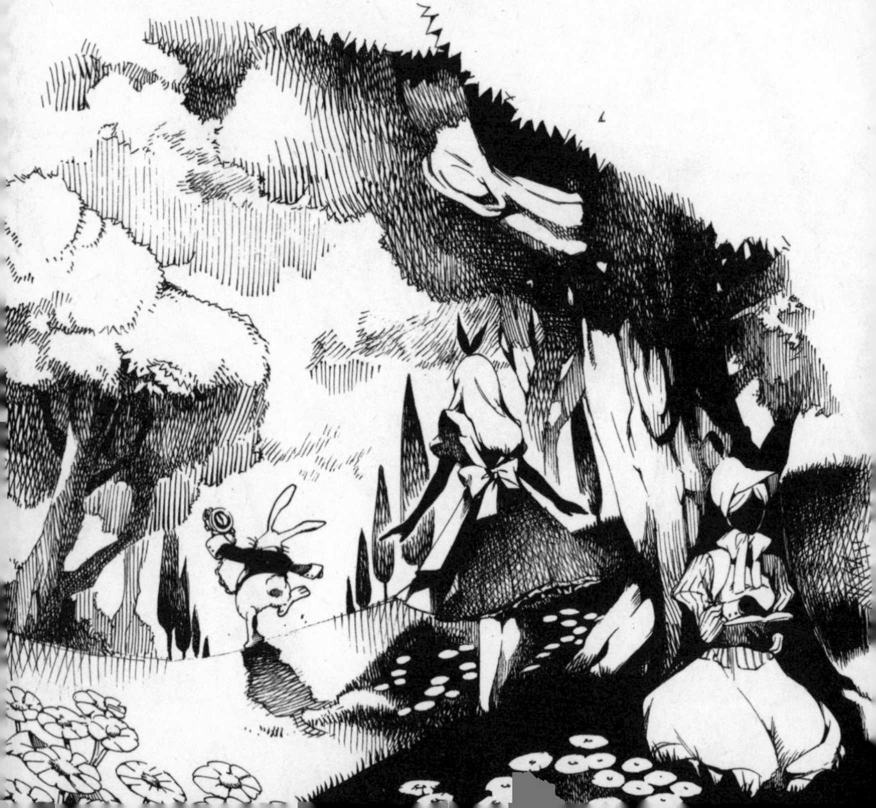

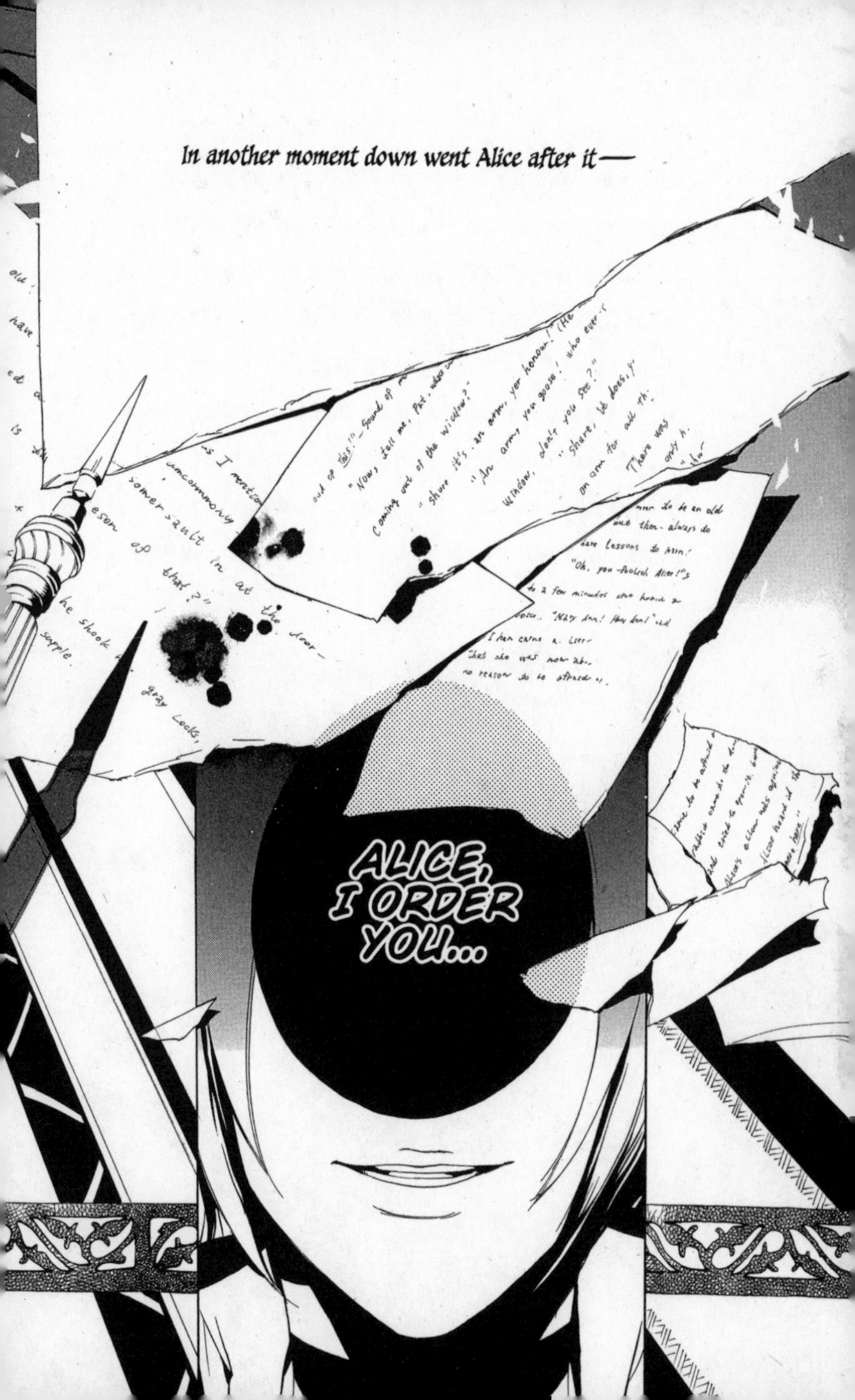
In another moment down went Alice after it—
ALICE, I ORDER YOU...

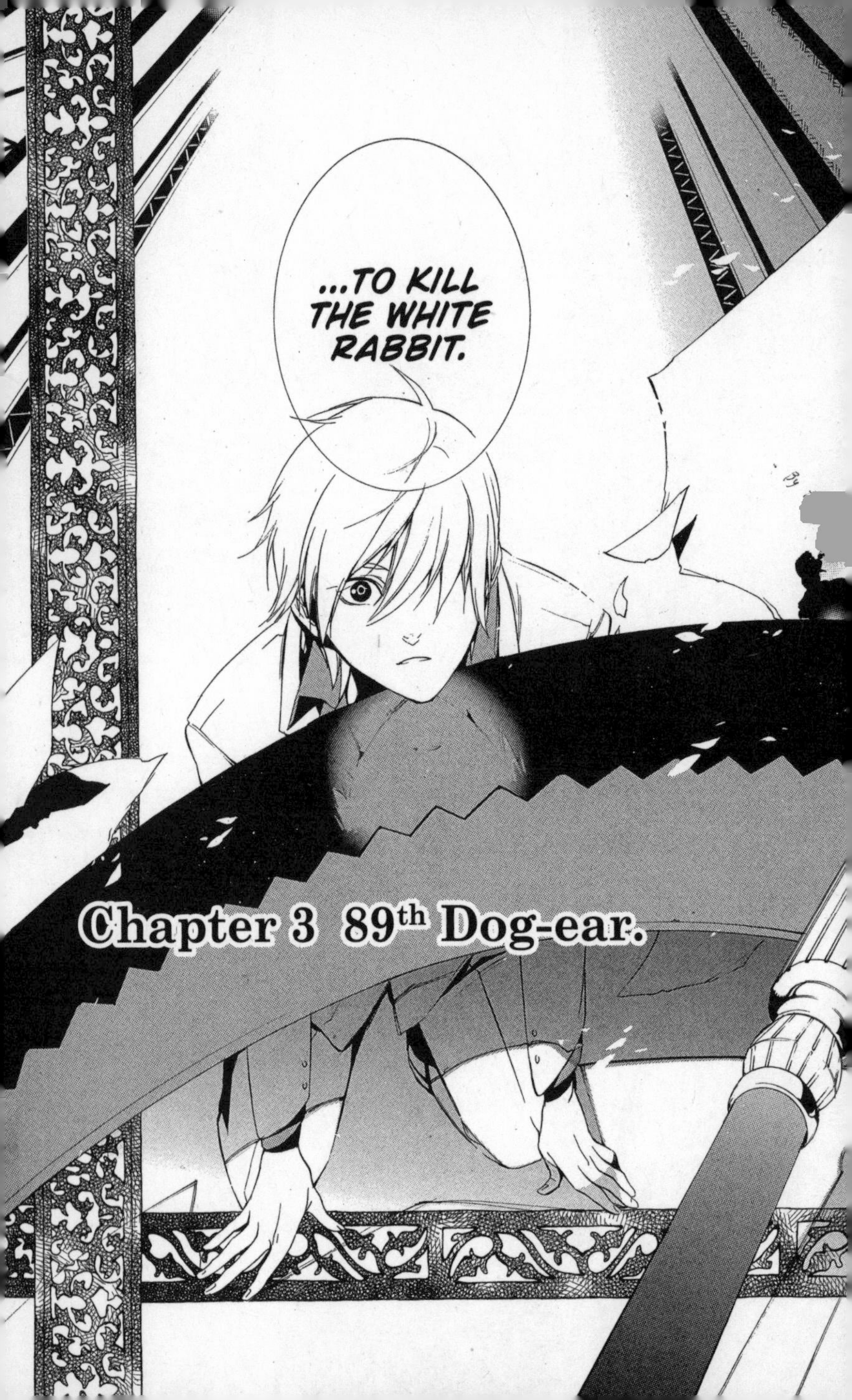
...TO KILL THE WHITE RABBIT.
Chapter 3 89th Dog-ear.

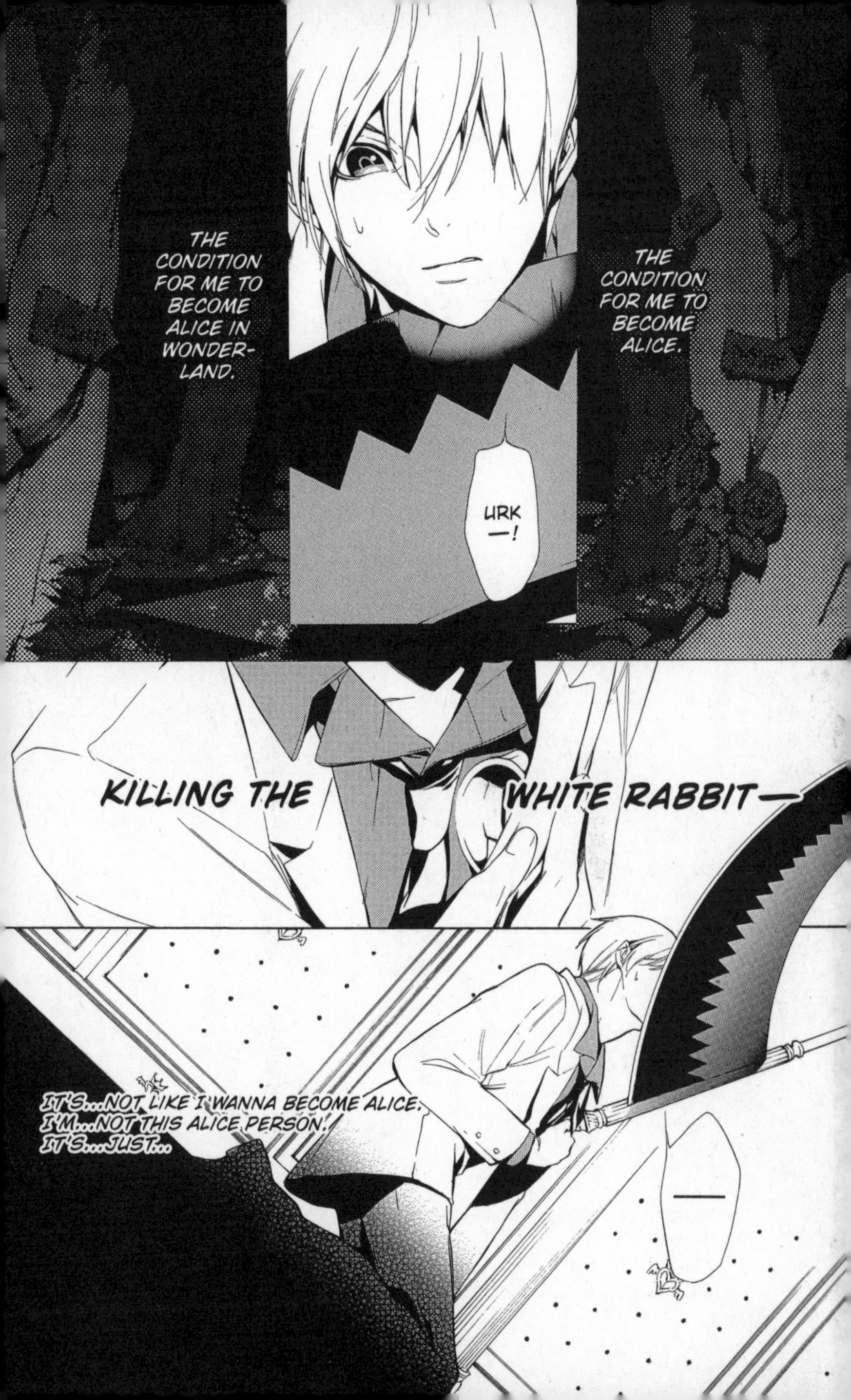
THE CONDITION FOR ME TO BECOME ALICE.
URK —!
THE CONDITION FOR ME TO BECOME ALICE IN WONDER-LAND.
KILLING THE WHITE RABBIT—
—
IT'S...NOT LIKE I WANNA BECOME ALICE. I'M...NOT THIS ALICE PERSON. IT'S...JUST...

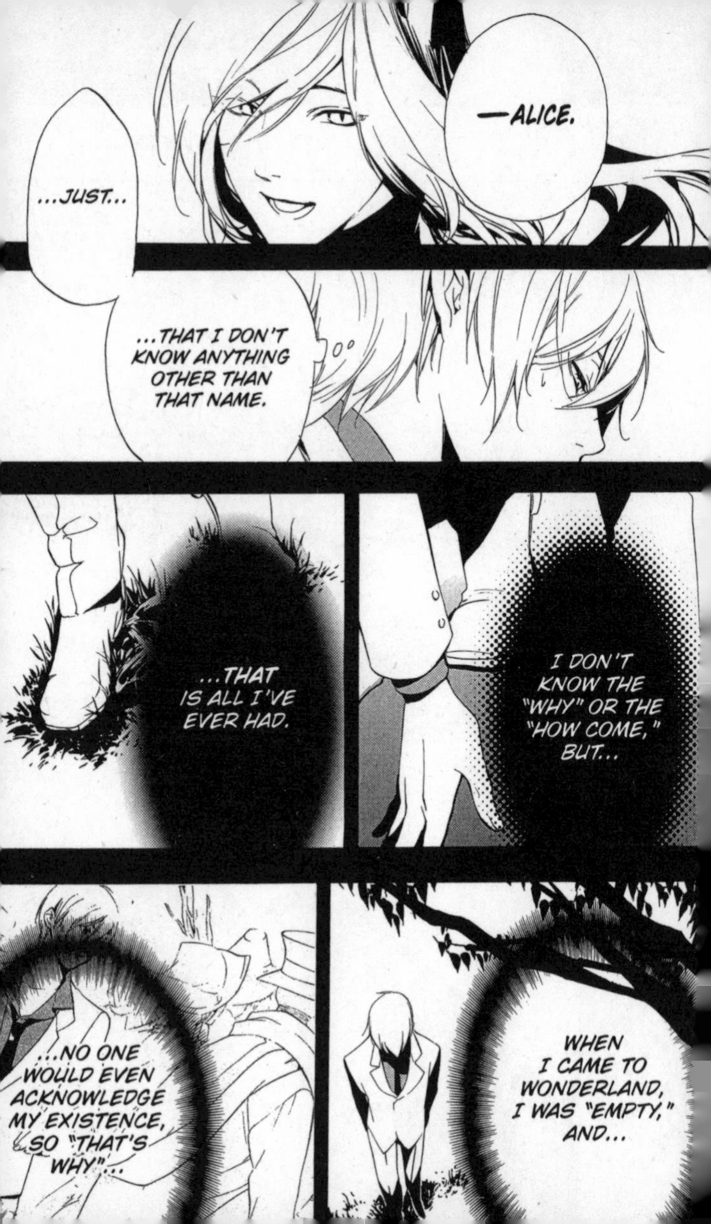
—ALICE.
...JUST...
...THAT I DON'T KNOW ANYTHING OTHER THAN THAT NAME.
I DON'T KNOW THE "WHY" OR THE "HOW COME," BUT...
...THAT IS ALL I'VE EVER HAD.
WHEN I CAME TO WONDERLAND, I WAS "EMPTY," AND...
...NO ONE WOULD EVEN ACKNOWLEDGE MY EXISTENCE, SO "THAT'S WHY"...

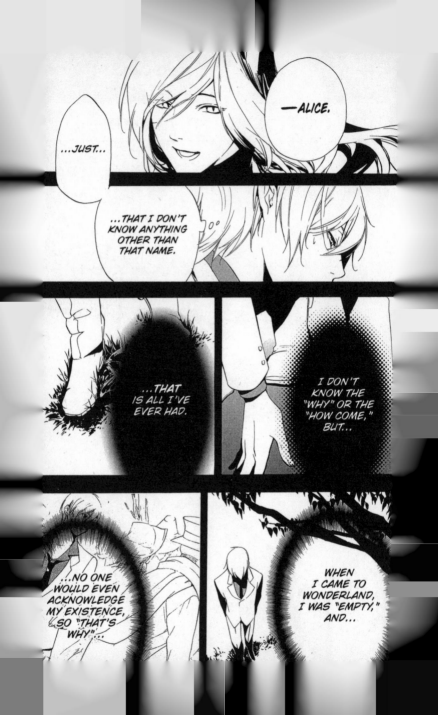

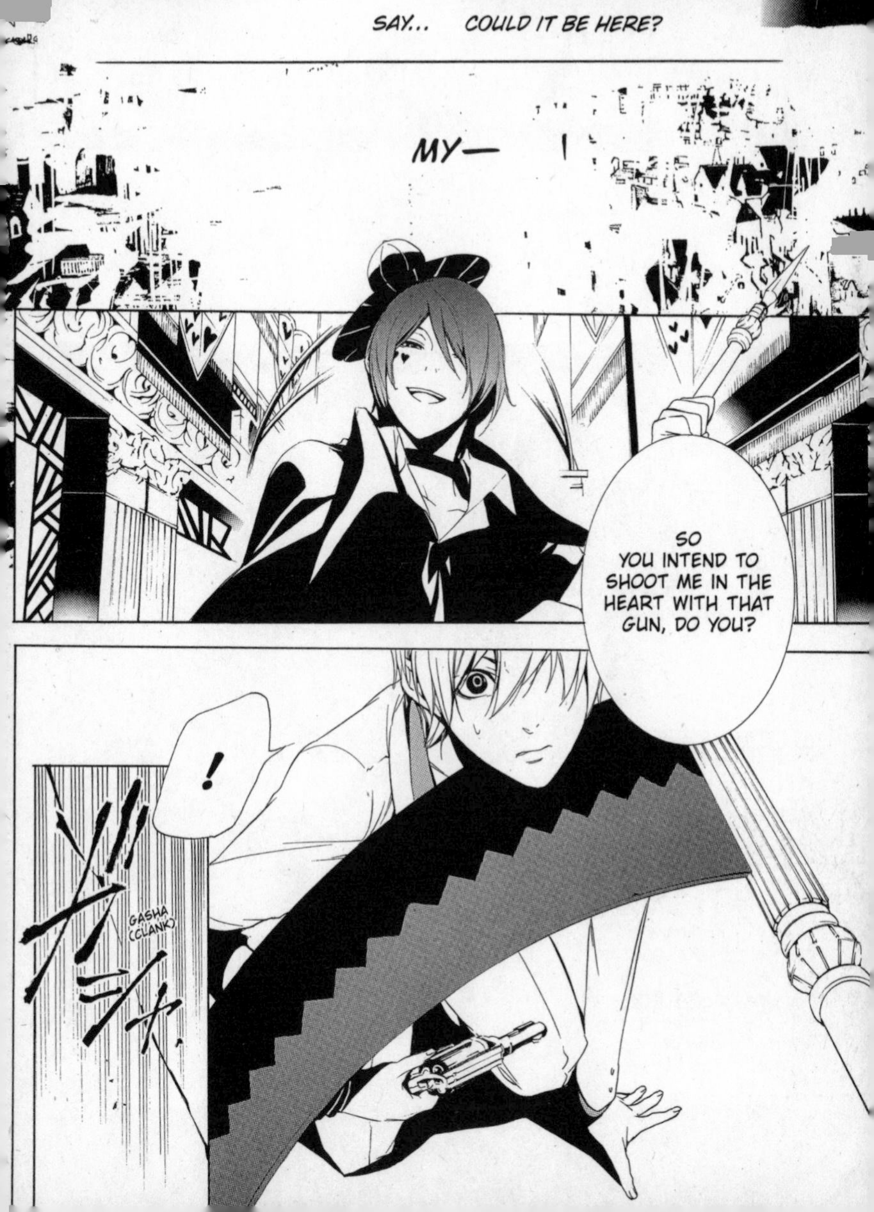
SAY... COULD IT BE HERE?
MY—
SO YOU INTEND TO SHOOT ME IN THE HEART WITH THAT GUN, DO YOU?
!
GASHA (CLANK)

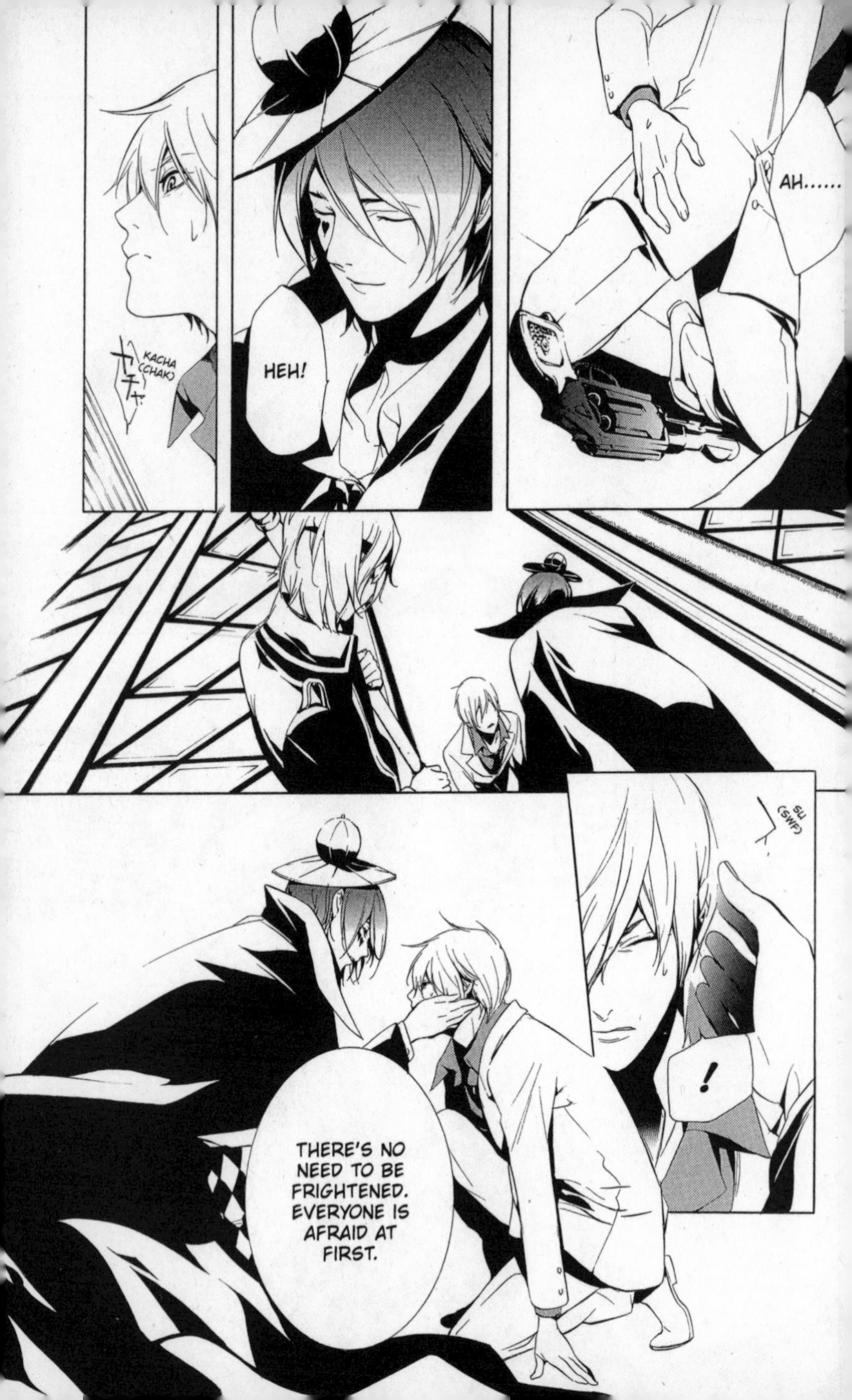
AH......
HEH!
KACHA (CHAK)
SU (SWF)
!
THERE'S NO NEED TO BE FRIGHTENED. EVERYONE IS AFRAID AT FIRST.

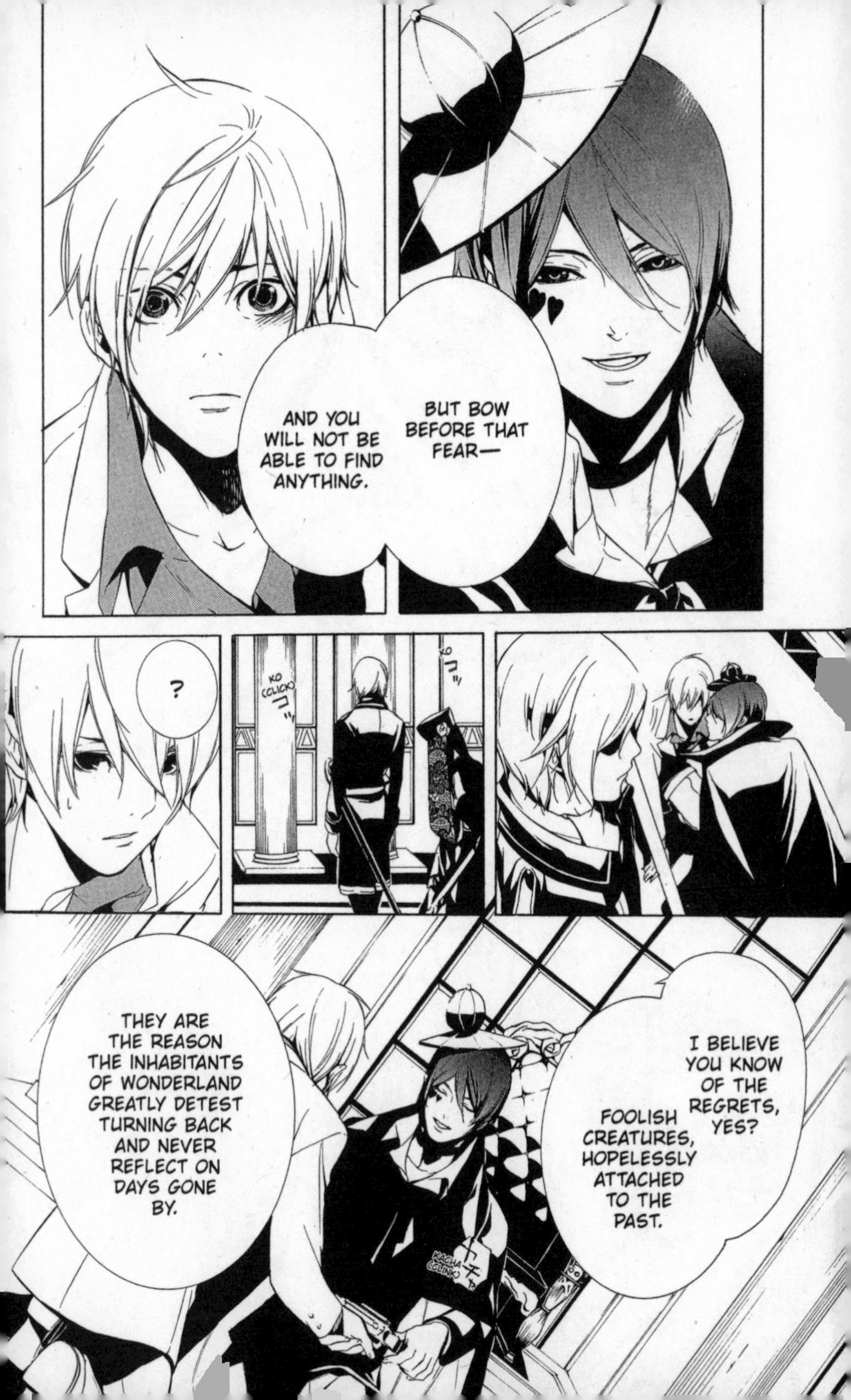
BUT BOW BEFORE THAT FEAR—
AND YOU WILL NOT BE ABLE TO FIND ANYTHING.
KO
KO (CLICK)
?
I BELIEVE YOU KNOW OF THE REGRETS, YES?
FOOLISH CREATURES, HOPELESSLY ATTACHED TO THE PAST.
KACHA (CLINK)
THEY ARE THE REASON THE INHABITANTS OF WONDERLAND GREATLY DETEST TURNING BACK AND NEVER REFLECT ON DAYS GONE BY.

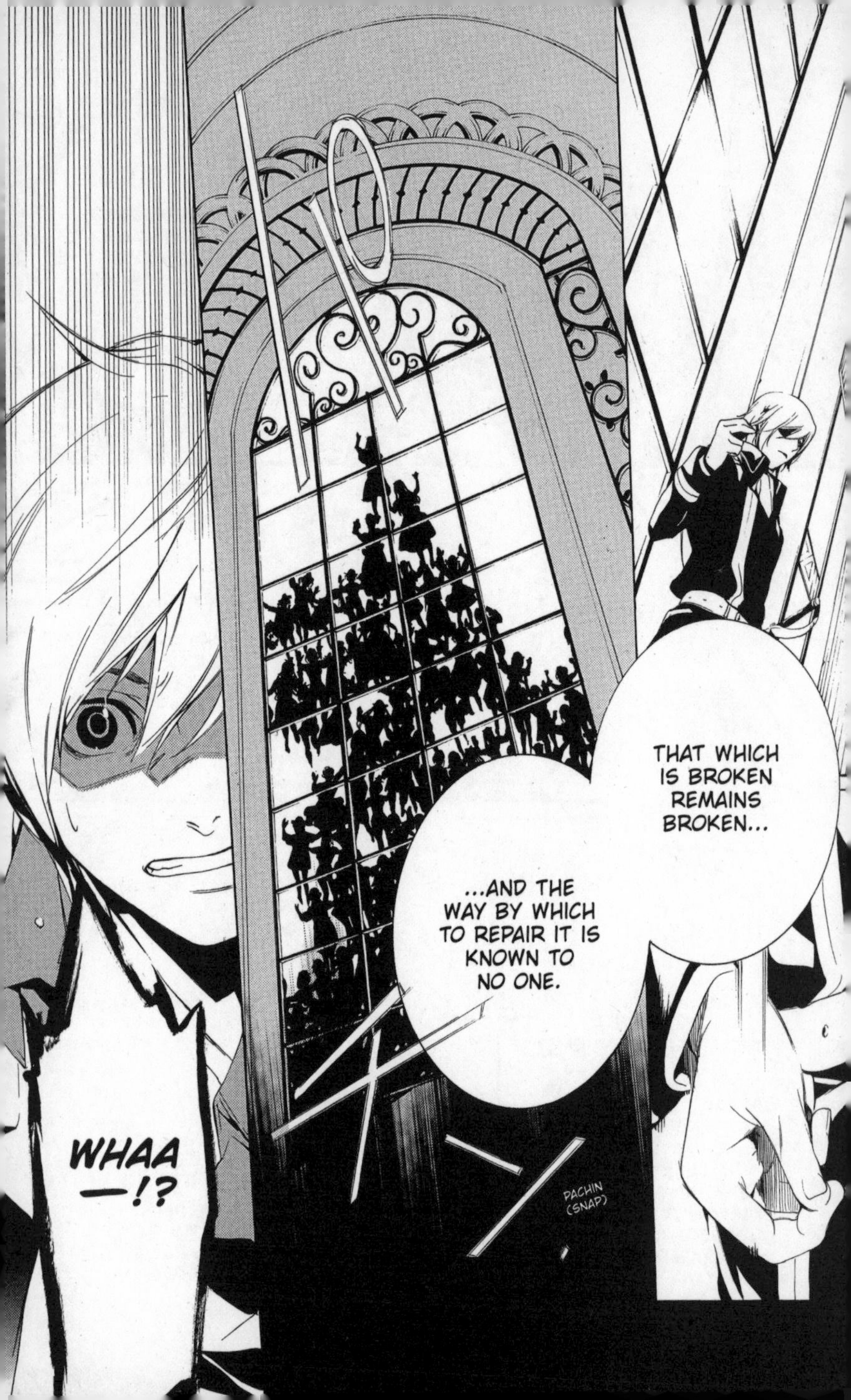
THAT WHICH IS BROKEN REMAINS BROKEN...
...AND THE WAY BY WHICH TO REPAIR IT IS KNOWN TO NO ONE.
PACHIN (SNAP)
WHAA—!?

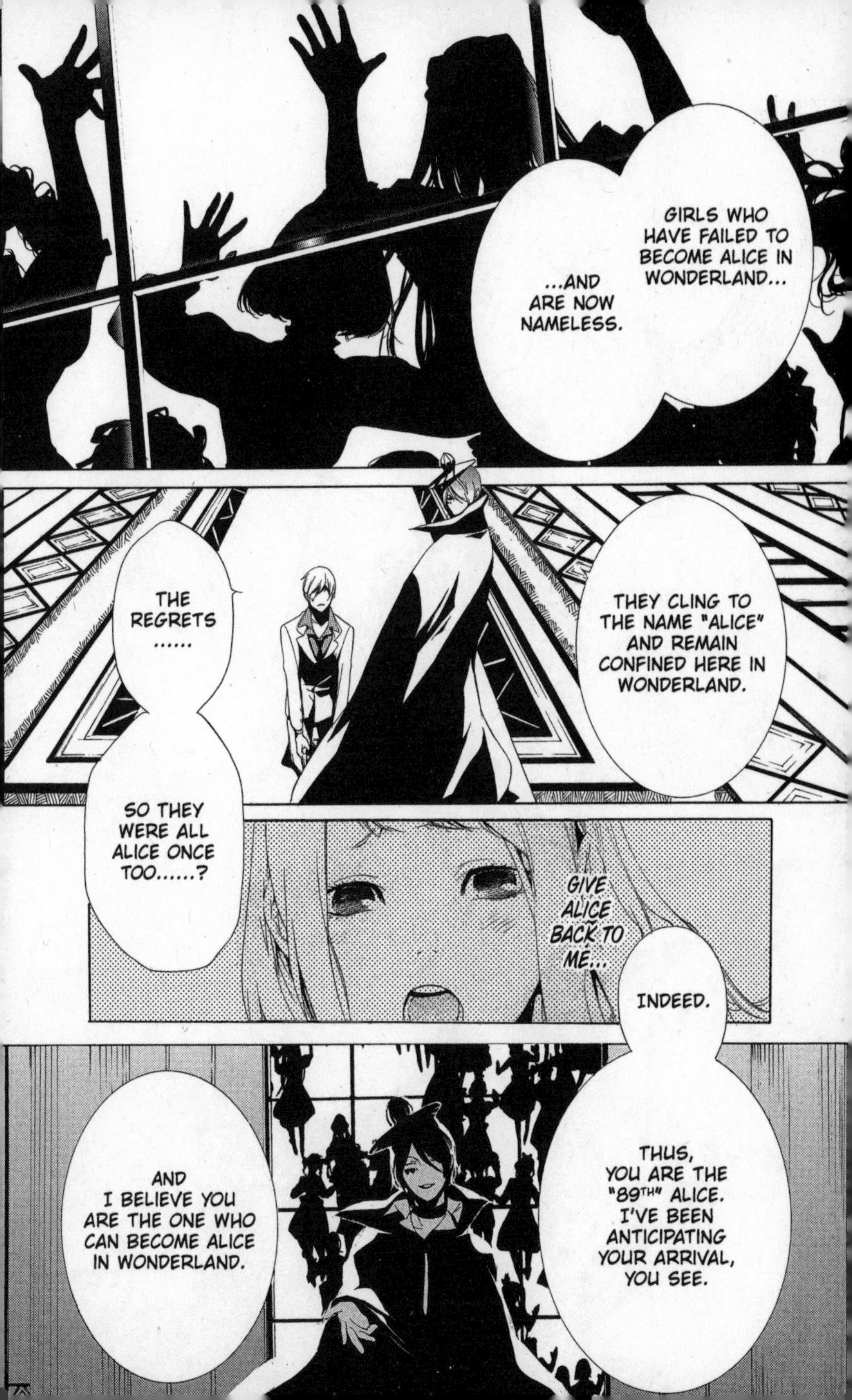
GIRLS WHO HAVE FAILED TO BECOME ALICE IN WONDERLAND...
...AND ARE NOW NAMELESS.
THEY CLING TO THE NAME "ALICE" AND REMAIN CONFINED HERE IN WONDERLAND.
THE REGRETS ......
SO THEY WERE ALL ALICE ONCE TOO......?
GIVE ALICE BACK TO ME...
INDEED.
THUS, YOU ARE THE "89TH" ALICE. I'VE BEEN ANTICIPATING YOUR ARRIVAL, YOU SEE.
AND I BELIEVE YOU ARE THE ONE WHO CAN BECOME ALICE IN WONDERLAND.

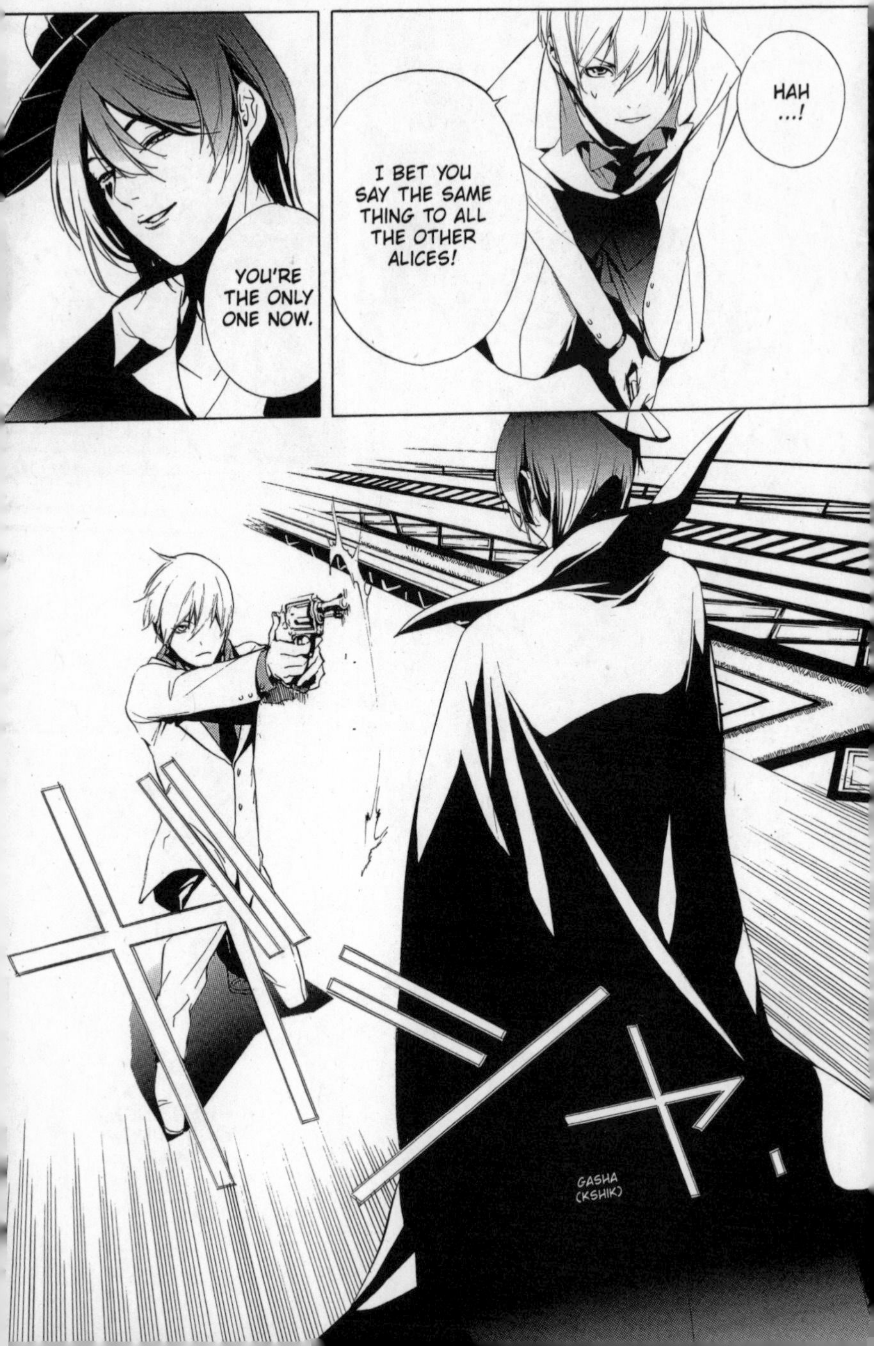
HAH ...!
I BET YOU SAY THE SAME THING TO ALL THE OTHER ALICES!
YOU'RE THE ONLY ONE NOW.
GASHA (KSHIK)

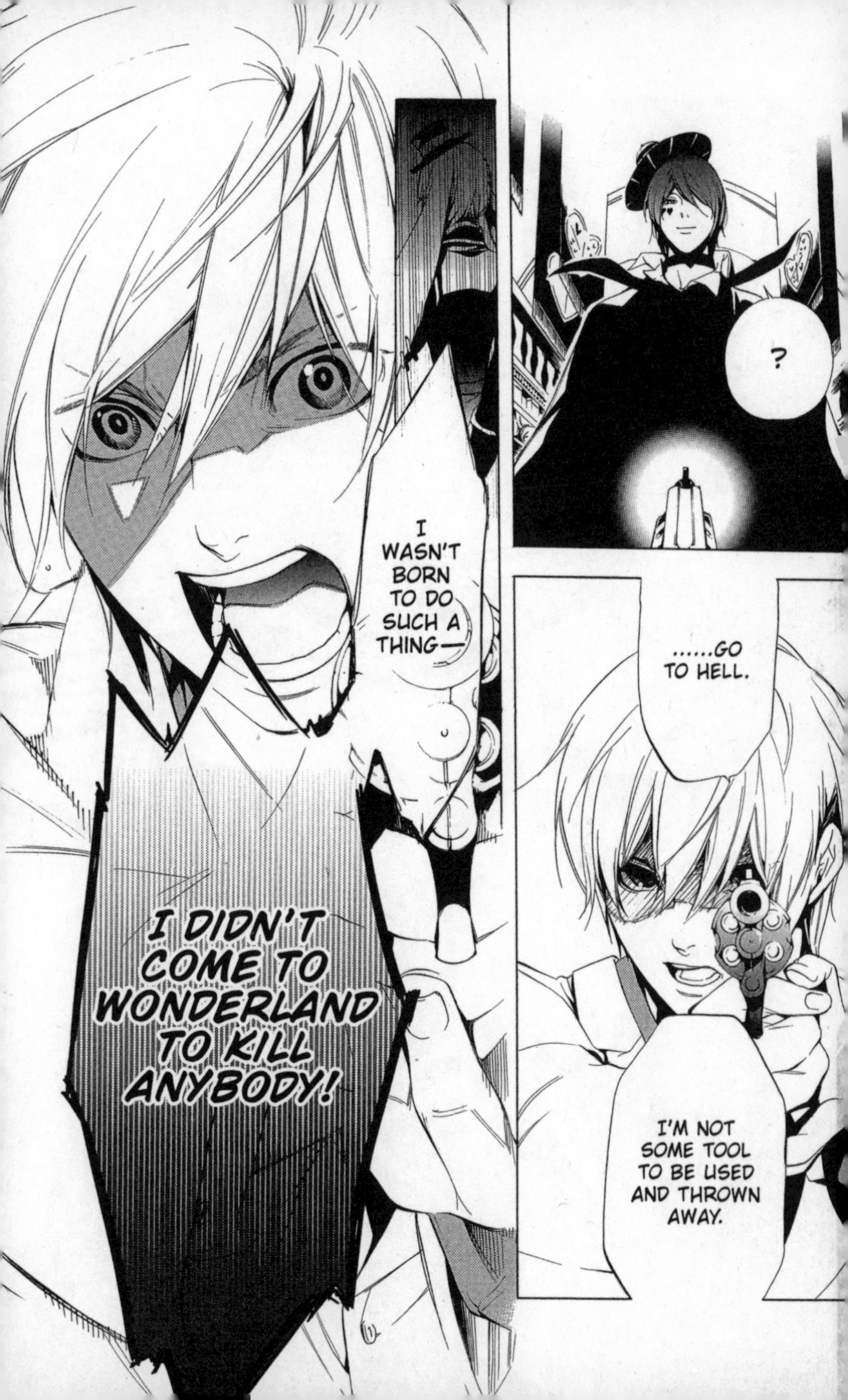
?
......GO TO HELL.
I'M NOT SOME TOOL TO BE USED AND THROWN AWAY.
I WASN'T BORN TO DO SUCH A THING—
I DIDN'T COME TO WONDERLAND TO KILL ANYBODY!

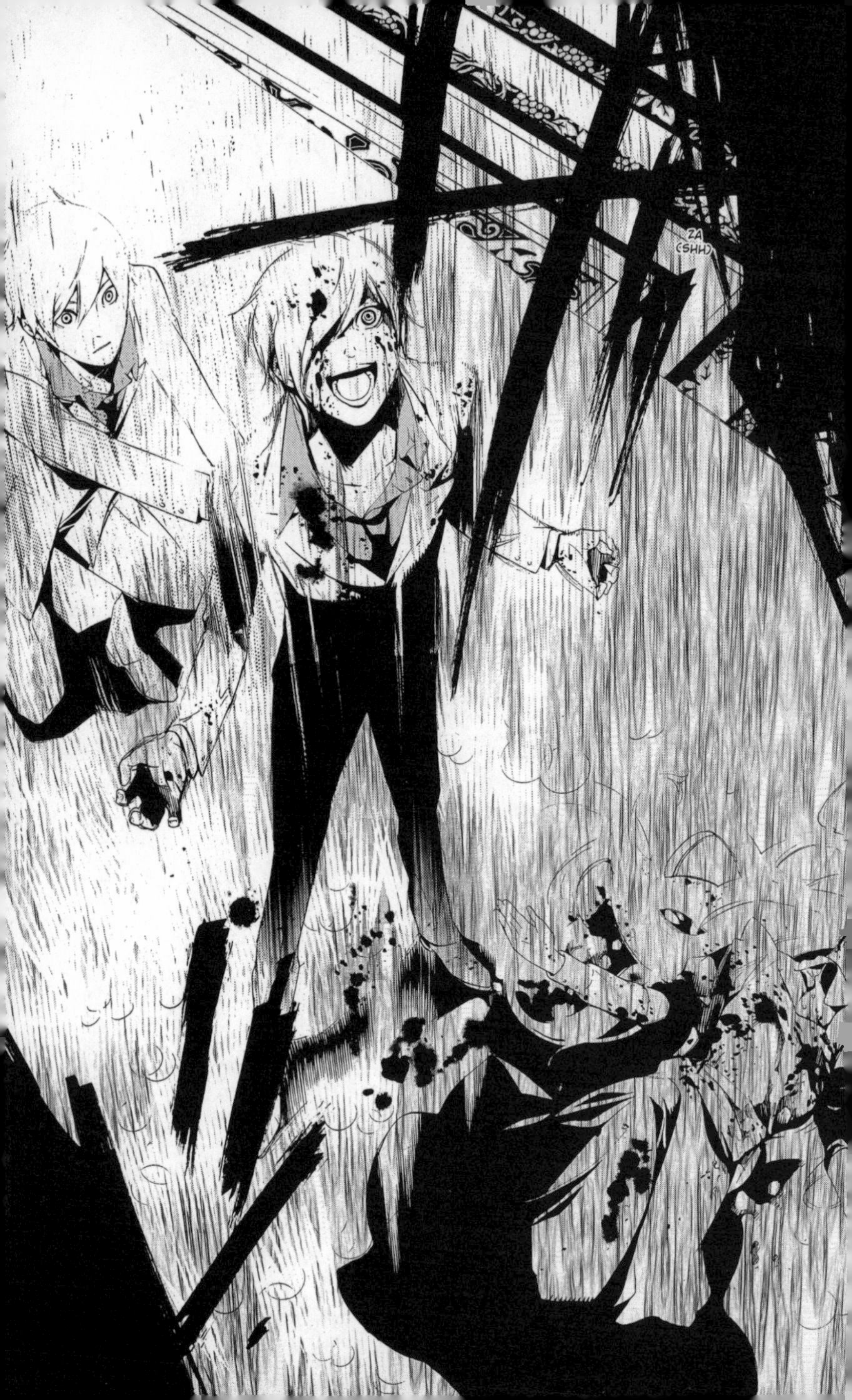
ZA
(SHH)

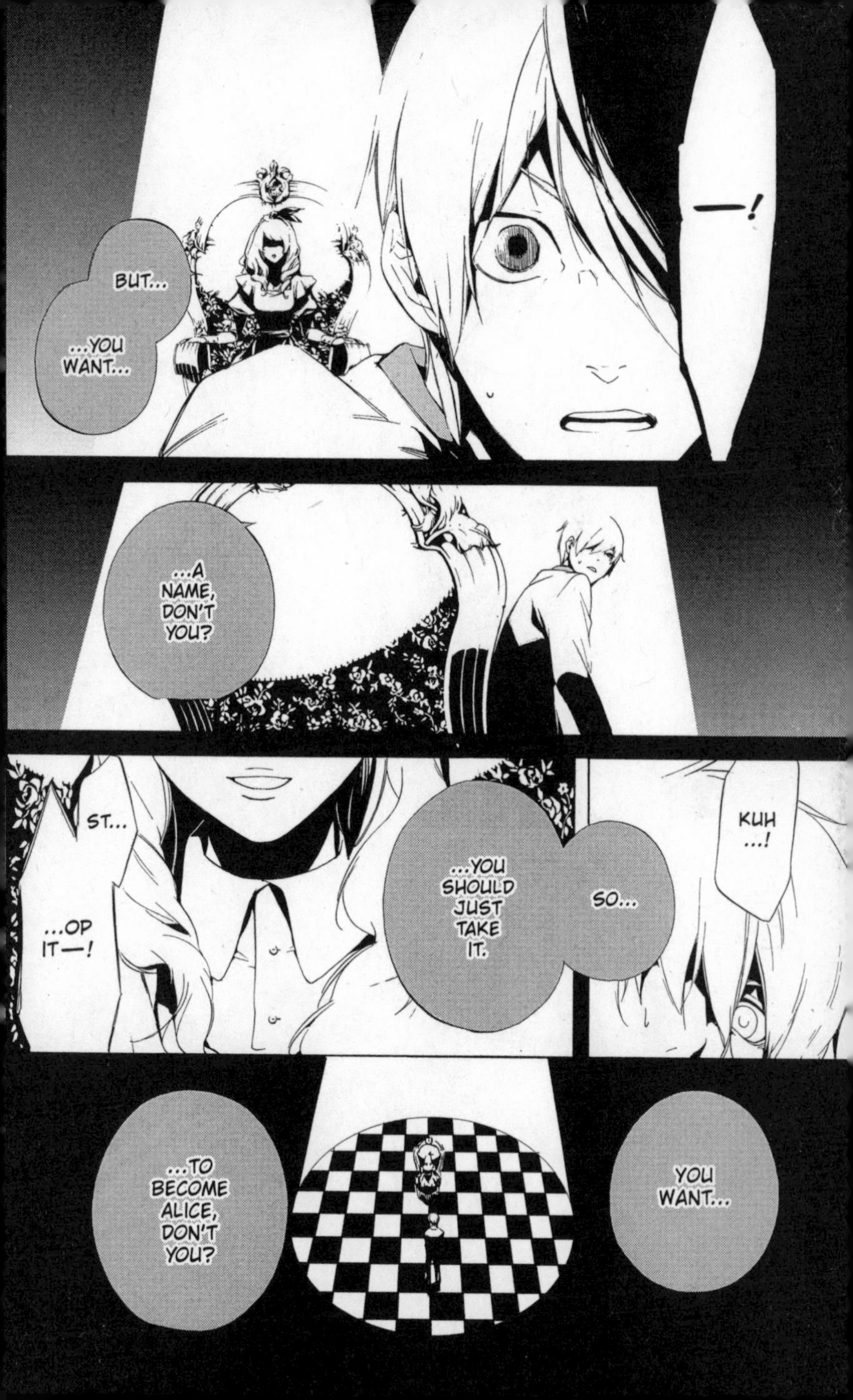
—!
BUT...
...YOU WANT...
...A NAME, DON'T YOU?
KUH ...!
SO...
...YOU SHOULD JUST TAKE IT.
ST...
...OP IT—!
YOU WANT...
...TO BECOME ALICE, DON'T YOU?

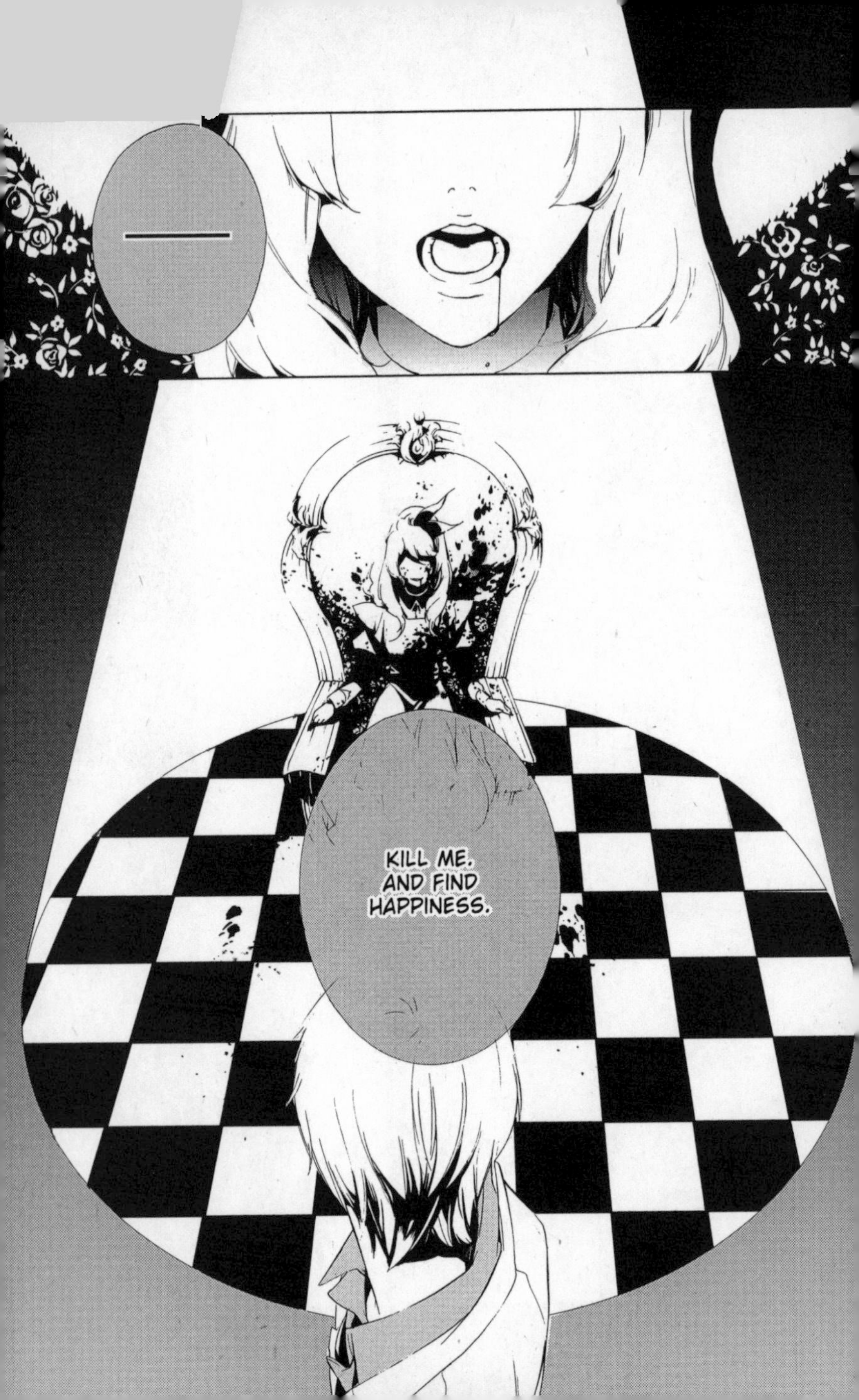
——
KILL ME. AND FIND HAPPINESS.

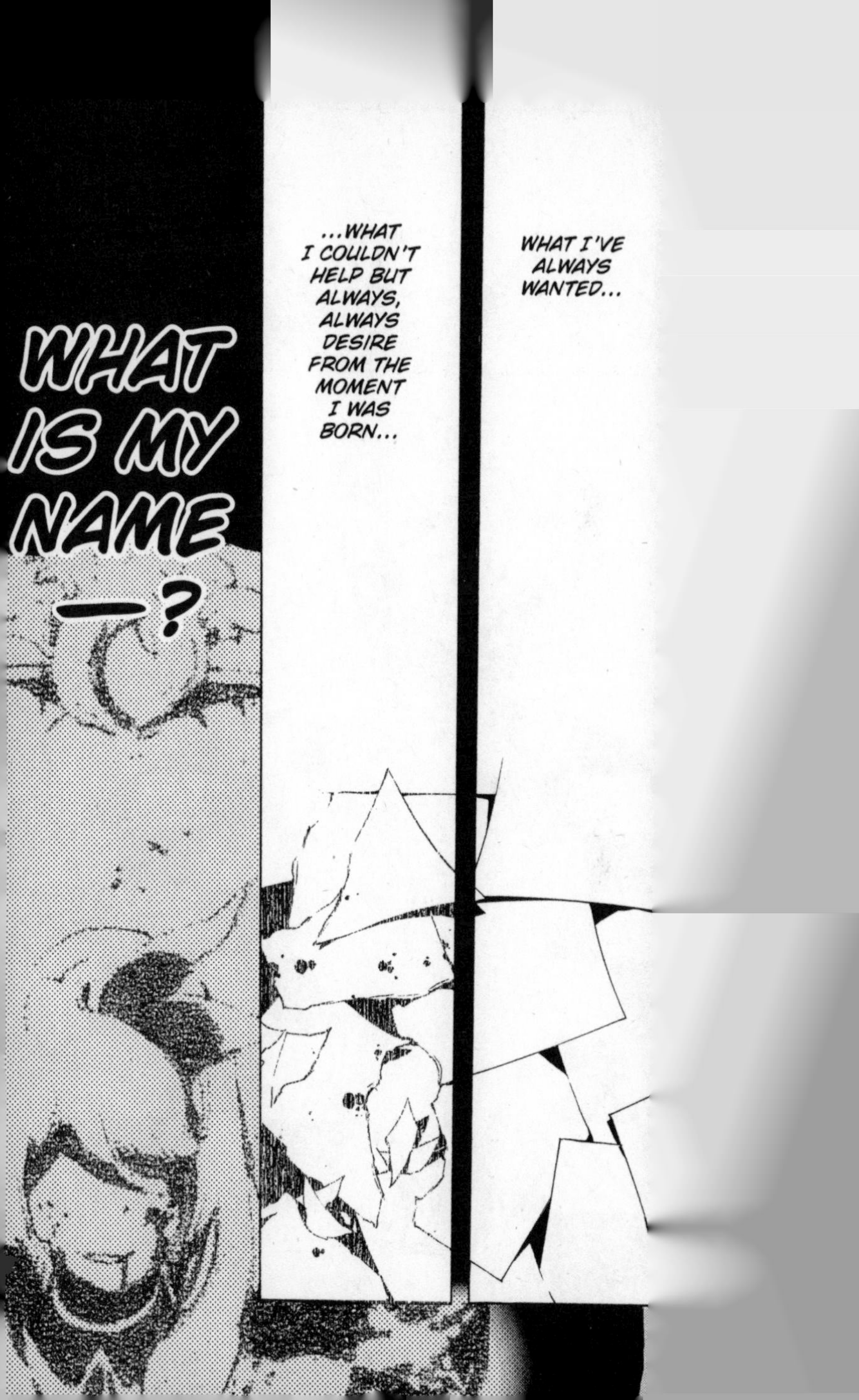
WHAT I'VE ALWAYS WANTED...
...WHAT I COULDN'T HELP BUT ALWAYS, ALWAYS DESIRE FROM THE MOMENT I WAS BORN...
WHAT IS MY NAME —?

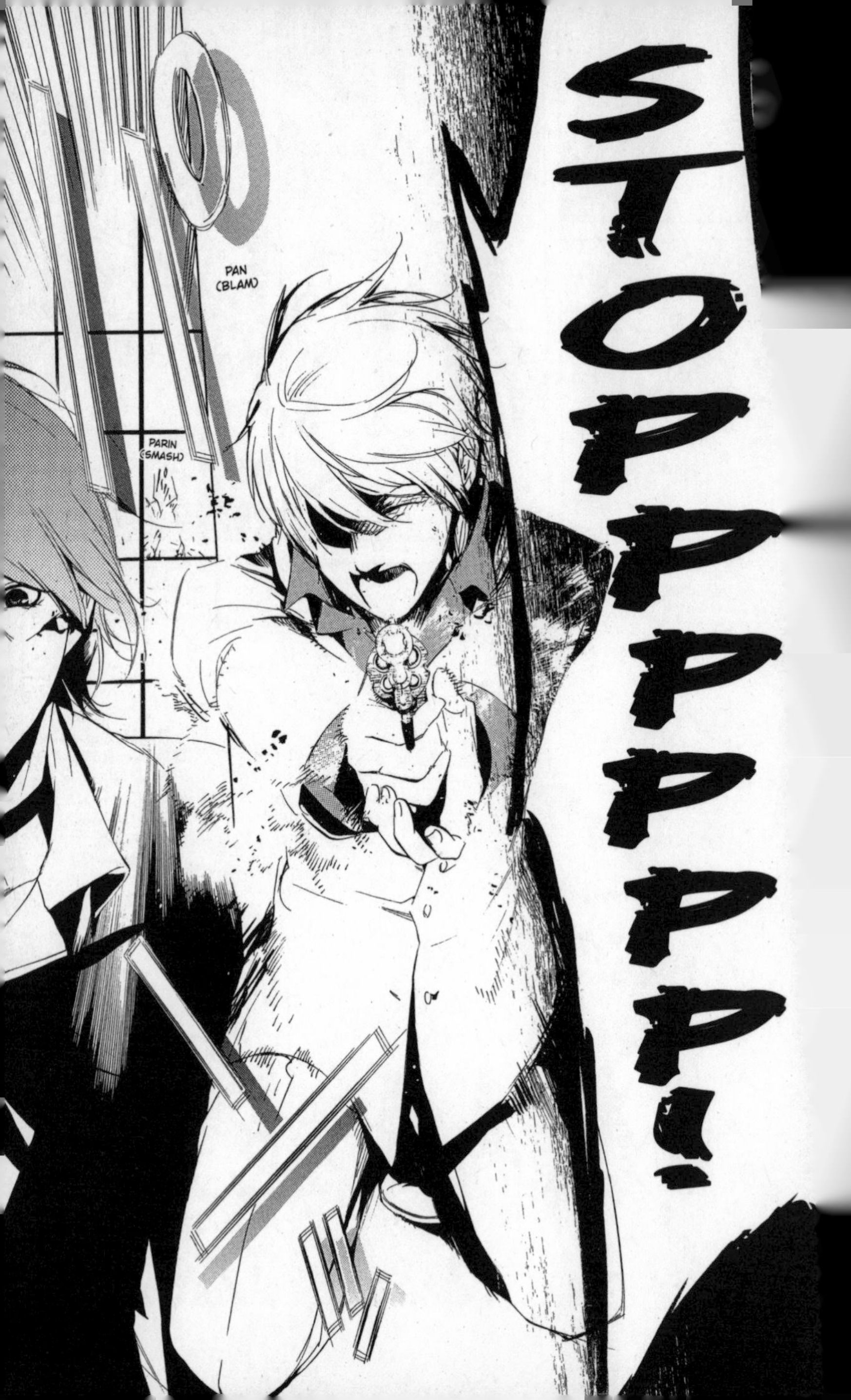
STOPPPPP!
PAN
(BLAM)
PARIN
(SMASH)

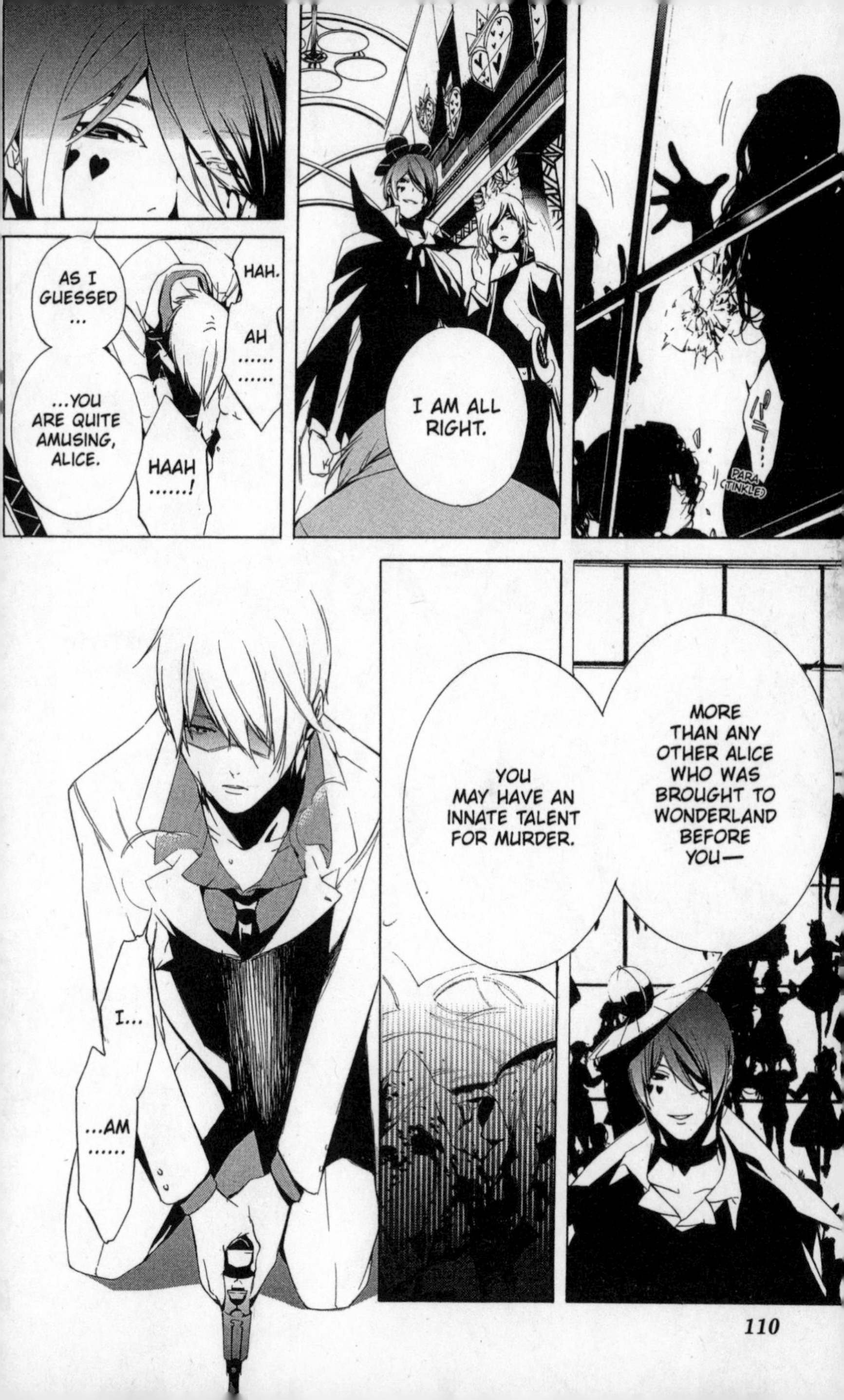
PARA (TINKLE)
I AM ALL RIGHT.
HAH.
AS I GUESSED...
AH......
......
...YOU ARE QUITE AMUSING, ALICE.
HAAH......!
MORE THAN ANY OTHER ALICE WHO WAS BROUGHT TO WONDERLAND BEFORE YOU—
YOU MAY HAVE AN INNATE TALENT FOR MURDER.
I...
...AM......

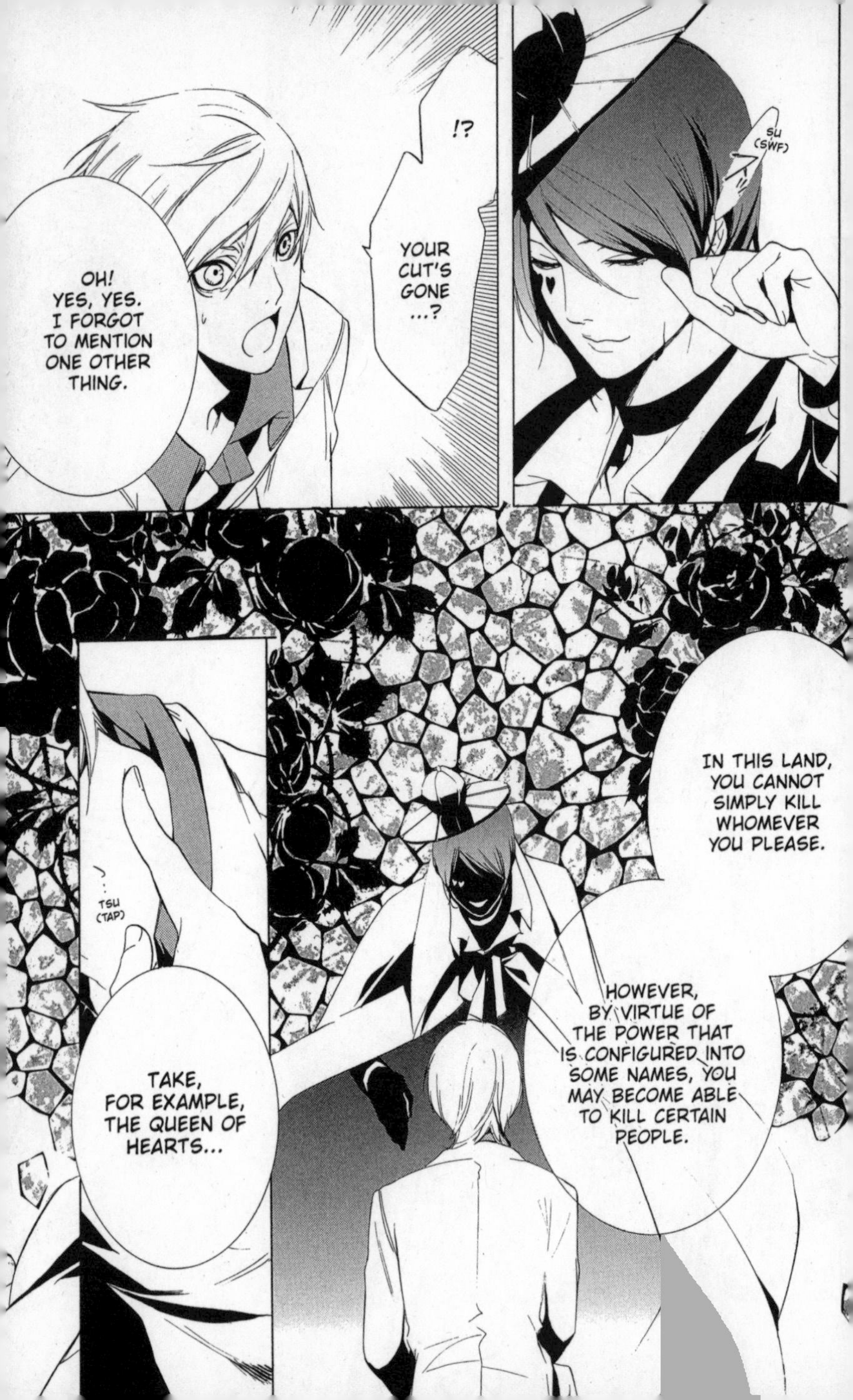
SU (SWF)
!?
YOUR CUT'S GONE ...?
OH! YES, YES. I FORGOT TO MENTION ONE OTHER THING.
IN THIS LAND, YOU CANNOT SIMPLY KILL WHOMEVER YOU PLEASE.
HOWEVER, BY VIRTUE OF THE POWER THAT IS CONFIGURED INTO SOME NAMES, YOU MAY BECOME ABLE TO KILL CERTAIN PEOPLE.
TSU (TAP)
TAKE, FOR EXAMPLE, THE QUEEN OF HEARTS...

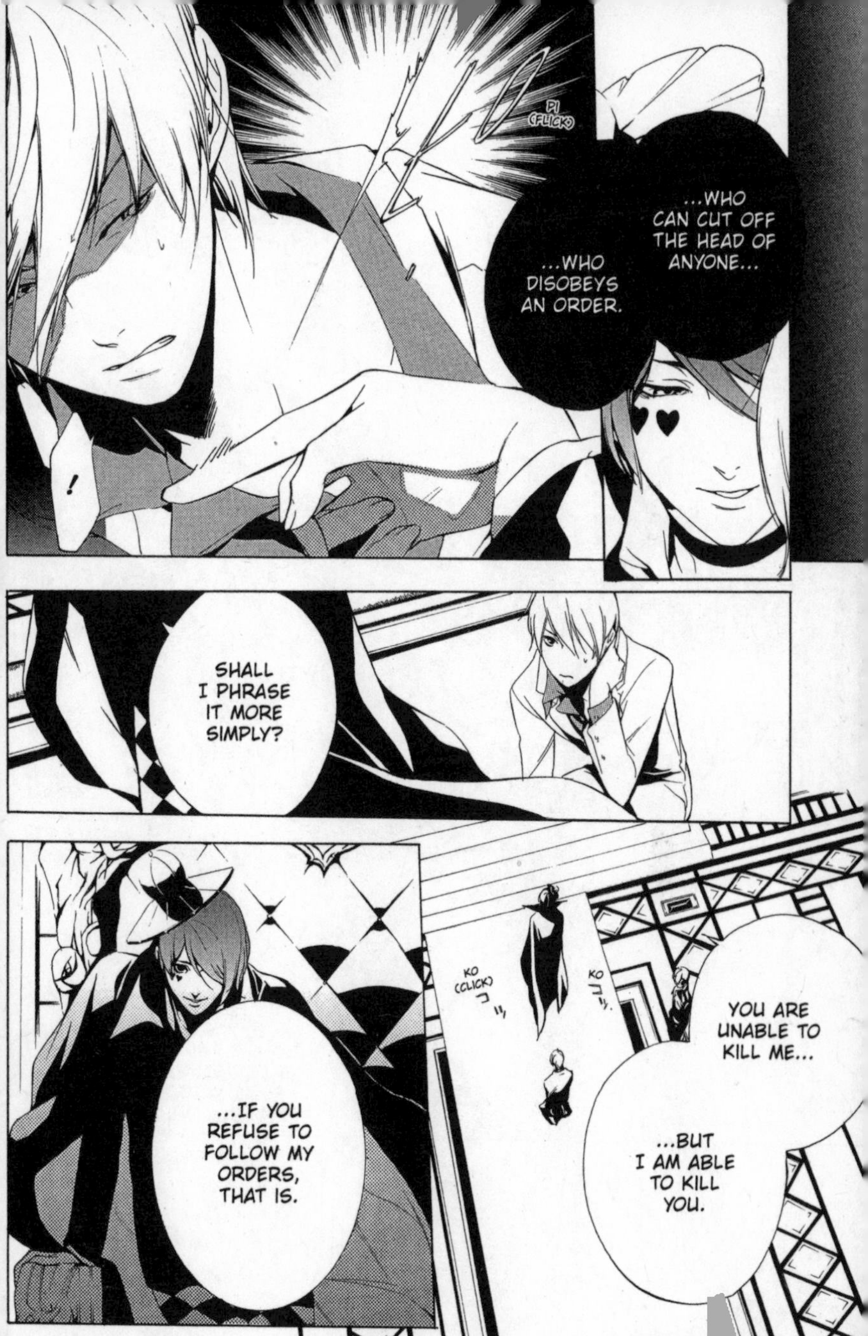
PI (FLICK)
...WHO CAN CUT OFF THE HEAD OF ANYONE...
...WHO DISOBEYS AN ORDER.
!
SHALL I PHRASE IT MORE SIMPLY?
KO (CLICK)
KO
YOU ARE UNABLE TO KILL ME...
...BUT I AM ABLE TO KILL YOU.
...IF YOU REFUSE TO FOLLOW MY ORDERS, THAT IS.

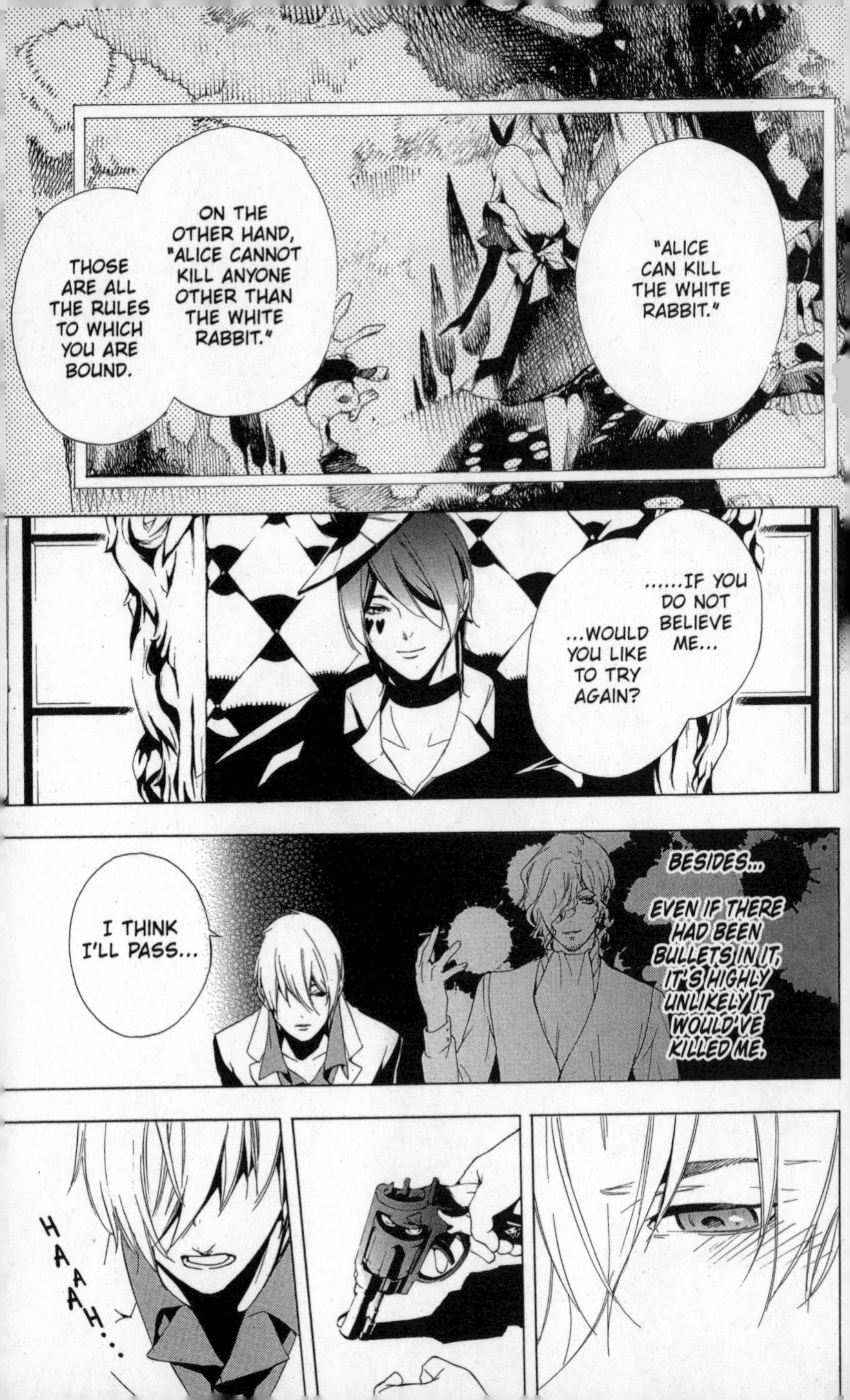
"ALICE CAN KILL THE WHITE RABBIT."
ON THE OTHER HAND, "ALICE CANNOT KILL ANYONE OTHER THAN THE WHITE RABBIT."
THOSE ARE ALL THE RULES TO WHICH YOU ARE BOUND.
......IF YOU DO NOT BELIEVE ME...
...WOULD YOU LIKE TO TRY AGAIN?
BESIDES...
EVEN IF THERE HAD BEEN BULLETS IN IT, IT'S HIGHLY UNLIKELY IT WOULD'VE KILLED ME.
I THINK I'LL PASS...
HAAAH...

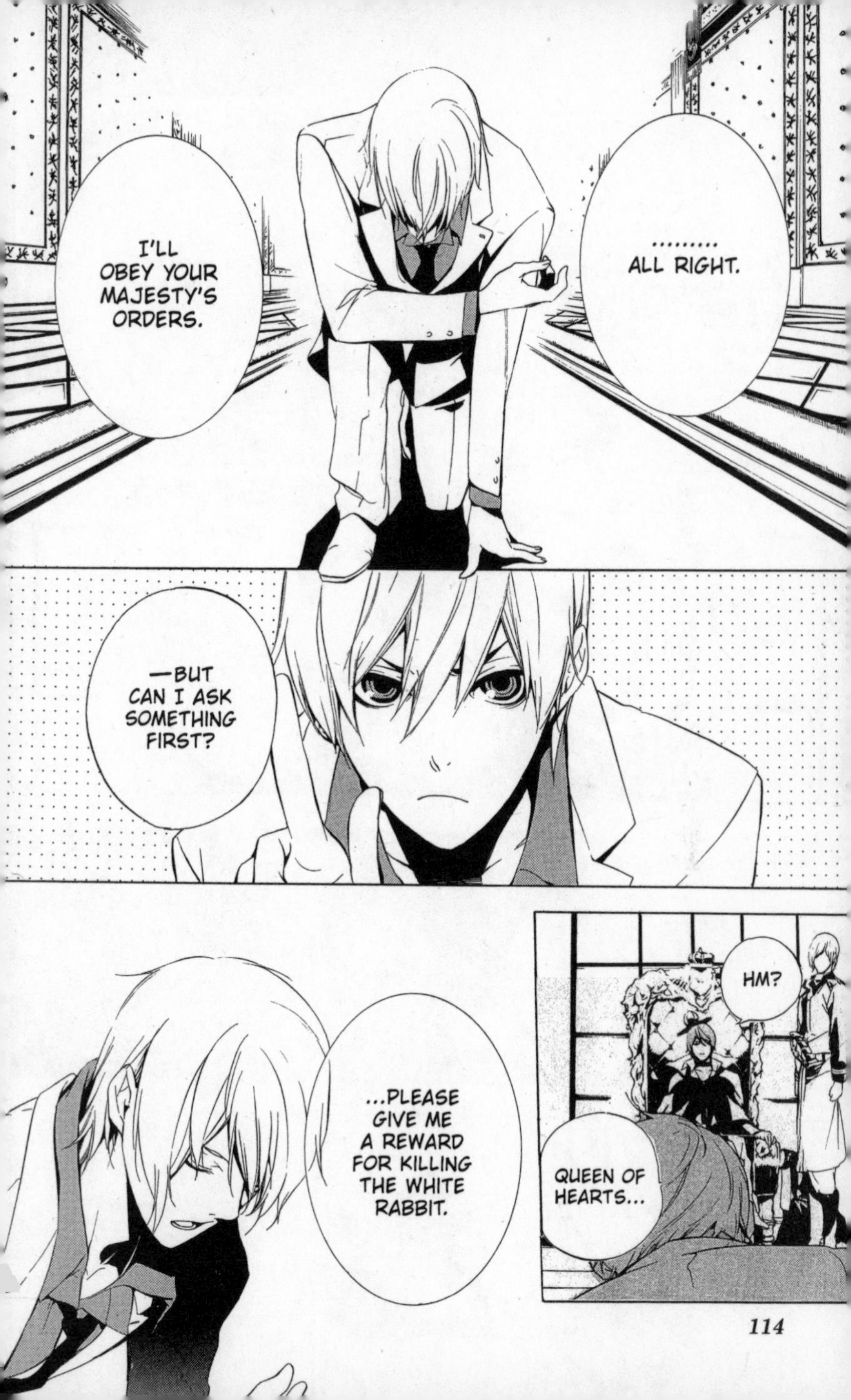
....
ALL RIGHT.
I'LL OBEY YOUR MAJESTY'S ORDERS.
—BUT CAN I ASK SOMETHING FIRST?
HM?
QUEEN OF HEARTS...
...PLEASE GIVE ME A REWARD FOR KILLING THE WHITE RABBIT.

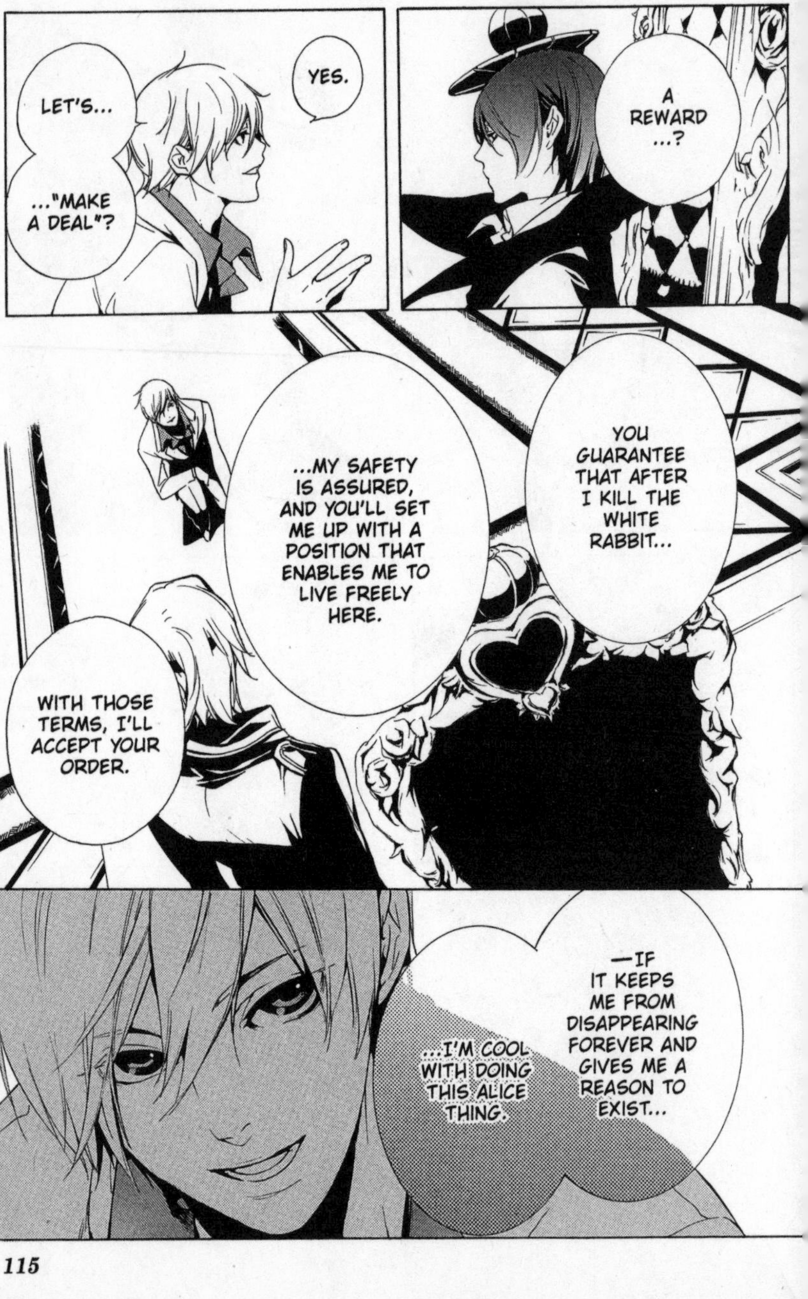
A REWARD ...?
YES.
LET'S...
..."MAKE A DEAL"?
YOU GUARANTEE THAT AFTER I KILL THE WHITE RABBIT...
...MY SAFETY IS ASSURED, AND YOU'LL SET ME UP WITH A POSITION THAT ENABLES ME TO LIVE FREELY HERE.
WITH THOSE TERMS, I'LL ACCEPT YOUR ORDER.
—IF IT KEEPS ME FROM DISAPPEARING FOREVER AND GIVES ME A REASON TO EXIST...
...I'M COOL WITH DOING THIS ALICE THING.

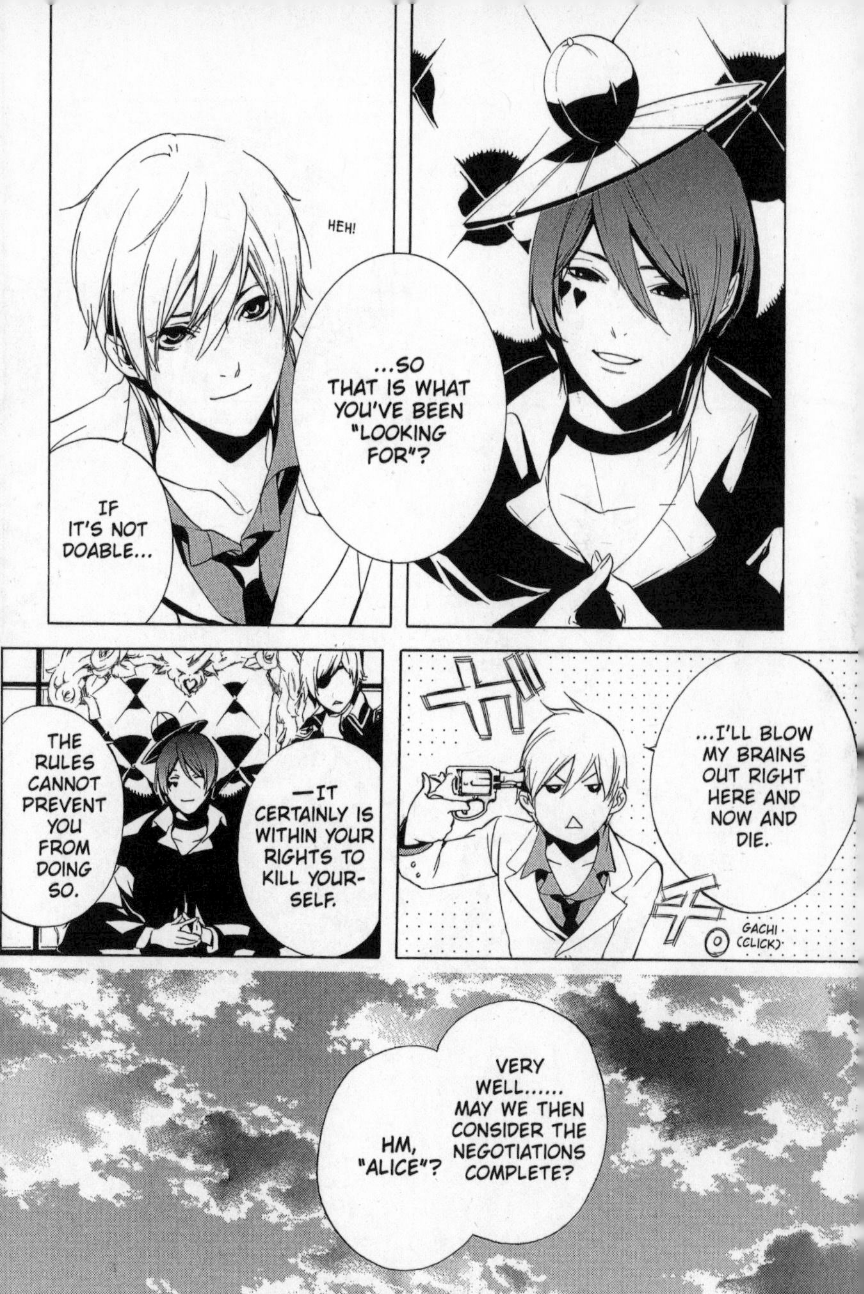
...SO THAT IS WHAT YOU'VE BEEN "LOOKING FOR"?
HEH!
IF IT'S NOT DOABLE...
...I'LL BLOW MY BRAINS OUT RIGHT HERE AND NOW AND DIE.
GACHI (CLICK)
—IT CERTAINLY IS WITHIN YOUR RIGHTS TO KILL YOUR-SELF.
THE RULES CANNOT PREVENT YOU FROM DOING SO.
VERY WELL...... MAY WE THEN CONSIDER THE NEGOTIATIONS COMPLETE?
HM, "ALICE"?

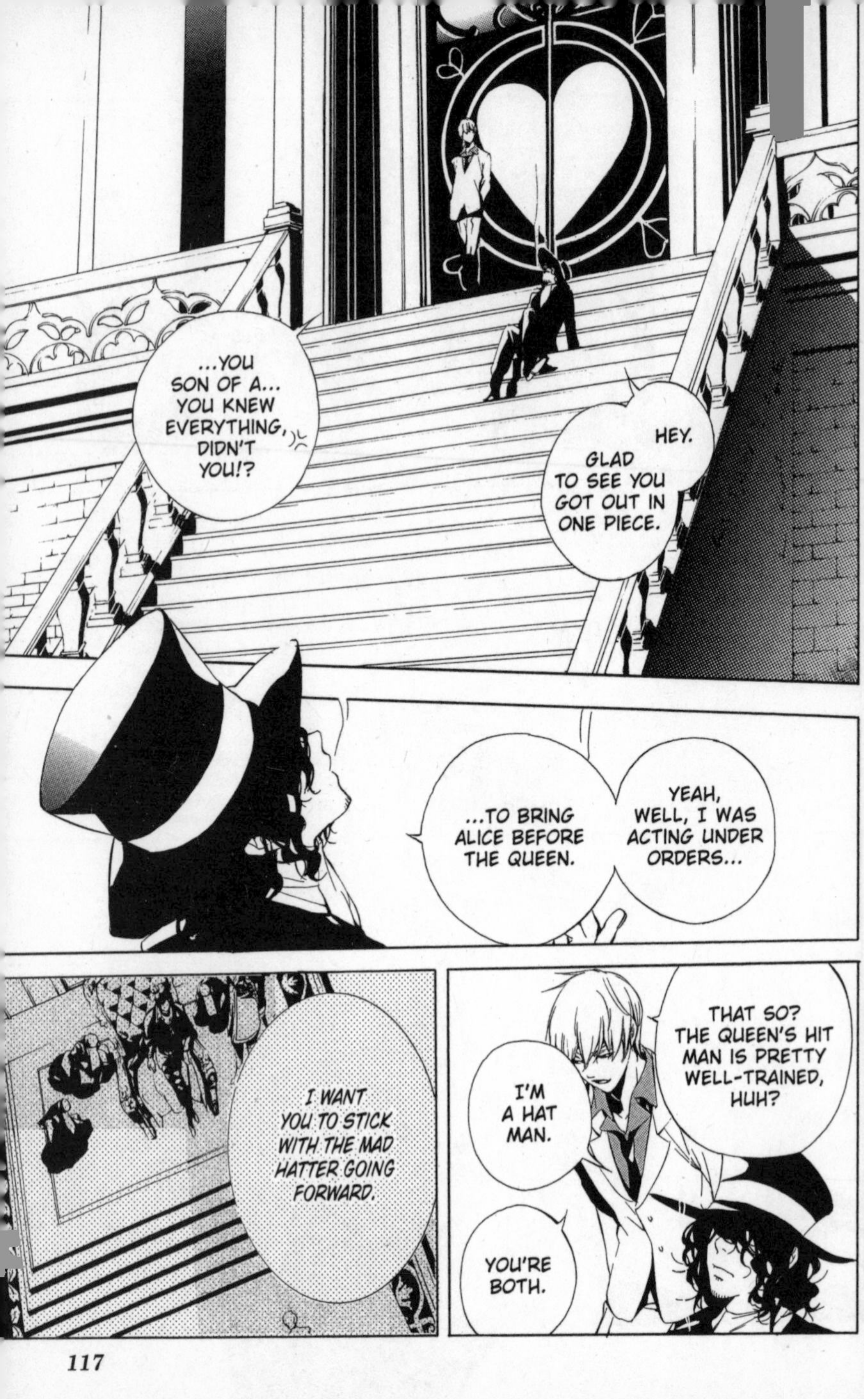
HEY. GLAD TO SEE YOU GOT OUT IN ONE PIECE.
...YOU SON OF A... YOU KNEW EVERYTHING, DIDN'T YOU!?
YEAH, WELL, I WAS ACTING UNDER ORDERS...
...TO BRING ALICE BEFORE THE QUEEN.
THAT SO? THE QUEEN'S HIT MAN IS PRETTY WELL-TRAINED, HUH?
I'M A HAT MAN.
YOU'RE BOTH.
I WANT YOU TO STICK WITH THE MAD HATTER GOING FORWARD.

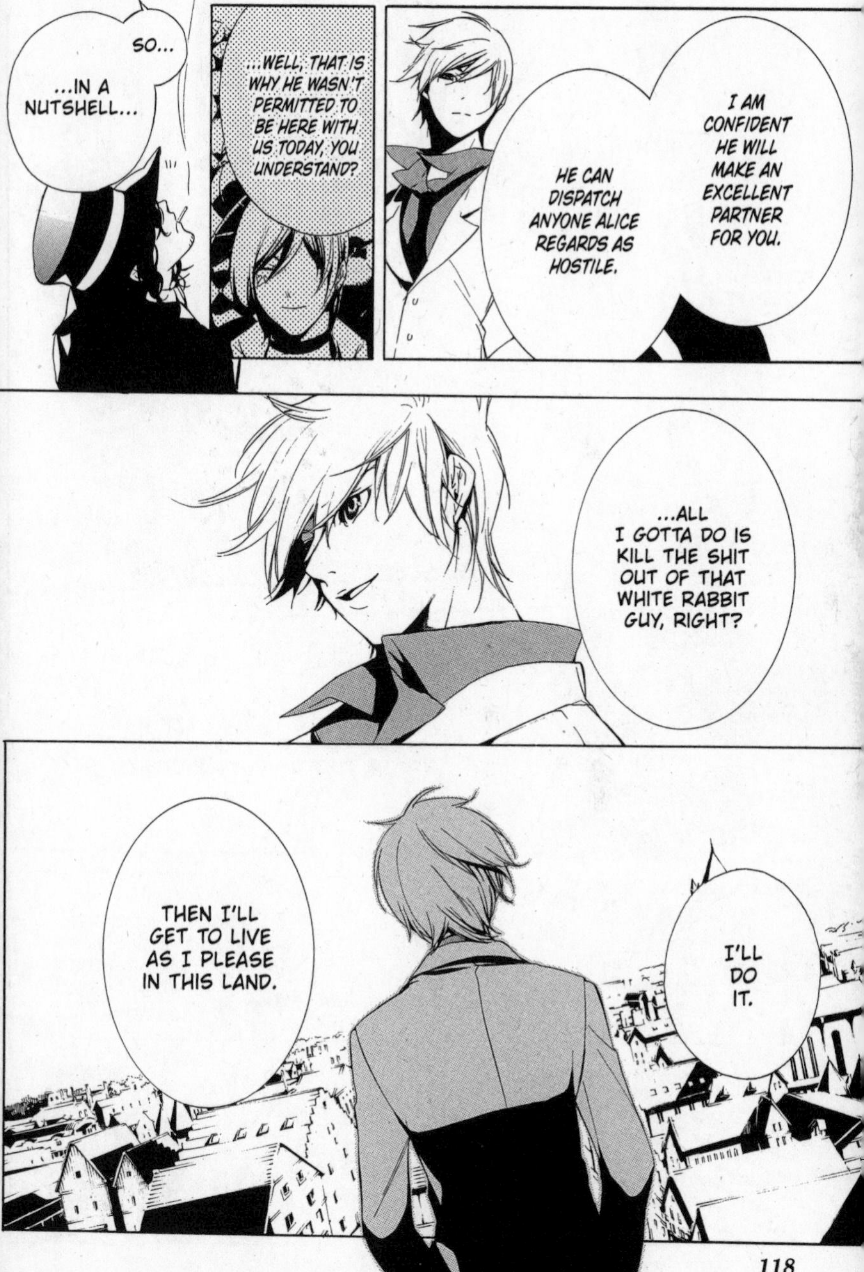
I AM CONFIDENT HE WILL MAKE AN EXCELLENT PARTNER FOR YOU.
HE CAN DISPATCH ANYONE ALICE REGARDS AS HOSTILE.
...WELL, THAT IS WHY HE WASN'T PERMITTED TO BE HERE WITH US TODAY, YOU UNDERSTAND?
SO...
...IN A NUTSHELL...
...ALL I GOTTA DO IS KILL THE SHIT OUT OF THAT WHITE RABBIT GUY, RIGHT?
I'LL DO IT.
THEN I'LL GET TO LIVE AS I PLEASE IN THIS LAND.

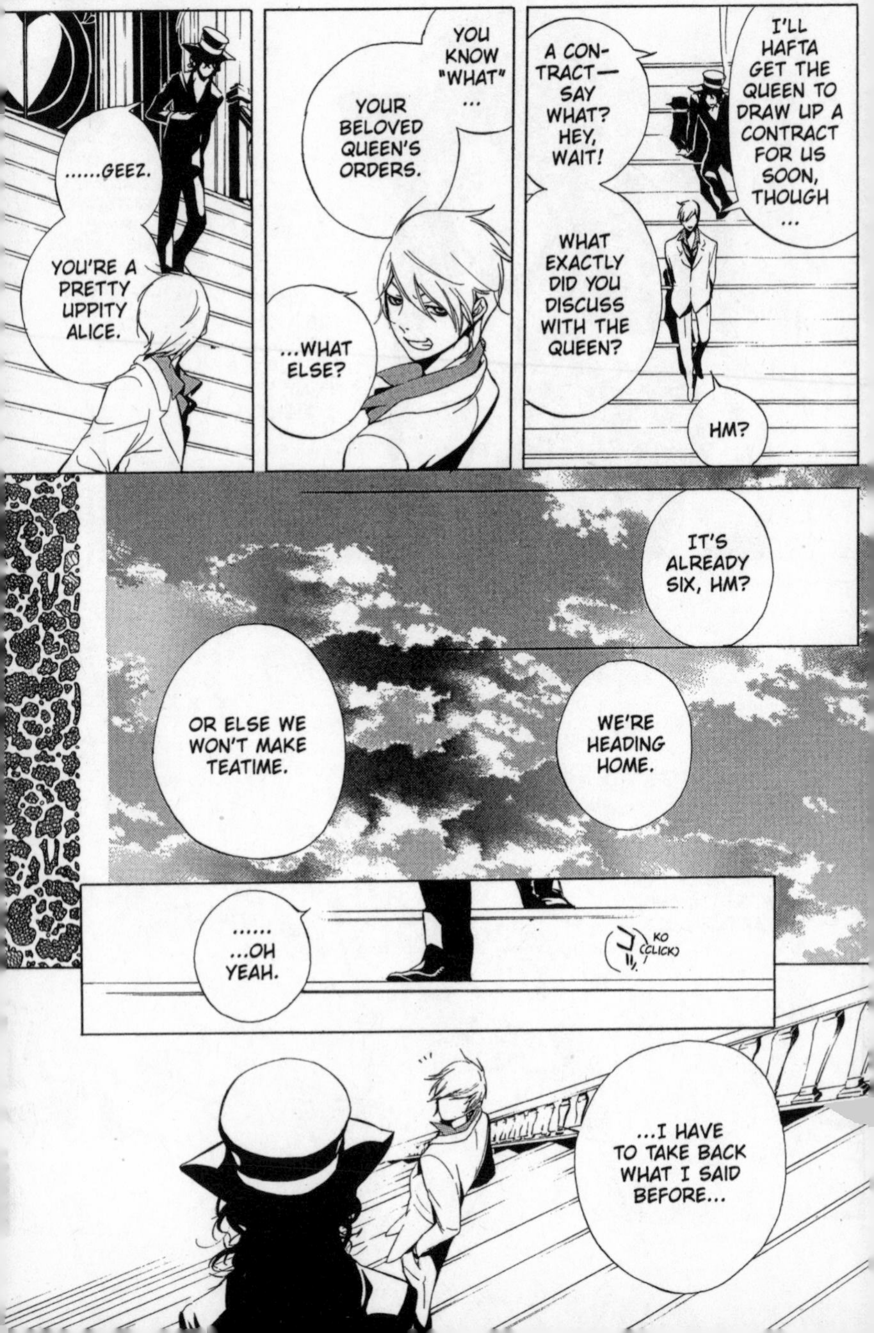
I'LL HAFTA GET THE QUEEN TO DRAW UP A CONTRACT FOR US SOON, THOUGH...
HM?
A CON-TRACT— SAY WHAT? HEY, WAIT!
WHAT EXACTLY DID YOU DISCUSS WITH THE QUEEN?
...WHAT ELSE?
YOUR BELOVED QUEEN'S ORDERS.
YOU KNOW "WHAT"...
......GEEZ.
YOU'RE A PRETTY UPPITY ALICE.
IT'S ALREADY SIX, HM?
WE'RE HEADING HOME.
OR ELSE WE WON'T MAKE TEATIME.
KO (CLICK)
....OH YEAH.
...I HAVE TO TAKE BACK WHAT I SAID BEFORE...

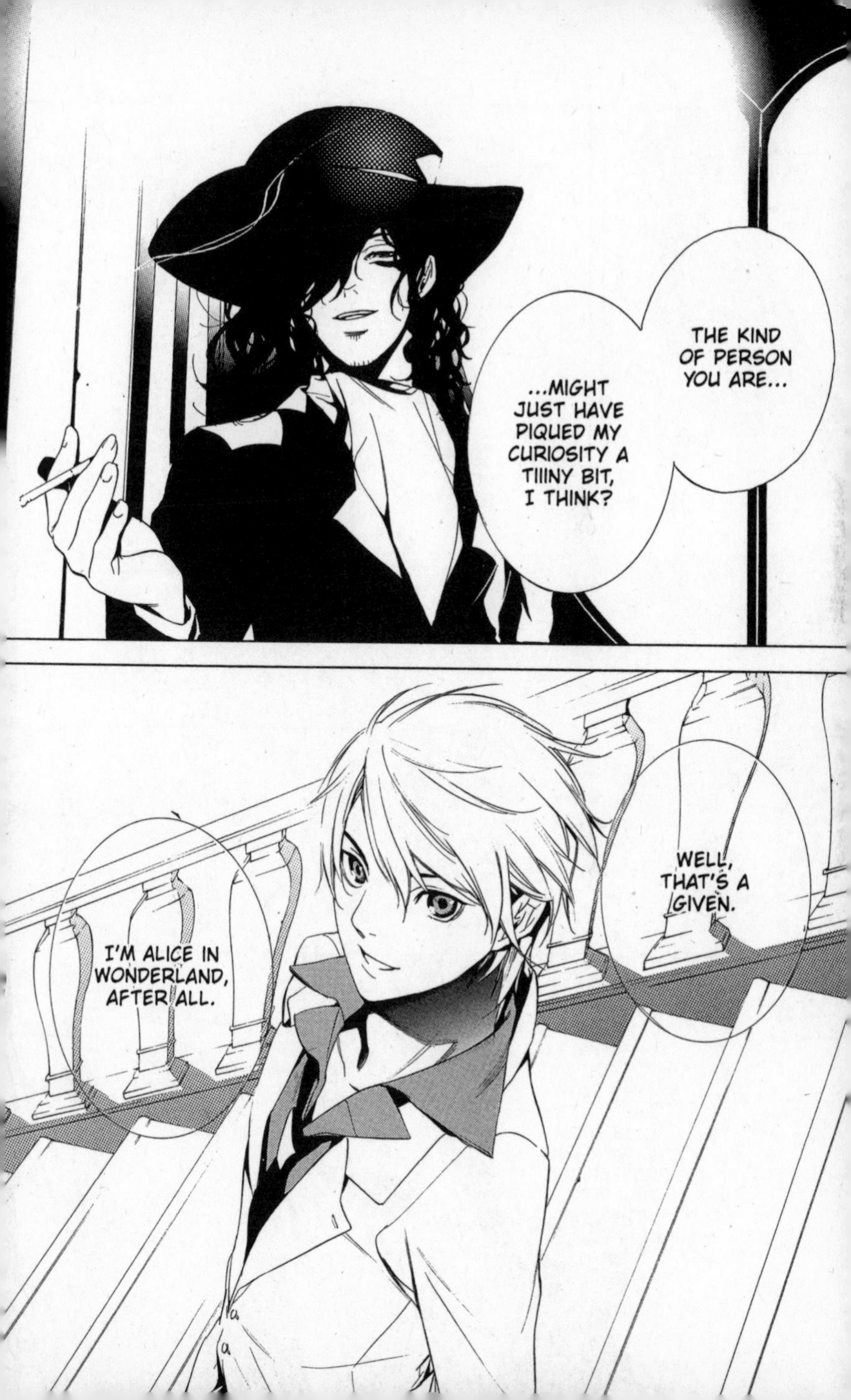
THE KIND OF PERSON YOU ARE...
...MIGHT JUST HAVE PIQUED MY CURIOSITY A TIIINY BIT, I THINK?
WELL, THAT'S A GIVEN.
I'M ALICE IN WONDERLAND, AFTER ALL.

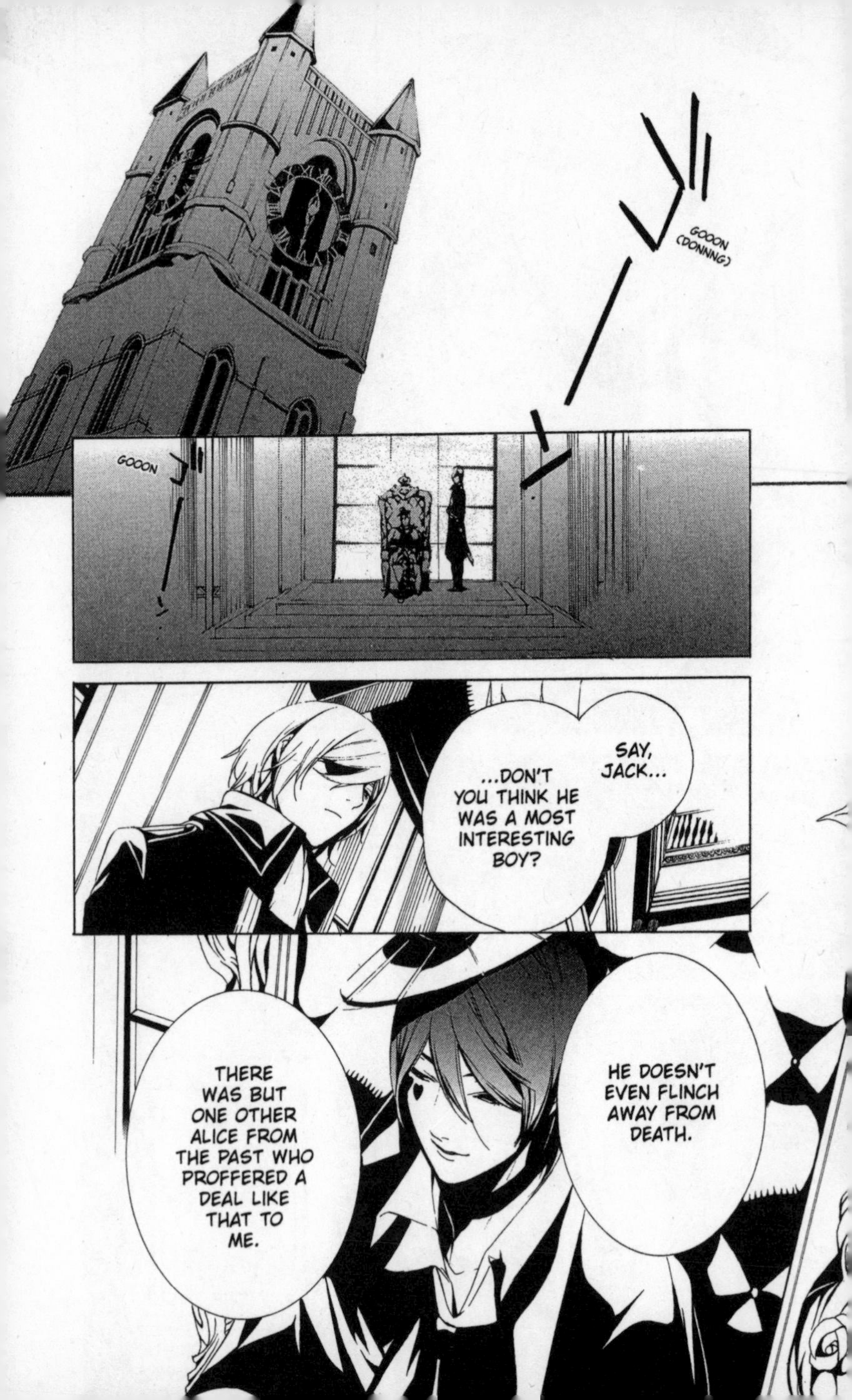
GOOOON (DONNNG)
GOOOON
SAY, JACK...
...DON'T YOU THINK HE WAS A MOST INTERESTING BOY?
HE DOESN'T EVEN FLINCH AWAY FROM DEATH.
THERE WAS BUT ONE OTHER ALICE FROM THE PAST WHO PROFFERED A DEAL LIKE THAT TO ME.

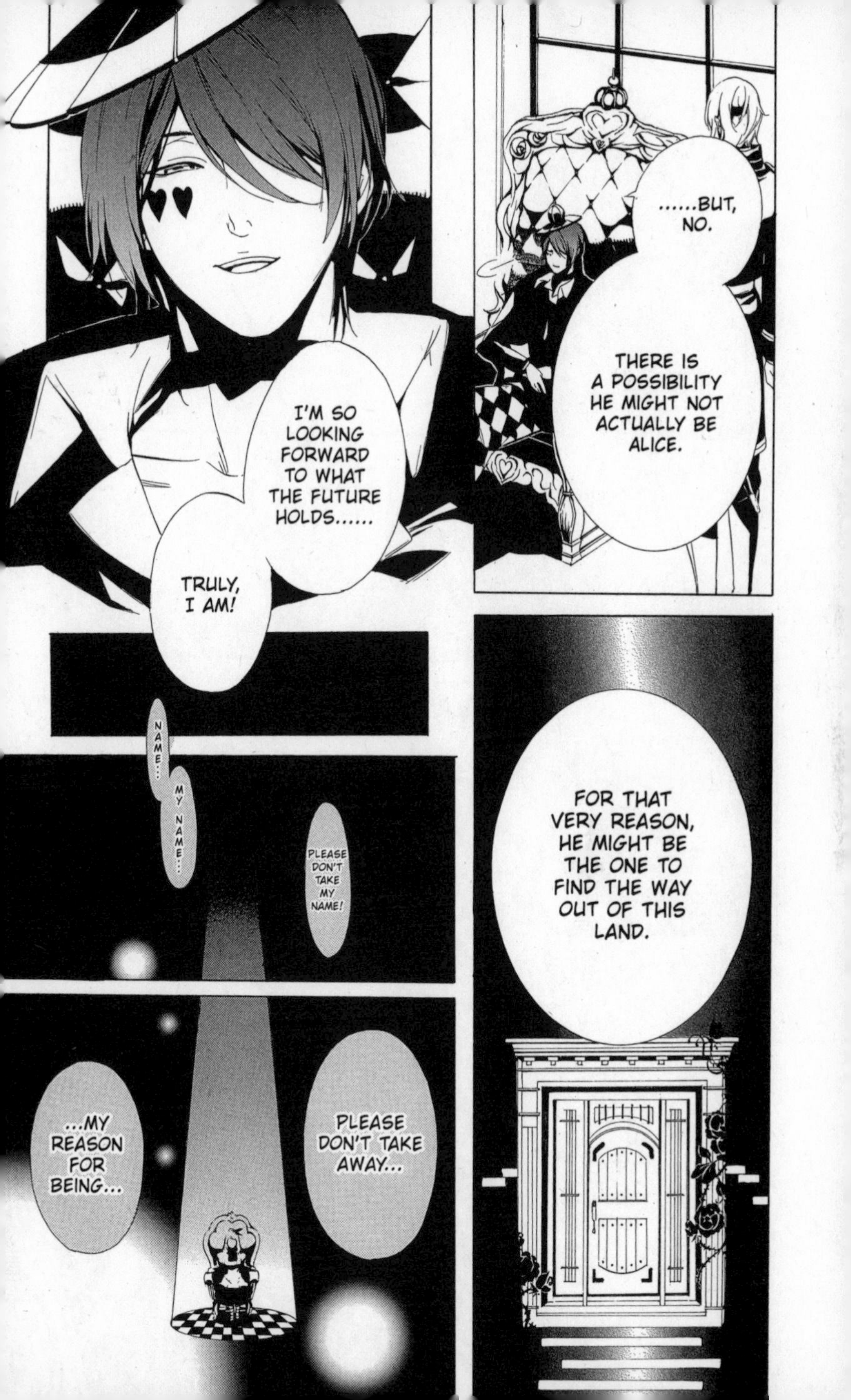
......BUT, NO.
THERE IS A POSSIBILITY HE MIGHT NOT ACTUALLY BE ALICE.
I'M SO LOOKING FORWARD TO WHAT THE FUTURE HOLDS......
TRULY, I AM!
FOR THAT VERY REASON, HE MIGHT BE THE ONE TO FIND THE WAY OUT OF THIS LAND.
NAME...
MY NAME...
PLEASE DON'T TAKE MY NAME!
PLEASE DON'T TAKE AWAY...
...MY REASON FOR BEING...

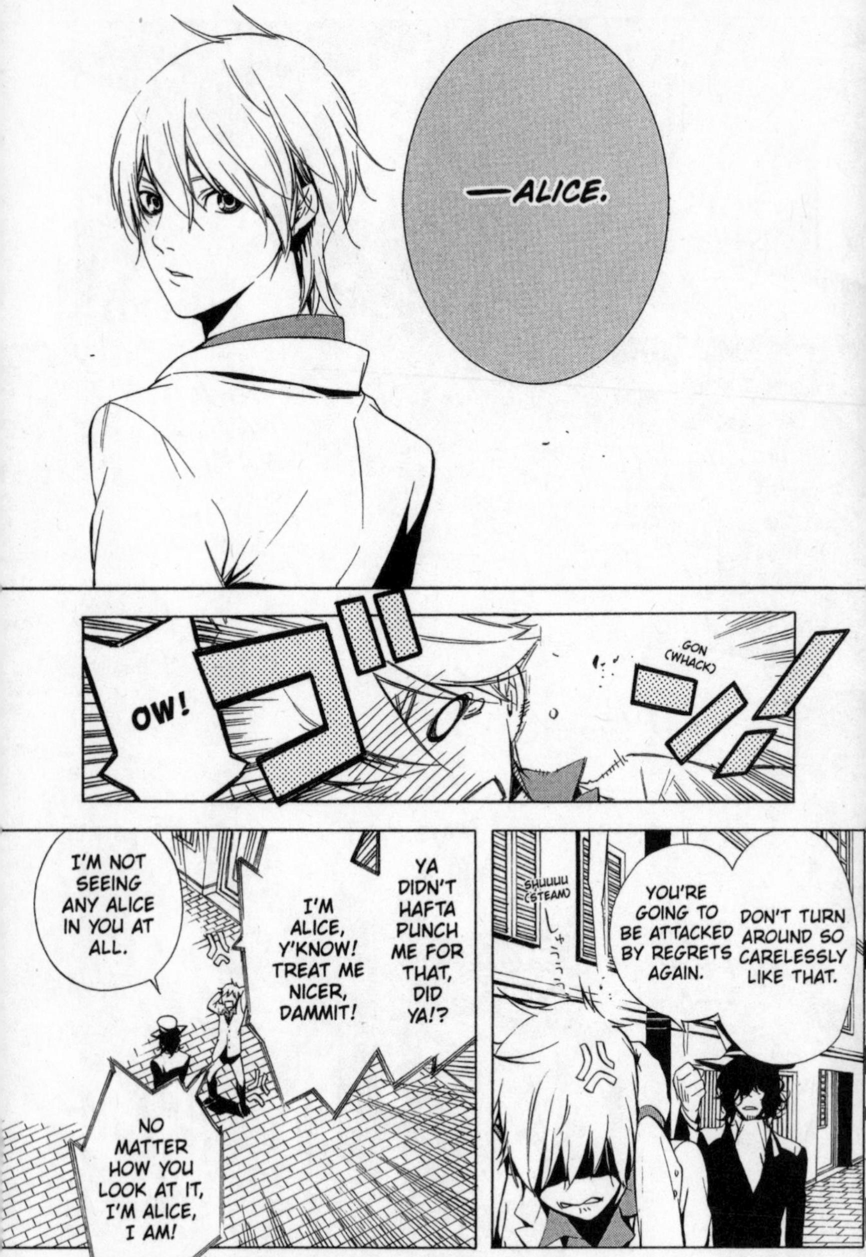
—ALICE.
GON (WHACK)
OW!
DON'T TURN AROUND SO CARELESSLY LIKE THAT.
YOU'RE GOING TO BE ATTACKED BY REGRETS AGAIN.
SHUUUU (STEAM)
YA DIDN'T HAFTA PUNCH ME FOR THAT, DID YA!?
I'M ALICE, Y'KNOW! TREAT ME NICER, DAMMIT!
I'M NOT SEEING ANY ALICE IN YOU AT ALL.
NO MATTER HOW YOU LOOK AT IT, I'M ALICE, I AM!

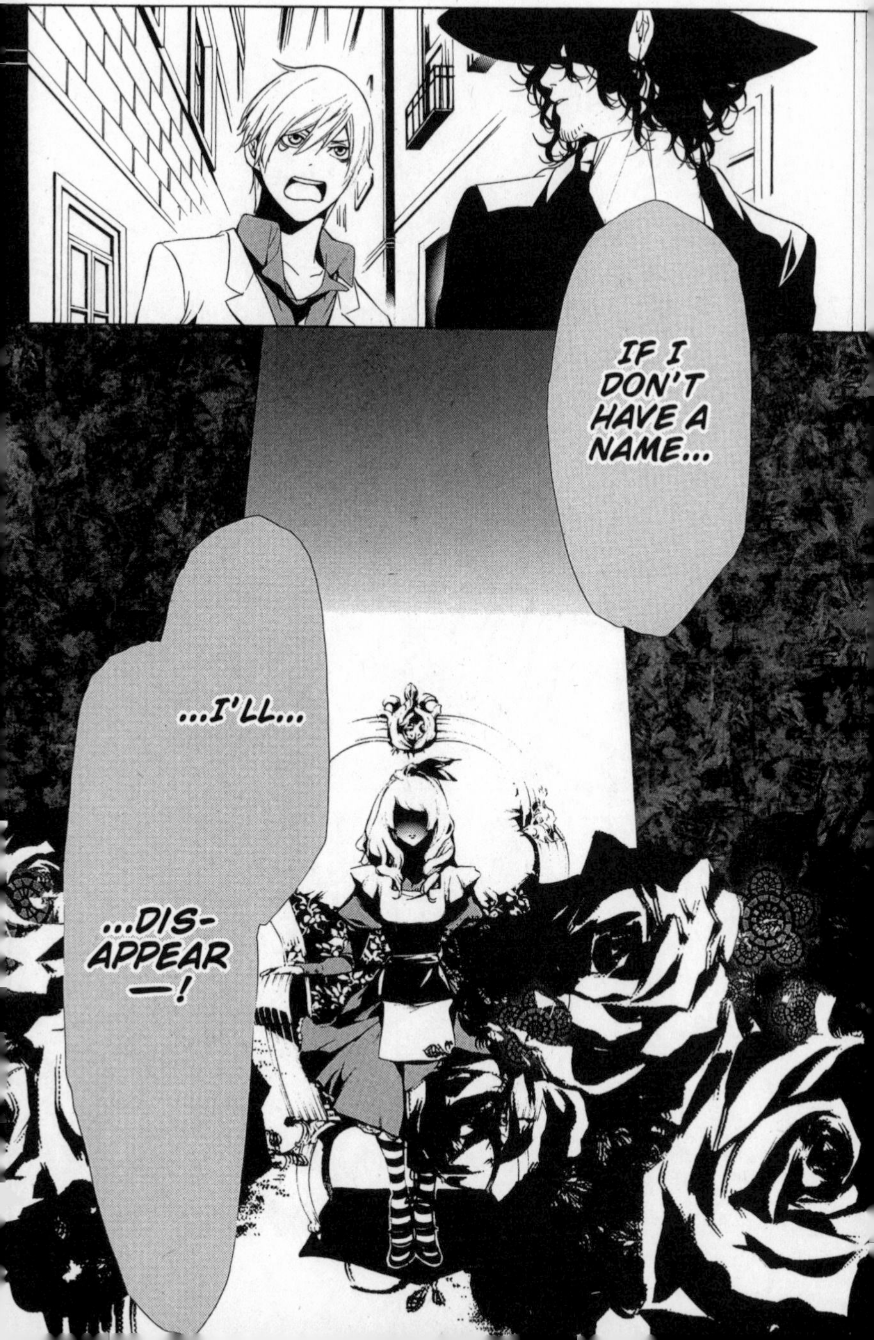
IF I DON'T HAVE A NAME...
...I'LL...
...DIS-APPEAR—!

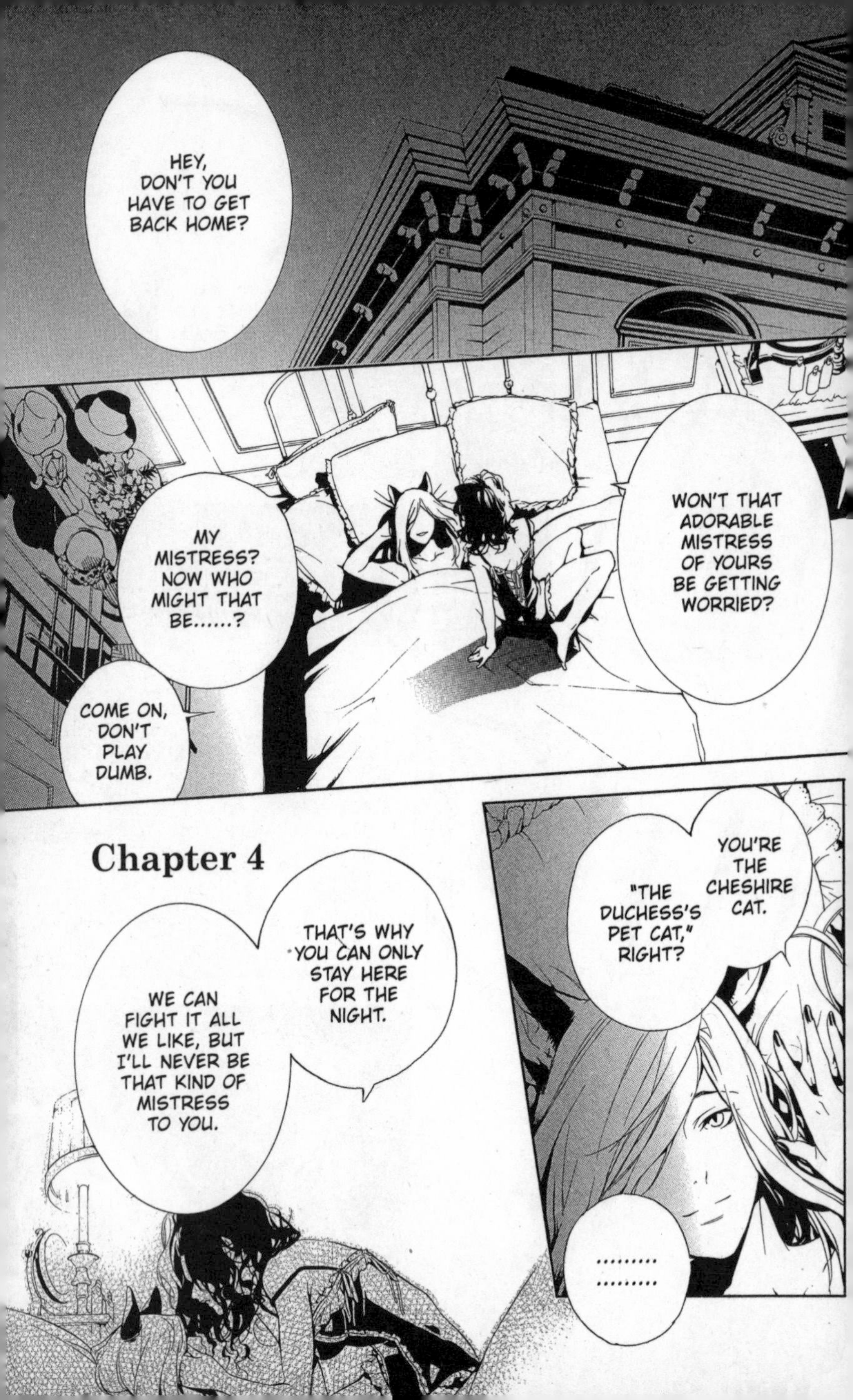
HEY, DON'T YOU HAVE TO GET BACK HOME?
WON'T THAT ADORABLE MISTRESS OF YOURS BE GETTING WORRIED?
MY MISTRESS? NOW WHO MIGHT THAT BE......?
COME ON, DON'T PLAY DUMB.
YOU'RE THE CHESHIRE CAT.
"THE DUCHESS'S PET CAT," RIGHT?
....
....
Chapter 4
THAT'S WHY YOU CAN ONLY STAY HERE FOR THE NIGHT.
WE CAN FIGHT IT ALL WE LIKE, BUT I'LL NEVER BE THAT KIND OF MISTRESS TO YOU.

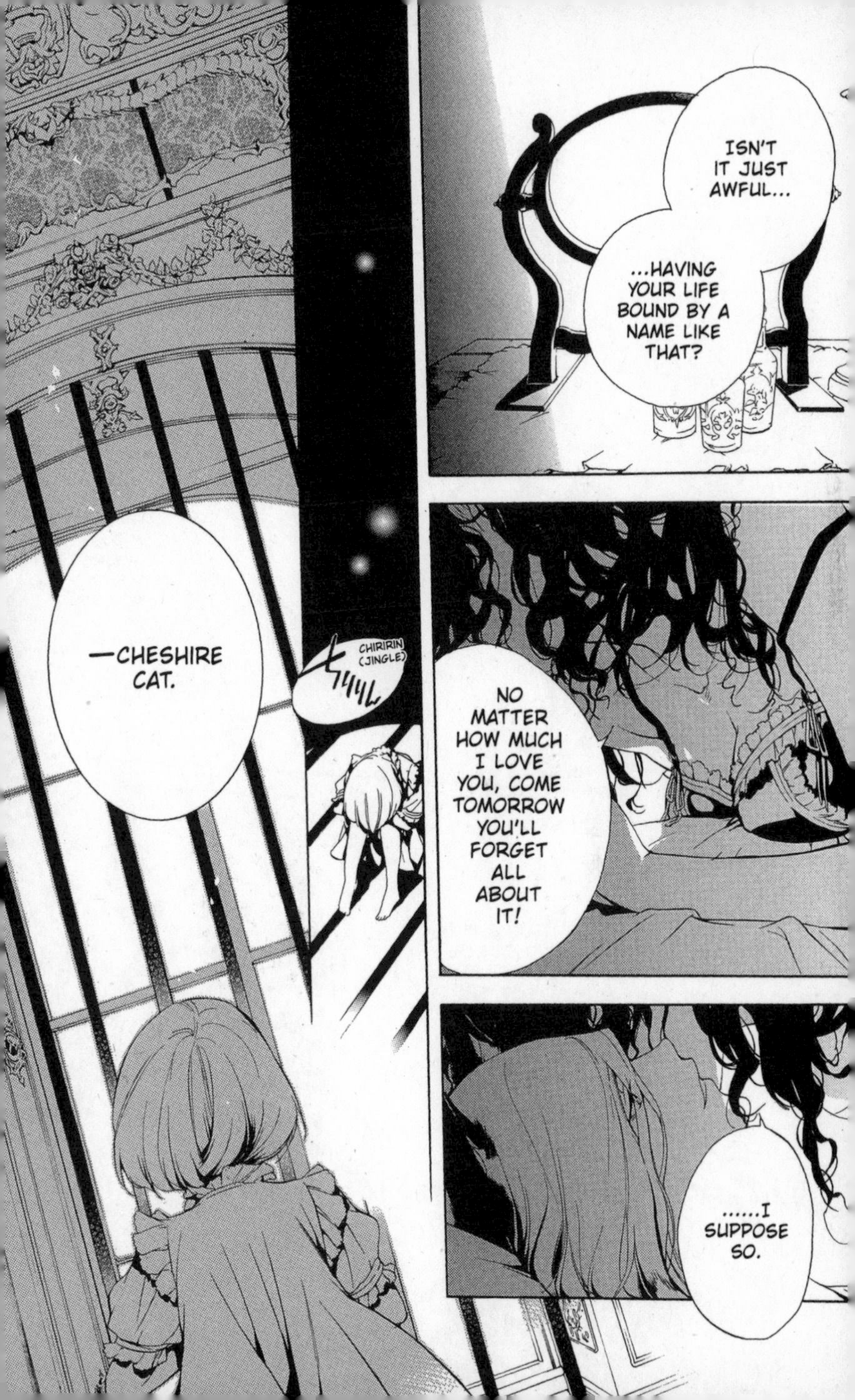
ISN'T IT JUST AWFUL...
...HAVING YOUR LIFE BOUND BY A NAME LIKE THAT?
NO MATTER HOW MUCH I LOVE YOU, COME TOMORROW YOU'LL FORGET ALL ABOUT IT!
......I SUPPOSE SO.
CHIRIRIN (JINGLE)
—CHESHIRE CAT.

Chapter 4
Grin like a Cheshire Cat.

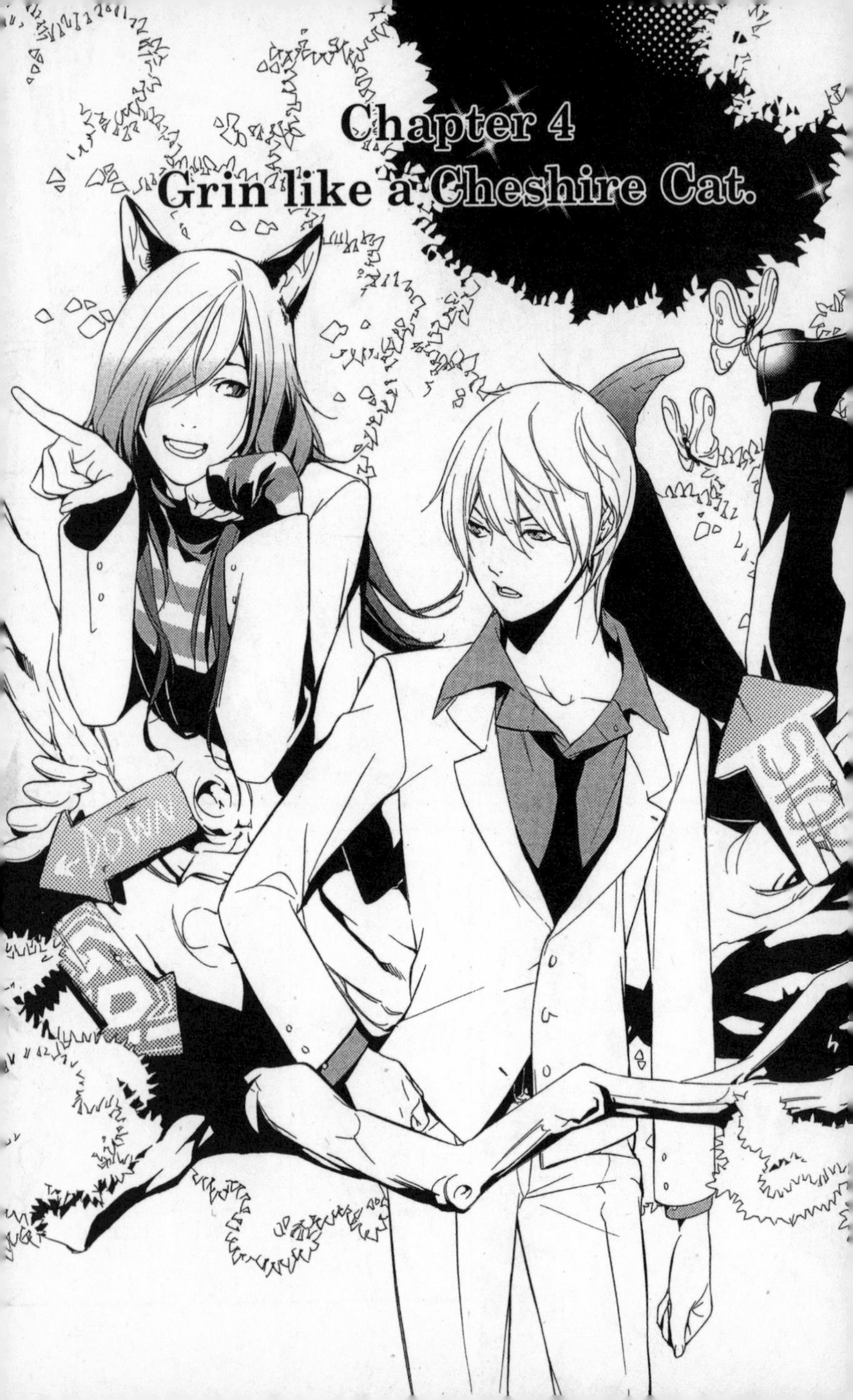
DOWN
GO!

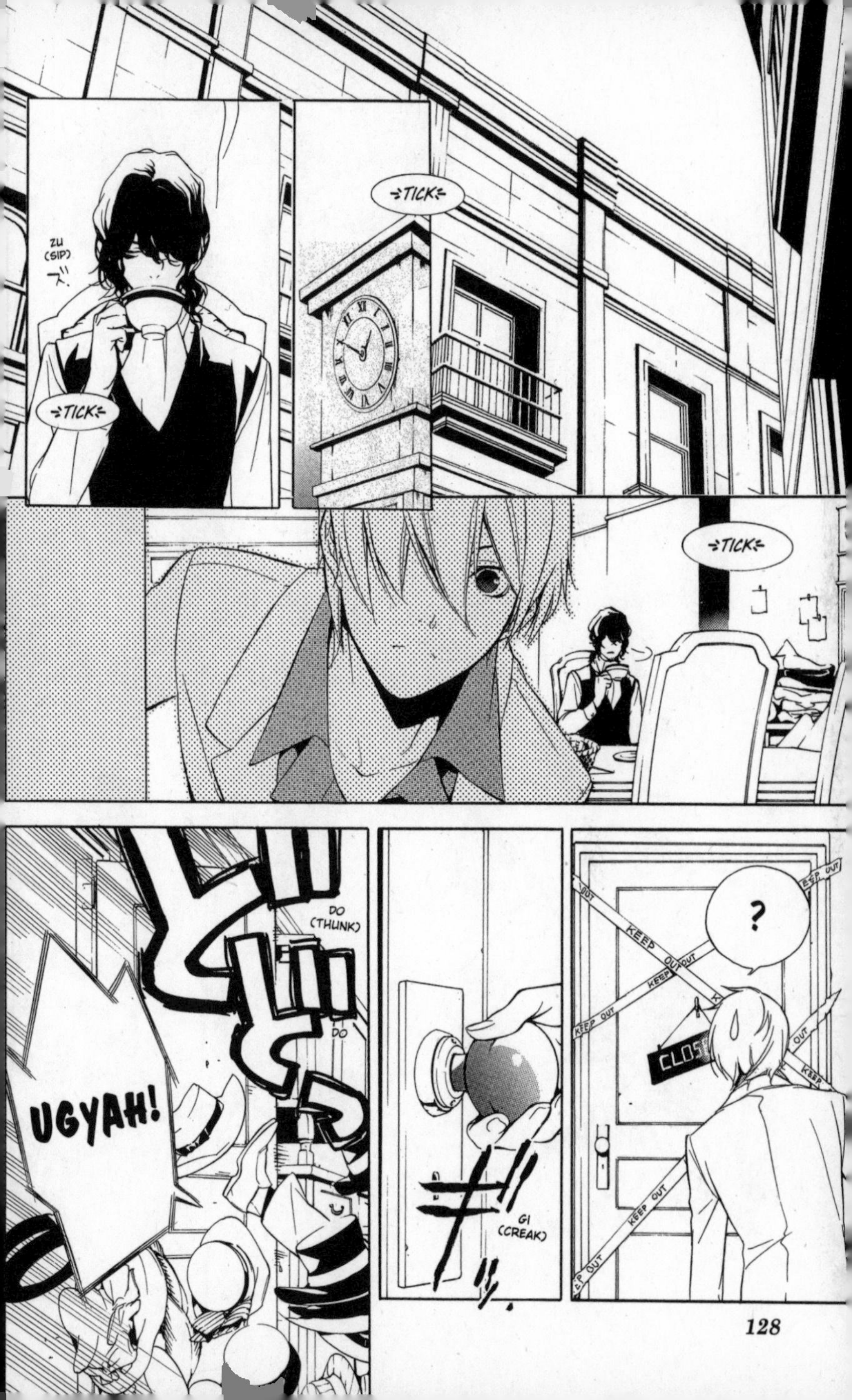
TICK
ZU (SIP)
TICK
TICK
?
KEEP OUT
CLOS
GI (CREAK)
DO (THUNK)
DO
UGYAH!

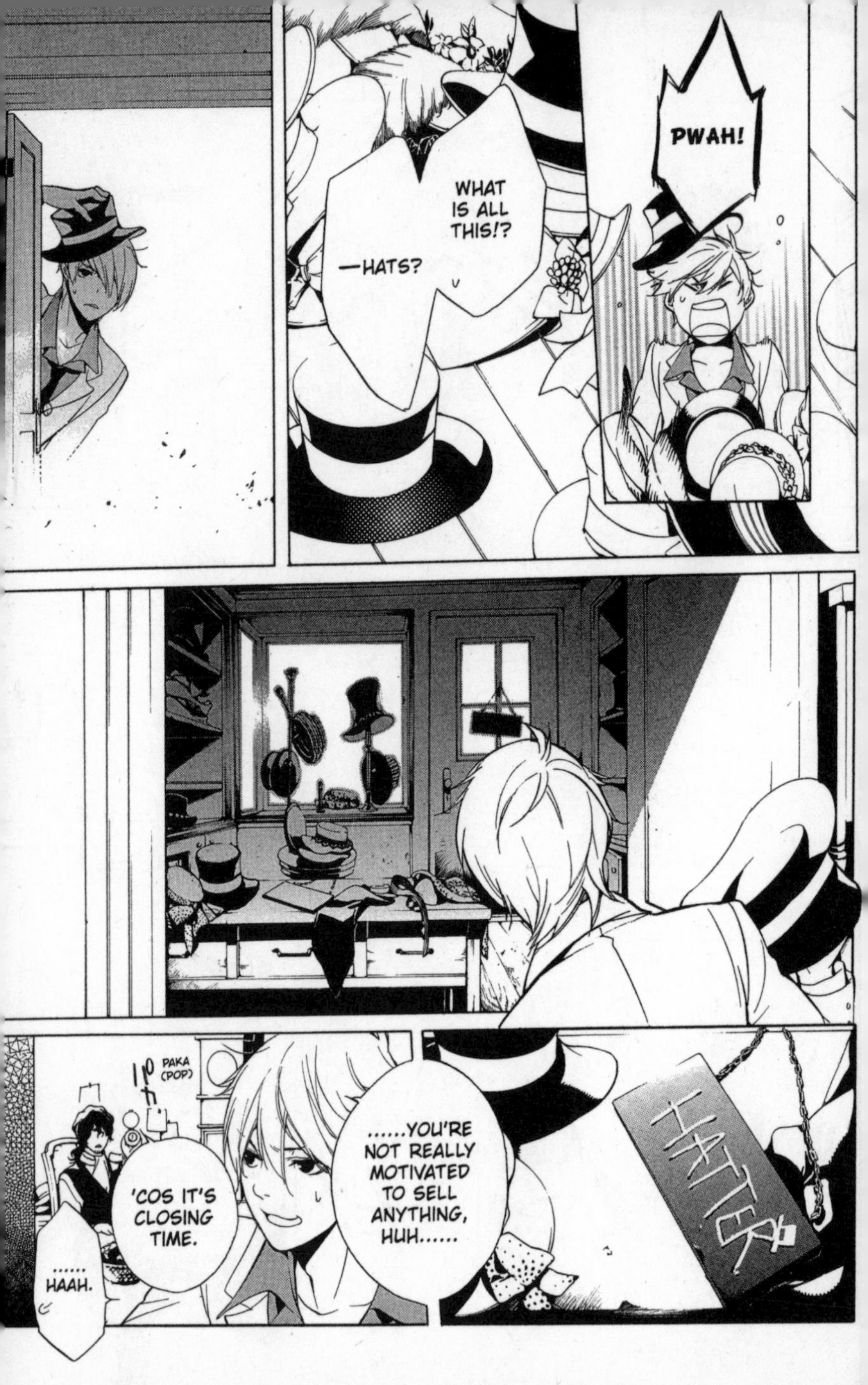
PWAH!
WHAT IS ALL THIS!?
—HATS?
......YOU'RE NOT REALLY MOTIVATED TO SELL ANYTHING, HUH......
'COS IT'S CLOSING TIME.
PAKA (POP)
...... HAAH.
HATTER

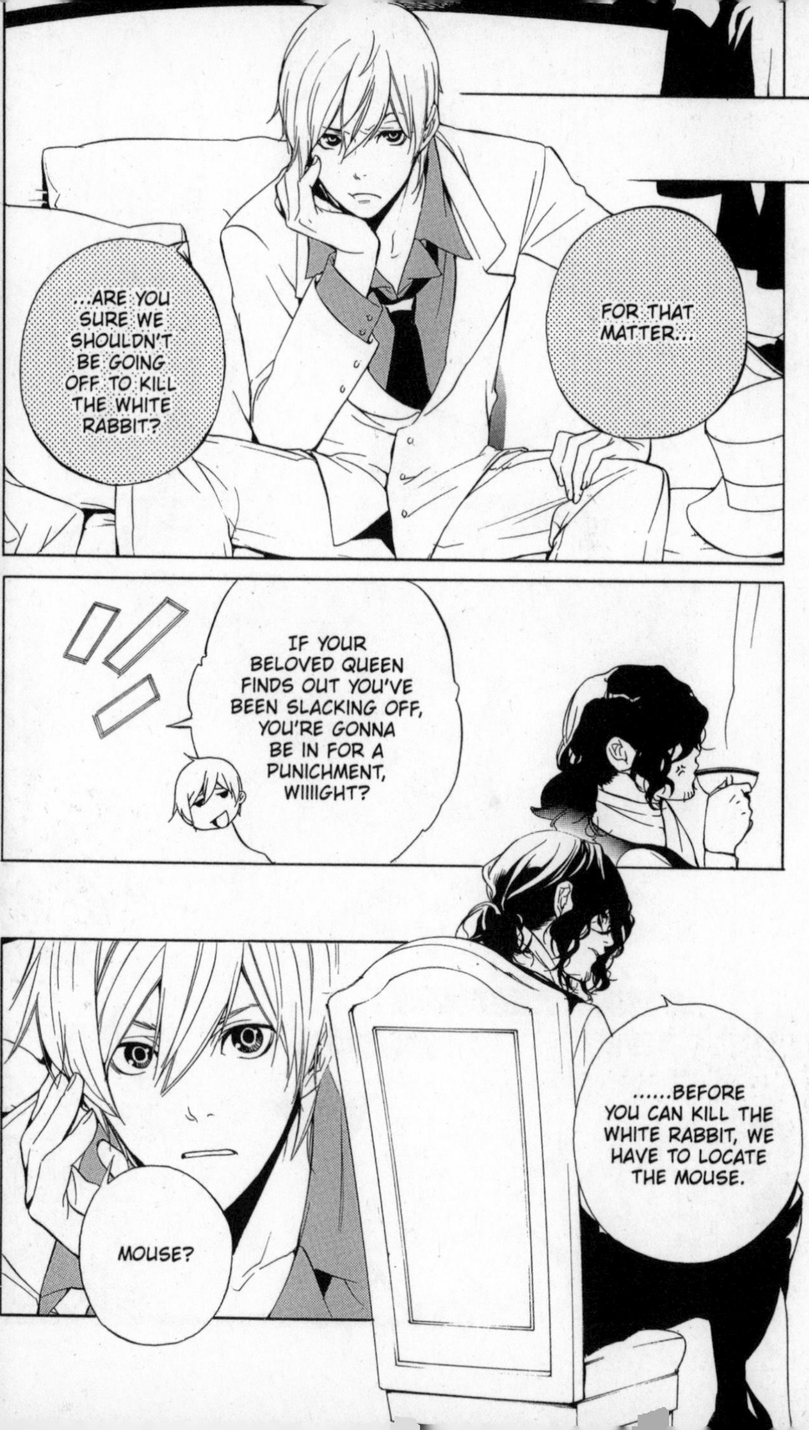
FOR THAT MATTER...
...ARE YOU SURE WE SHOULDN'T BE GOING OFF TO KILL THE WHITE RABBIT?
IF YOUR BELOVED QUEEN FINDS OUT YOU'VE BEEN SLACKING OFF, YOU'RE GONNA BE IN FOR A PUNICHMENT, WIIIIGHT?
......BEFORE YOU CAN KILL THE WHITE RABBIT, WE HAVE TO LOCATE THE MOUSE.
MOUSE?

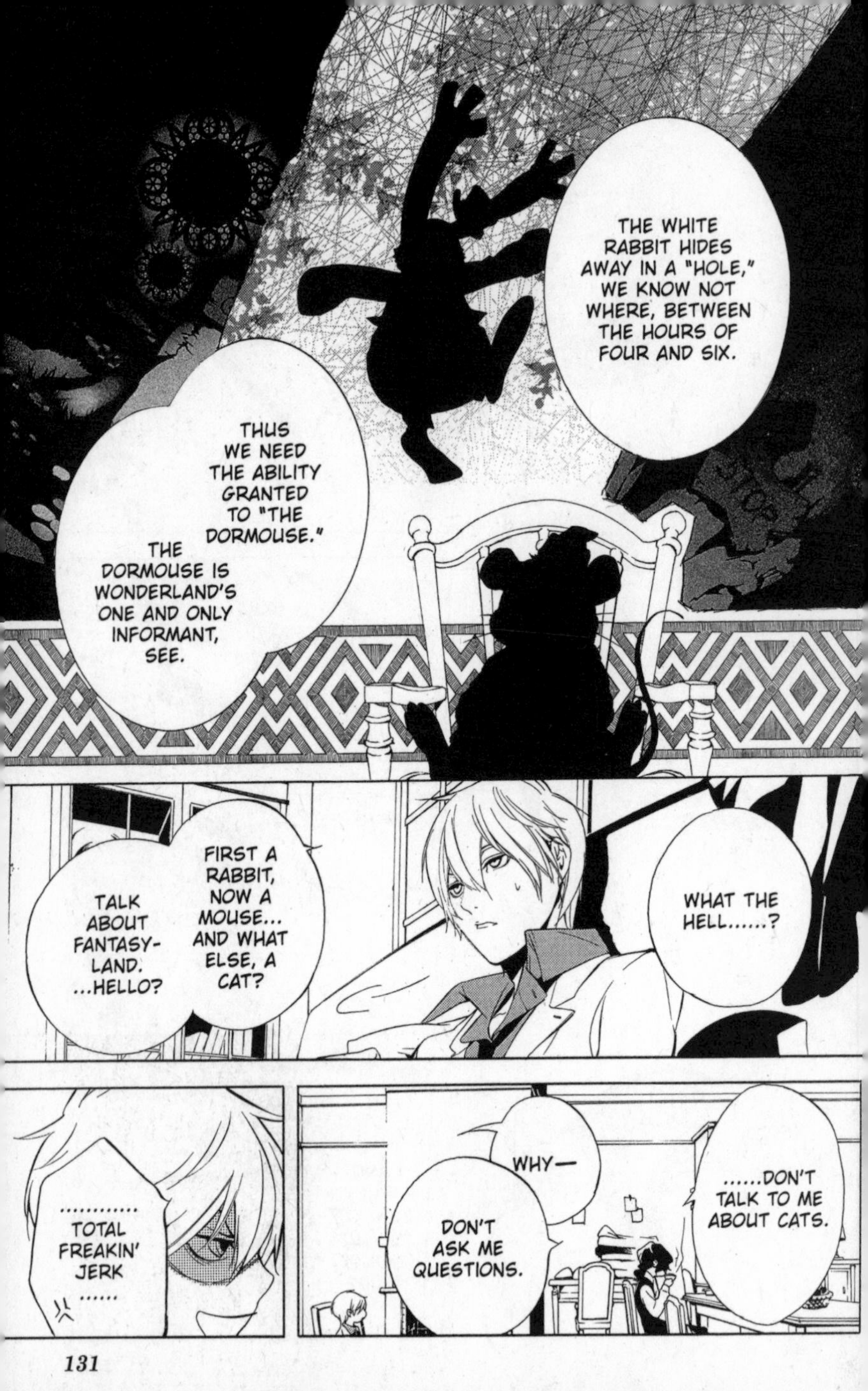
THE WHITE RABBIT HIDES AWAY IN A "HOLE," WE KNOW NOT WHERE, BETWEEN THE HOURS OF FOUR AND SIX.
THUS WE NEED THE ABILITY GRANTED TO "THE DORMOUSE."
THE DORMOUSE IS WONDERLAND'S ONE AND ONLY INFORMANT, SEE.
WHAT THE HELL......?
FIRST A RABBIT, NOW A MOUSE... AND WHAT ELSE, A CAT?
TALK ABOUT FANTASY-LAND. ...HELLO?
......DON'T TALK TO ME ABOUT CATS.
WHY—
DON'T ASK ME QUESTIONS.
.... TOTAL FREAKIN' JERK ......

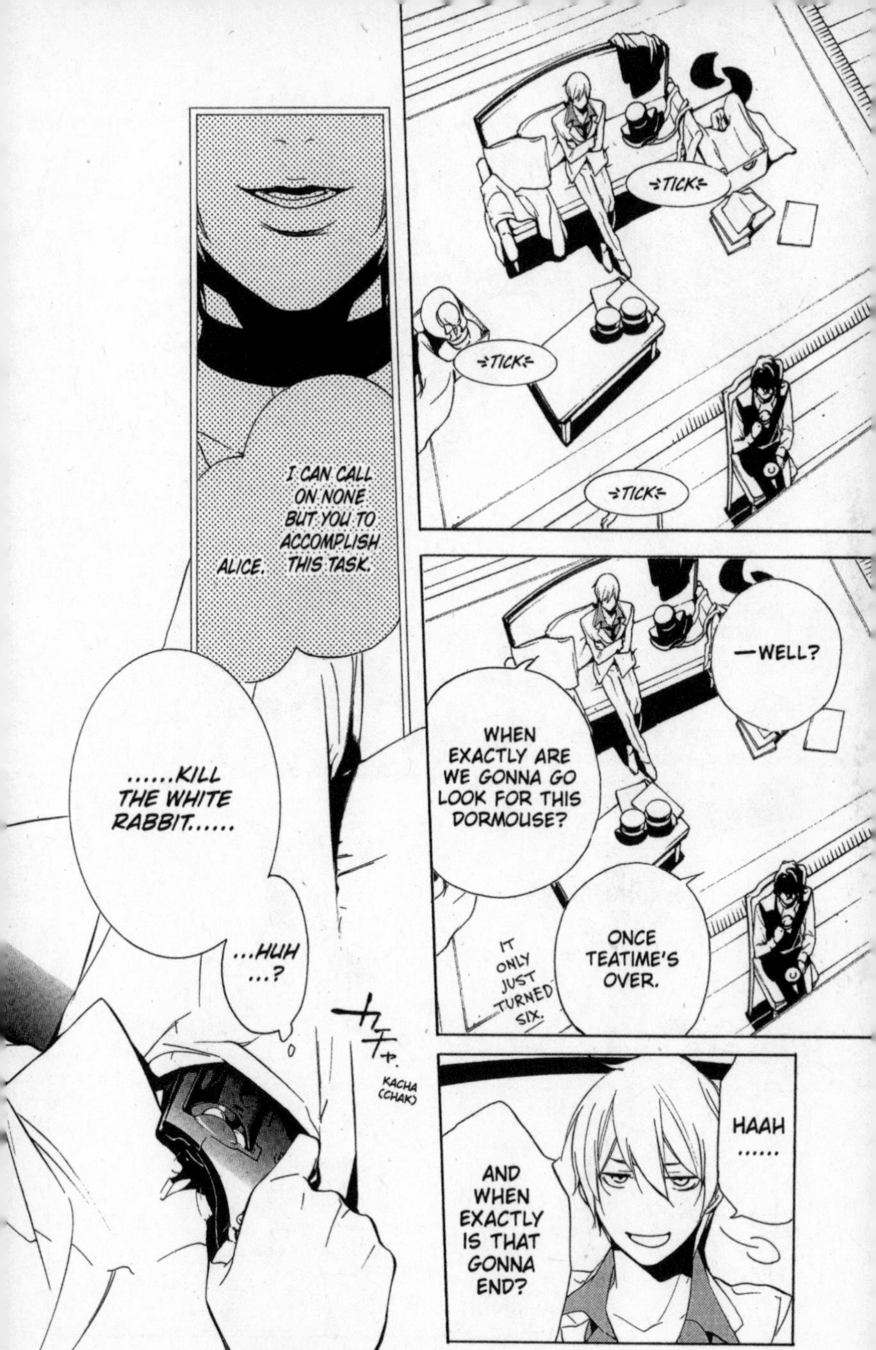
TICK
TICK
TICK
—WELL?
WHEN EXACTLY ARE WE GONNA GO LOOK FOR THIS DORMOUSE?
ONCE TEATIME'S OVER.
IT ONLY JUST TURNED SIX.
HAAH ......
AND WHEN EXACTLY IS THAT GONNA END?
I CAN CALL ON NONE BUT YOU TO ACCOMPLISH THIS TASK.
ALICE.
......KILL THE WHITE RABBIT......
...HUH ...?
KACHA (CHAK)

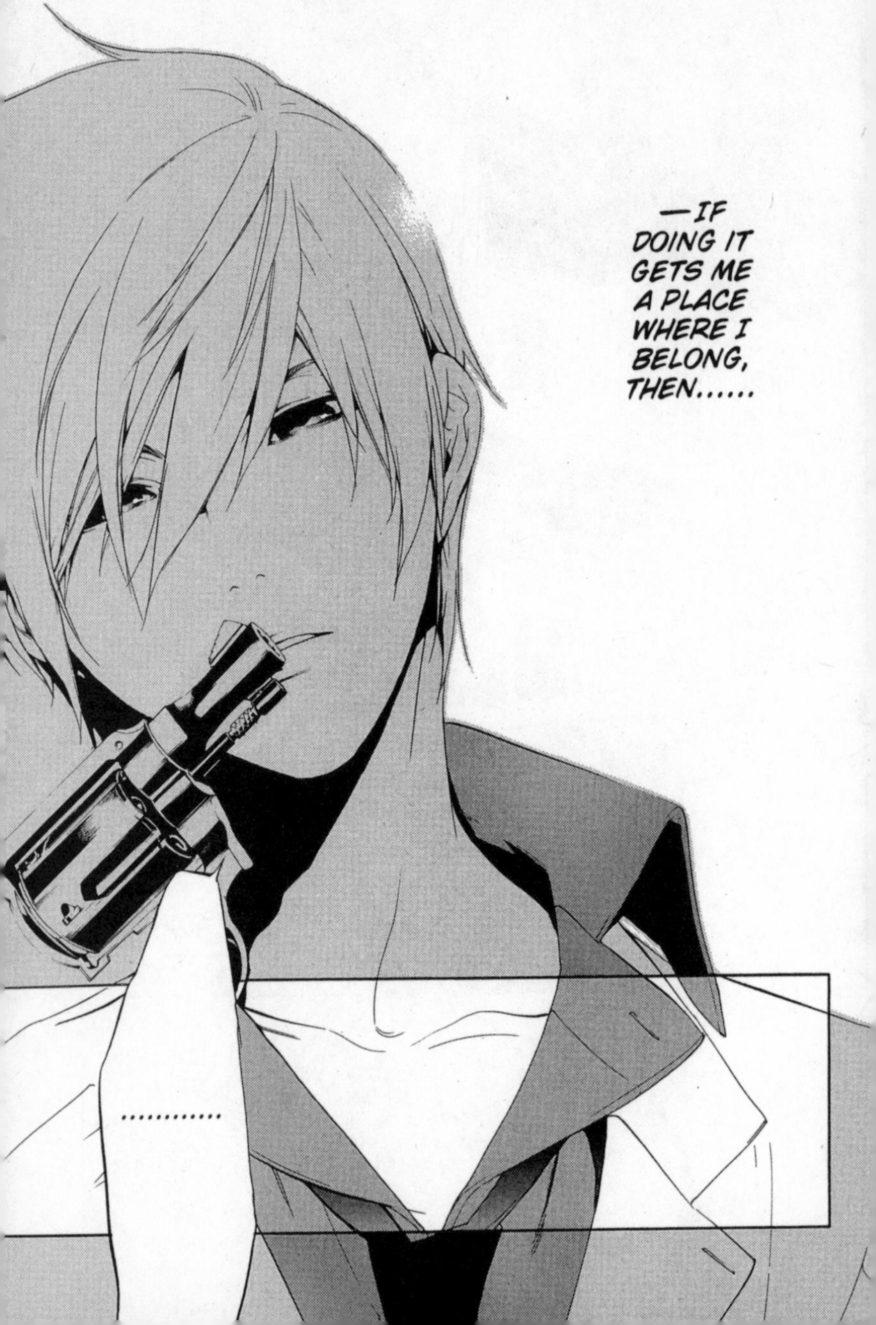
—IF DOING IT GETS ME A PLACE WHERE I BELONG, THEN......
....

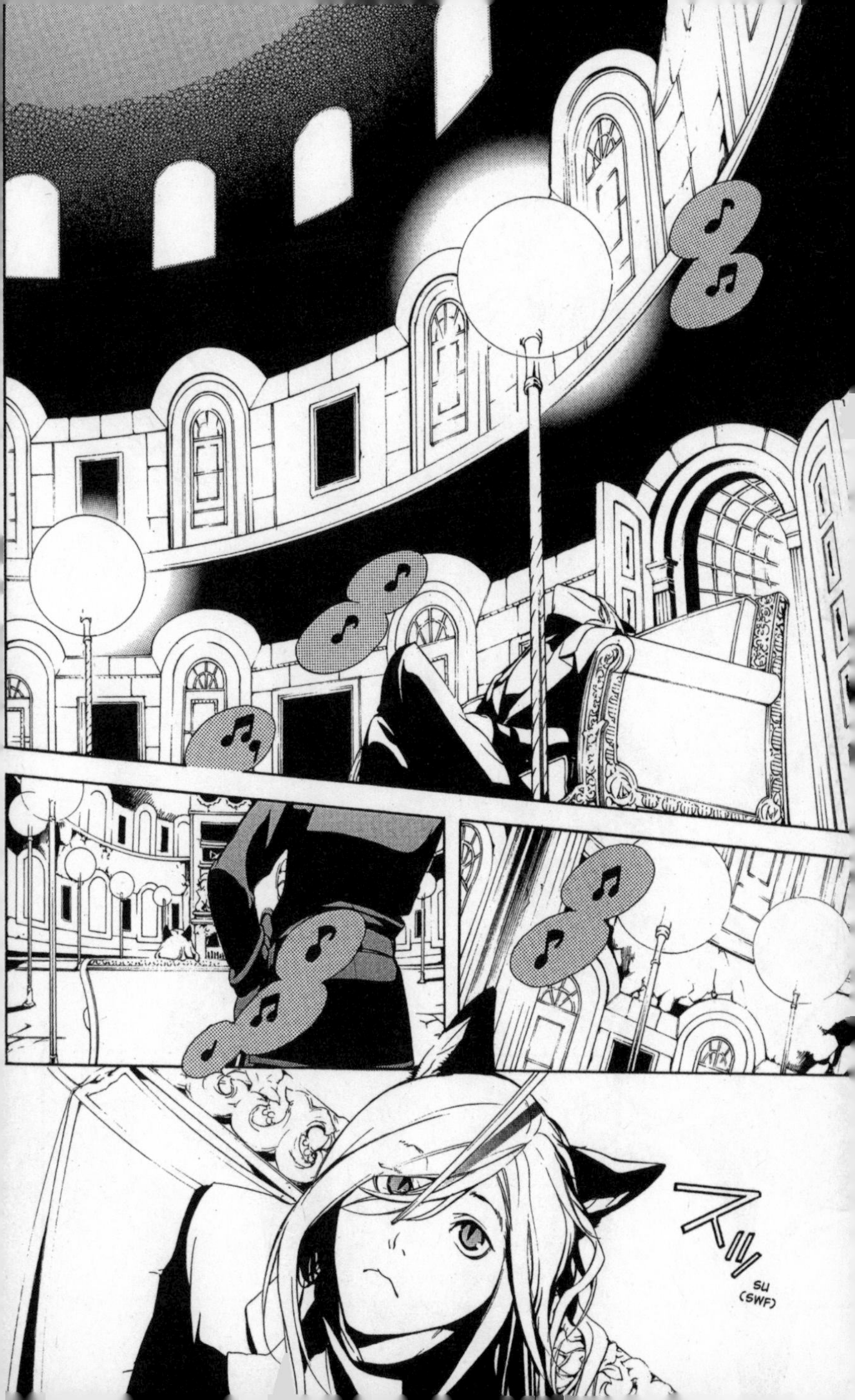
SU
(SWF)

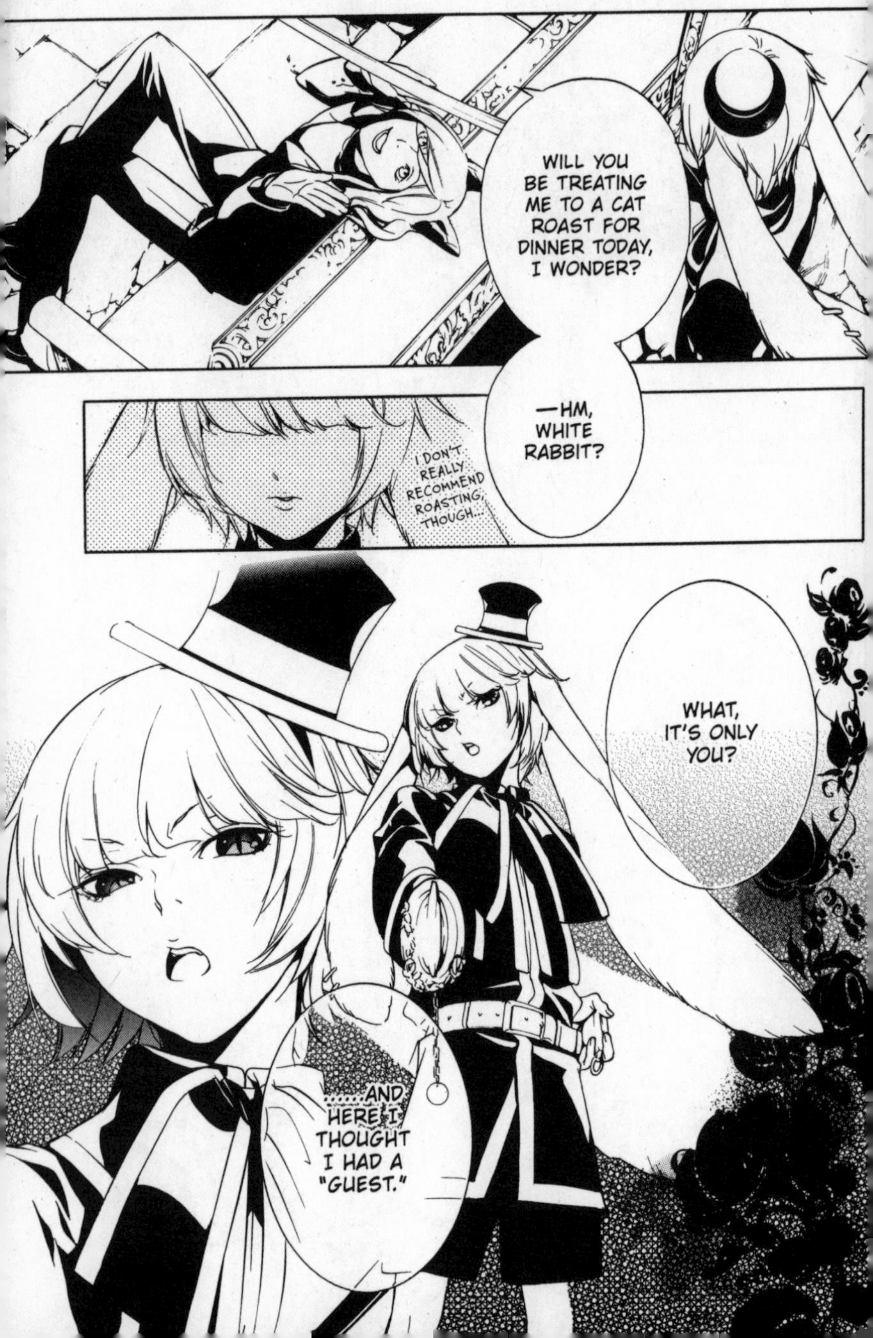
WILL YOU BE TREATING ME TO A CAT ROAST FOR DINNER TODAY, I WONDER?
—HM, WHITE RABBIT?
I DON'T REALLY RECOMMEND ROASTING, THOUGH...
WHAT, IT'S ONLY YOU?
......AND HERE I THOUGHT I HAD A "GUEST."

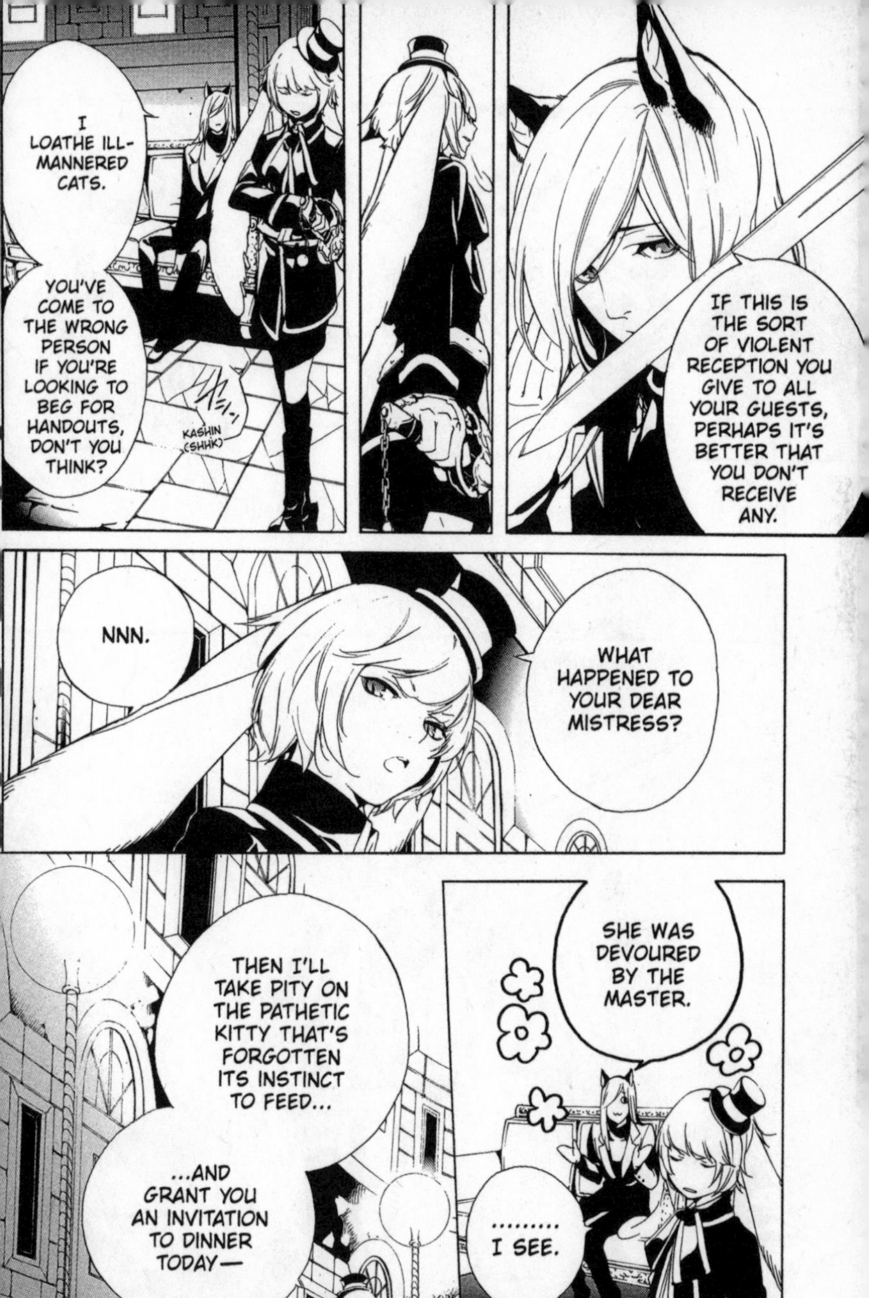
IF THIS IS THE SORT OF VIOLENT RECEPTION YOU GIVE TO ALL YOUR GUESTS, PERHAPS IT'S BETTER THAT YOU DON'T RECEIVE ANY.
I LOATHE ILL-MANNERED CATS.
YOU'VE COME TO THE WRONG PERSON IF YOU'RE LOOKING TO BEG FOR HANDOUTS, DON'T YOU THINK?
KASHIN (SHHK)
WHAT HAPPENED TO YOUR DEAR MISTRESS?
NNN.
SHE WAS DEVOURED BY THE MASTER.
.... I SEE.
THEN I'LL TAKE PITY ON THE PATHETIC KITTY THAT'S FORGOTTEN ITS INSTINCT TO FEED...
...AND GRANT YOU AN INVITATION TO DINNER TODAY—

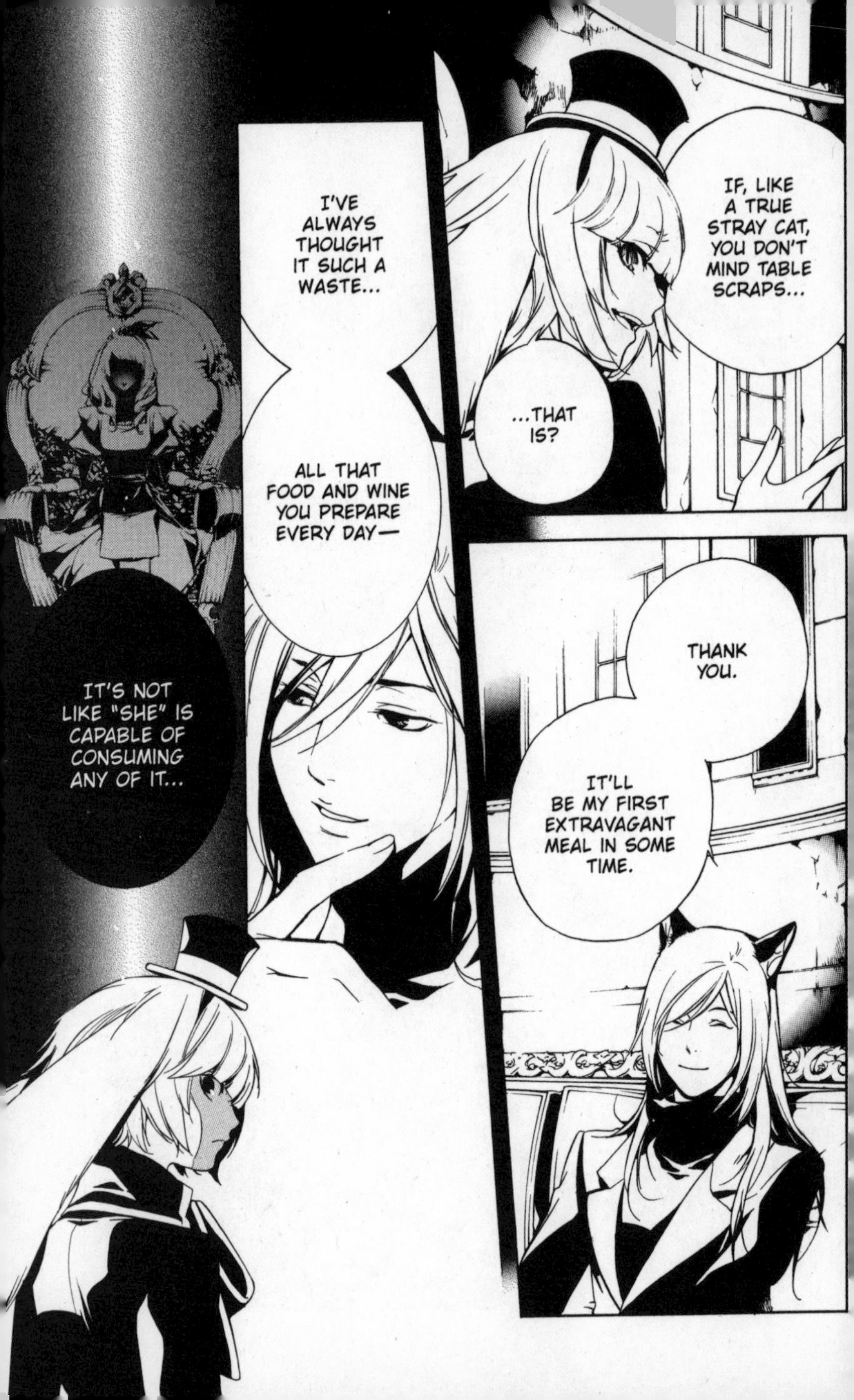
IF, LIKE A TRUE STRAY CAT, YOU DON'T MIND TABLE SCRAPS...
...THAT IS?
I'VE ALWAYS THOUGHT IT SUCH A WASTE...
ALL THAT FOOD AND WINE YOU PREPARE EVERY DAY—
IT'S NOT LIKE "SHE" IS CAPABLE OF CONSUMING ANY OF IT...
THANK YOU.
IT'LL BE MY FIRST EXTRAVAGANT MEAL IN SOME TIME.

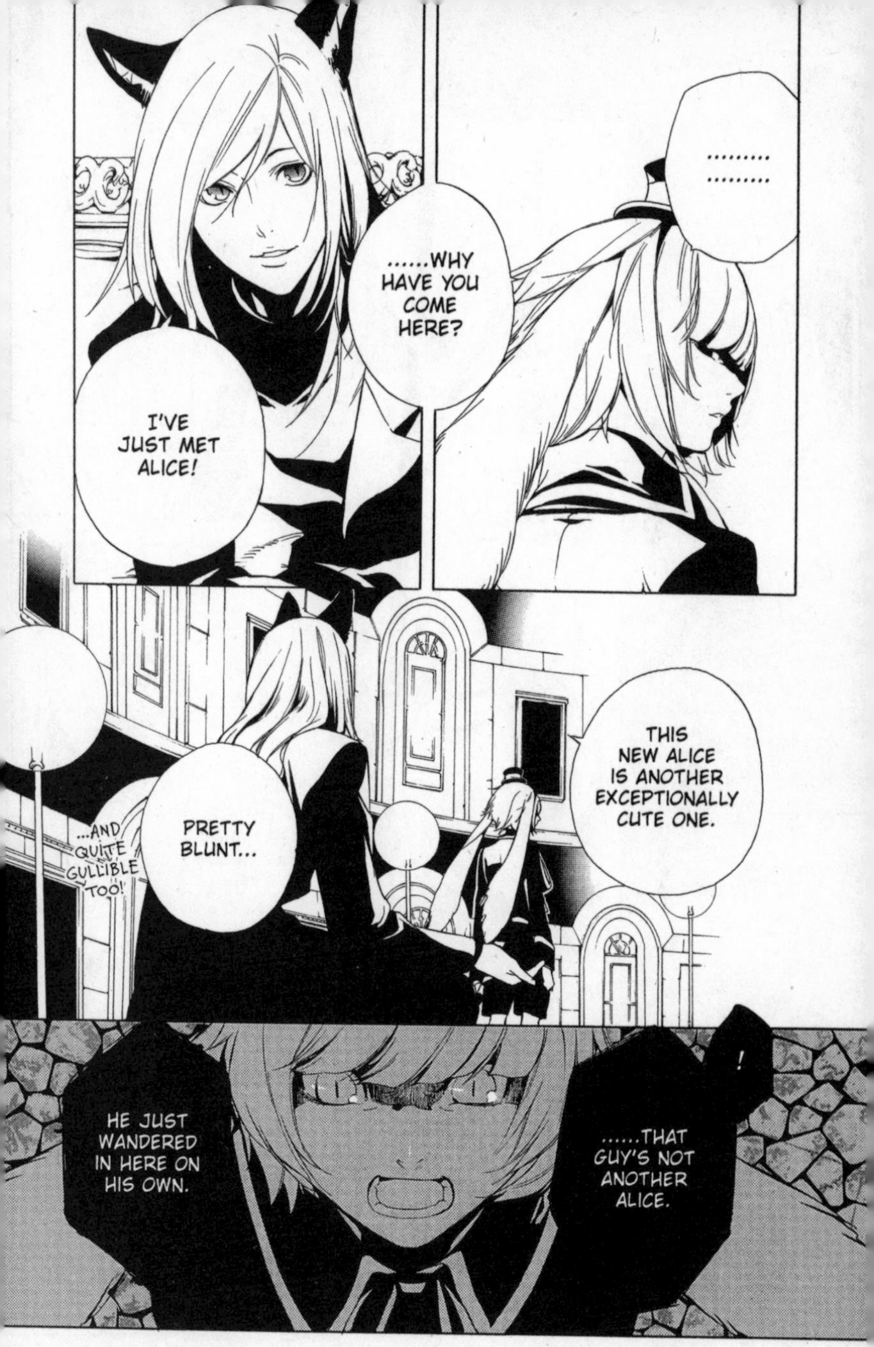

....
....
......WHY HAVE YOU COME HERE?
I'VE JUST MET ALICE!
THIS NEW ALICE IS ANOTHER EXCEPTIONALLY CUTE ONE.
PRETTY BLUNT...
...AND QUITE GULLIBLE TOO!
!
......THAT GUY'S NOT ANOTHER ALICE.
HE JUST WANDERED IN HERE ON HIS OWN.

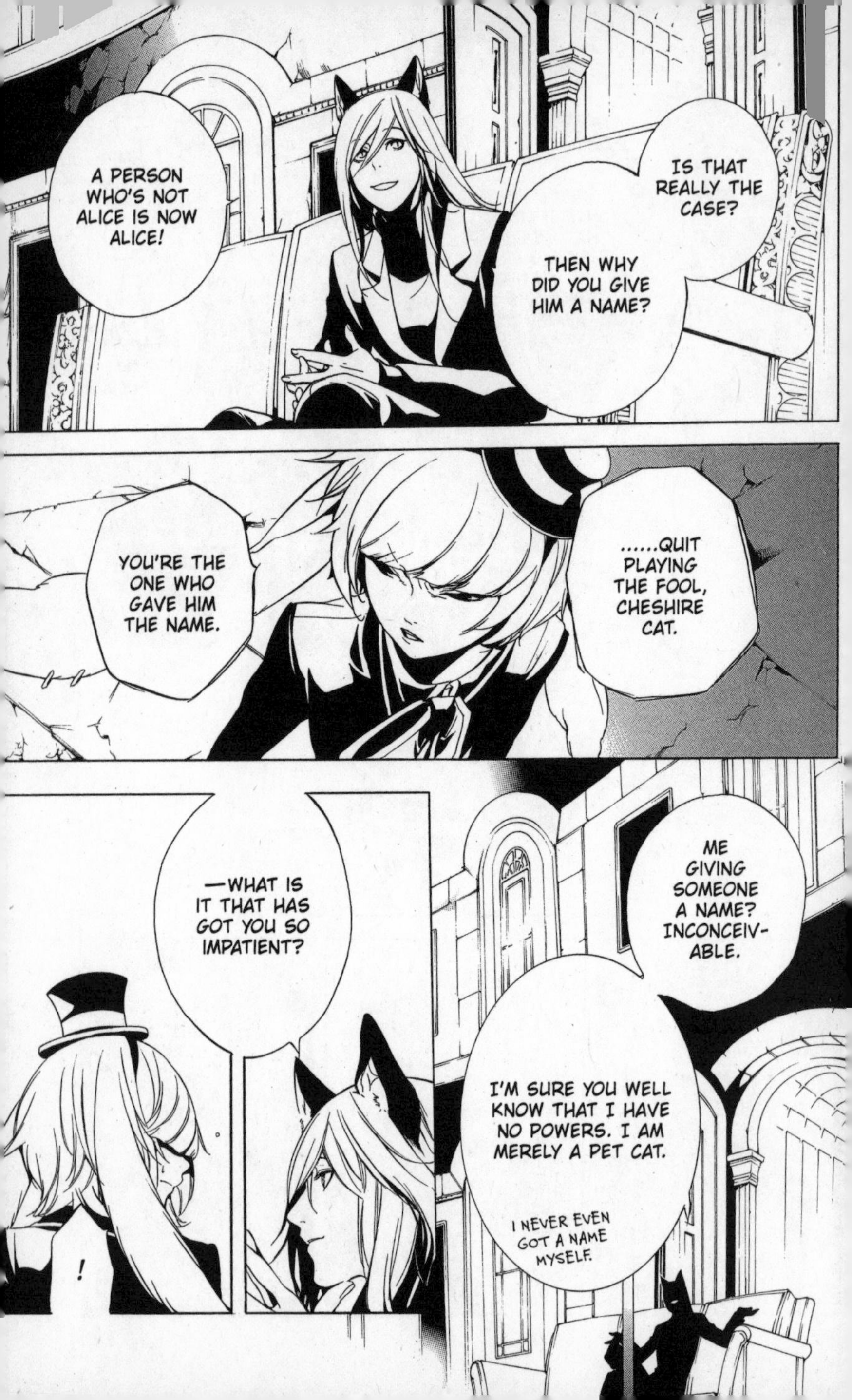
IS THAT REALLY THE CASE?
THEN WHY DID YOU GIVE HIM A NAME?
A PERSON WHO'S NOT ALICE IS NOW ALICE!
......QUIT PLAYING THE FOOL, CHESHIRE CAT.
YOU'RE THE ONE WHO GAVE HIM THE NAME.
ME GIVING SOMEONE A NAME? INCONCEIV-ABLE.
I'M SURE YOU WELL KNOW THAT I HAVE NO POWERS. I AM MERELY A PET CAT.
I NEVER EVEN GOT A NAME MYSELF.
—WHAT IS IT THAT HAS GOT YOU SO IMPATIENT?
!

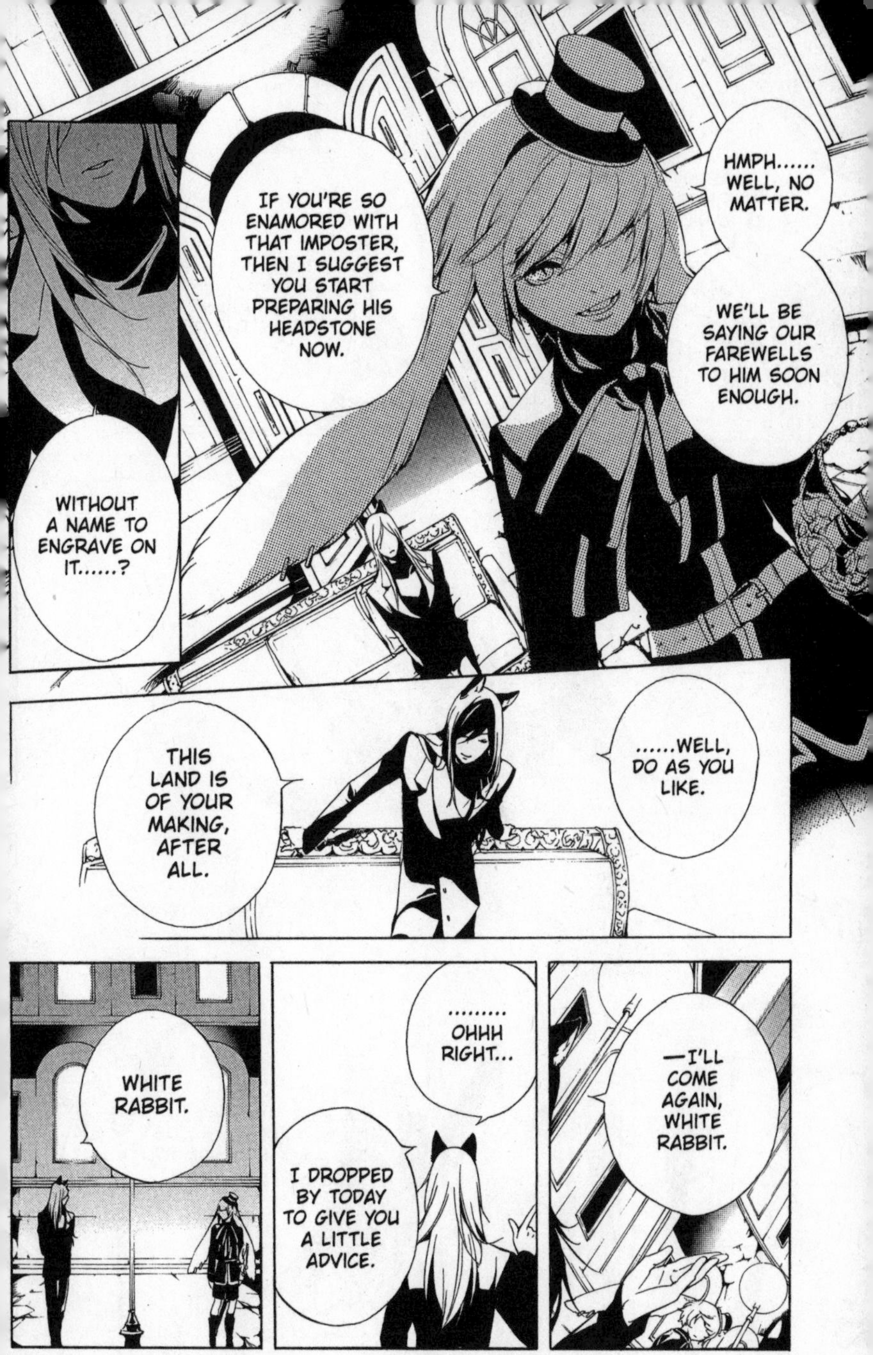
HMPH...... WELL, NO MATTER.
WE'LL BE SAYING OUR FAREWELLS TO HIM SOON ENOUGH.
IF YOU'RE SO ENAMORED WITH THAT IMPOSTER, THEN I SUGGEST YOU START PREPARING HIS HEADSTONE NOW.
WITHOUT A NAME TO ENGRAVE ON IT......?
......WELL, DO AS YOU LIKE.
THIS LAND IS OF YOUR MAKING, AFTER ALL.
—I'LL COME AGAIN, WHITE RABBIT.
.... OHHH RIGHT...
I DROPPED BY TODAY TO GIVE YOU A LITTLE ADVICE.
WHITE RABBIT.

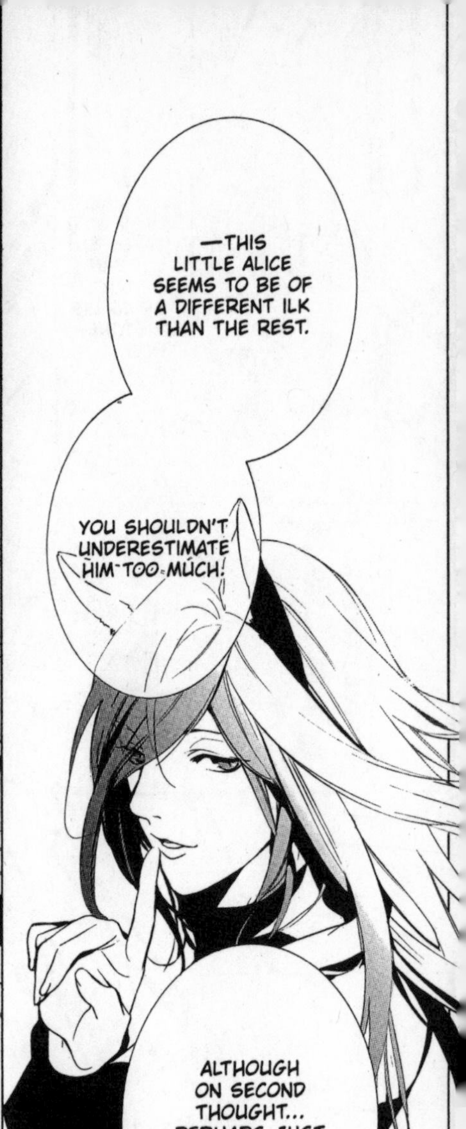
—THIS LITTLE ALICE SEEMS TO BE OF A DIFFERENT ILK THAN THE REST.
YOU SHOULDN'T UNDERESTIMATE HIM TOO MUCH!
ALTHOUGH ON SECOND THOUGHT... PERHAPS JUST THIS ONCE YOU SHOULD?
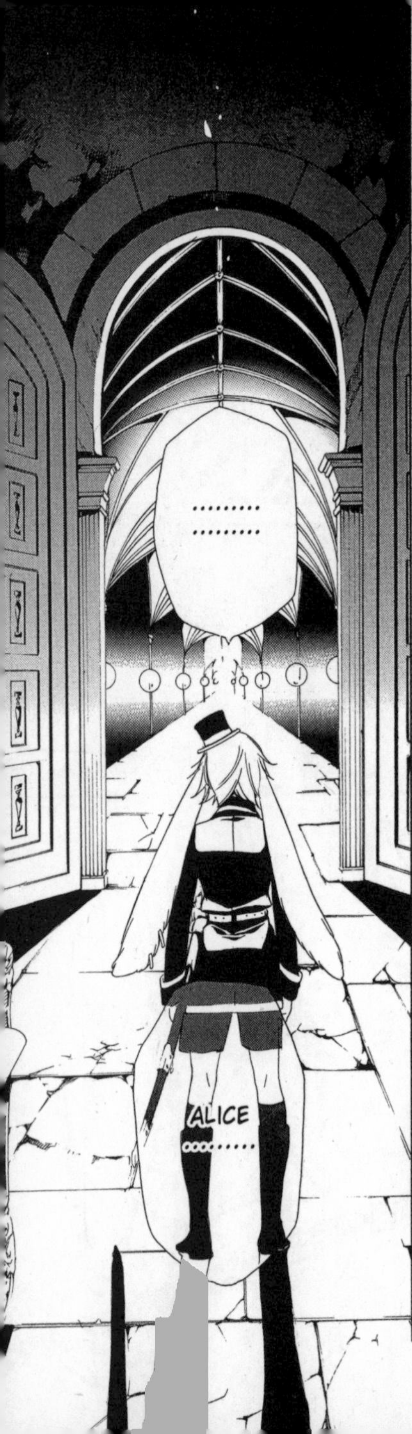
....
....
ALICE ....

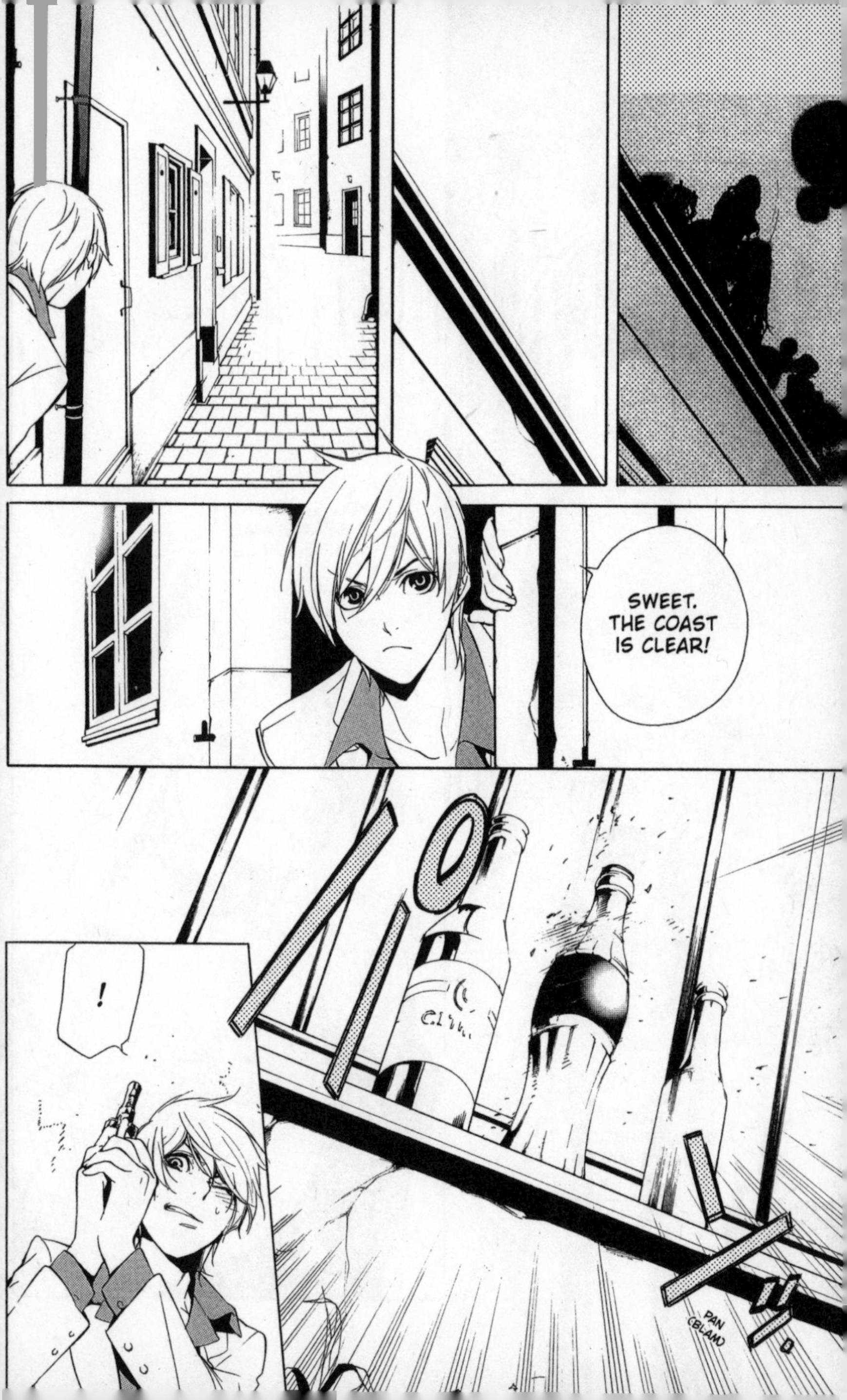
SWEET. THE COAST IS CLEAR!
!
PAN
(BLAM)

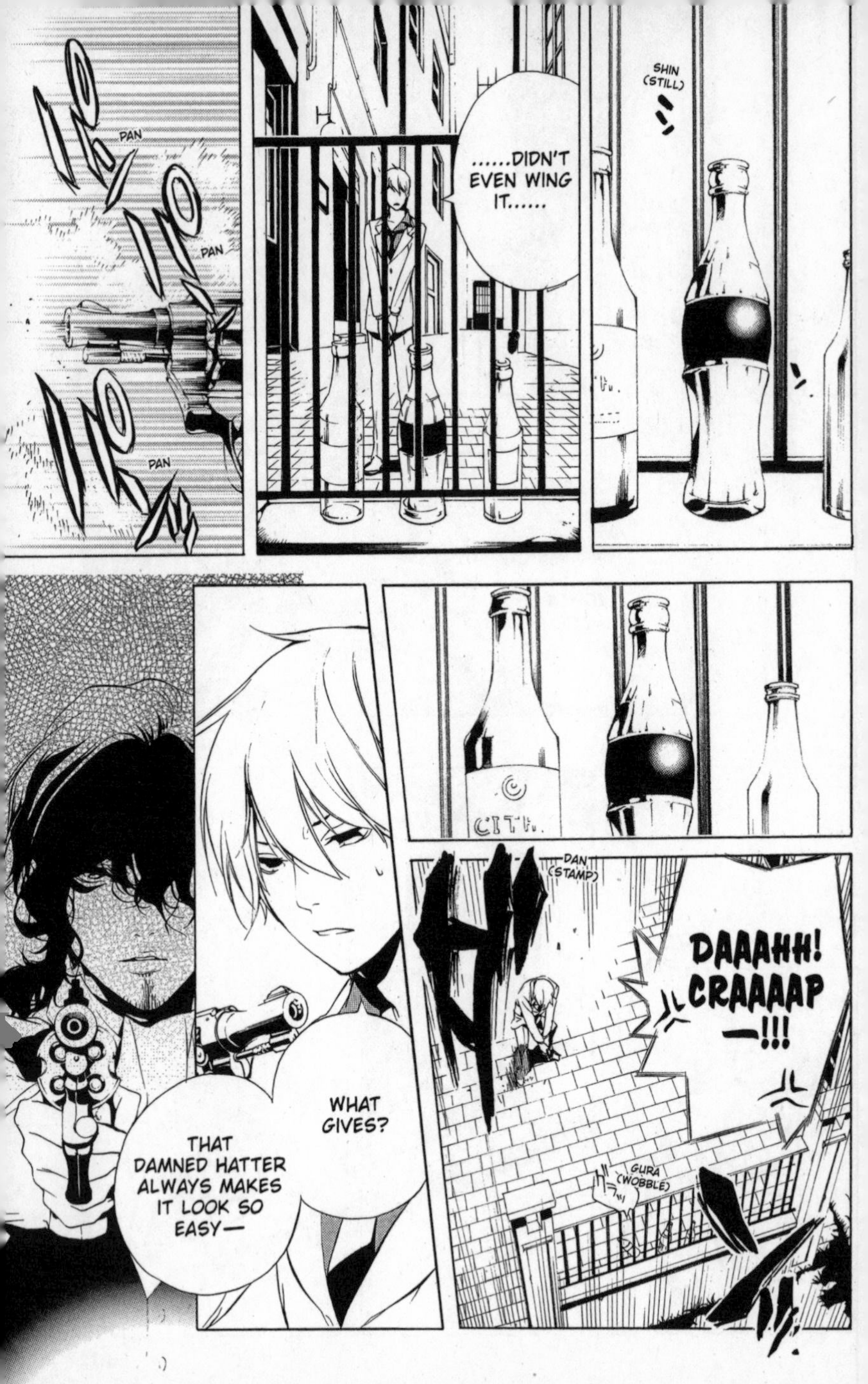
SHIN (STILL)
......DIDN'T EVEN WING IT......
PAN
PAN
PAN
DAN (STAMP)
DAAAHH! CRAAAAP—!!!
GURA (WOBBLE)
WHAT GIVES?
THAT DAMNED HATTER ALWAYS MAKES IT LOOK SO EASY—

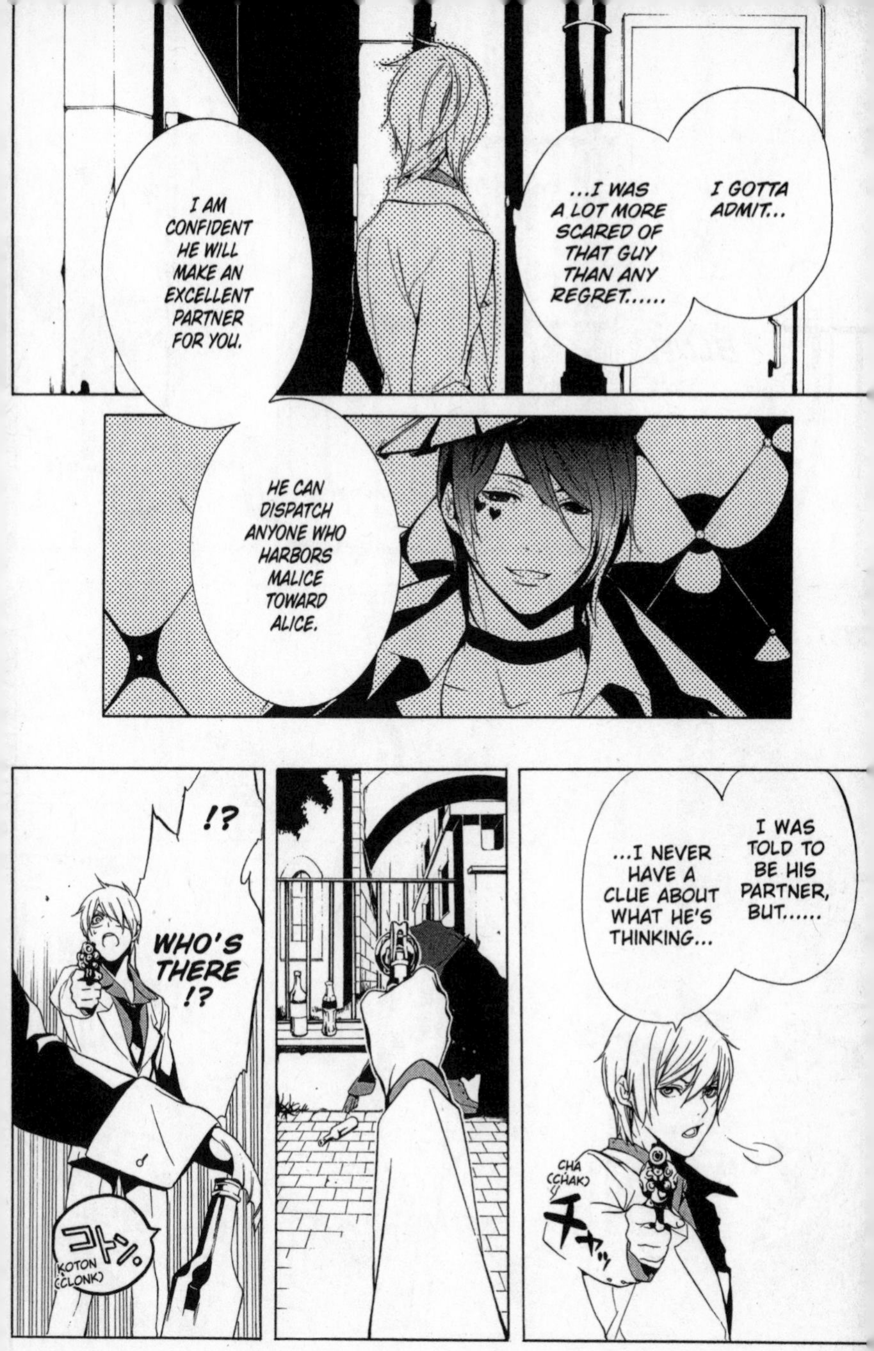

I GOTTA ADMIT...
...I WAS A LOT MORE SCARED OF THAT GUY THAN ANY REGRET......
I AM CONFIDENT HE WILL MAKE AN EXCELLENT PARTNER FOR YOU.
HE CAN DISPATCH ANYONE WHO HARBORS MALICE TOWARD ALICE.
I WAS TOLD TO BE HIS PARTNER, BUT......
...I NEVER HAVE A CLUE ABOUT WHAT HE'S THINKING...
チャッ
CHA (CHAK)
!?
WHO'S THERE !?
コトン。
KOTON (CLONK)

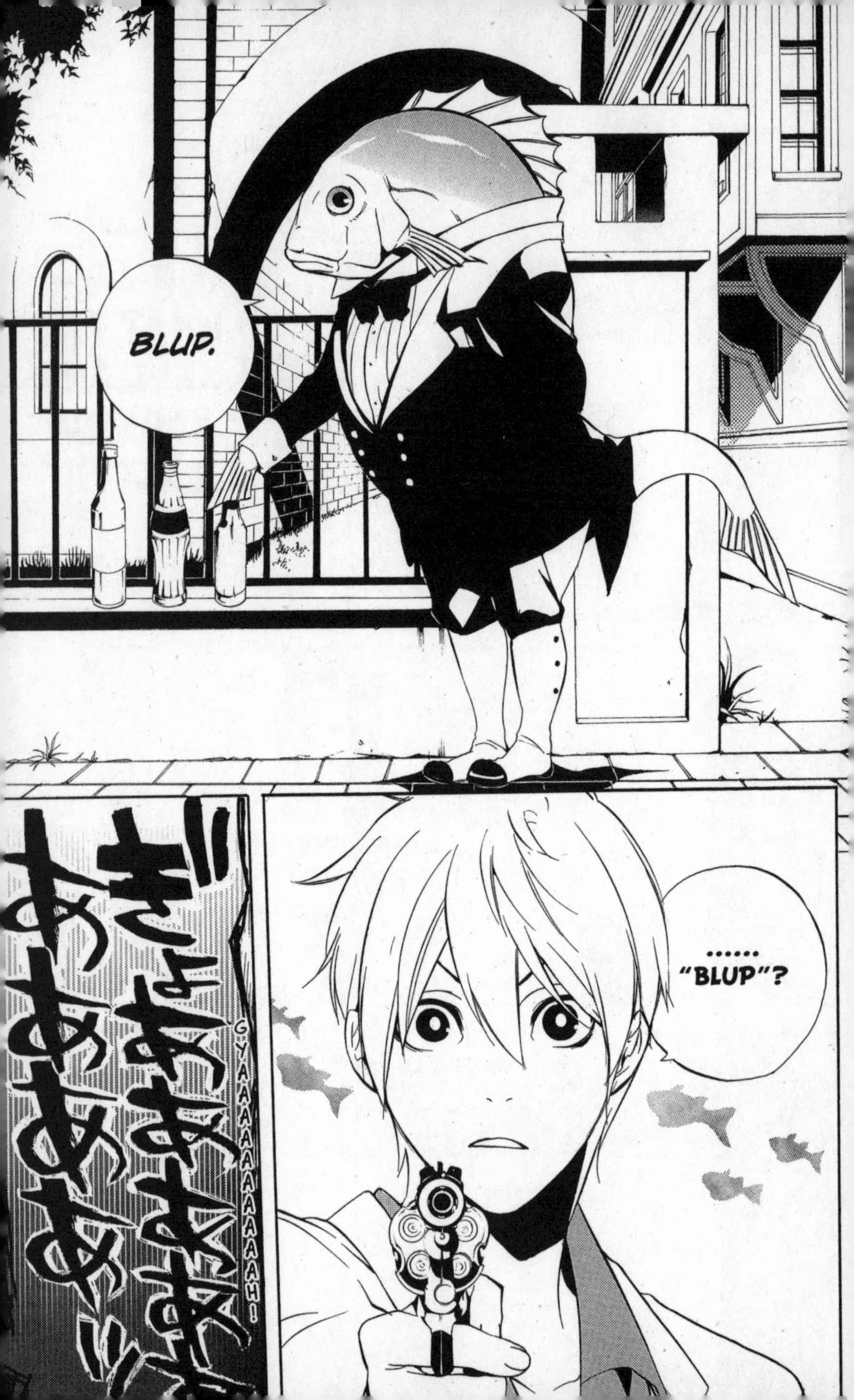
BLUP.
......"BLUP"?
GYAAAAAAAAAAH!

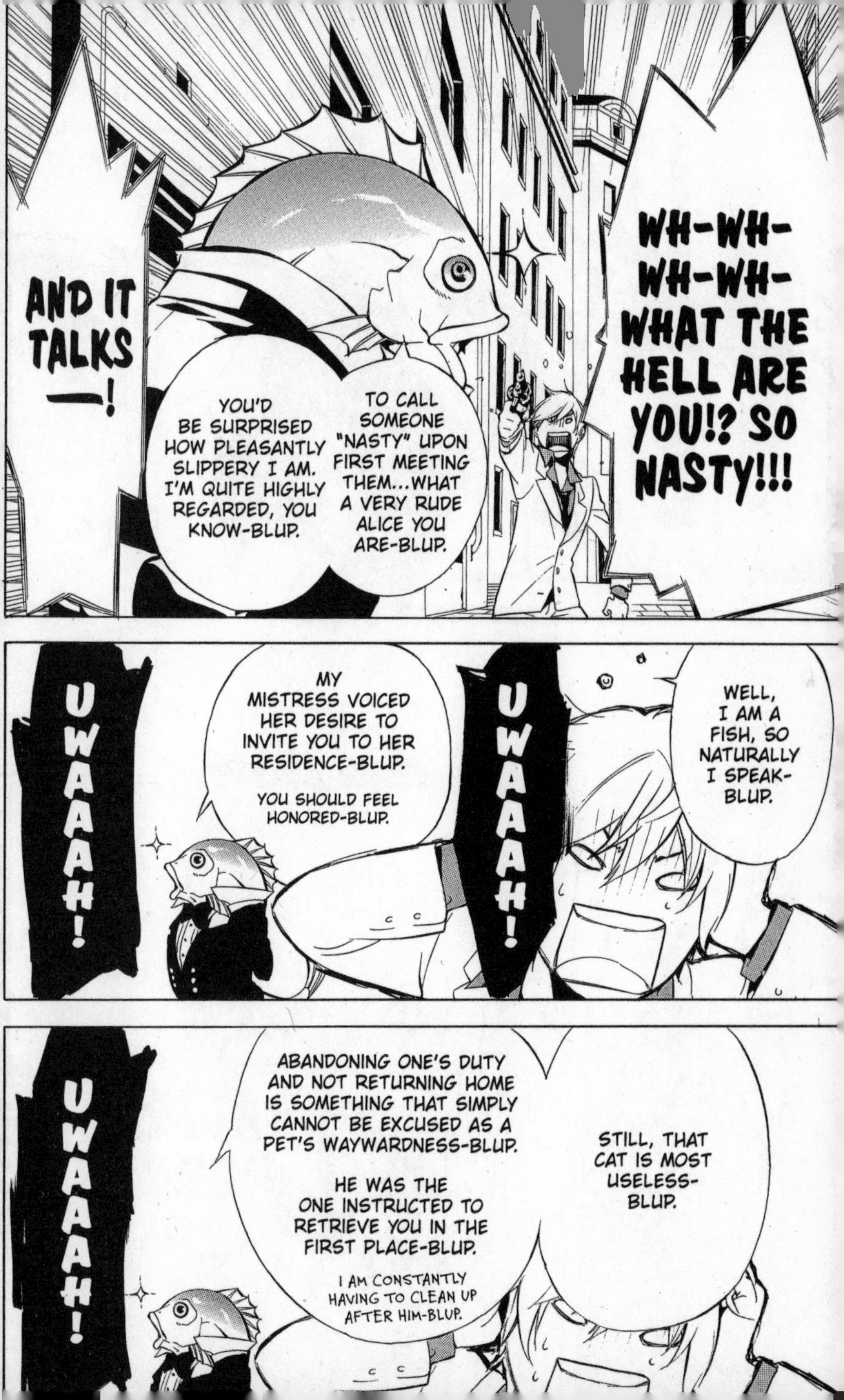
WH-WH-WH-WH-WHAT THE HELL ARE YOU!? SO NASTY!!!
TO CALL SOMEONE "NASTY" UPON FIRST MEETING THEM...WHAT A VERY RUDE ALICE YOU ARE-BLUP.
YOU'D BE SURPRISED HOW PLEASANTLY SLIPPERY I AM. I'M QUITE HIGHLY REGARDED, YOU KNOW-BLUP.
AND IT TALKS—!
WELL, I AM A FISH, SO NATURALLY I SPEAK-BLUP.
UWAAAAH!
MY MISTRESS VOICED HER DESIRE TO INVITE YOU TO HER RESIDENCE-BLUP.
YOU SHOULD FEEL HONORED-BLUP.
UWAAAAH!
STILL, THAT CAT IS MOST USELESS-BLUP.
ABANDONING ONE'S DUTY AND NOT RETURNING HOME IS SOMETHING THAT SIMPLY CANNOT BE EXCUSED AS A PET'S WAYWARDNESS-BLUP.
HE WAS THE ONE INSTRUCTED TO RETRIEVE YOU IN THE FIRST PLACE-BLUP.
I AM CONSTANTLY HAVING TO CLEAN UP AFTER HIM-BLUP.
UWAAAAH!

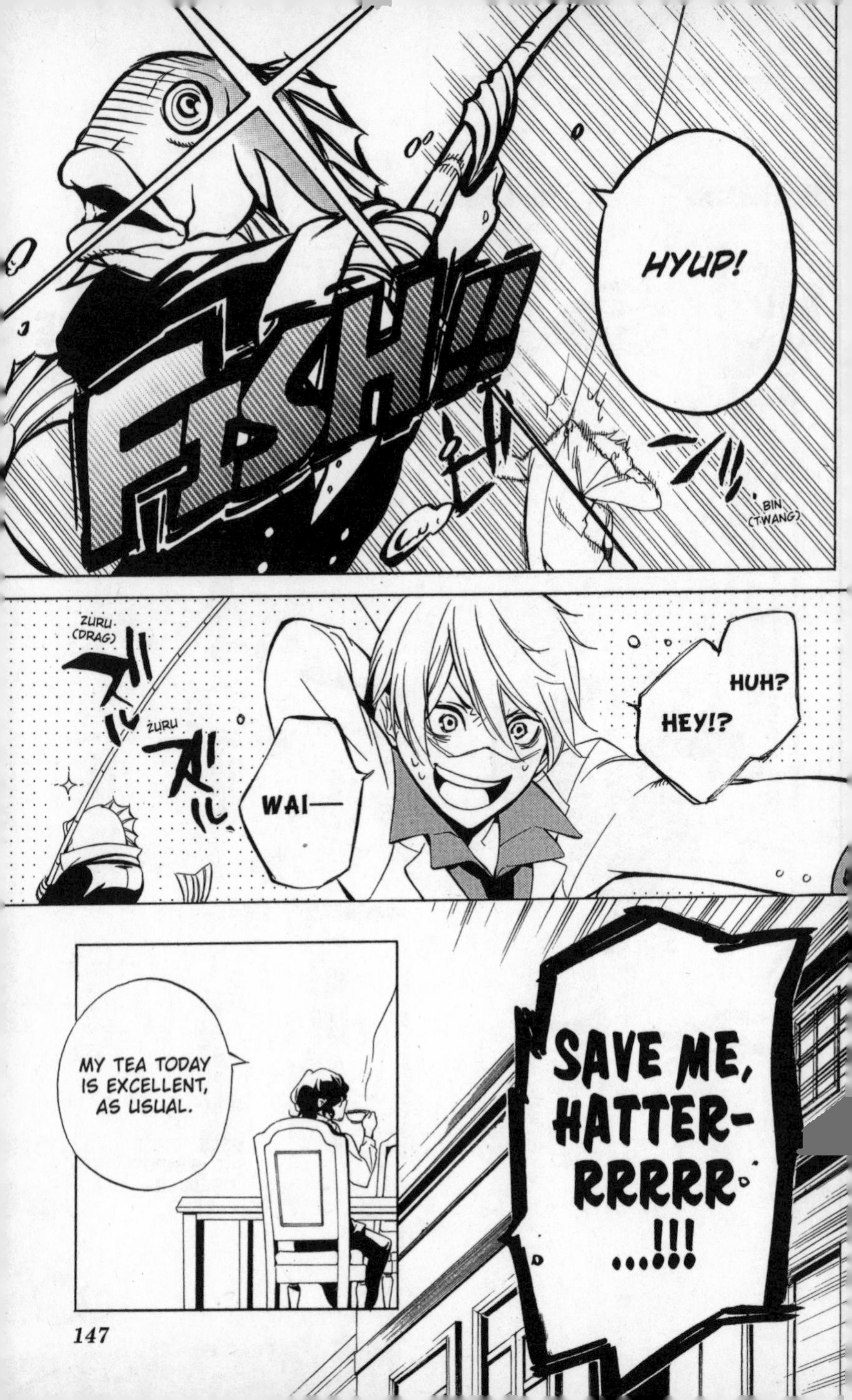
HYUP!
FSH!!
BIN (T-WANG)
HUH?
HEY!?
WAI—
ZURU (DRAG)
ZURU
SAVE ME, HATTER-RRRRR ...!!!
MY TEA TODAY IS EXCELLENT, AS USUAL.

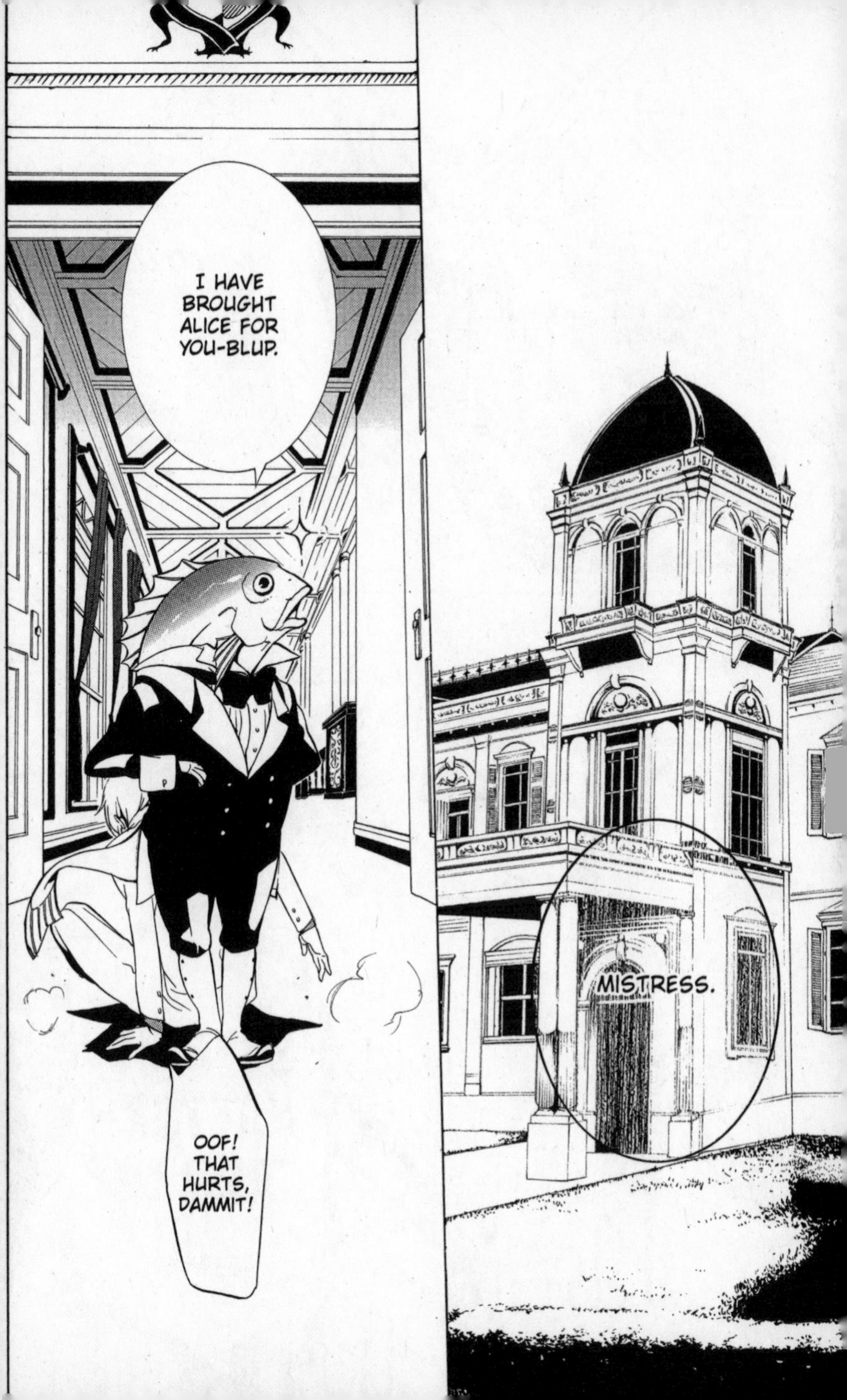
MISTRESS.
I HAVE BROUGHT ALICE FOR YOU-BLUP.
OOF! THAT HURTS, DAMMIT!

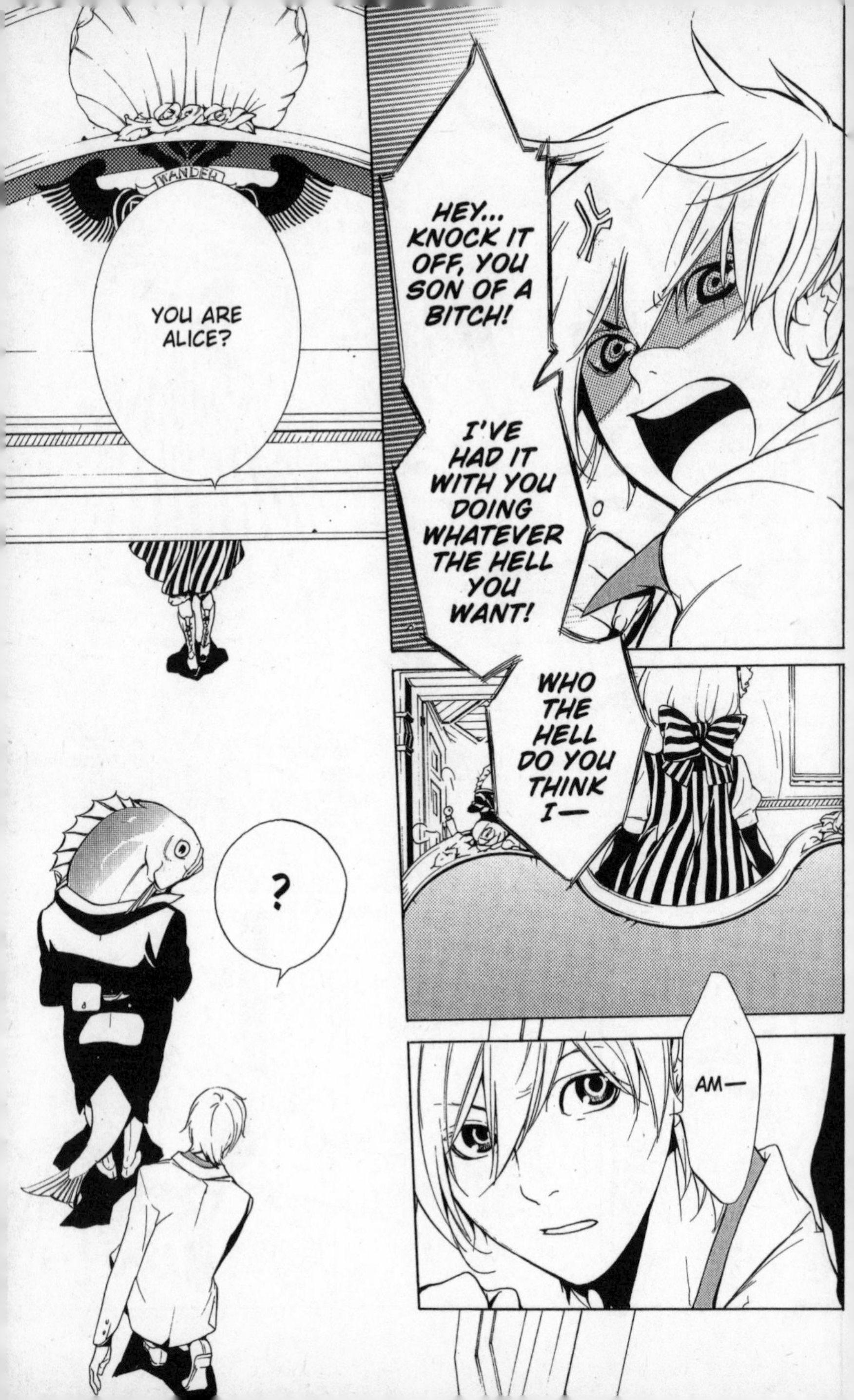
HEY... KNOCK IT OFF, YOU SON OF A BITCH!
I'VE HAD IT WITH YOU DOING WHATEVER THE HELL YOU WANT!
WHO THE HELL DO YOU THINK I—
AM—
WANDER
YOU ARE ALICE?
?

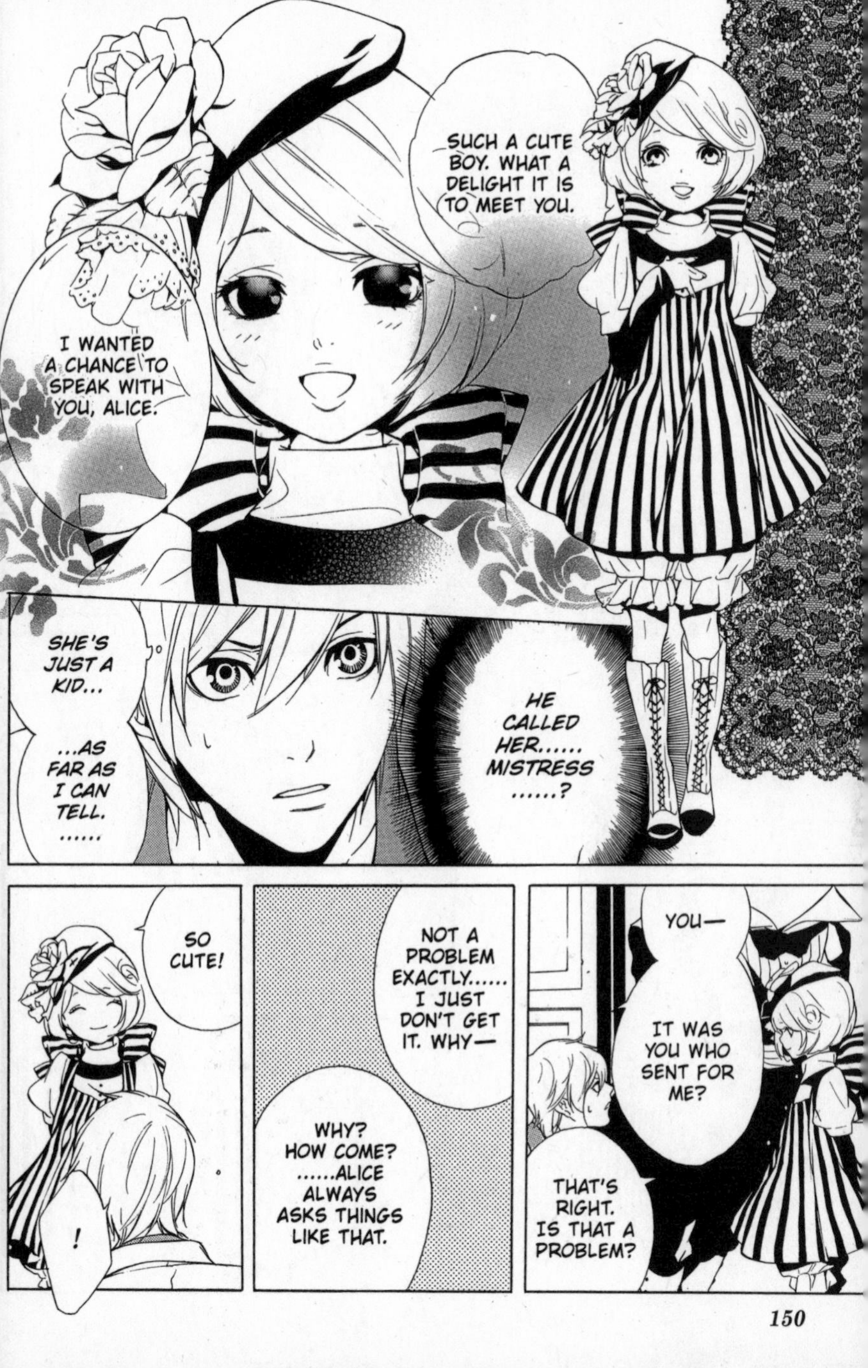
SUCH A CUTE BOY. WHAT A DELIGHT IT IS TO MEET YOU.
I WANTED A CHANCE TO SPEAK WITH YOU, ALICE.
HE CALLED HER...... MISTRESS......?
SHE'S JUST A KID...
...AS FAR AS I CAN TELL. ......
YOU—
IT WAS YOU WHO SENT FOR ME?
THAT'S RIGHT. IS THAT A PROBLEM?
NOT A PROBLEM EXACTLY...... I JUST DON'T GET IT. WHY—
WHY? HOW COME? ......ALICE ALWAYS ASKS THINGS LIKE THAT.
SO CUTE!
!

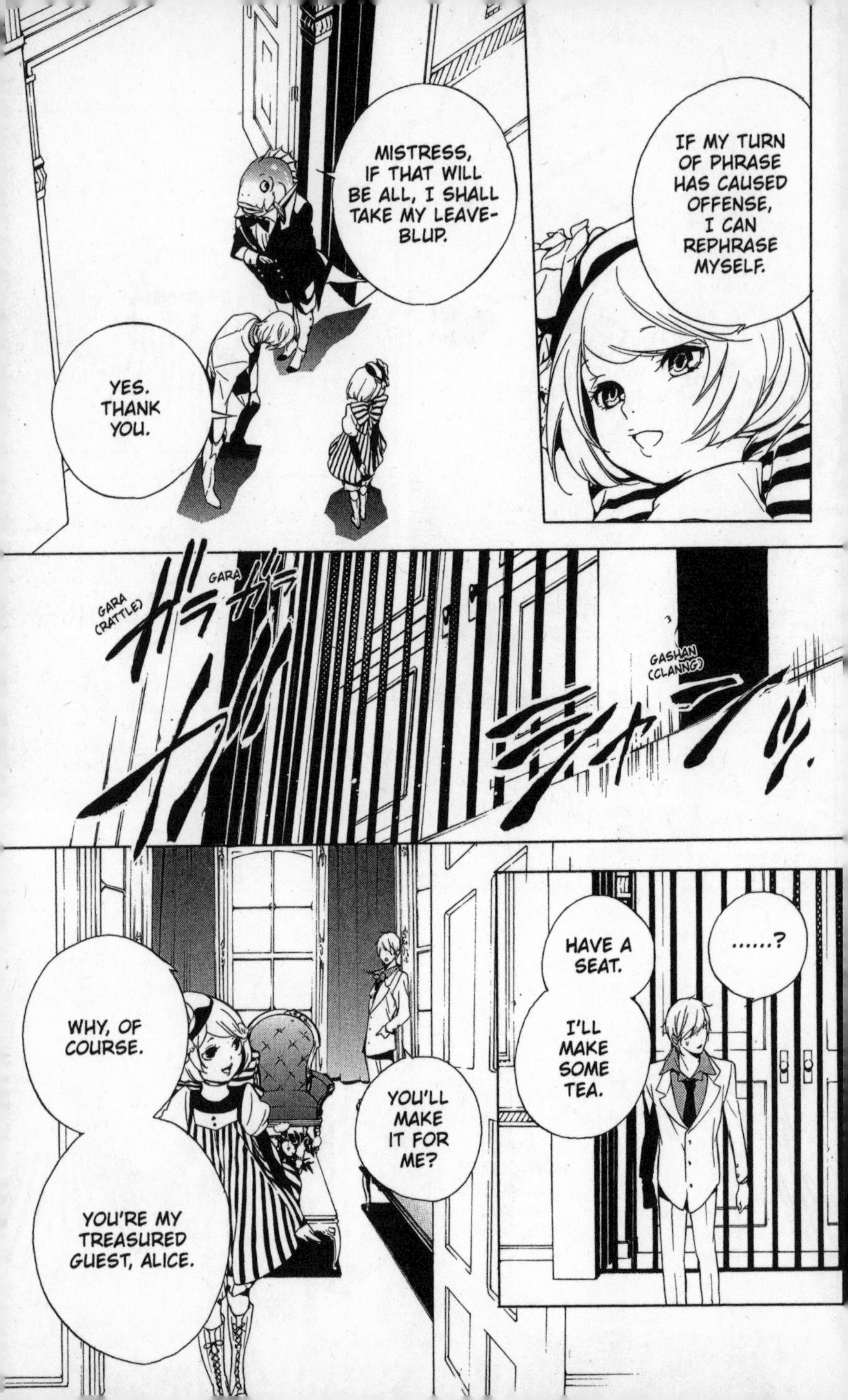
IF MY TURN OF PHRASE HAS CAUSED OFFENSE, I CAN REPHRASE MYSELF.
MISTRESS, IF THAT WILL BE ALL, I SHALL TAKE MY LEAVE-BLUP.
YES. THANK YOU.
GASHAN (CLANNG)
GARA
GARA (RATTLE)
......?
HAVE A SEAT.
I'LL MAKE SOME TEA.
YOU'LL MAKE IT FOR ME?
WHY, OF COURSE.
YOU'RE MY TREASURED GUEST, ALICE.

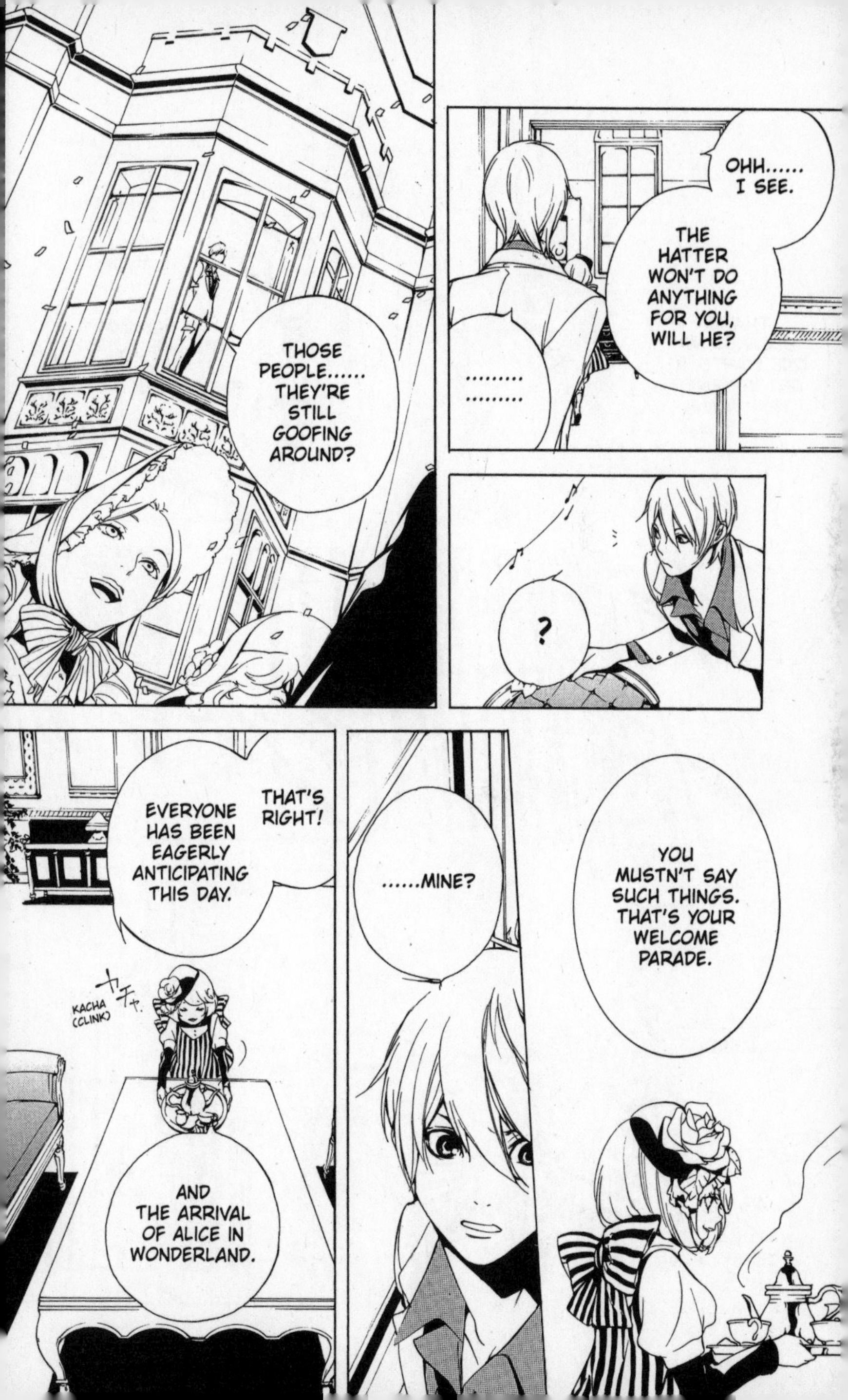
OHH...... I SEE.
THE HATTER WON'T DO ANYTHING FOR YOU, WILL HE?
....
?
THOSE PEOPLE...... THEY'RE STILL GOOFING AROUND?
YOU MUSTN'T SAY SUCH THINGS. THAT'S YOUR WELCOME PARADE.
......MINE?
THAT'S RIGHT!
EVERYONE HAS BEEN EAGERLY ANTICIPATING THIS DAY.
KACHA (CLINK)
AND THE ARRIVAL OF ALICE IN WONDERLAND.

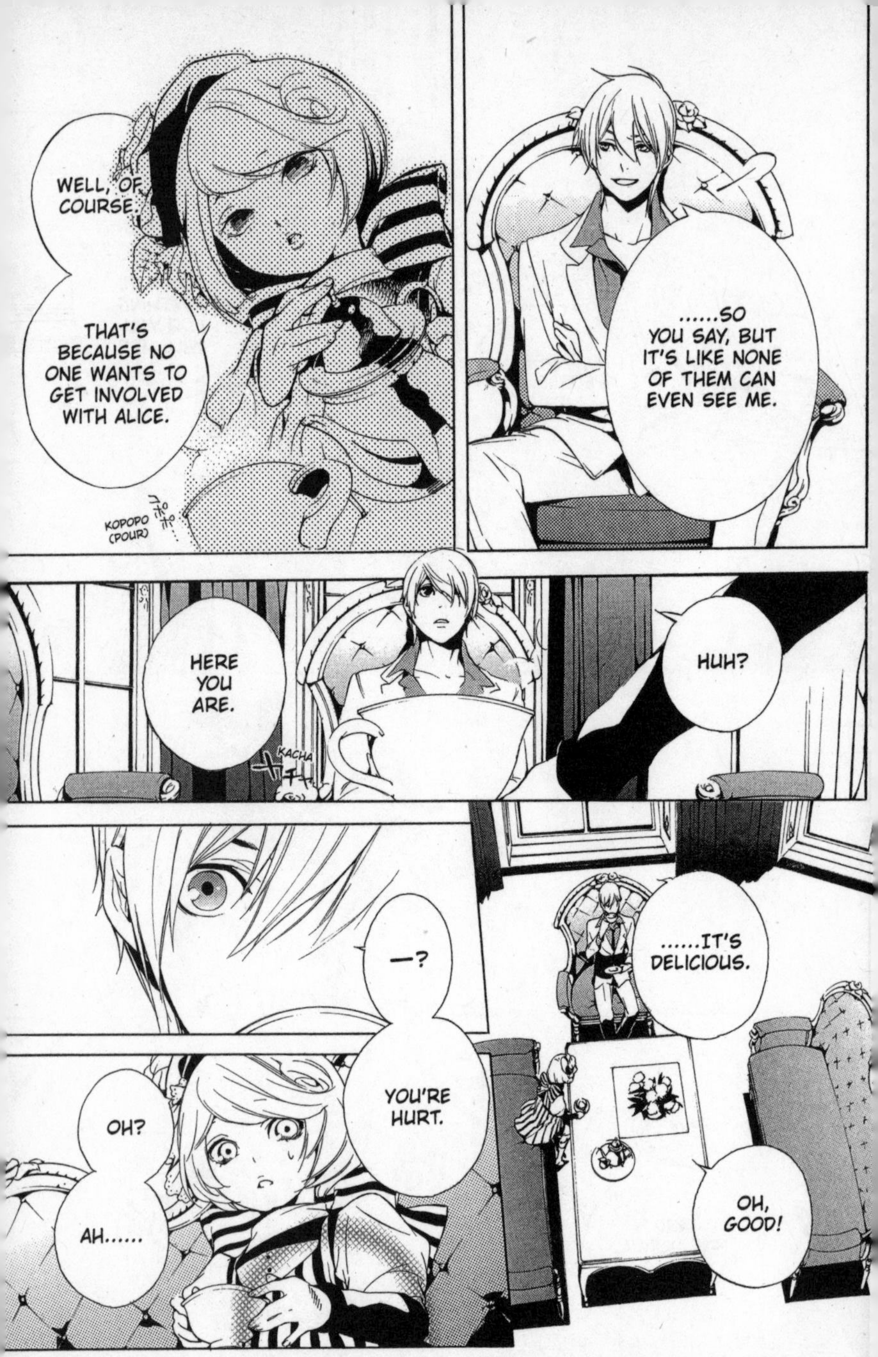
......SO YOU SAY, BUT IT'S LIKE NONE OF THEM CAN EVEN SEE ME.
WELL, OF COURSE.
THAT'S BECAUSE NO ONE WANTS TO GET INVOLVED WITH ALICE.
KOPOPO (POUR)
HUH?
HERE YOU ARE.
KACHA
......IT'S DELICIOUS.
OH, GOOD!
—?
YOU'RE HURT.
OH?
AH......

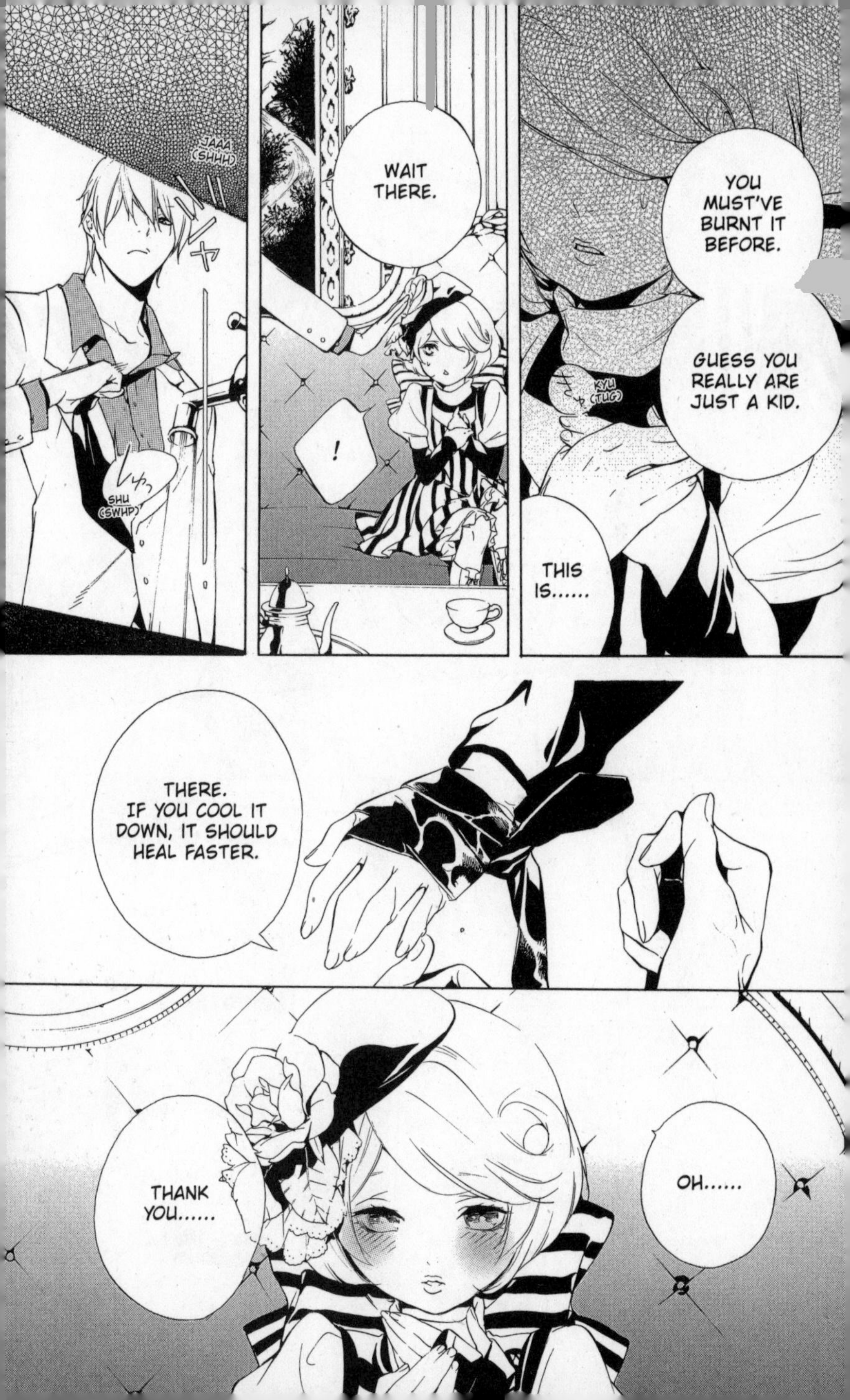
YOU MUST'VE BURNT IT BEFORE.
GUESS YOU REALLY ARE JUST A KID.
KYU (TUG)
THIS IS......
WAIT THERE.
!
JAAA (SHHH)
SHU (SWHP)
THERE. IF YOU COOL IT DOWN, IT SHOULD HEAL FASTER.
OH......
THANK YOU......

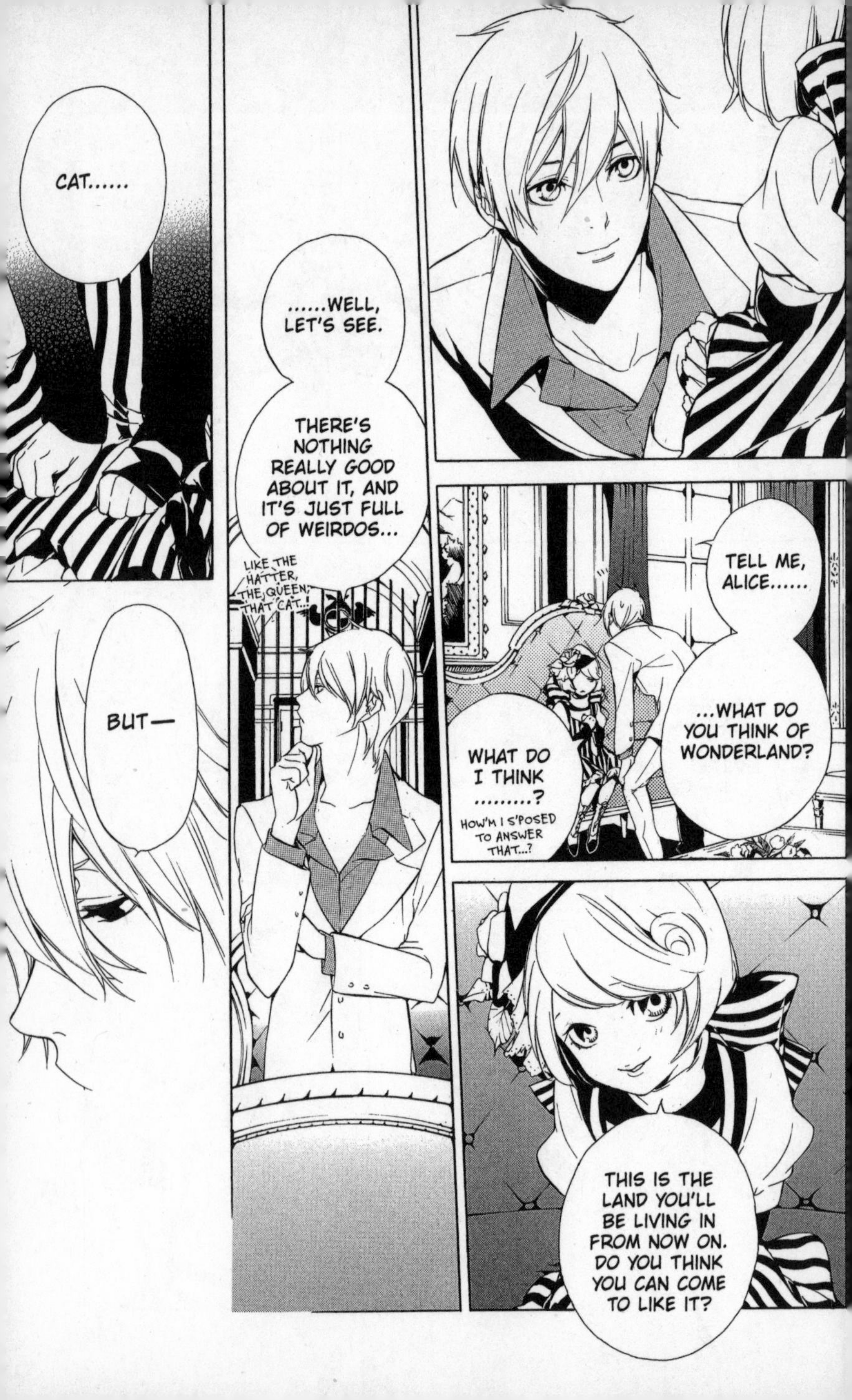
TELL ME, ALICE......
...WHAT DO YOU THINK OF WONDERLAND?
WHAT DO I THINK ....?
HOW'M I S'POSED TO ANSWER THAT...?
THIS IS THE LAND YOU'LL BE LIVING IN FROM NOW ON. DO YOU THINK YOU CAN COME TO LIKE IT?
......WELL, LET'S SEE.
THERE'S NOTHING REALLY GOOD ABOUT IT, AND IT'S JUST FULL OF WEIRDOS...
LIKE THE HATTER, THE QUEEN, THAT CAT...!
CAT......
BUT—

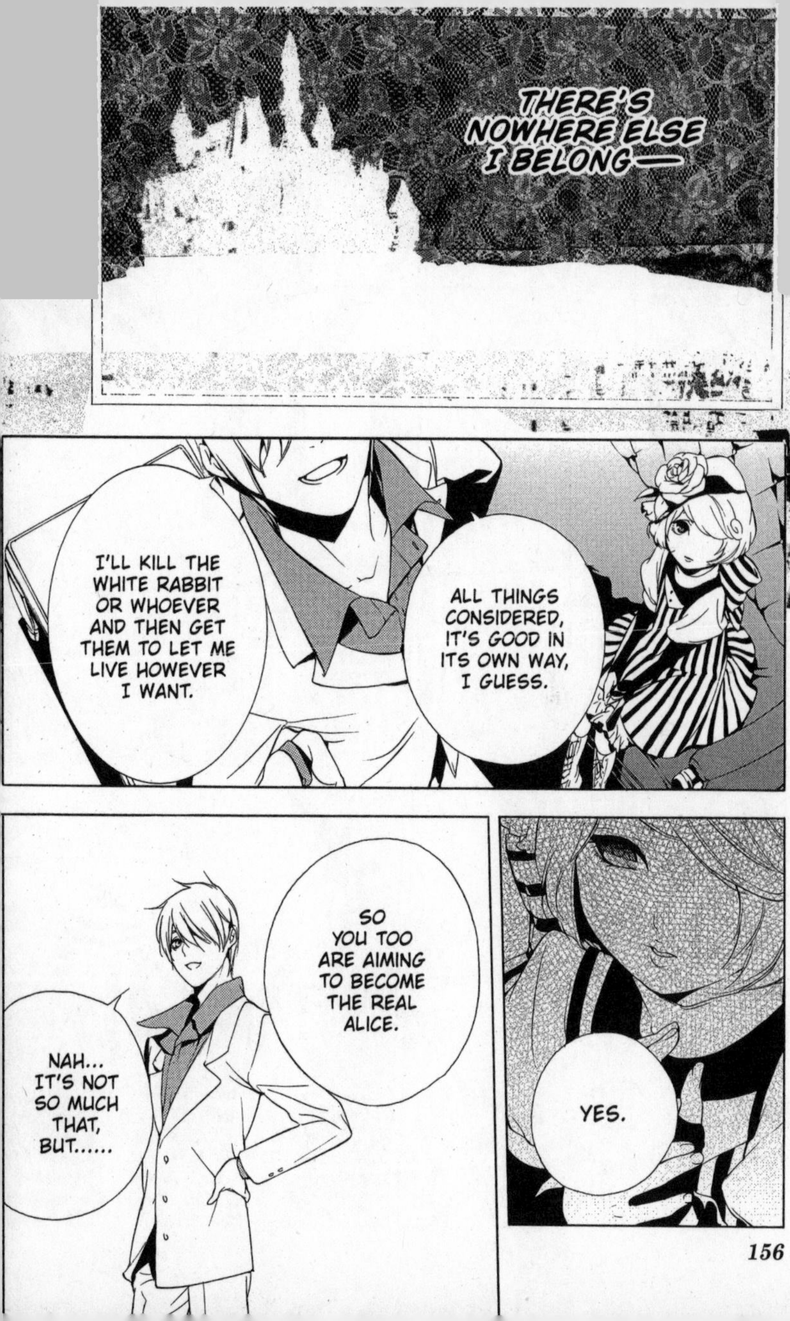
THERE'S NOWHERE ELSE I BELONG—
ALL THINGS CONSIDERED, IT'S GOOD IN ITS OWN WAY, I GUESS.
I'LL KILL THE WHITE RABBIT OR WHOEVER AND THEN GET THEM TO LET ME LIVE HOWEVER I WANT.
YES.
SO YOU TOO ARE AIMING TO BECOME THE REAL ALICE.
NAH... IT'S NOT SO MUCH THAT, BUT......

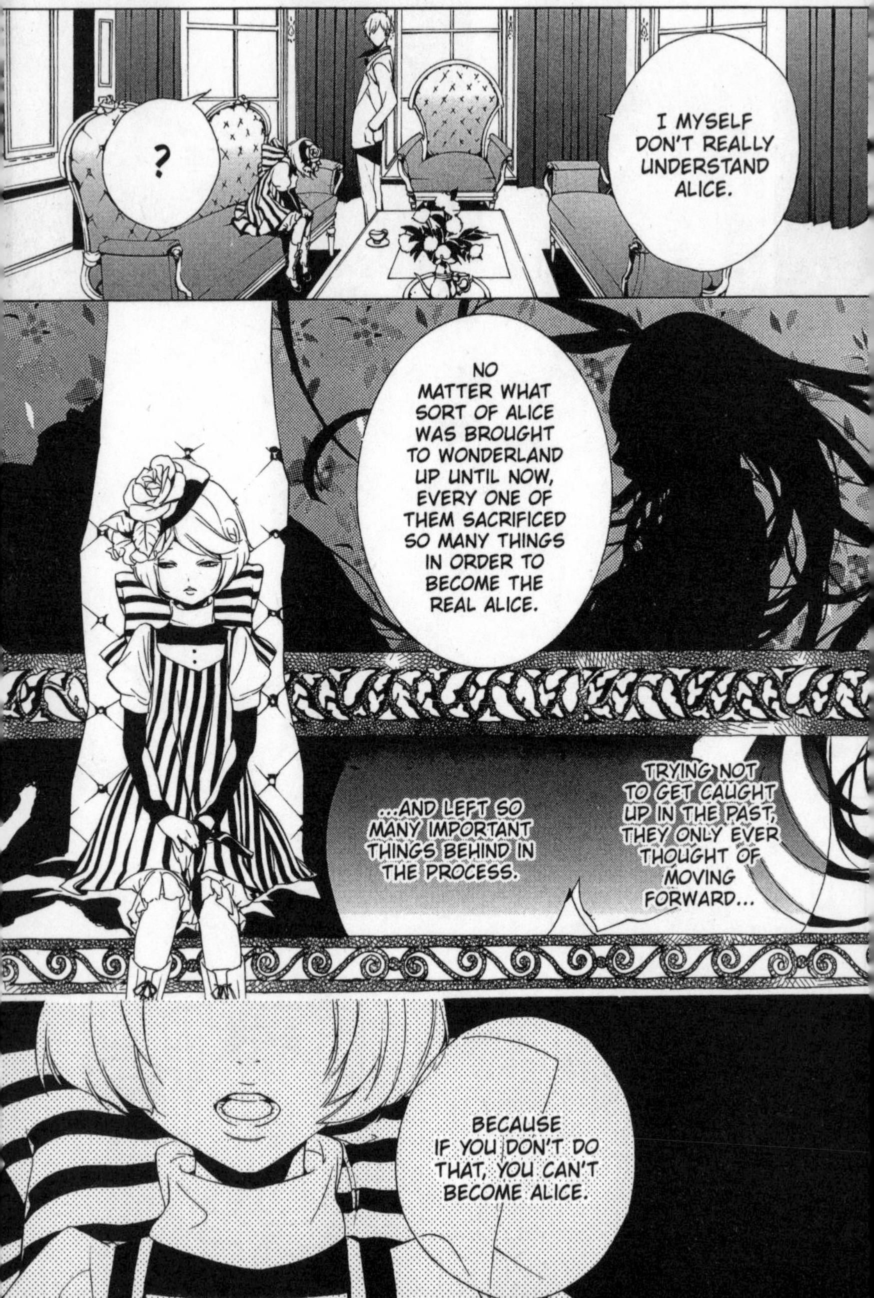
I MYSELF DON'T REALLY UNDERSTAND ALICE.
?
NO MATTER WHAT SORT OF ALICE WAS BROUGHT TO WONDERLAND UP UNTIL NOW, EVERY ONE OF THEM SACRIFICED SO MANY THINGS IN ORDER TO BECOME THE REAL ALICE.
TRYING NOT TO GET CAUGHT UP IN THE PAST, THEY ONLY EVER THOUGHT OF MOVING FORWARD...
...AND LEFT SO MANY IMPORTANT THINGS BEHIND IN THE PROCESS.
BECAUSE IF YOU DON'T DO THAT, YOU CAN'T BECOME ALICE.

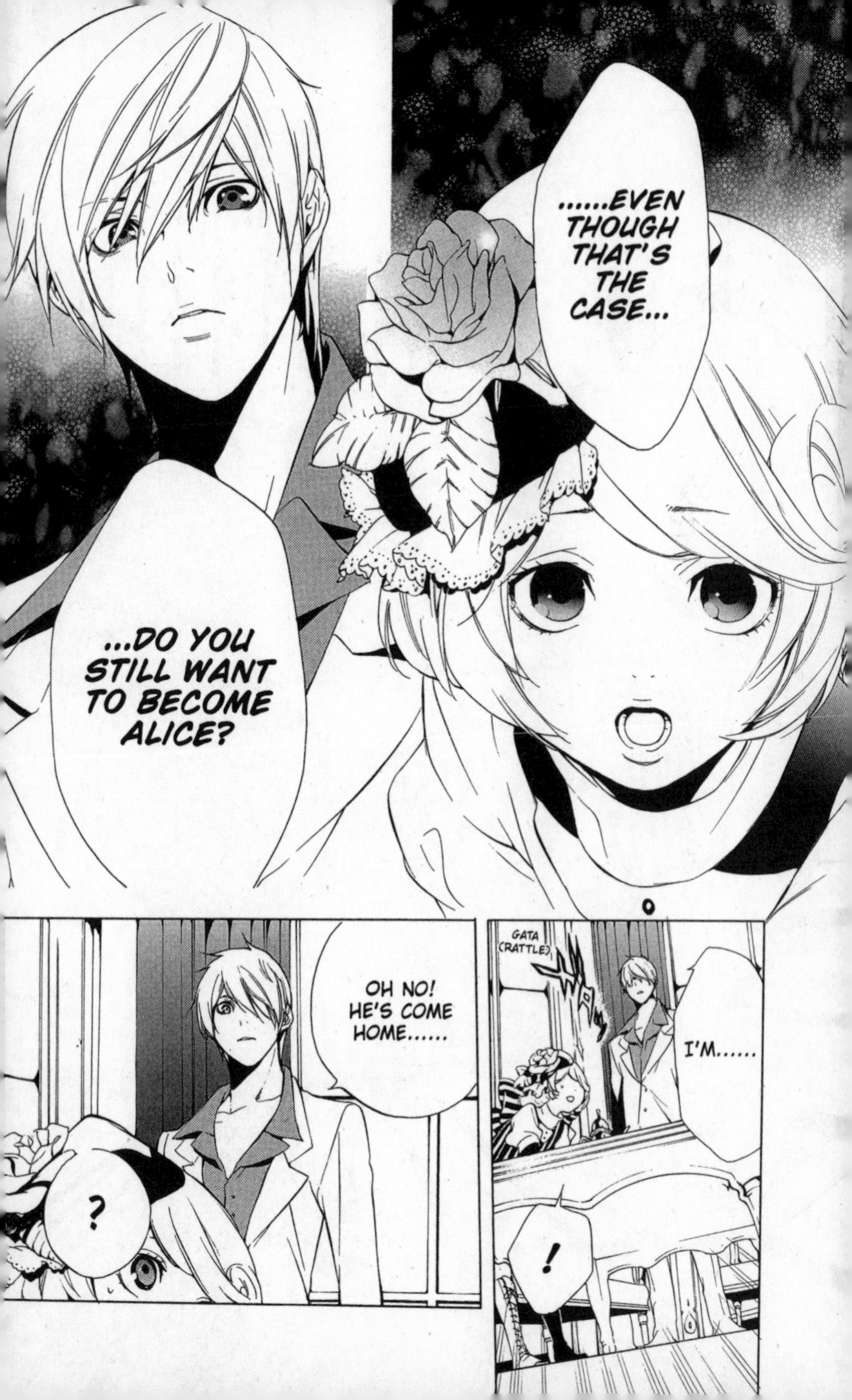
......EVEN THOUGH THAT'S THE CASE...
...DO YOU STILL WANT TO BECOME ALICE?
GATA (RATTLE)
I'M......
!
OH NO! HE'S COME HOME......
?

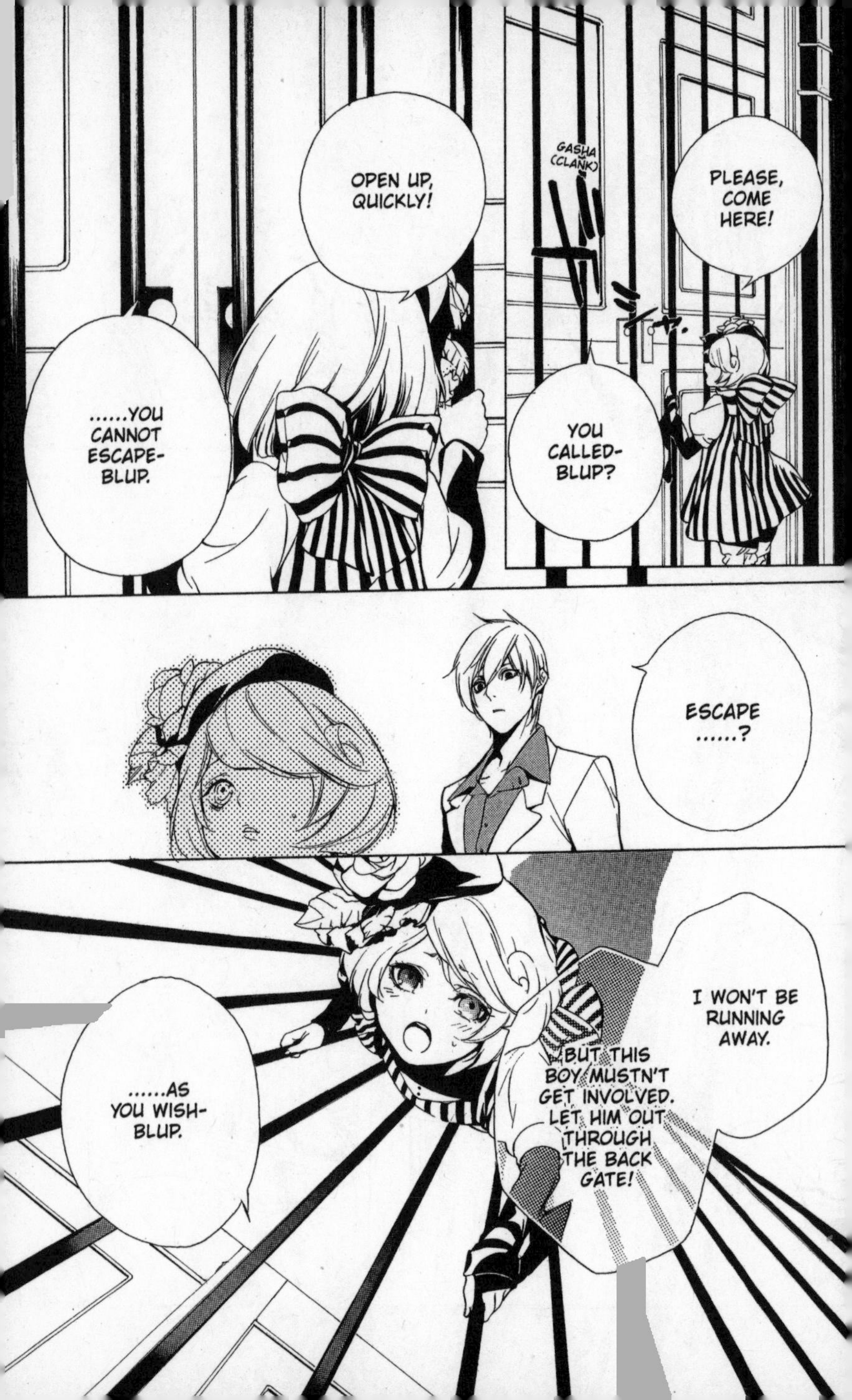
PLEASE, COME HERE!
GASHA (CLANK)
OPEN UP, QUICKLY!
YOU CALLED-BLUP?
......YOU CANNOT ESCAPE-BLUP.
ESCAPE ......?
I WON'T BE RUNNING AWAY.
BUT THIS BOY MUSTN'T GET INVOLVED. LET HIM OUT THROUGH THE BACK GATE!
......AS YOU WISH-BLUP.

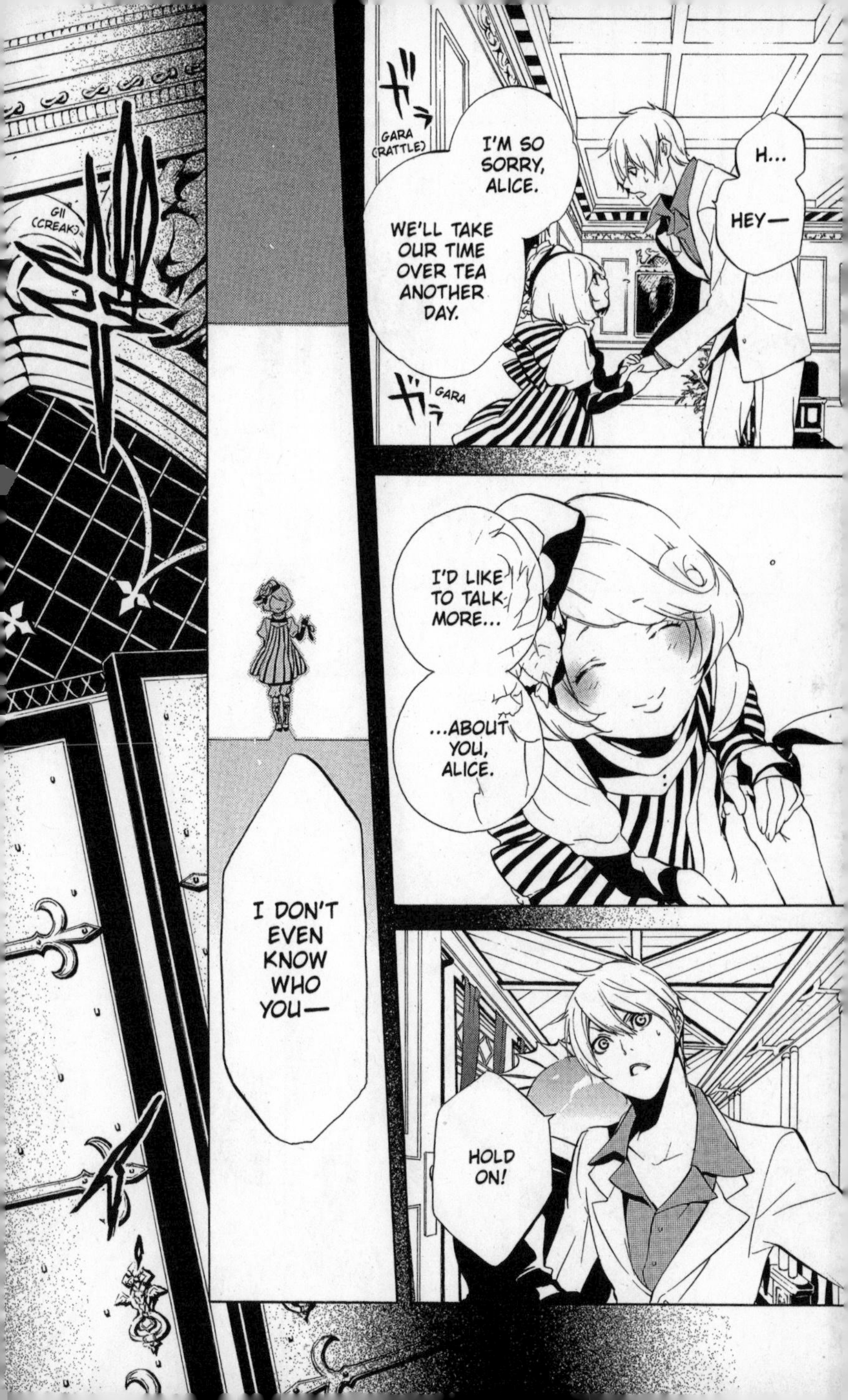
H...
HEY—
GARA (RATTLE)
I'M SO SORRY, ALICE.
WE'LL TAKE OUR TIME OVER TEA ANOTHER DAY.
GARA
I'D LIKE TO TALK MORE...
...ABOUT YOU, ALICE.
HOLD ON!
I DON'T EVEN KNOW WHO YOU—
GII (CREAK)

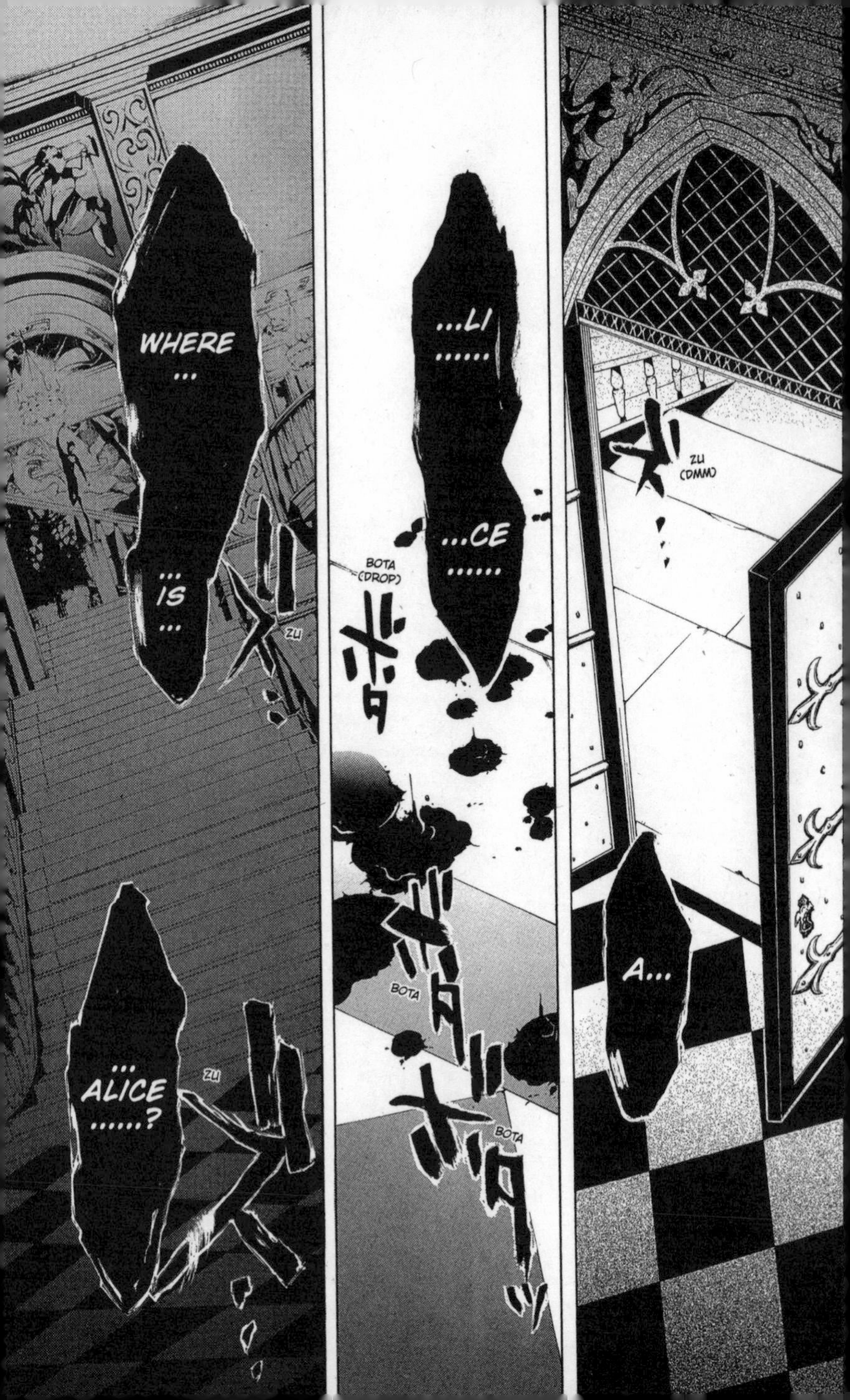
ZU (DMM)
A...
...LI ......
...CE ......
BOTA (DROP)
BOTA
BOTA
WHERE ...
... IS ...
ZU
... ALICE ......?
ZU

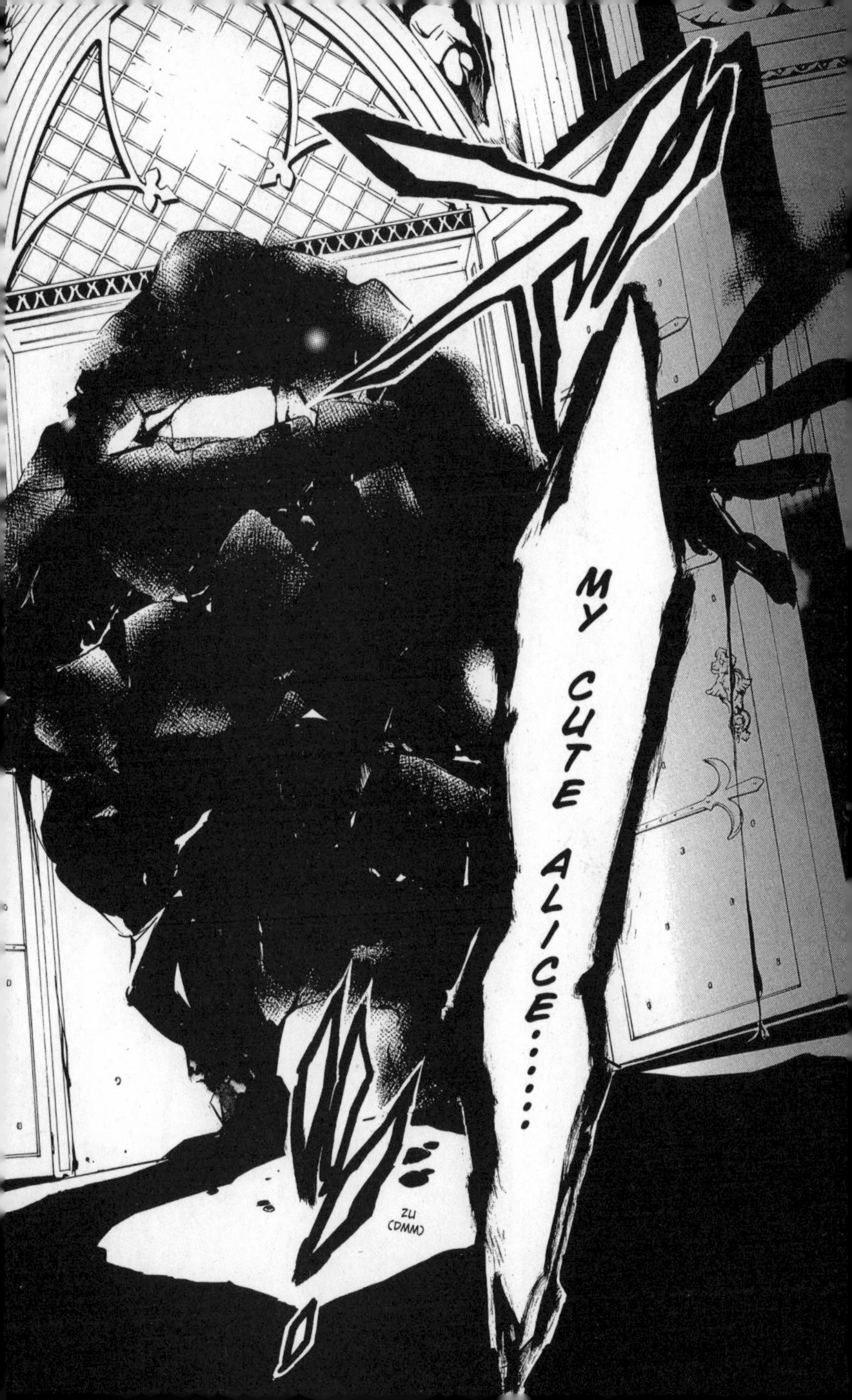
MY CUTE ALICE......
ZU
(DMM)

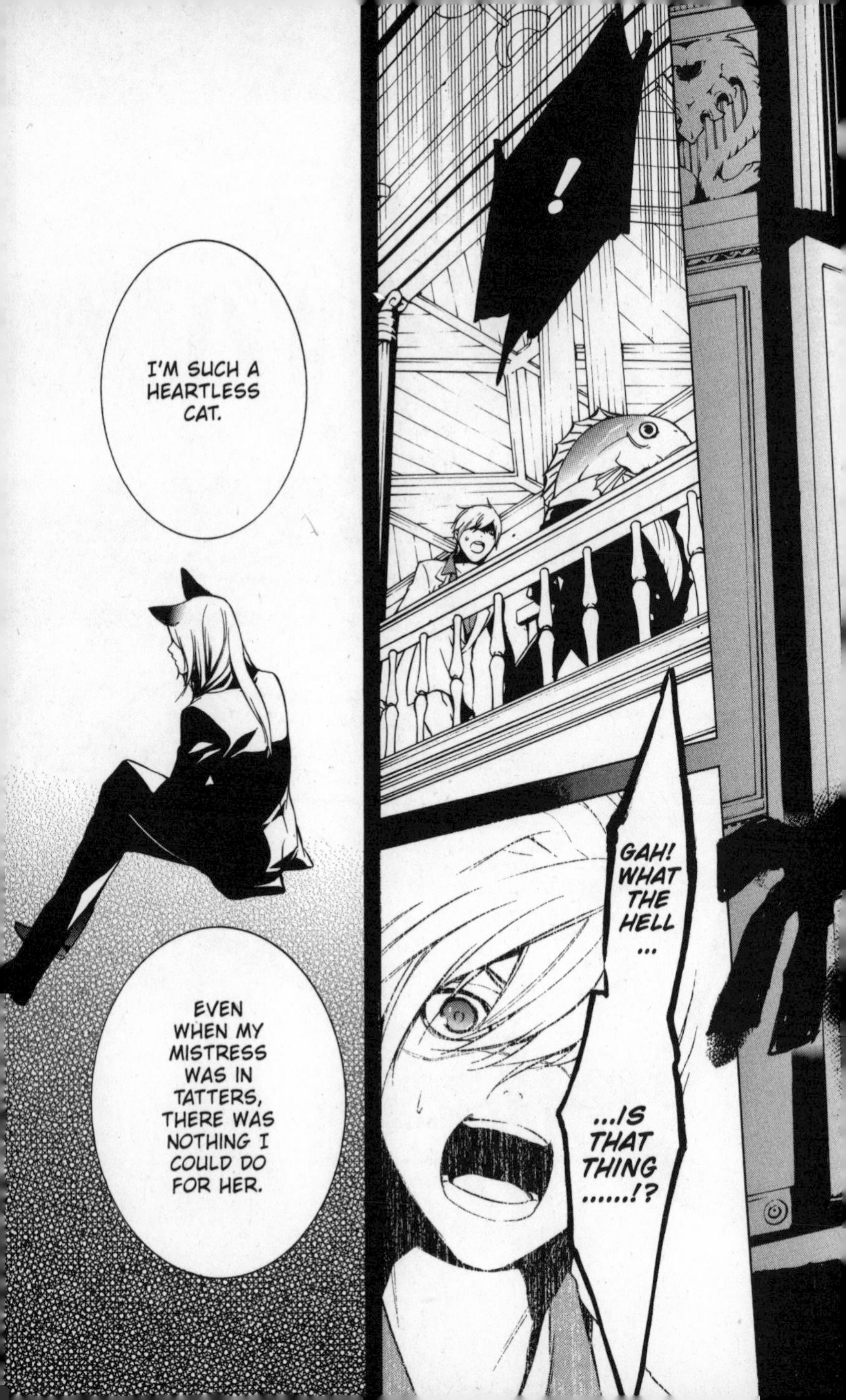
!
GAH! WHAT THE HELL ...
...IS THAT THING ......!?
I'M SUCH A HEARTLESS CAT.
EVEN WHEN MY MISTRESS WAS IN TATTERS, THERE WAS NOTHING I COULD DO FOR HER.

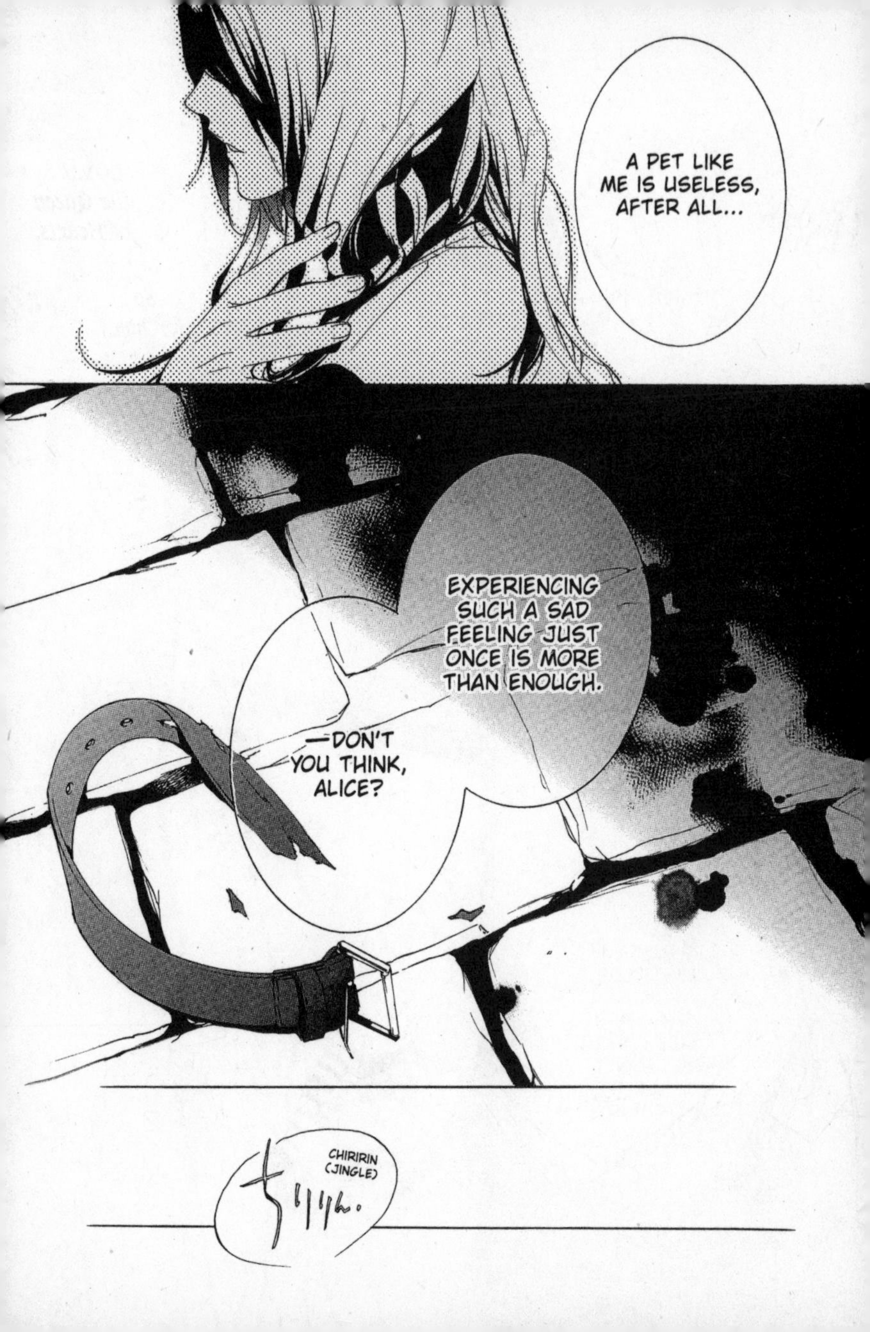
A PET LIKE ME IS USELESS, AFTER ALL...
EXPERIENCING SUCH A SAD FEELING JUST ONCE IS MORE THAN ENOUGH.
—DON'T YOU THINK, ALICE?
CHIRIRIN (JINGLE)

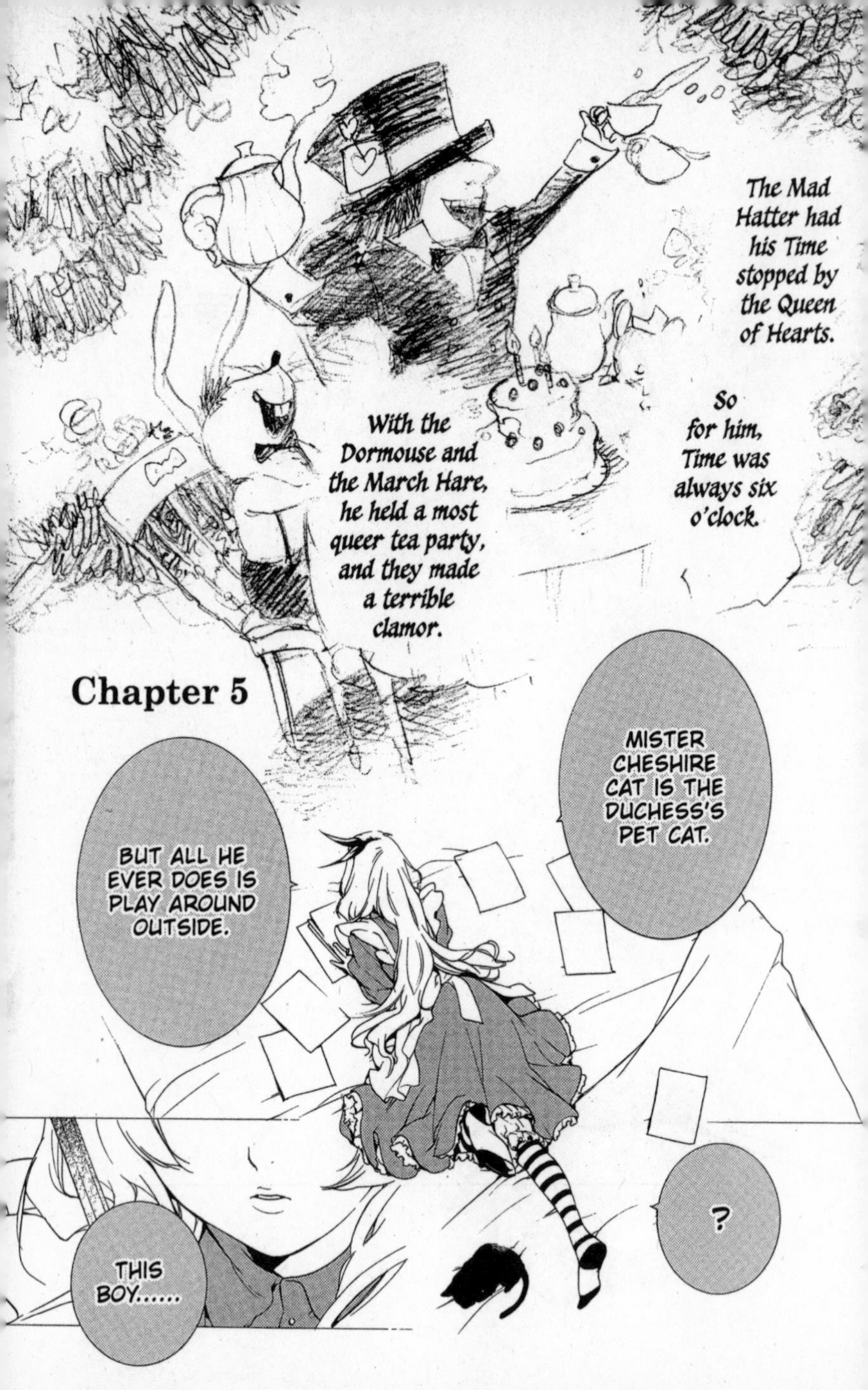
The Mad Hatter had his Time stopped by the Queen of Hearts.
So for him, Time was always six o'clock.
With the Dormouse and the March Hare, he held a most queer tea party, and they made a terrible clamor.
Chapter 5
MISTER CHESHIRE CAT IS THE DUCHESS'S PET CAT.
BUT ALL HE EVER DOES IS PLAY AROUND OUTSIDE.
?
THIS BOY......

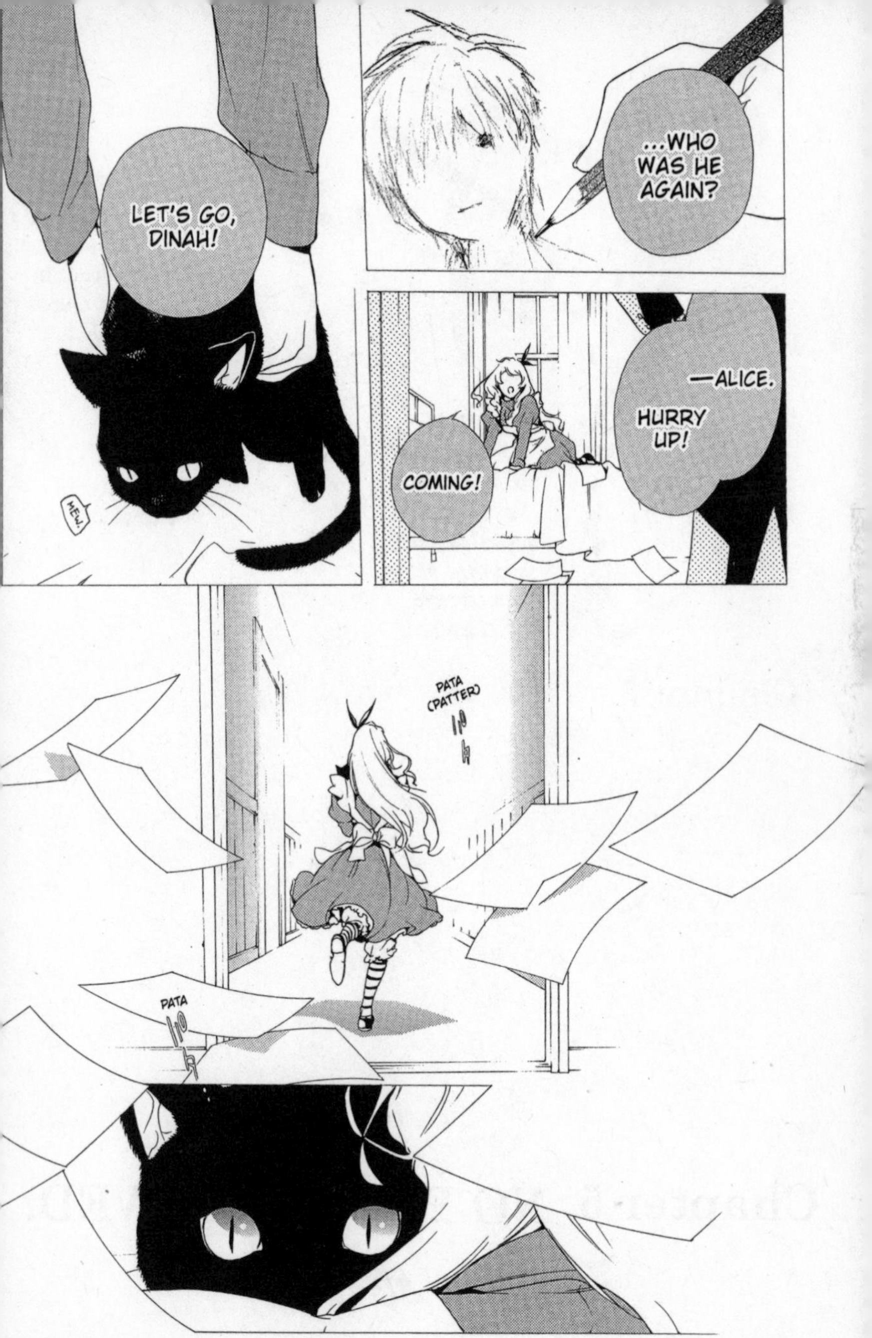
...WHO WAS HE AGAIN?
—ALICE.
HURRY UP!
COMING!
LET'S GO, DINAH!
MEW.
PATA (PATTER)
PATA

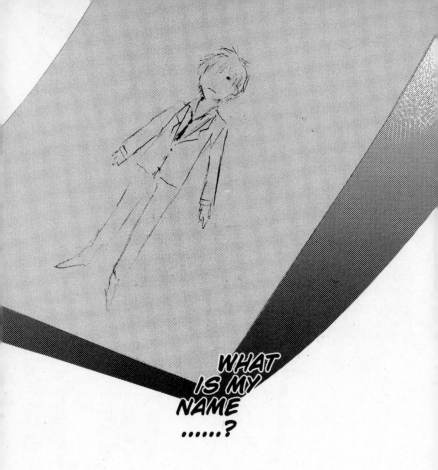

WHAT
IS MY
NAME
......?

Chapter 5 NO PETS ALLOWED.

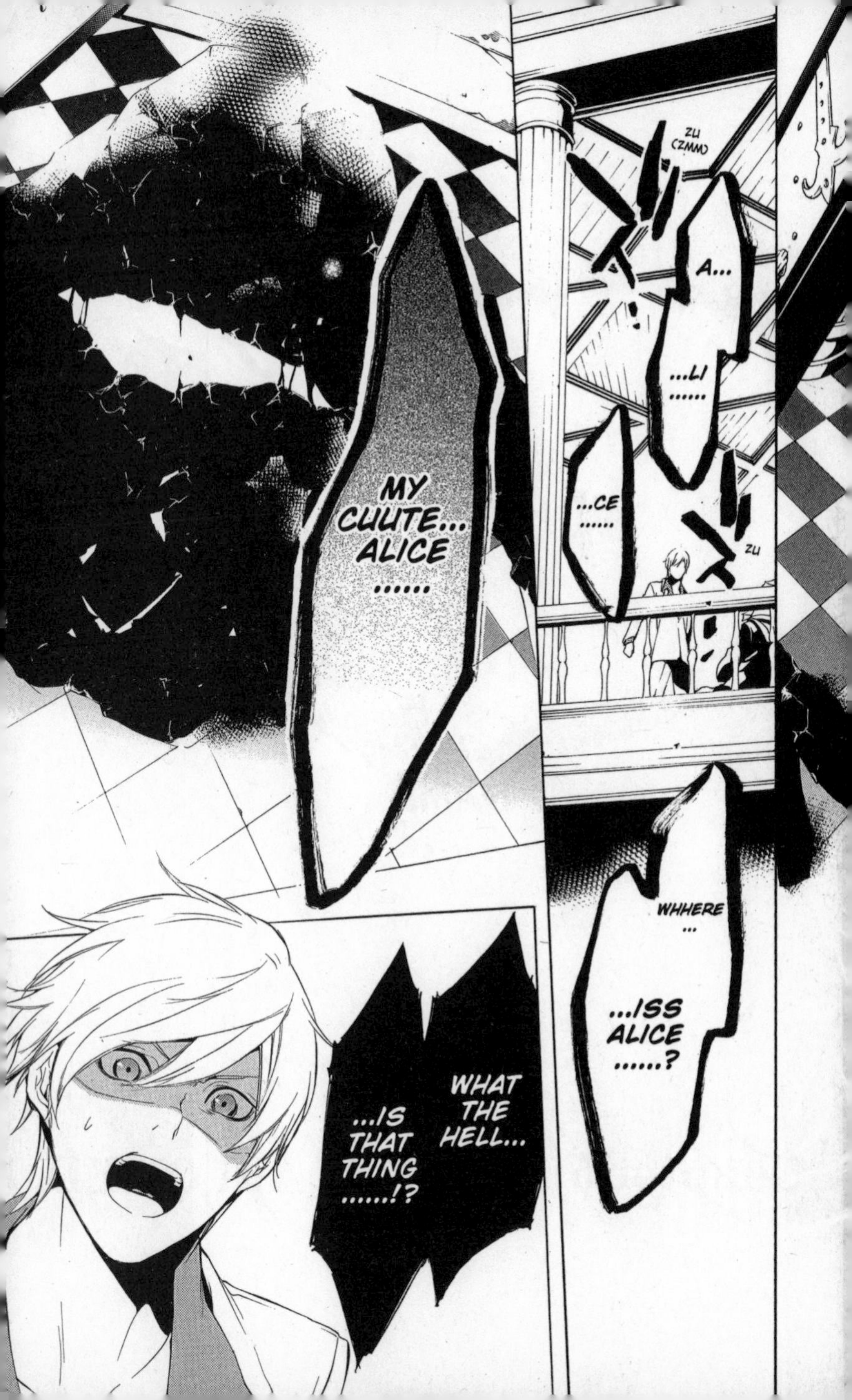
ZU (ZMM)
A...
...LI ......
...CE ......
ZU
WHHERE ... ...ISS ALICE ......?
MY CUUTE... ALICE ......
WHAT THE HELL...
...IS THAT THING ......!?

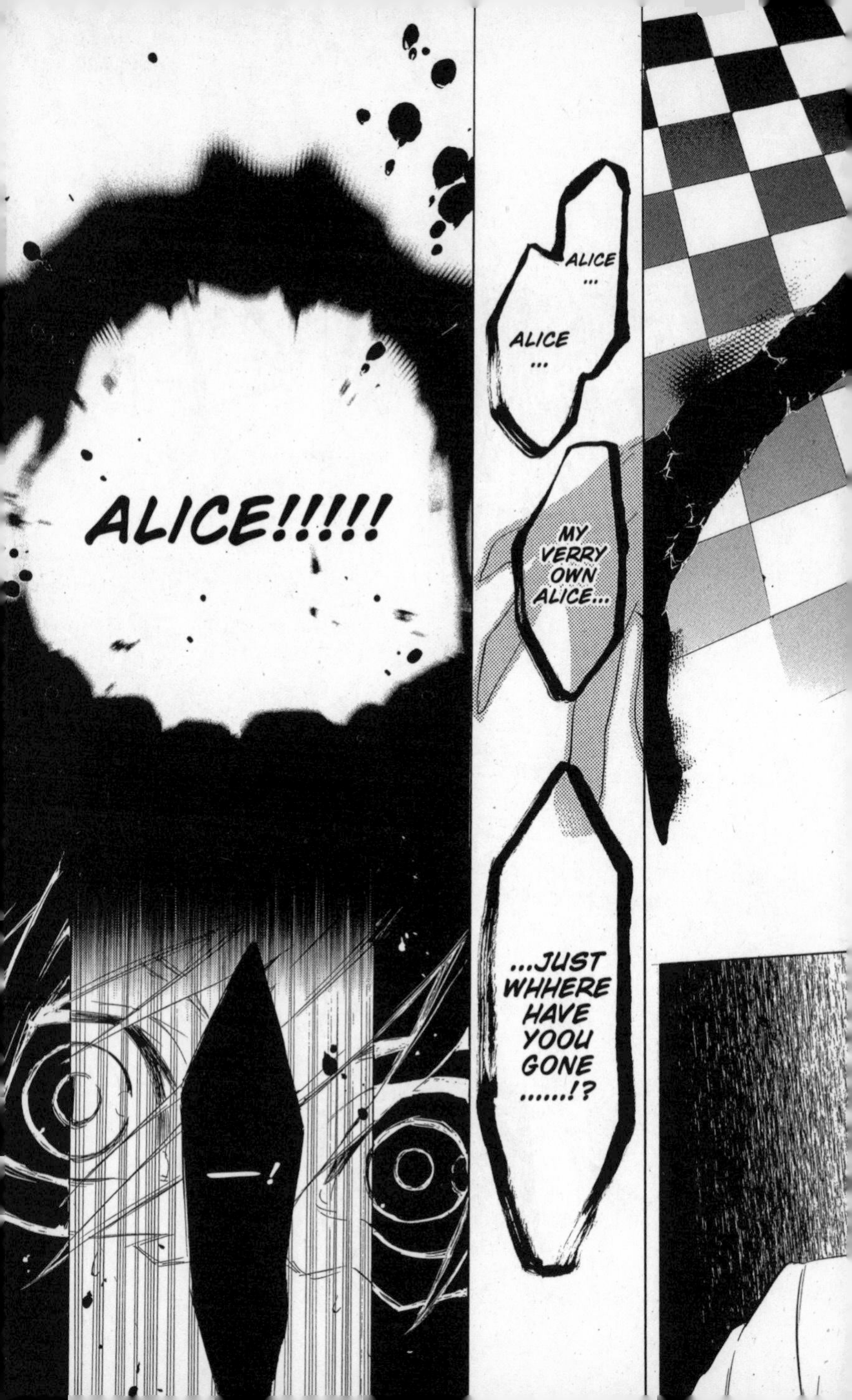
ALICE ... ALICE ...
MY VERRY OWN ALICE...
...JUST WHHERE HAVE YOOU GONE ......!?
ALICE!!!!!
—!

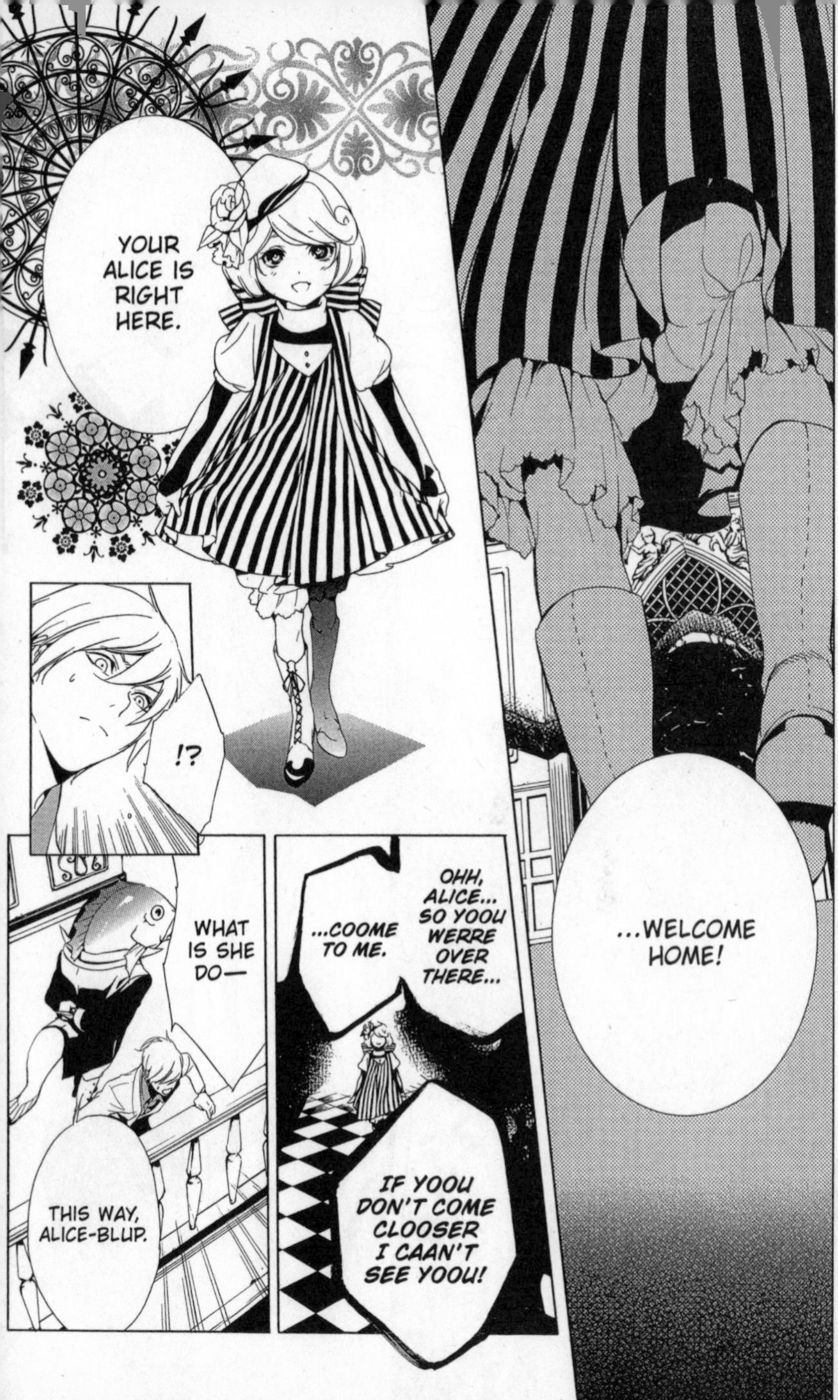
...WELCOME HOME!
YOUR ALICE IS RIGHT HERE.
!?
OHH, ALICE... SO YOOU WERRE OVER THERE...
...COOME TO ME.
IF YOOU DON'T COME CLOOSER I CAAN'T SEE YOOU!
WHAT IS SHE DO—
THIS WAY, ALICE-BLUP.

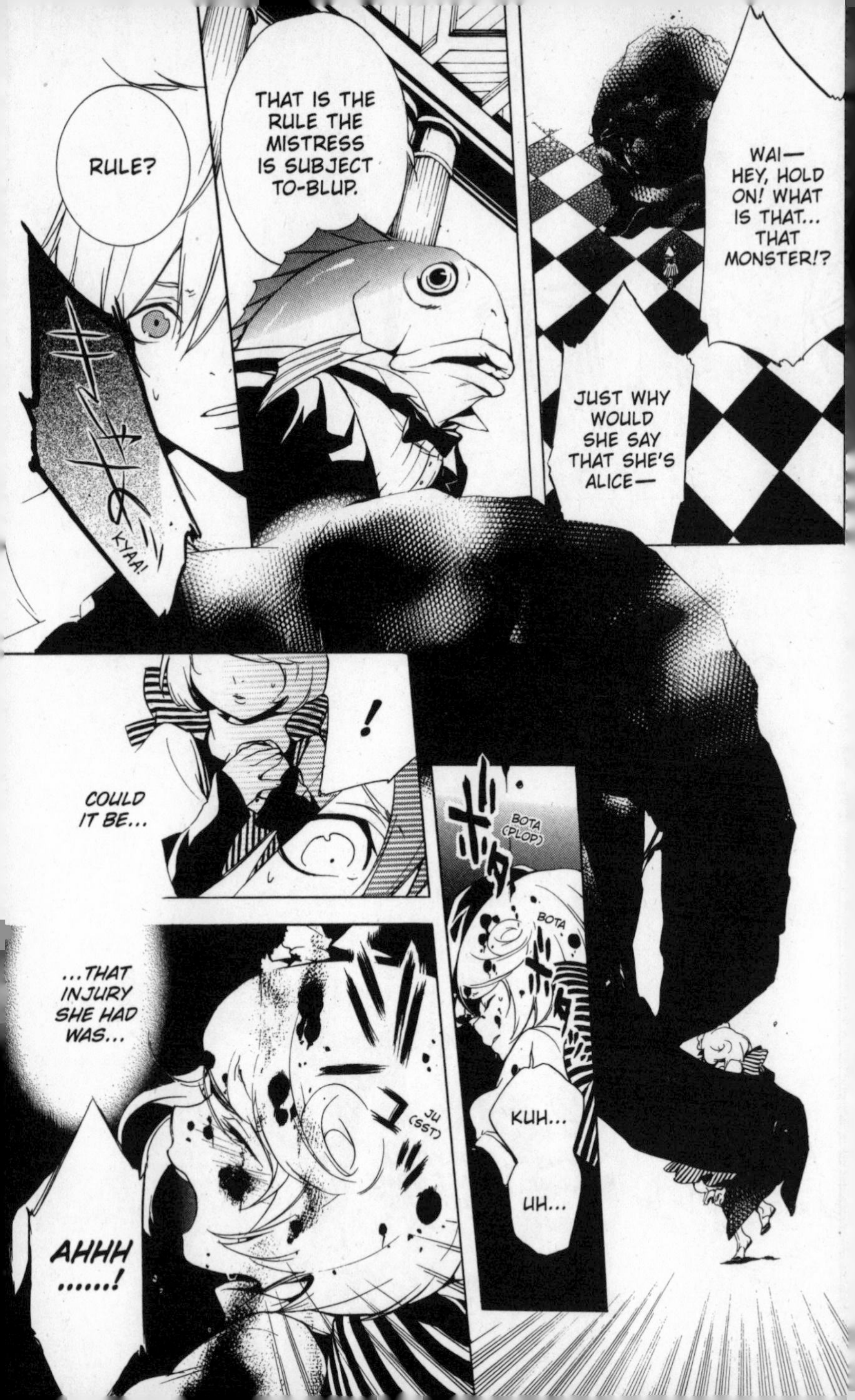
WAI— HEY, HOLD ON! WHAT IS THAT... THAT MONSTER!?
JUST WHY WOULD SHE SAY THAT SHE'S ALICE—
THAT IS THE RULE THE MISTRESS IS SUBJECT TO-BLUP.
RULE?
KYAA!
BOTA (PLOP)
BOTA
KUH...
UH...
!
COULD IT BE...
...THAT INJURY SHE HAD WAS...
JU (SST)
AHHH ......!

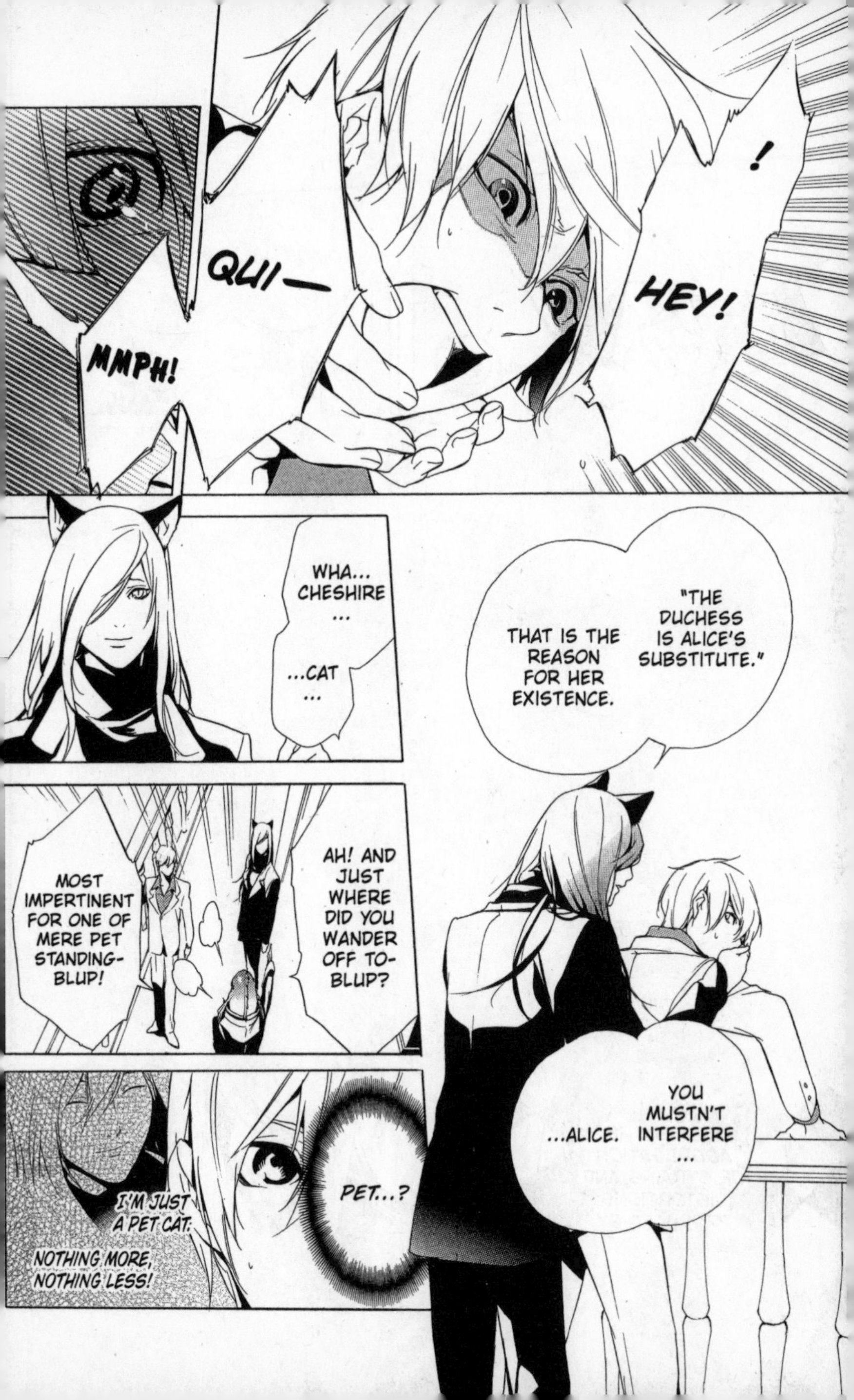
!
HEY!
QUI—
MMPH!
"THE DUCHESS IS ALICE'S SUBSTITUTE."
THAT IS THE REASON FOR HER EXISTENCE.
YOU MUSTN'T INTERFERE ...
...ALICE.
WHA... CHESHIRE ... ...CAT ...
AH! AND JUST WHERE DID YOU WANDER OFF TO-BLUP?
MOST IMPERTINENT FOR ONE OF MERE PET STANDING-BLUP!
PET...?
I'M JUST A PET CAT.
NOTHING MORE, NOTHING LESS!

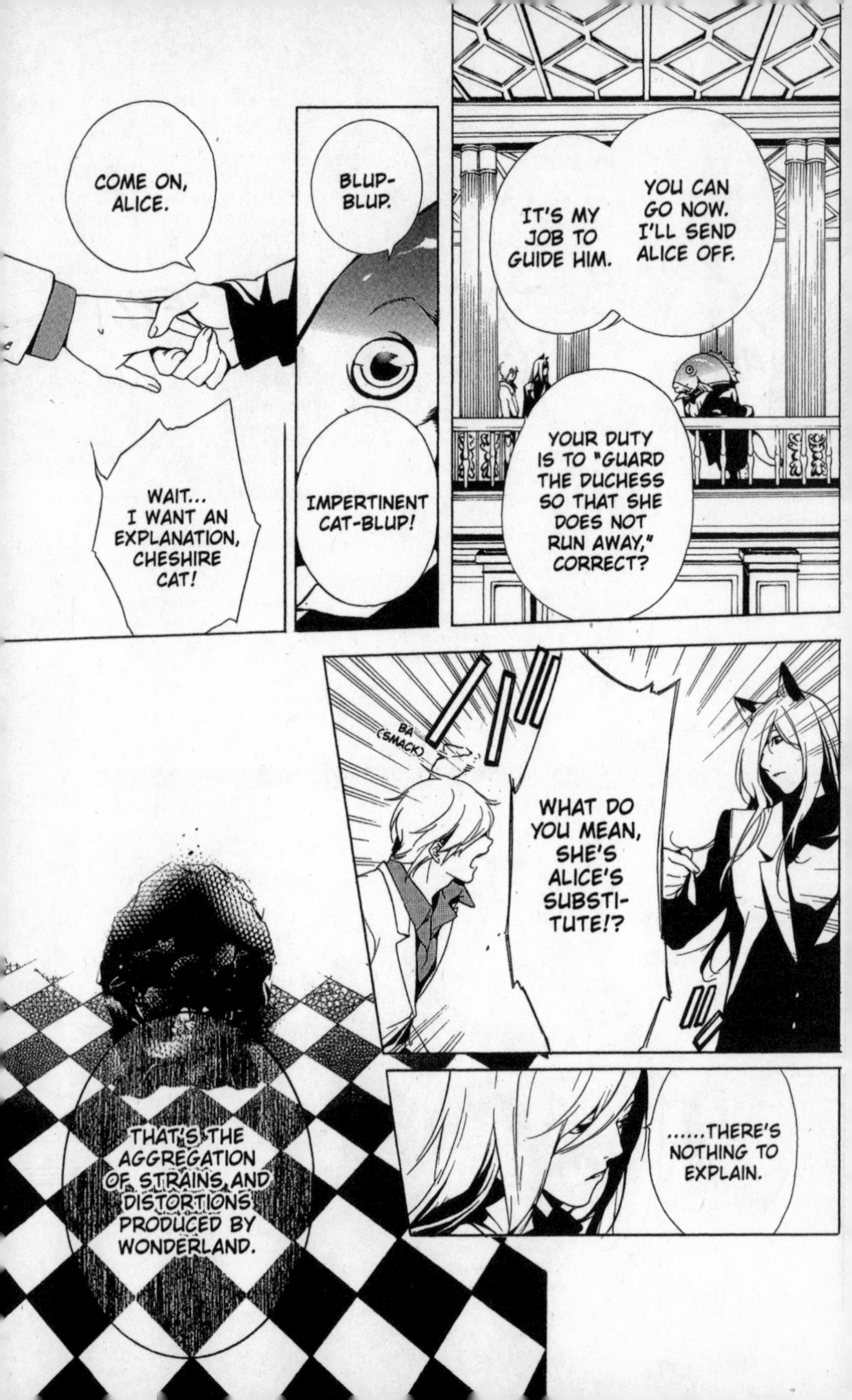
YOU CAN GO NOW. I'LL SEND ALICE OFF.
IT'S MY JOB TO GUIDE HIM.
YOUR DUTY IS TO "GUARD THE DUCHESS SO THAT SHE DOES NOT RUN AWAY," CORRECT?
BLUP-BLUP.
IMPERTINENT CAT-BLUP!
COME ON, ALICE.
WAIT... I WANT AN EXPLANATION, CHESHIRE CAT!
BA (SMACK)
WHAT DO YOU MEAN, SHE'S ALICE'S SUBSTITUTE!?
......THERE'S NOTHING TO EXPLAIN.
THAT'S THE AGGREGATION OF STRAINS AND DISTORTIONS PRODUCED BY WONDERLAND.

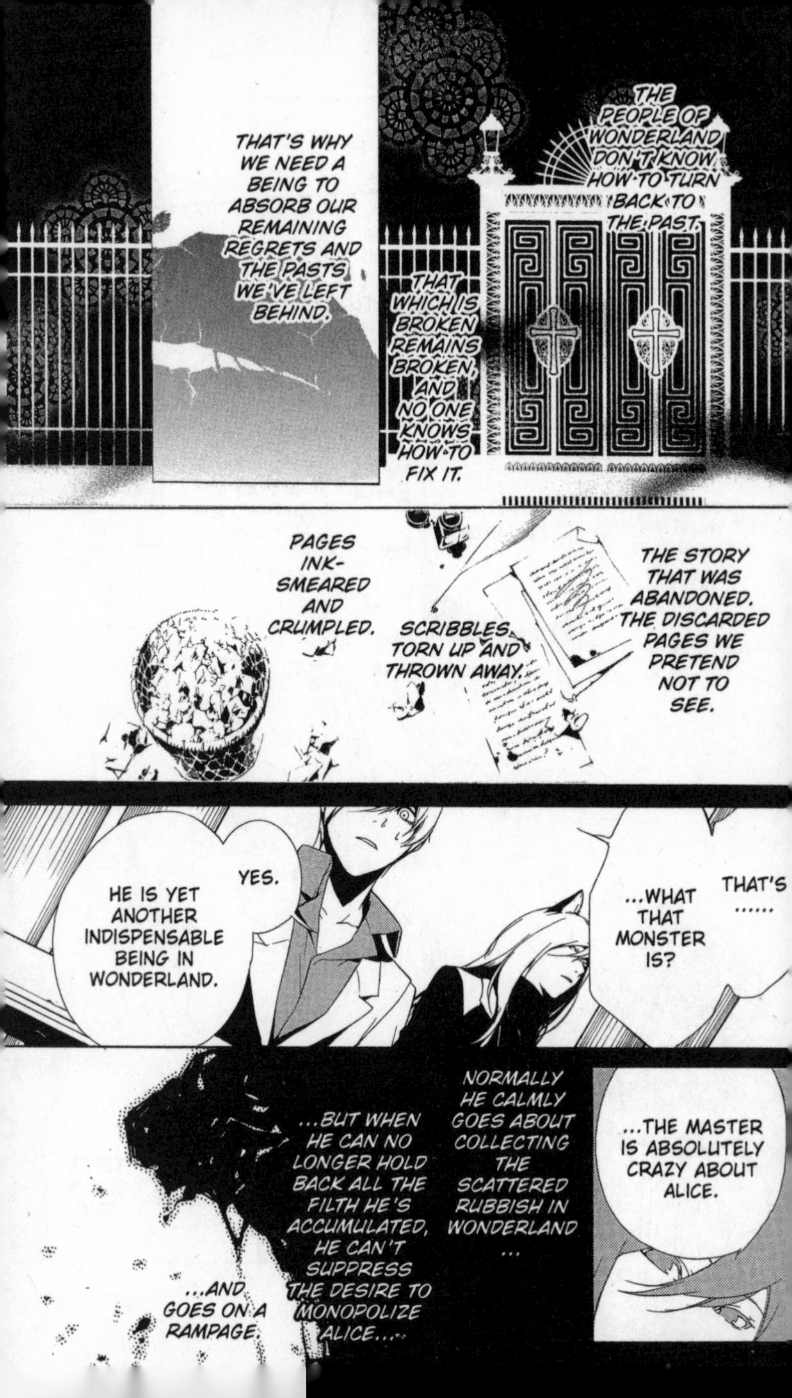
THE PEOPLE OF WONDERLAND DON'T KNOW HOW TO TURN BACK TO THE PAST.
THAT WHICH IS BROKEN REMAINS BROKEN, AND NO ONE KNOWS HOW TO FIX IT.
THAT'S WHY WE NEED A BEING TO ABSORB OUR REMAINING REGRETS AND THE PASTS WE'VE LEFT BEHIND.
THE STORY THAT WAS ABANDONED. THE DISCARDED PAGES WE PRETEND NOT TO SEE.
SCRIBBLES TORN UP AND THROWN AWAY.
PAGES INK-SMEARED AND CRUMPLED.
THAT'S ......
...WHAT THAT MONSTER IS?
YES.
HE IS YET ANOTHER INDISPENSABLE BEING IN WONDERLAND.
...THE MASTER IS ABSOLUTELY CRAZY ABOUT ALICE.
NORMALLY HE CALMLY GOES ABOUT COLLECTING THE SCATTERED RUBBISH IN WONDERLAND ...
...BUT WHEN HE CAN NO LONGER HOLD BACK ALL THE FILTH HE'S ACCUMULATED, HE CAN'T SUPPRESS THE DESIRE TO MONOPOLIZE ALICE...
...AND GOES ON A RAMPAGE.

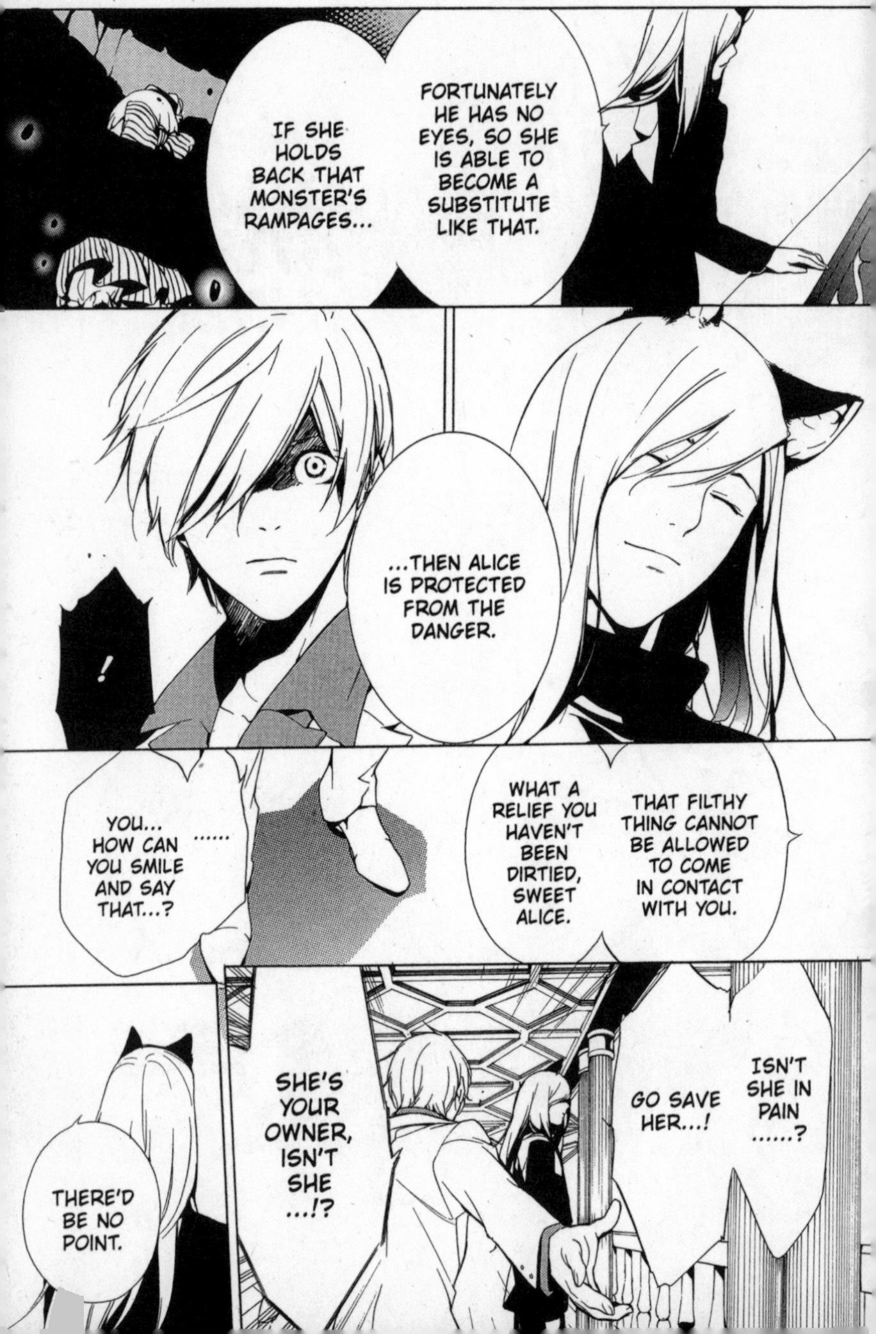
FORTUNATELY HE HAS NO EYES, SO SHE IS ABLE TO BECOME A SUBSTITUTE LIKE THAT.
IF SHE HOLDS BACK THAT MONSTER'S RAMPAGES...
...THEN ALICE IS PROTECTED FROM THE DANGER.
!
THAT FILTHY THING CANNOT BE ALLOWED TO COME IN CONTACT WITH YOU.
WHAT A RELIEF YOU HAVEN'T BEEN DIRTIED, SWEET ALICE.
......
YOU... HOW CAN YOU SMILE AND SAY THAT...?
ISN'T SHE IN PAIN ......?
GO SAVE HER...!
SHE'S YOUR OWNER, ISN'T SHE ...!?
THERE'D BE NO POINT.

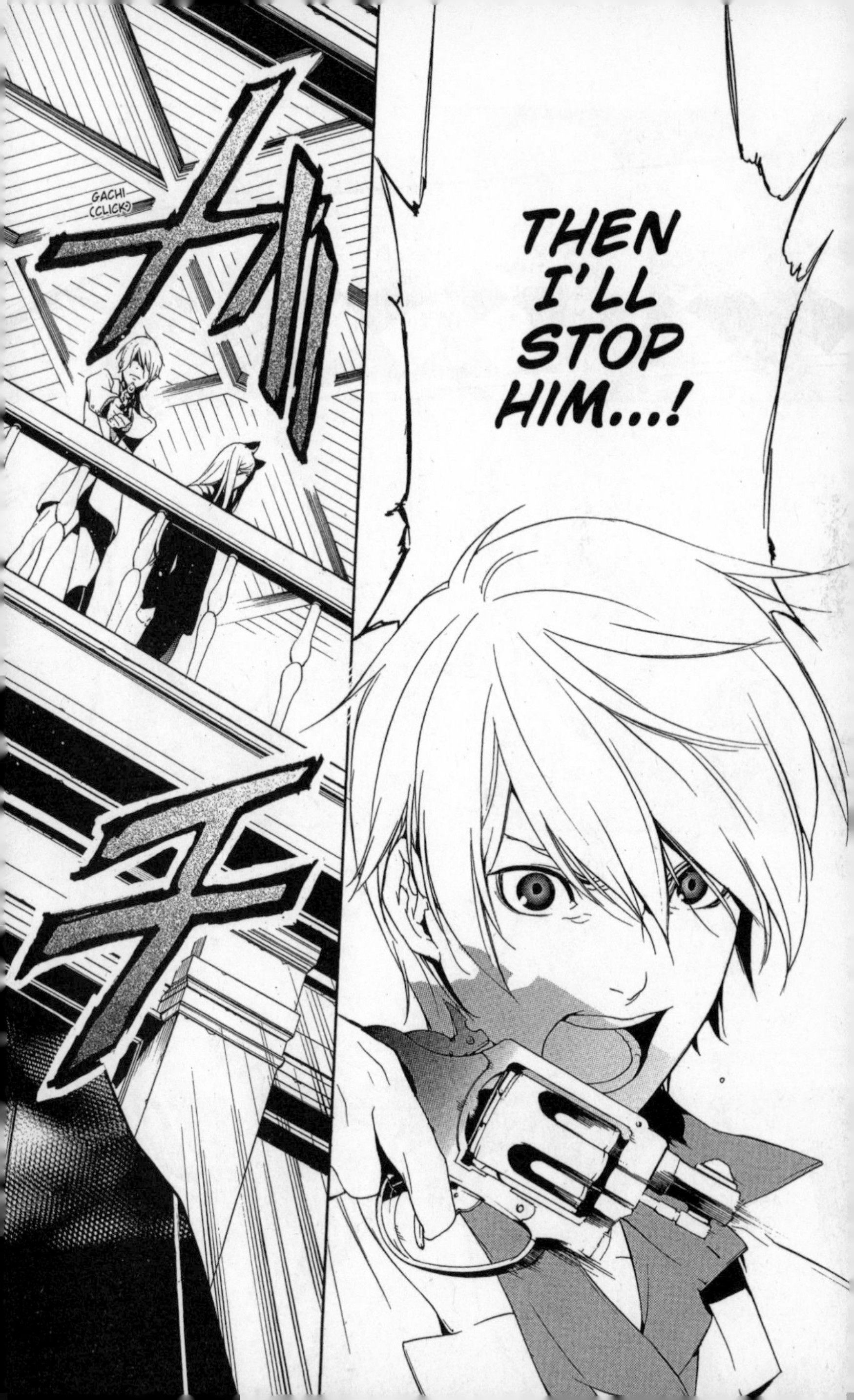
THEN I'LL STOP HIM...!
ガチ
GACHI (CLICK)

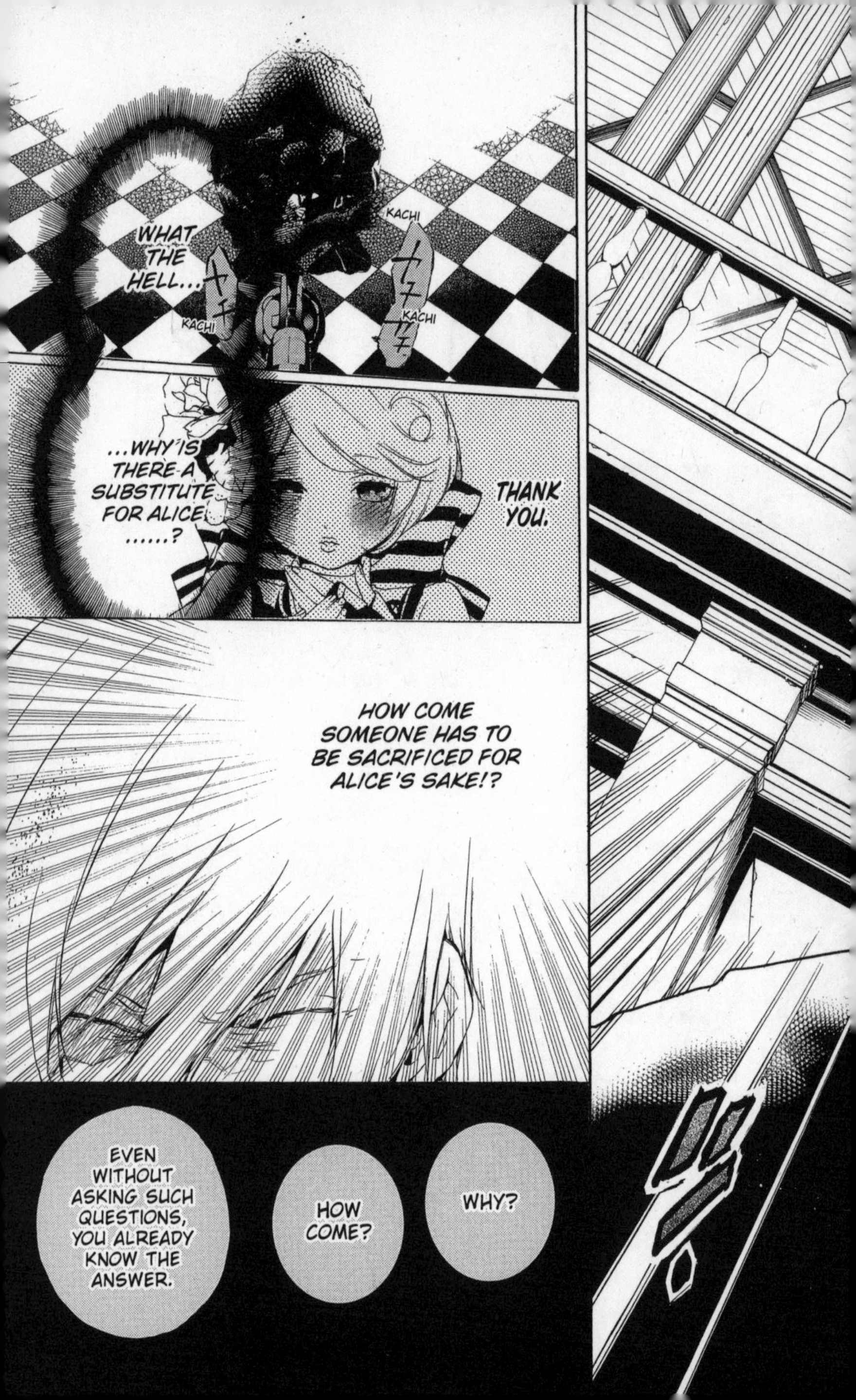
KACHI
KACHI
WHAT THE HELL...
KACHI
THANK YOU.
...WHY IS THERE A SUBSTITUTE FOR ALICE ......?
HOW COME SOMEONE HAS TO BE SACRIFICED FOR ALICE'S SAKE!?
WHY?
HOW COME?
EVEN WITHOUT ASKING SUCH QUESTIONS, YOU ALREADY KNOW THE ANSWER.

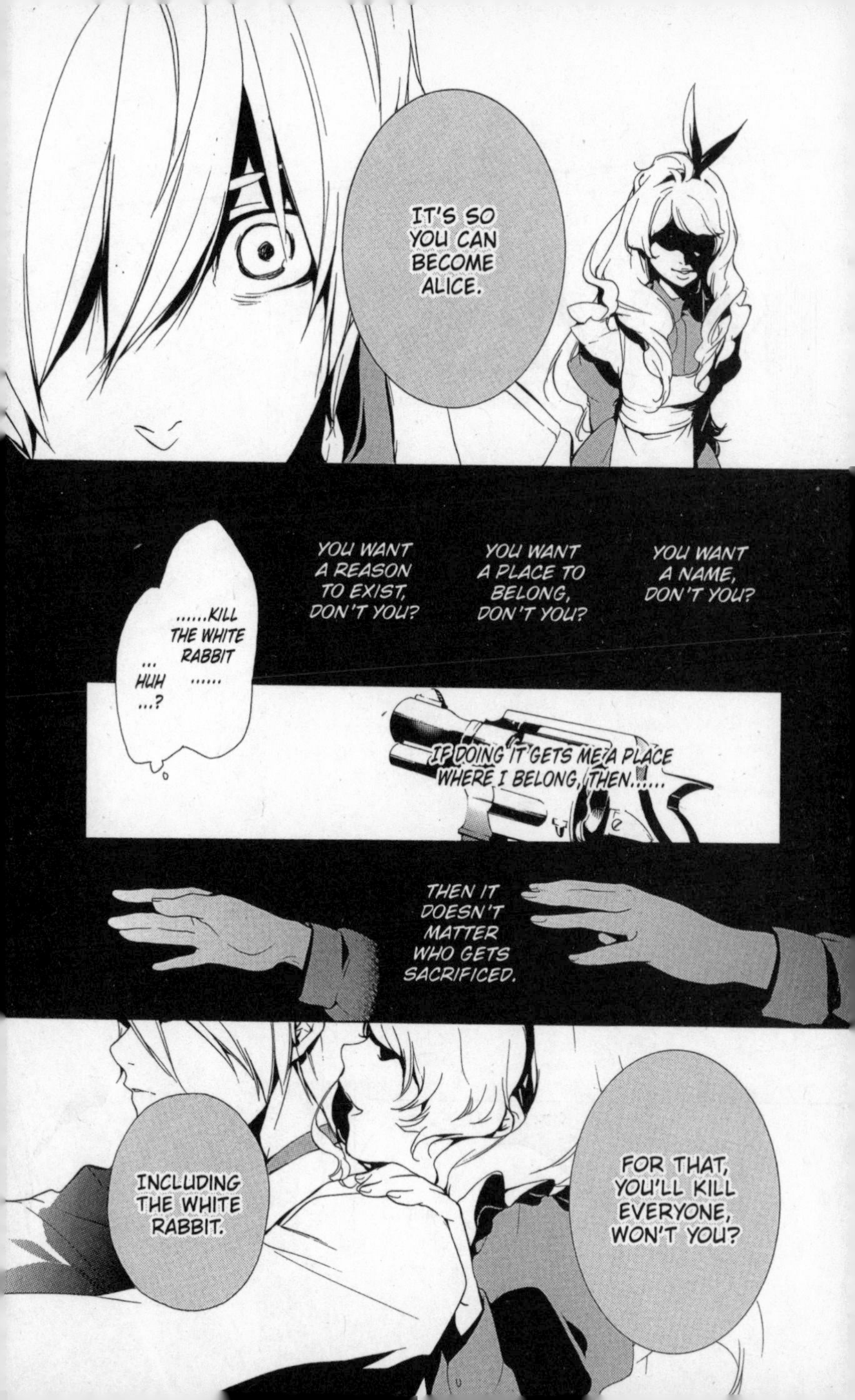
IT'S SO YOU CAN BECOME ALICE.
YOU WANT A NAME, DON'T YOU?
YOU WANT A PLACE TO BELONG, DON'T YOU?
YOU WANT A REASON TO EXIST, DON'T YOU?
......KILL THE WHITE RABBIT ......
... HUH ...?
IF DOING IT GETS ME A PLACE WHERE I BELONG, THEN......
THEN IT DOESN'T MATTER WHO GETS SACRIFICED.
FOR THAT, YOU'LL KILL EVERYONE, WON'T YOU?
INCLUDING THE WHITE RABBIT.

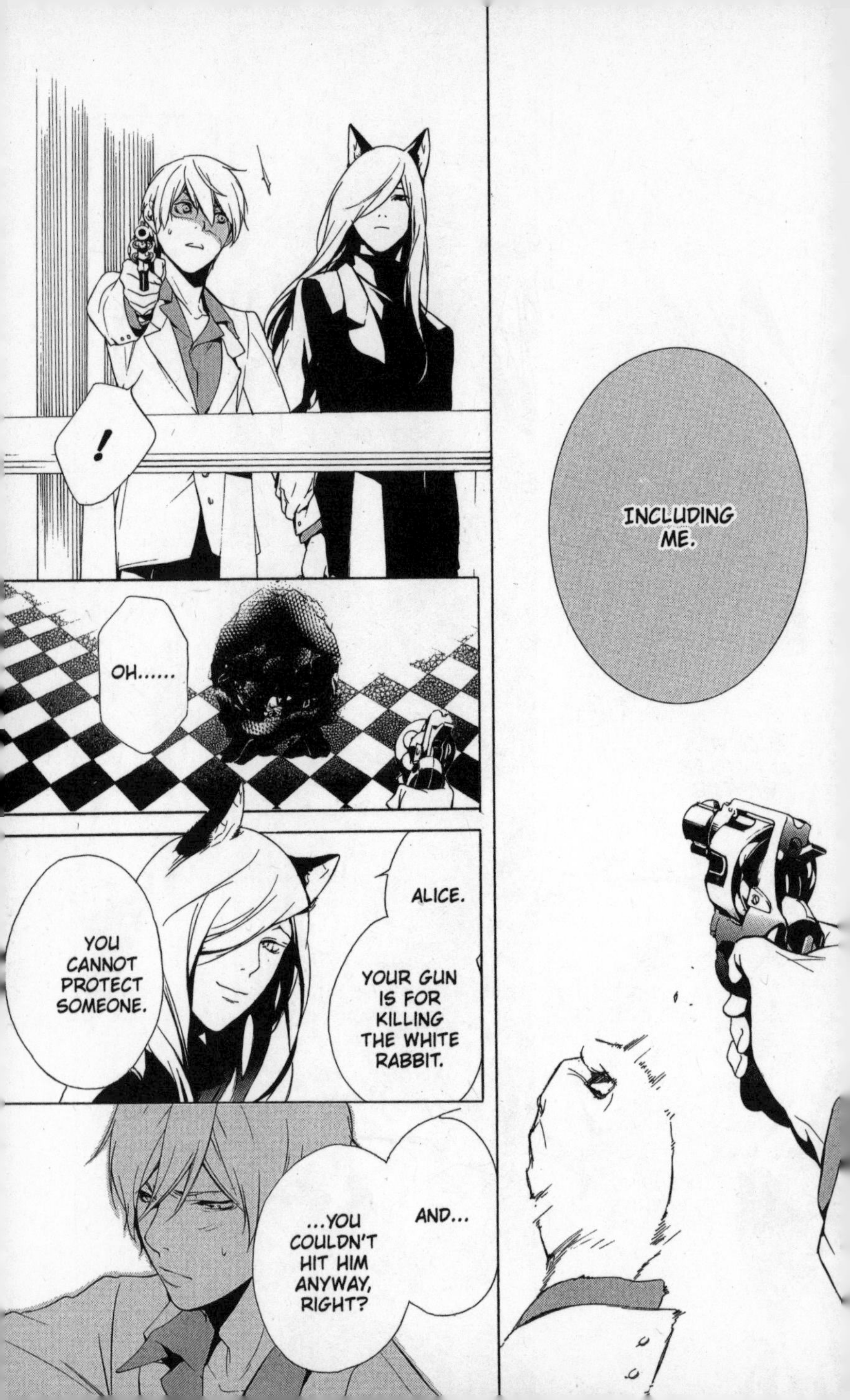
INCLUDING ME.
!
OH......
ALICE.
YOUR GUN IS FOR KILLING THE WHITE RABBIT.
YOU CANNOT PROTECT SOMEONE.
AND...
...YOU COULDN'T HIT HIM ANYWAY, RIGHT?

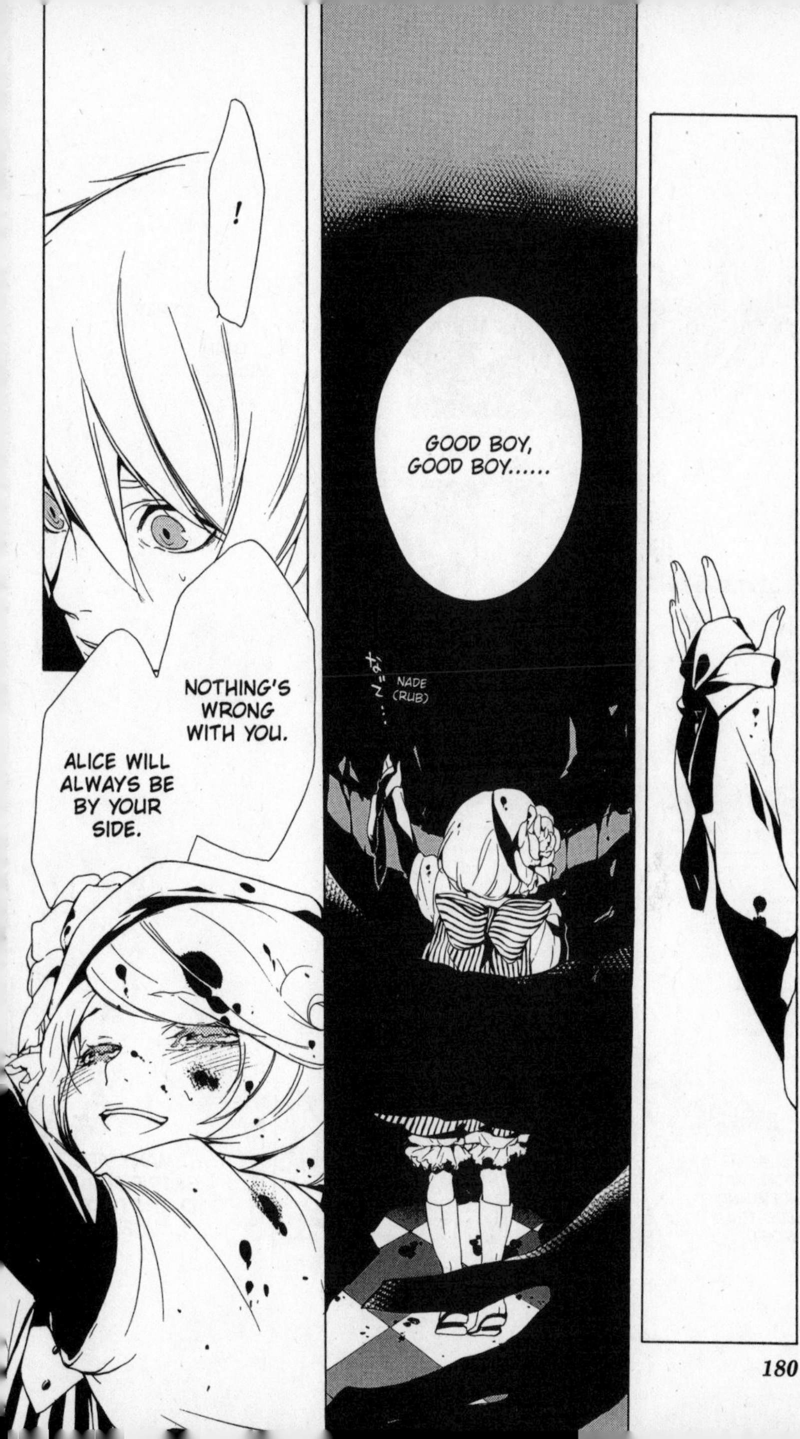
GOOD BOY, GOOD BOY......
なで…
NADE (RUB)
!
NOTHING'S WRONG WITH YOU.
ALICE WILL ALWAYS BE BY YOUR SIDE.

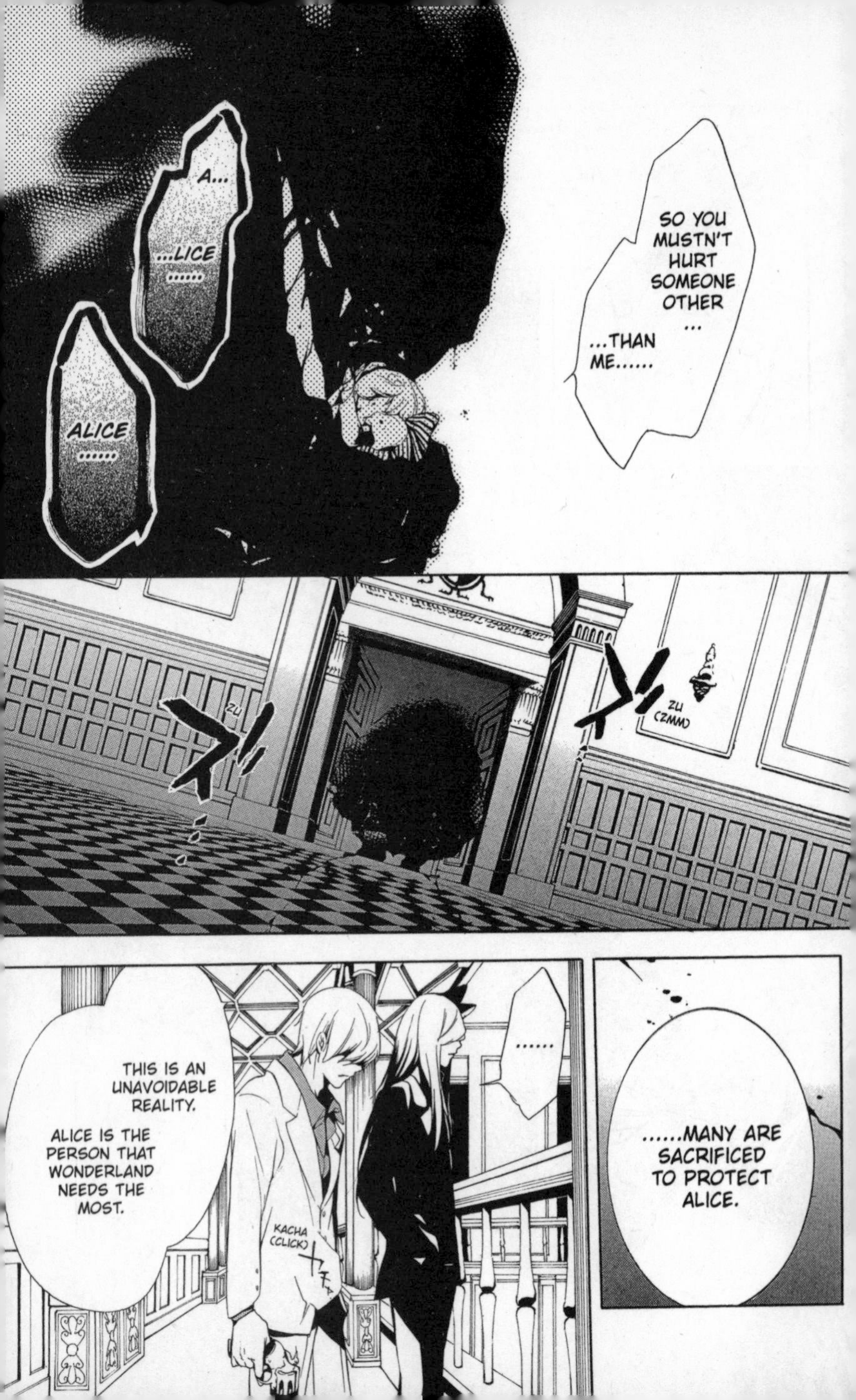
SO YOU MUSTN'T HURT SOMEONE OTHER ... ...THAN ME......
A... ...LICE ......
ALICE ......
ZU (ZMM)
ZU
......MANY ARE SACRIFICED TO PROTECT ALICE.
......
THIS IS AN UNAVOIDABLE REALITY.
ALICE IS THE PERSON THAT WONDERLAND NEEDS THE MOST.
KACHA (CLICK)

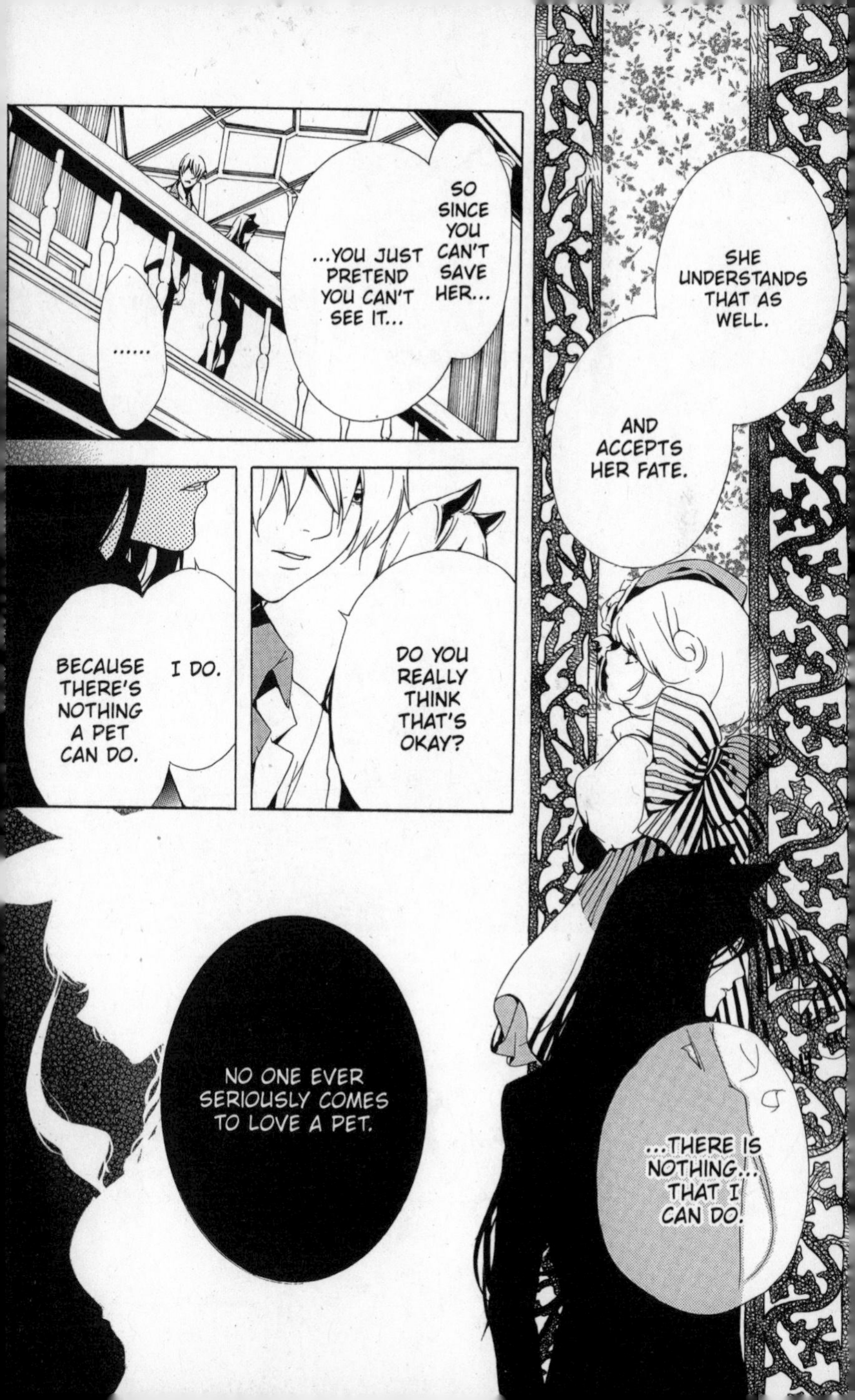
SHE UNDERSTANDS THAT AS WELL.
AND ACCEPTS HER FATE.
SO SINCE YOU CAN'T SAVE HER...
...YOU JUST PRETEND YOU CAN'T SEE IT...
......
DO YOU REALLY THINK THAT'S OKAY?
I DO.
BECAUSE THERE'S NOTHING A PET CAN DO.
...THERE IS NOTHING... THAT I CAN DO.
NO ONE EVER SERIOUSLY COMES TO LOVE A PET.

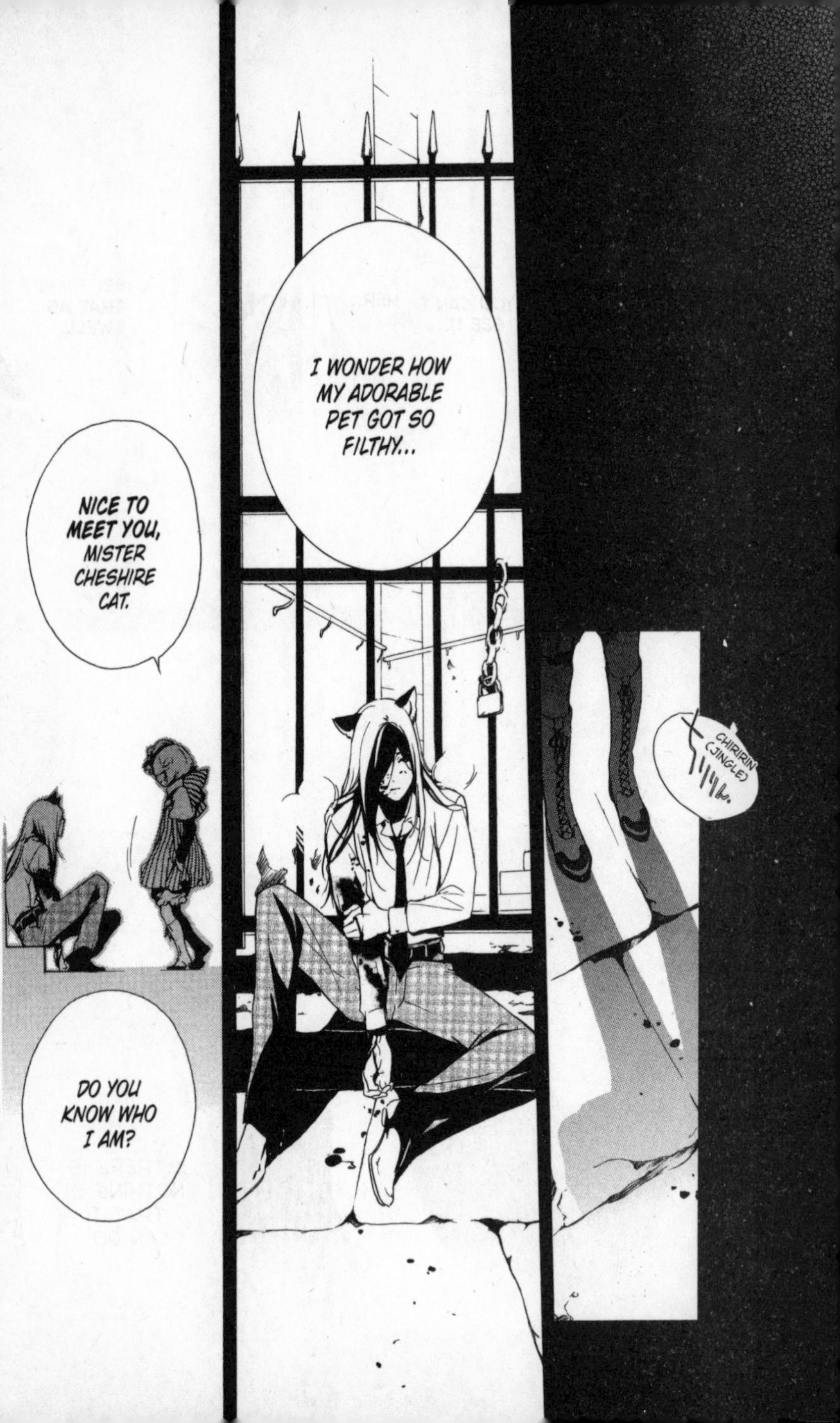
CHIRIRIN (JINGLE)
I WONDER HOW MY ADORABLE PET GOT SO FILTHY...
NICE TO MEET YOU, MISTER CHESHIRE CAT.
DO YOU KNOW WHO I AM?

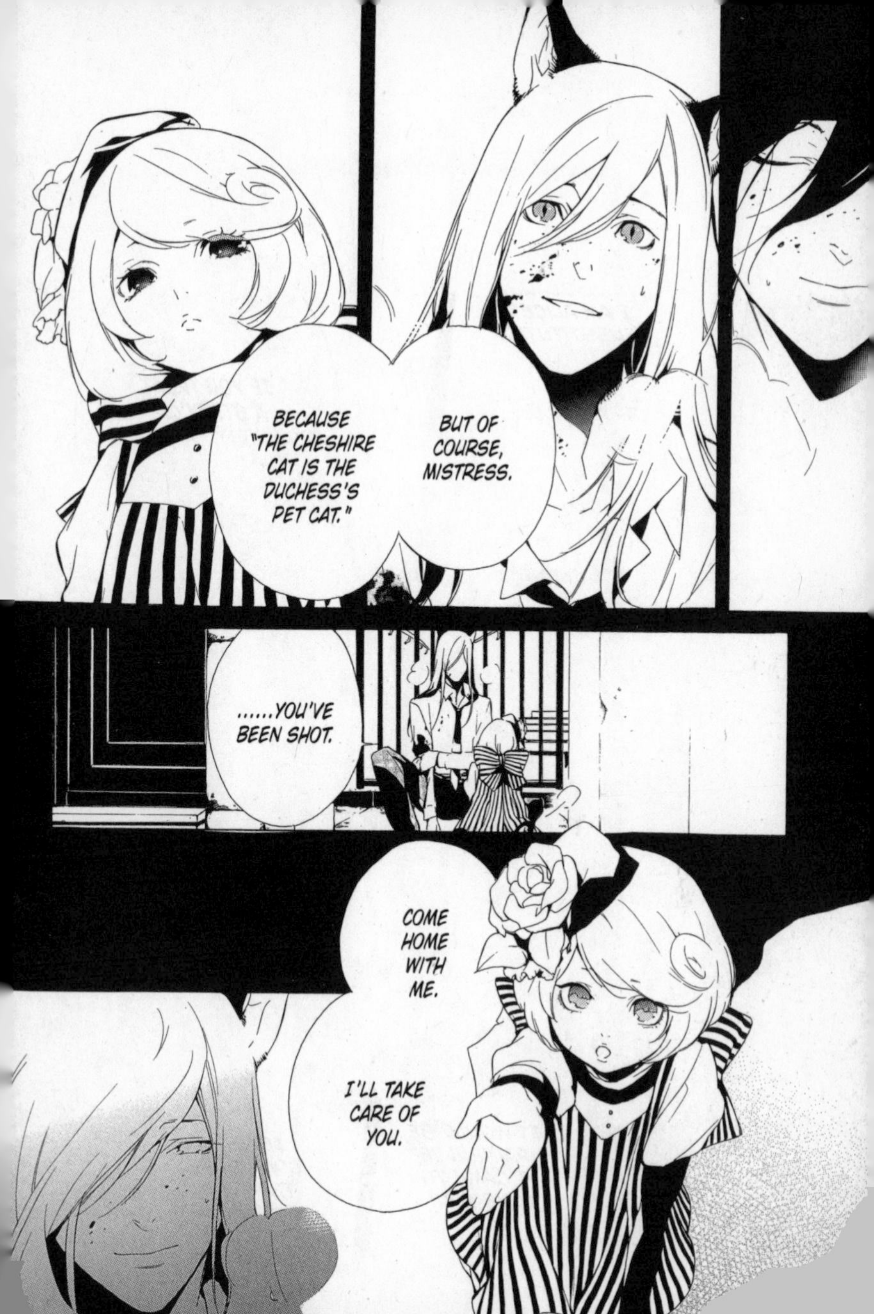
BUT OF COURSE, MISTRESS.
BECAUSE "THE CHESHIRE CAT IS THE DUCHESS'S PET CAT."
......YOU'VE BEEN SHOT.
COME HOME WITH ME.
I'LL TAKE CARE OF YOU.

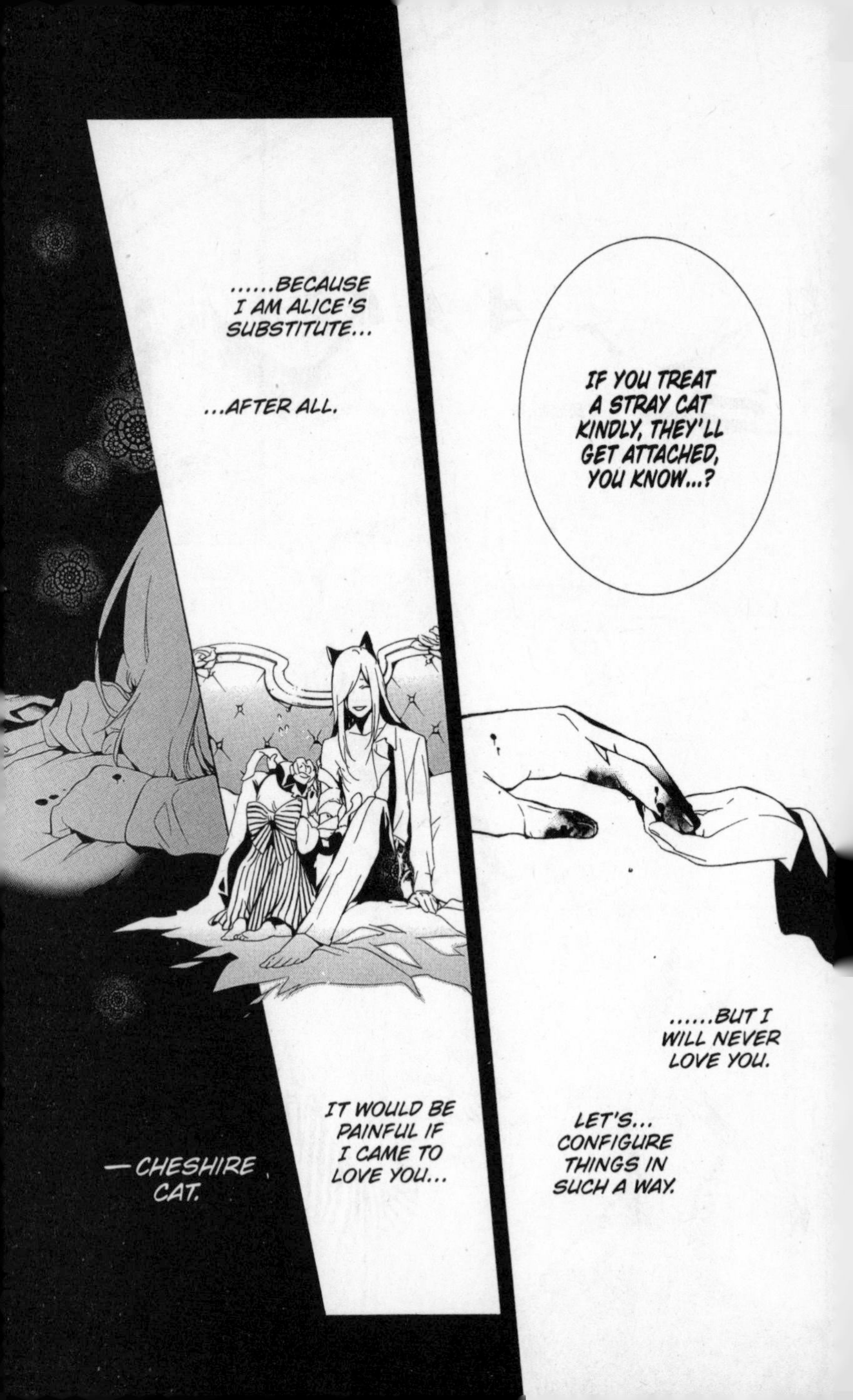
IF YOU TREAT A STRAY CAT KINDLY, THEY'LL GET ATTACHED, YOU KNOW...?
......BUT I WILL NEVER LOVE YOU.
LET'S... CONFIGURE THINGS IN SUCH A WAY.
......BECAUSE I AM ALICE'S SUBSTITUTE...
...AFTER ALL.
IT WOULD BE PAINFUL IF I CAME TO LOVE YOU...
—CHESHIRE CAT.

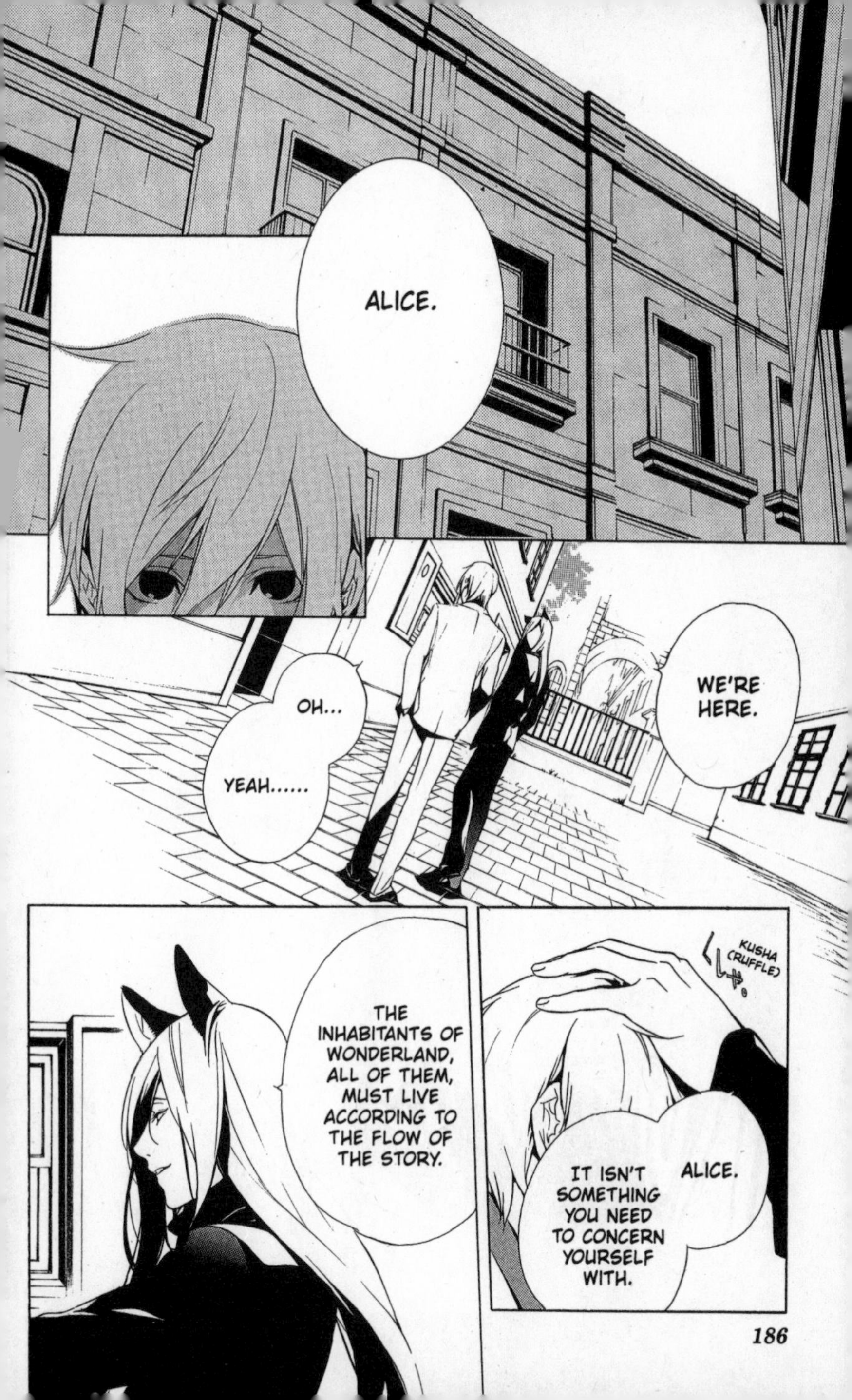
ALICE.
WE'RE HERE.
OH...
YEAH......
KUSHA (RUFFLE)
ALICE.
IT ISN'T SOMETHING YOU NEED TO CONCERN YOURSELF WITH.
THE INHABITANTS OF WONDERLAND, ALL OF THEM, MUST LIVE ACCORDING TO THE FLOW OF THE STORY.

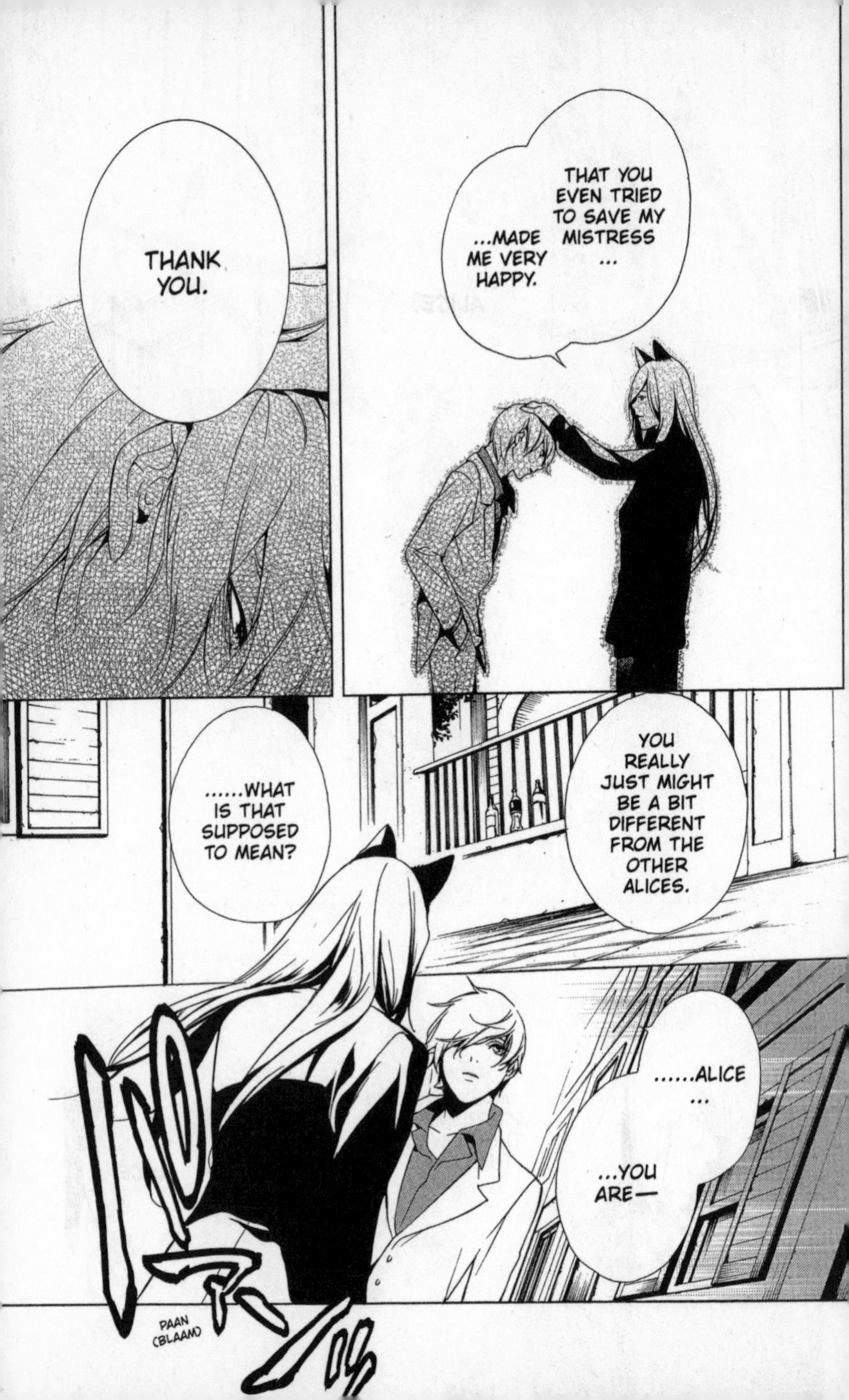
THAT YOU EVEN TRIED TO SAVE MY MISTRESS ...
...MADE ME VERY HAPPY.
THANK YOU.
YOU REALLY JUST MIGHT BE A BIT DIFFERENT FROM THE OTHER ALICES.
......WHAT IS THAT SUPPOSED TO MEAN?
......ALICE ...
...YOU ARE—
PAAN (BLAAM)

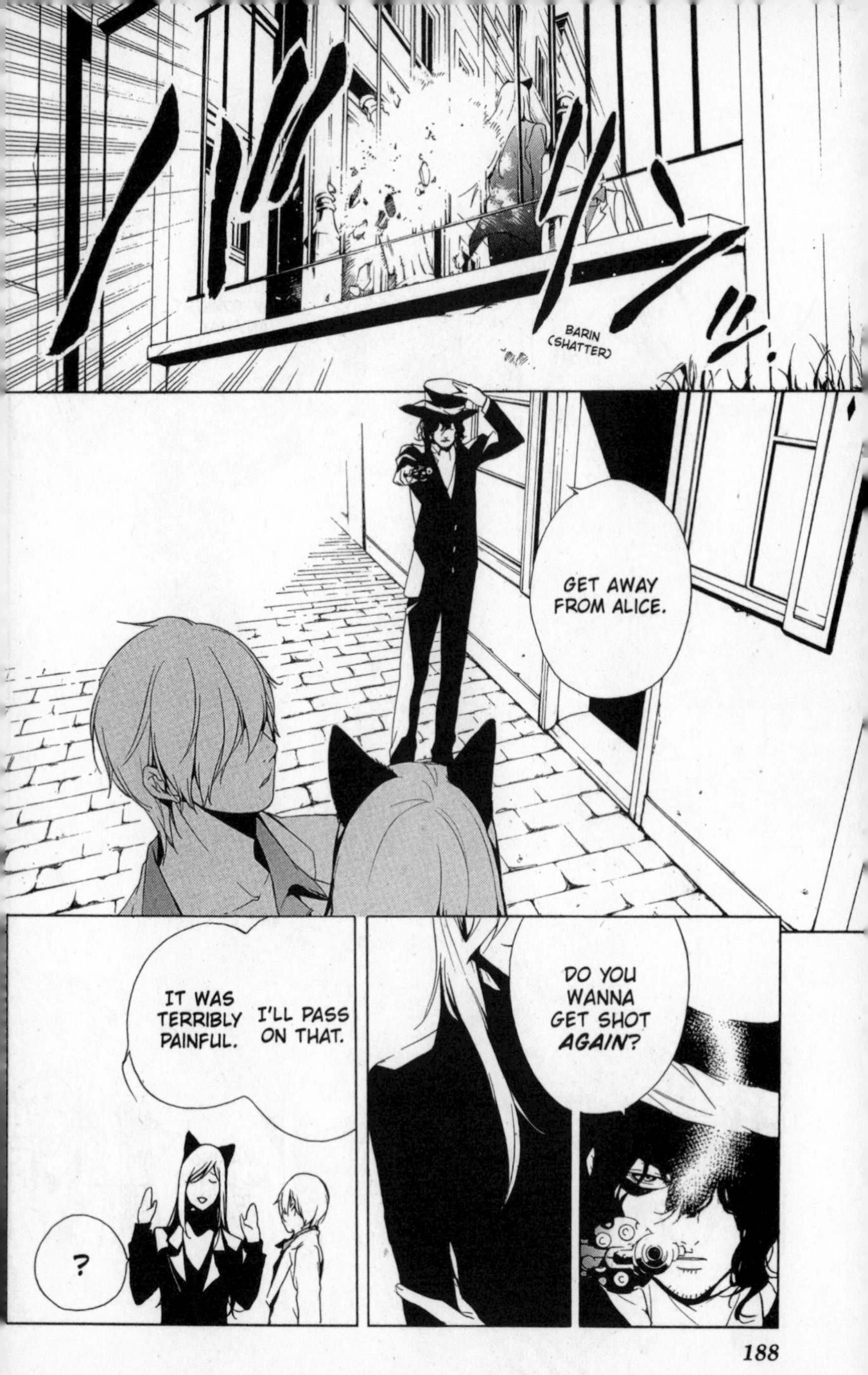
BARIN (SHATTER)
GET AWAY FROM ALICE.
DO YOU WANNA GET SHOT AGAIN?
I'LL PASS ON THAT.
IT WAS TERRIBLY PAINFUL.
?

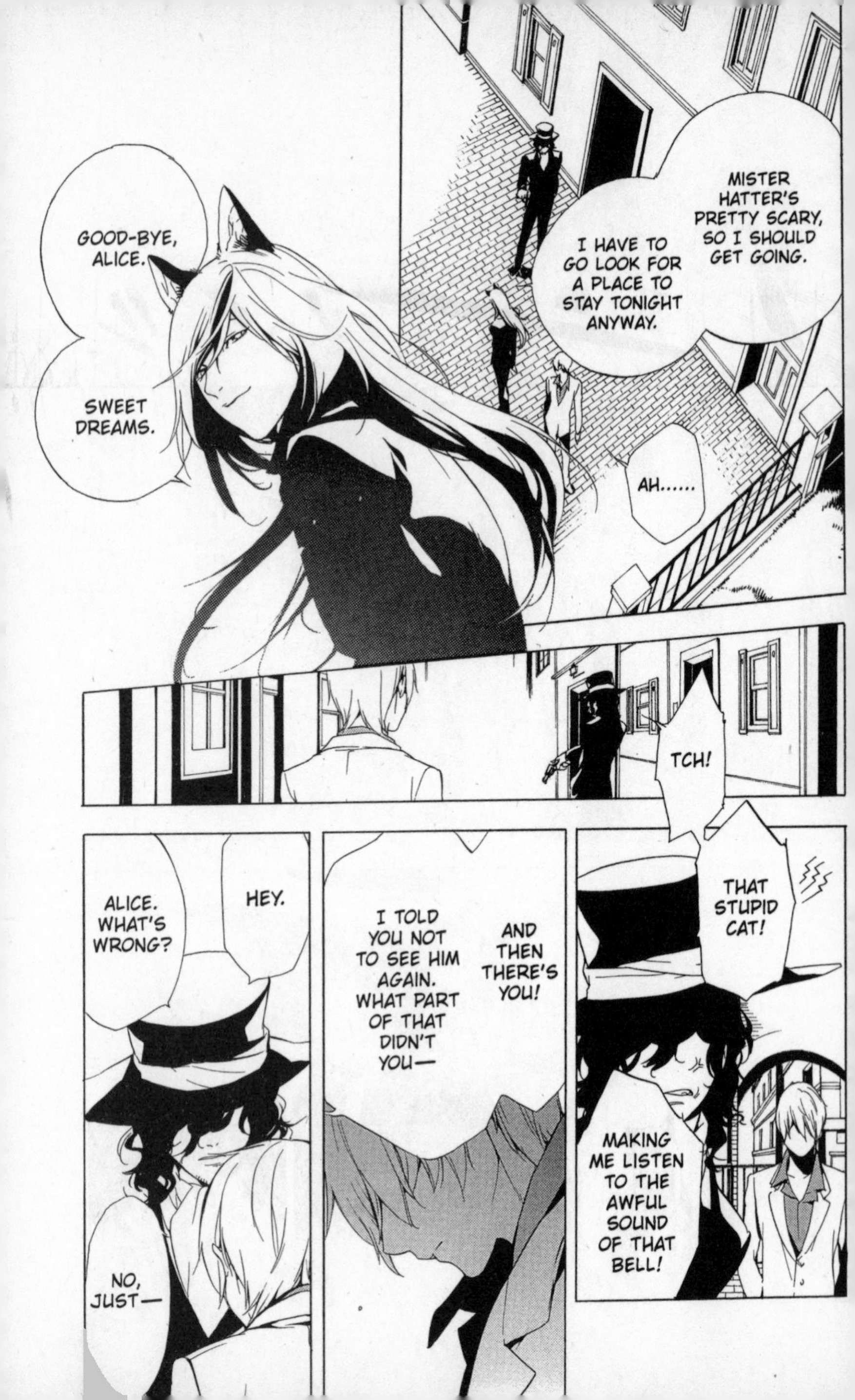
MISTER HATTER'S PRETTY SCARY, SO I SHOULD GET GOING.
I HAVE TO GO LOOK FOR A PLACE TO STAY TONIGHT ANYWAY.
GOOD-BYE, ALICE.
SWEET DREAMS.
AH......
TCH!
THAT STUPID CAT!
MAKING ME LISTEN TO THE AWFUL SOUND OF THAT BELL!
AND THEN THERE'S YOU!
I TOLD YOU NOT TO SEE HIM AGAIN. WHAT PART OF THAT DIDN'T YOU—
HEY.
ALICE. WHAT'S WRONG?
NO, JUST—

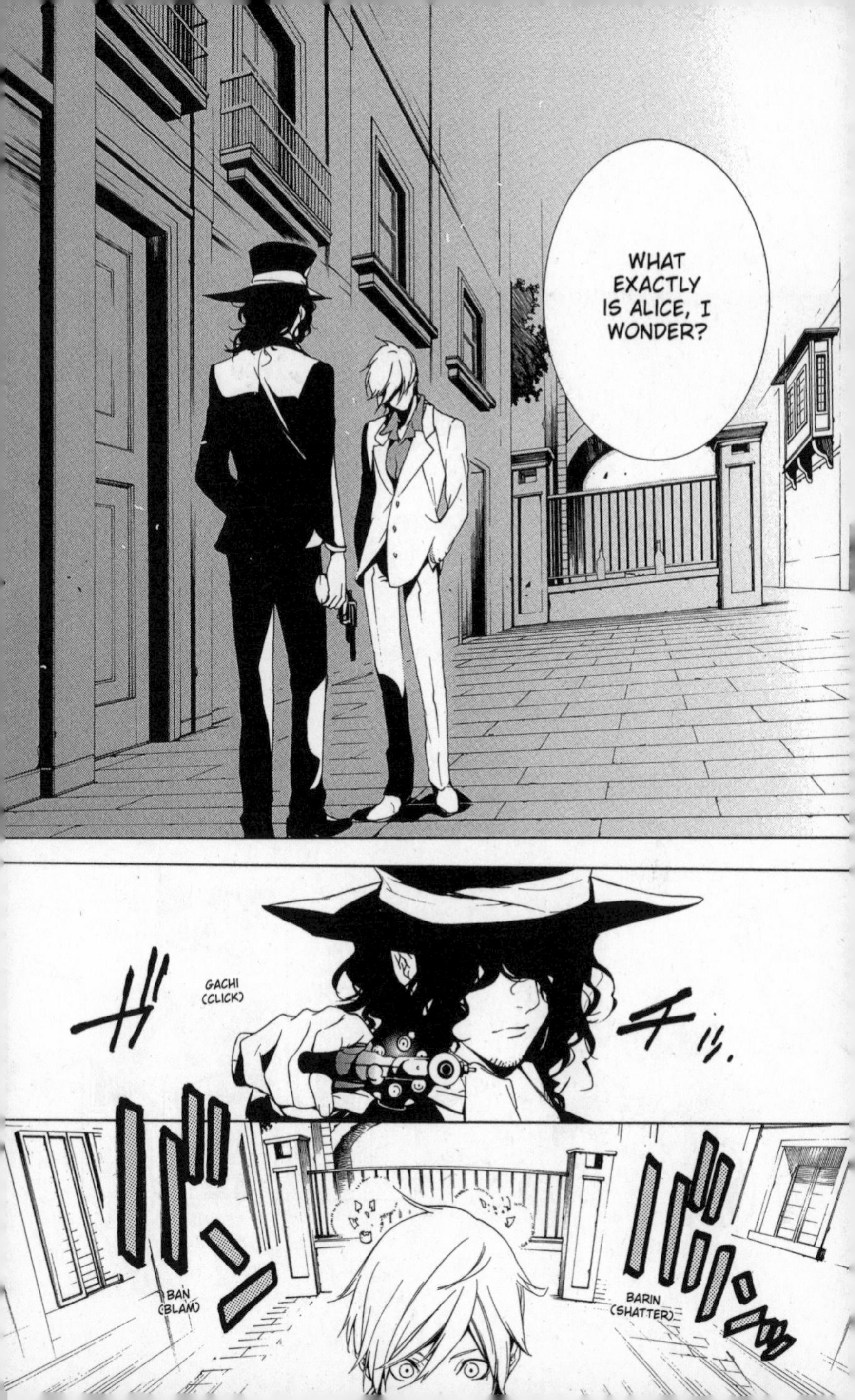
WHAT EXACTLY IS ALICE, I WONDER?
GACHI (CLICK)
BARIN (SHATTER)
BAN (BLAM)

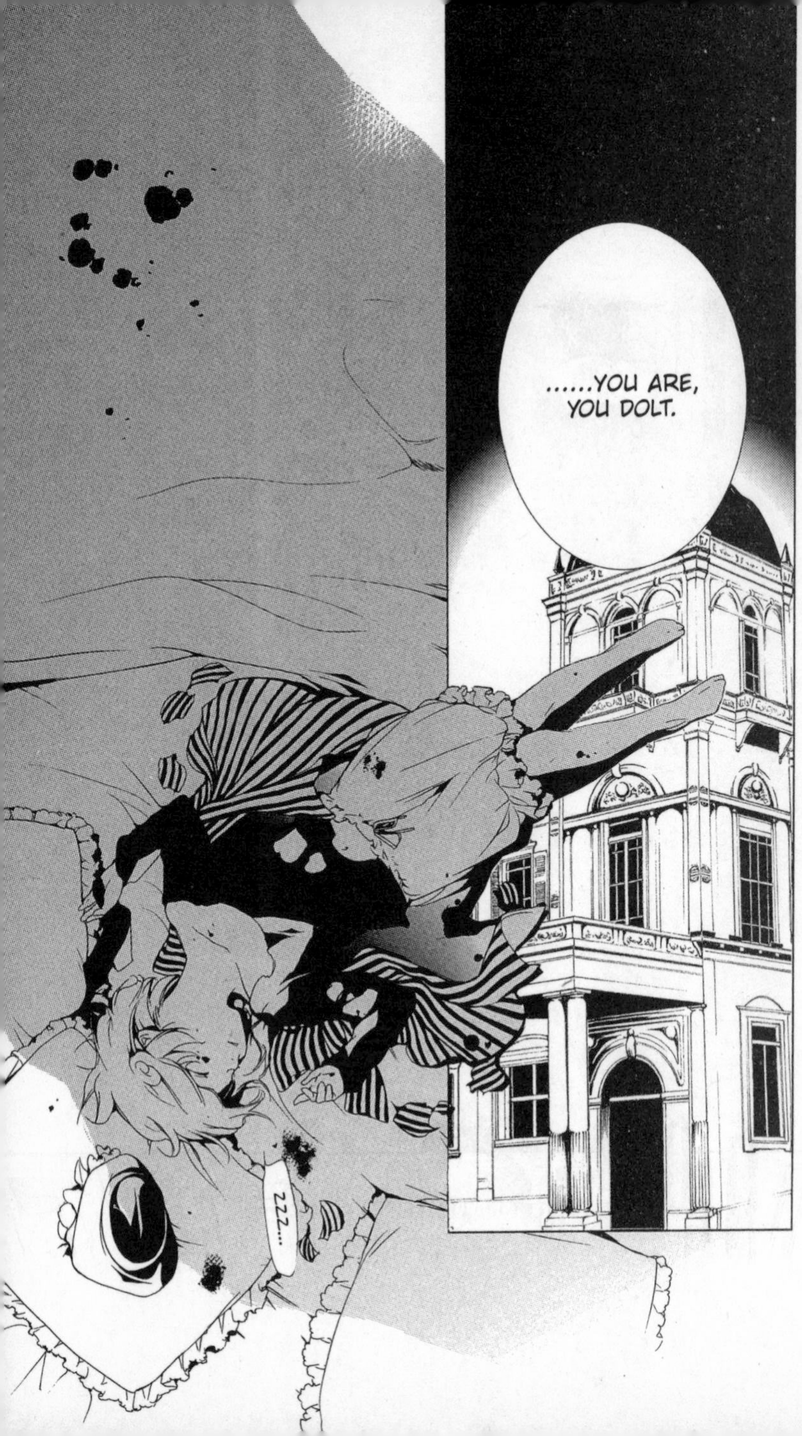
......YOU ARE, YOU DOLT.
ZZZ...

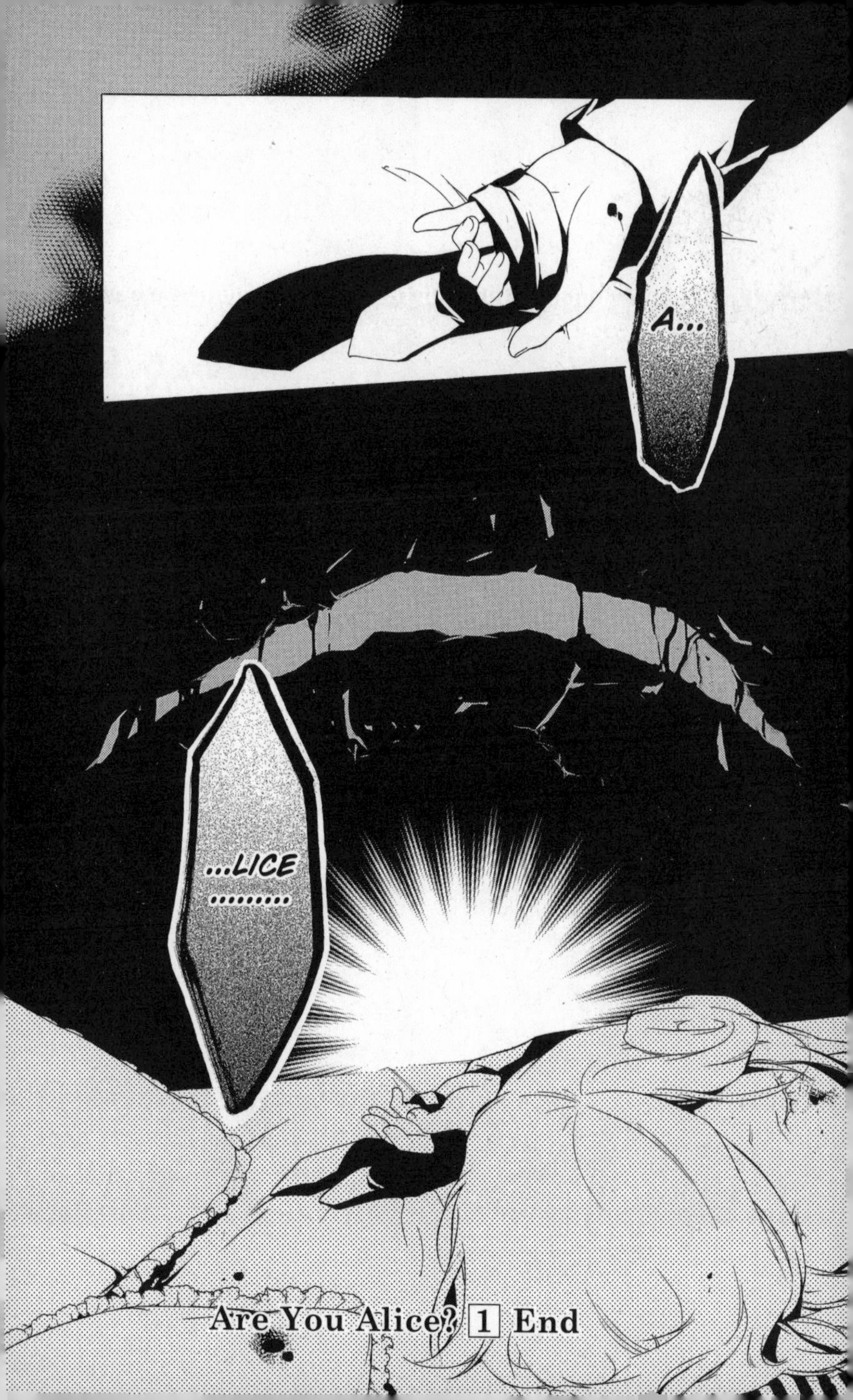
A...
...LICE
....
Are You Alice? 1 End

The world of *Are You Alice?* was brought to life with "a drama CD for your listening enjoyment," but now I'm adding "a manga for your reading enjoyment," to the property as well.

Katagiri-sensei took the ever-mysterious characters from Wonderland and powerfully threw them back at me with all her might. I'm so lucky to be able to worship these rich characters that appear before me in every chapter.

If I can do justice to this story of the Alice who isn't Alice for the sake of Alice, I would be very happy indeed.

And with that, I hope to see you again in Volume 2!

Ai Ninomiya

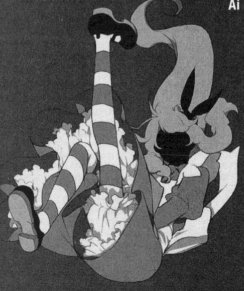

ARE YOU ALICE? 1

IKUMI KATAGIRI
AI NINOMIYA

Translation and Lettering: Alexis Eckerman

Are you Alice? © 2010 by Ai Ninomiya / Ikumi Katagiri. All rights reserved. First published in Japan in 2010 by ICHIJINSHA. English translation rights arranged with ICHIJINSHA through Tuttle-Mori Agency, Inc., Tokyo.

Translation © 2013 by Hachette Book Group, Inc.

Yen Press
Hachette Book Group
1290 Avenue of the Americas, New York, NY 10104

www.HachetteBookGroup.com
www.YenPress.com

Yen Press is an imprint of Hachette Book Group, Inc. The Yen Press name and logo are trademarks of Hachette Book Group, Inc.

First Yen Press Edition: May 2013

ISBN: 978-0-316-25095-5

10 9 8 7

BVG

Printed in the United States of America